ROMANTIC FICTION AND LITERARY EXCESS IN THE MINERVA PRESS ERA

Jane Austen's ironic reference to 'the trash with which the press now groans' is only one of innumerable Romantic complaints about fiction's newly overwhelming presence. This book draws on evidence from over one hundred Romantic novels to explore the changes in publishing, reviewing, reading, and writing that accompanied the unprecedented growth in novel publication during the Romantic period. With particular focus on the infamous Minerva Press, the most prolific fiction-producer of the age, Hannah Hudson puts its popular authors in dialogue with writers such as Walter Scott, Ann Radcliffe, Maria Edgeworth, and William Godwin. Using paratextual materials including reviews, advertisements, and authorial prefaces, this book establishes the ubiquity of Romantic anxieties about literary 'excess', showing how beliefs about fictional overproduction created new literary hierarchies. Ultimately, Hudson argues that this so-called excess was a driving force in fictional experimentation and the advertising and publication practices that shaped the genre's reception.

HANNAH DOHERTY HUDSON is Associate Professor of English at Suffolk University in Boston.

CAMBRIDGE STUDIES IN ROMANTICISM

Founding Editor
Marilyn Butler, *University of Oxford*

General Editor
James Chandler, *University of Chicago*

This series aims to foster the best new work in one of the most challenging fields within English literary studies. From the early 1780s to the early 1830s, a formidable array of talented men and women took to literary composition, not just in poetry, which some of them famously transformed, but in many modes of writing. The expansion of publishing created new opportunities for writers, and the political stakes of what they wrote were raised again by what Wordsworth called those 'great national events' that were 'almost daily taking place': the French Revolution, the Napoleonic and American wars, urbanization, industrialization, religious revival, an expanded empire abroad, and the reform movement at home. This was an enormous ambition, even when it pretended otherwise. The relations between science, philosophy, religion, and literature were reworked in texts such as *Frankenstein* and *Biographia Literaria*; gender relations in *A Vindication of the Rights of Woman* and *Don Juan*; journalism by Cobbett and Hazlitt; and poetic form, content, and style by the Lake School and the Cockney School. Outside Shakespeare studies, probably no body of writing has produced such a wealth of commentary or done so much to shape the responses of modern criticism. This indeed is the period that saw the emergence of those notions of literature and of literary history, especially national literary history, on which modern scholarship in English has been founded.

The categories produced by Romanticism have also been challenged by recent historicist arguments. The task of the series is to engage both with a challenging corpus of Romantic writings and with the changing field of criticism they have helped to shape. As with other literary series published by Cambridge University Press, this one will represent the work of both younger and more established scholars on either side of the Atlantic and elsewhere.

See the end of the book for a complete list of published titles.

ROMANTIC FICTION AND LITERARY EXCESS IN THE MINERVA PRESS ERA

HANNAH DOHERTY HUDSON

Suffolk University

Shaftesbury Road, Cambridge CB2 8EA, United Kingdom

One Liberty Plaza, 20th Floor, New York, NY 10006, USA

477 Williamstown Road, Port Melbourne, VIC 3207, Australia

314–321, 3rd Floor, Plot 3, Splendor Forum, Jasola District Centre, New Delhi – 110025, India

103 Penang Road, #05–06/07, Visioncrest Commercial, Singapore 238467

Cambridge University Press is part of Cambridge University Press & Assessment, a department of the University of Cambridge.

We share the University's mission to contribute to society through the pursuit of education, learning and research at the highest international levels of excellence.

www.cambridge.org
Information on this title: www.cambridge.org/9781009321938

DOI: 10.1017/9781009321921

First published 2023
First paperback edition 2025

A catalogue record for this publication is available from the British Library

ISBN   978-1-009-32196-9   Hardback
ISBN   978-1-009-32193-8   Paperback

Cambridge University Press & Assessment has no responsibility for the persistence or accuracy of URLs for external or third-party internet websites referred to in this publication and does not guarantee that any content on such websites is, or will remain, accurate or appropriate.

For Jared and Eliot

Contents

Figures

Acknowledgements

It is difficult to know where to begin – or end – the acknowledgements for a work of this size, researched, written, and revised over a period of many years. I'm grateful for the support and words of encouragement, big and small, I've received from so many different sources over the years; consider this sentence the well-deserved and heartfelt thanks to everyone I've missed or forgotten in the paragraphs below (rest assured that I will remember the omission, probably in the middle of the night, immediately after it is too late to update the manuscript).

This book began as a dissertation at Stanford, under the guidance of Terry Castle, Denise Gigante, and John Bender, all of whom have shaped my ideas and writing through their own work. Many other faculty and staff in the department helped me along the way, not least Blakey Vermeule and the inimitable Judy Candell. Perhaps the greatest gift of my PhD program is the friendship and professional camaraderie of my fellow students. This project benefitted in its very earliest days from the comments and encouragement of Stephen Osadetz, Claude Willan, Natalie Phillips, Andrew Bricker, Jenna Sutton, and James Wood; it would never have become the book it is now without the ongoing and priceless advice, support, and generous feedback of Bronwen Tate, Bridget Whearty, Jillian Hess, and Rebecca Richardson.

My research on the Minerva Press has benefitted immeasurably from a number of scholarships, fellowships, and research grants, including dissertation fellowships from the Mellon Foundation and the American Council of Learned Societies, as well as Summer Seminar funding from the National Endowment of the Humanities (NEH), an Archival Research award from Stanford's English department, a Graduate Research Opportunity grant from Stanford University, and a visiting fellowship at the Chawton House Library. As an assistant professor at the University of Texas at San Antonio, I was fortunate to be supported by a Labatt Fellowship, and at Suffolk University, my current institutional home, my research has been supported by several Summer Research Stipends and Faculty Research Assistant grants, which have allowed me the great privilege of training and working with outstanding undergraduates over the course of this book project. To my research assistants, Amanda Zarni, Anna Pravdica, Samantha Chase, and Alyssa McInnis: thank you so much for your meticulous work and your inspiring energy and intellect! My knowledge of historical books and the publishing process has benefitted greatly from the Rare Book School courses I've taken in the past few years; I am very grateful for the Access 2021 Scholarship and the Director's Scholarship that allowed me to attend these classes.

I have been fortunate throughout my career to be surrounded by fellow scholars who encouraged the potential in my work. As a graduate student I was lucky to be accepted to that NEH Summer Seminar, and the scholarly community that has grown from that experience, fondly known as 'Austen Camp', has stayed with me to this day. I'm grateful to Devoney Looser, Danielle Spratt, Jodi Wyett, and all of my other fellow participants in that seminar for their intellectual generosity as this book has taken shape. I've found similar scholarly community among the ever-growing group of other researchers working on the Minerva Press, first Elizabeth Neiman, but now also Yael Shapira, JoEllen DeLucia, Tina Morin, Megan Peiser, and many others whom I've had the pleasure of meeting or reading over the years. The American Society for Eighteenth-Century Studies has been a welcoming scholarly home for me since graduate school, and I'm grateful for both the Women's Caucus and the Bender lunch attendees for providing friendly faces in my early years at the conference. The Suffolk University English department has been the most supportive scholarly home imaginable in the years I've been finishing the book – I'm so thankful to all my colleagues, past and present, for their kindness, humour, and encouragement.

The research for this book has taken place over many years and in many libraries. I thank the rare book librarians and staff at the British Library, the Cambridge University Library, the Bodleian Library at Oxford, the Stanford University Library, the University of Missouri's Ellis Library, the Pforzheimer Collection at the New York Public Library, Harvard's Houghton and Widener Libraries, the Chawton Library, and the Spencer Research Library at the University of Kansas for their assistance. Barbara Bieck at the New York Society Library generously took photos of an eccentric William Lane publication for me in the midst of the pandemic, and I thank her and the NYSL, as well as the Lewis Walpole Library, the Beinecke, the Houghton, and the University of Aberdeen, for providing the images that illustrate this book and its cover. Large sections of the book were written or revised in the peaceful environs of the Boston Athenaeum and the Cambridge Public Library. In addition to the support from my doctoral institution and subsequent employers, I am grateful for the library access and research resources provided by visiting/affiliate status in the University of Cambridge's English Faculty (2010–2011) and Harvard University's English department.

Sections of Chapter 3 appear as a part of the article 'Imitation, Intertextuality, and the Minerva Press Novel', published in *Romantic Textualities: Literature and Print Culture, 1780–1840* 23 (Summer 2020); additionally, some reworked sections from my article 'Robert Bage's Novel Merchandise: Commercialism, Gender, and Form in Late Eighteenth-Century Fiction', published in *The Eighteenth-Century Novel*, vol. IX (New York: AMS Press, 2012), appear in Chapter 2. I thank both journals for allowing me to include these pieces here. I'm grateful to Bethany Thomas and Jim Chandler for their interest in the book and their guidance through the writing and editing process. Thank you to George Laver for his help in answering my myriad questions, to Laura Portwood-Stacer for her helpful advice and resources, to both of my anonymous reviewers for their detailed and helpful feedback on the manuscript, and to everyone at Cambridge University Press who have shepherded the book through publication. It has also benefitted from the comments and questions of numerous people – journal editors, anonymous readers, audience members, and fellow panellists and conferences – who have encountered the project in various forms along the way.

Last but certainly not least, I am grateful to and for my family. Mary, Jim, and Jean Doherty have always been my most steadfast supporters, and my work has been buoyed by the encouragement of all the members of my extended family, especially John Battista and Justine McCabe. Peabody Terrace, Dragonfly, and Kayleigh Shuler have served as extensions of our family, providing the all-important childcare that allowed me to write. And Jared and Eliot Hudson have been with me day by day (and often elbow-by-elbow in the pandemic years) as I've written and revised this book: I love and especially thank you both.

Note on the Text

I have attempted to cite eighteenth- and nineteenth-century periodicals in a way that balances clarity and ease of reference with historical accuracy; thus, I generally include volume, month, year, and page numbers, where these are provided in the original source, but may not include issue number or date unless the original magazine or review uses this mode of numbering. Similarly, since the vast majority of periodical articles were published anonymously, I list these in the periodicals section of the Bibliography by article title or the title of the book being reviewed rather than by innumerable 'Anonymous' entries, unless the periodical specifically identifies an author, initial, or pseudonym. (Though I follow the original publication in naming or not naming contributors, in many cases, particularly for the larger reviews like the *Monthly* and the *Critical Review*, the identities of originally anonymous contributors have been retrospectively established by other scholars; see, e.g., Benjamin Christie Nangle on the *Monthly Review*.) Attributions for novels that differ from their identification at first publication, unless otherwise noted, are taken from the *English Short-Title Catalog* or *British Fiction 1800–1829: A Database of Production, Circulation and Reception*. Readers seeking information on a specific Romantic novel should consult both the index and the two primary source sections of the bibliography; novels appearing in the index may be included in either or both sections, depending on whether they are cited directly or mentioned only within the context of a periodical review.

My references do not differentiate between digitized and paper copies of the printed materials I cite in most cases (as I have frequently consulted multiple versions of the same text in different locations and formats and different readers are likely to have access to different copies); however, when individual copies do differ in ways that are relevant to my argument, for instance, through the inclusion of marginalia or missing advertisements in a specific copy, or when important physical features are not visible in a digitized version, I indicate the specifics and locations of these variations in the text. Born-digital materials and unique archival materials are cited by webpage and shelf-mark, respectively.

Abbreviations

AR	*The Analytical Review*
CR	*The Critical Review*
DBF	*British Fiction 1800–1829: A Database of Production, Circulation and Reception*
ECCO	*Eighteenth-Century Collections Online*
EM	*The European Magazine*
ER	*The English Review*
ESTC	*English Short-Title Catalog*
GM	*The Gentleman's Magazine*
LM	*The Lady's Magazine*
MR	*The Monthly Review*
NCCO	*Nineteenth-Century Collections Online*
UMKP	*Universal Magazine of Knowledge and Pleasure*

Introduction
The Minerva Press Era

What a number of *Novels* are continually poured from the prolific press ...! —'General Observations on Modern Novels,' *The Lady's Magazine* (1787)[1]

Never, surely, was there an age in which novels were more generally read than the present. —Mary Meeke, preface to *Midnight Weddings* (1802)[2]

[I]t is apparent, that novel reading, under proper restrictions, is not injurious to the morals; on the contrary, both amusing and instructive: the only danger is that of running into excess. —'On Novel Reading', *The Kaleidoscope* (1821)[3]

In a letter to the editor of the *Universal Magazine* in 1793, the pseudonymous 'Lucius' held forth on novels at some length.[4] Bemoaning the fact that 'a taste for reading the most superficial novels is ... on the increase', he specifically decried 'that collection of trash incessantly poured out from our professed manufactories, where fresh novels are advertised for in quantities!'[5] While Lucius is considerably more alarmist about the dangers of novel-reading than the author of my final epigraph, his preoccupation with volume, (im)moderation, popularity, and prolificity is shared by all of the epigraph writers and, indeed, echoes across countless other discussions of novels and novel-reading in the Romantic period. As this book demonstrates, the belief that there were simply too many novels, that their proliferation was threatening (economically, morally, physically), and that their numbers necessitated an ongoing process of categorizing, managing, and evaluating them pervaded the Romantic period. To understand the development of the novel around the turn of the nineteenth century, I will argue in these pages, thus requires us both to acknowledge and to resist the centrality of this discourse, understanding how it shaped the period's fiction and how it still urges us, so often successfully, to replicate its historical hierarchies and structures of value.

Discussions of fiction from this period almost invariably describe it in terms that emphasize its sheer quantity. Romantic novels, in such accounts, aren't written or crafted, they are churned out, poured forth in torrents or mass-produced; they don't simply appear but swarm and deluge, springing up like mushrooms or many-headed hydras.[6] Both novelists and presses are described as prolific in a way that interferes alarmingly with readerly agency: readers, we are told, do not seek out these novels of their own volition, but are flooded with them, addicted to them, or bewildered by them. '[T]he larger our libraries are the greater the impossibility of knowing what they consist of', as another contributor to the *Lady's Magazine* declared in 1789.[7] While the long novel was certainly nothing new in England by the end of the eighteenth century, now critics complained that every novel, however thin the plot, ran into three, five, or even seven thick volumes, sometimes because of the author's 'superfluous garrulity',[8] sometimes through the use of deplorable stratagems such as page layouts with 'tremendous breadth of margin',[9] which helped to populate those increasingly large libraries by spreading a small number of words into a great number of volumes. As the range of descriptions listed here suggests, anxiety about literary overproduction may begin with complaints about the numbers of books published, but it rapidly extends into discussions of narrative length, readerly attention span, the appetite of the reading public for new fiction, and even the motivations of book publishers. Both the material characteristics of book production and the emotional implications of widespread reading are portrayed as underlying reasons for, but also inevitable outcomes of, rising numbers of novels on the market.

A sense of literary overload is obviously neither unique to Romantic-era England nor inspired exclusively by novels. It has always been possible for an individual reader to feel overwhelmed (or for undesirable authors to seem too numerous), and the advent of early modern printing technologies made such feelings all the more frequent. The seventeenth and early eighteenth centuries, in particular, saw an increase in printed material – and complaints about its volume – that in many ways foreshadow the end-of-century characterizations I document here.[10] Alexander Pope's satirical poem *The Dunciad*, for instance, famously mocks the age's 'groaning shelves' and skewers both authorial prolixity and the sheer mass of printed matter with references to 'whole pile[s]' of books and volumes 'of amplest size'.[11] Throughout the poem, Pope returns to some recurrent themes: the overproduction of printed material, the poor quality of much literary work, and the grossly commercial motivations of authors, concerns echoed by other writers and critics of the 1720s and 1730s. These refrains continued into the mid-eighteenth century, as scholars including Christina Lupton have documented.[12] But the later eighteenth century, particularly the years after 1780, saw a surge in printed material that outpaced all previous growth, and the complaints about excess that accompanied this change both intensified and multiplied.[13] By the end of the eighteenth century, a contemporary writer could describe books with reasonable justification as 'heaped upon the world, not in small quantities, but in multitudes'.[14] David Higgins pithily describes this period as 'an era marked by an exponential increase in the availability of printed matter'; as Andrew Piper has argued, this shift is fundamental to the literary and philosophical developments of the early nineteenth century: 'Romanticism is what happens when there are suddenly a great deal more books to read, when indeed there are *too many* books to read.'[15]

Though all sorts of printed materials were available in newly overwhelming quantities during this time, in this book I explore the ways that the novel was specifically susceptible to critique on these grounds.[16] As a relatively new genre, a seemingly extraneous and unnecessary genre (always at risk of being perceived as shameful entertainer rather than beneficial educator), and a genre strongly associated with 'undesirable' literary developments including professional women authors and working-class literacy, it was the novel, as scholars including Melissa Sodeman, Ina Ferris, and Emma Clery have suggested, that was seen as both a primary symptom and a cause of this new age of overwhelming abundance.[17] And while Romantic critiques of the novel on these grounds often take the form of vague and rhetorically loaded complaints, like Lucius's, they do have a clear bibliographical basis: as the data in *The English Novel* (2000) so compellingly demonstrates, even as rates of literacy among English readers increased at the end of the eighteenth century, so too – dramatically – did the number of novels on the market.[18] The story of this rise is inseparable from the history of one publishing house, the Minerva Press, which operated in London between 1790 and 1820.

The Minerva Press has a complicated relationship to the Romantic era's perceptions of fictional overproduction. The Minerva's founder, William Lane, entered the London book trade in the 1770s, selling books from his father's poultry shop before starting his own business.[19] In 1790, he founded the Minerva Press, quickly adopting a distinctive black-letter imprint that distinguished his title pages from those of other publishers (see Figure 1).[20]

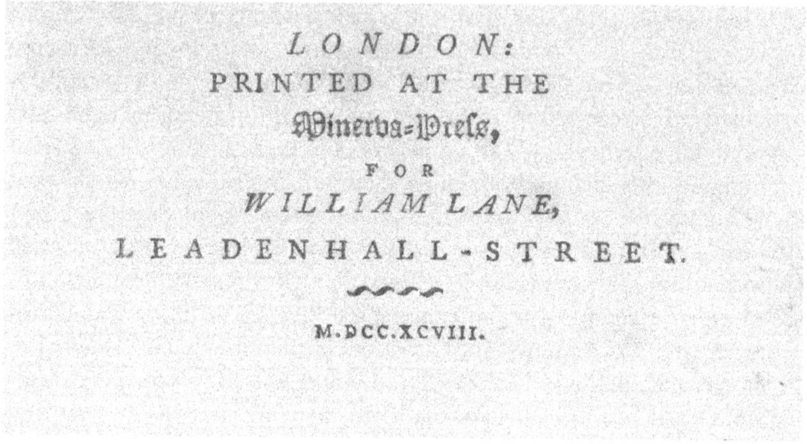
LONDON:
PRINTED AT THE
Minerva-Press,
FOR
WILLIAM LANE,
LEADENHALL-STREET.
M.DCC.XCVIII.

Figure 1 Detail, title page, *Phedora*, vol. I, *EC8 C3818 798p. Houghton Library, Harvard University.

Located in the commercial environs of Leadenhall Street (also home to the East India Company) rather than the more traditional book-selling locations around St Paul's Churchyard and the West End,[21] the Press invited mockery for both its literary pretensions and its orientation towards profit, a conjunction epitomized by the infamous golden statue of Minerva that Lane hung over the door of his premises.[22] There is a strong air of snobbery around much of the criticism directed at the Minerva Press: Lane's humble beginnings were a target of derision, as were the untalented women said to read and write the Press's novels.[23] Writing in 1815, W. H. Ireland managed to mock both Lane's working-class past and the intellect of his present readers with the quip: 'instead of Minerva, a goose should have been the designation of its far-famed press'.[24] With its dual implications of an ungentlemanly proximity to poultry shops and the unearned wealth produced by the goose that laid the golden egg, the insult simultaneously brings to mind familiar descriptions of young women readers as 'silly geese' – certainly not the images Lane's ambitious imprint hoped to evoke.

The press also attracted attention for another reason: within a few years, it was producing more novels than any other publisher in England. In part this success was due to Lane's savvy business model, which combined a publishing house with multiple in-house printing presses and a large and famous circulating library, not to mention a newspaper and a thriving mail-order business for ready-made small libraries.[25] The Minerva Press published six novels in its first year, and twenty-two the year after, rapidly picking up momentum over the course of the decade.[26] By 1800, it was clear that the Minerva Press was out-producing every other source of novels in the market, a dominance that would characterize its thirty-year lifespan, although the Press's actual output rose and fell substantially in different years during this period.[27] Bibliographic research tells us that Lane, his successor A. K. Newman, and the Minerva Press published around 600 novels between 1790 and 1820, amounting to more than a quarter of all the new novels in England, and more than five times as many as any other single publisher during that time period.[28] This feat is remarkable both for being unprecedented in the history of the English novel and for the rapidity with which the Press increased its production and relative market share. While in the entirety of the 1770s barely 300 novels were published in England, by the 1790s that number had more than doubled, and much of that growth is attributable to the Minerva.[29] It is unsurprising, then, that the Minerva Press should have been strongly associated with the Romantic age's fictional excesses: in many ways, it produced them.

The connection between the Minerva Press and Romantic views on novels and novel-reading is, however, more complicated than a simple numerical statement of the press's vast output can explain. Even as the Minerva increased the sheer number of new novels, both through its own publications and by spurring competition in other publishers, it also came to be associated with everything about novels that society most feared and rejected. Its novels were characterized, variously, as lurid, boring, and derivative; sensational, unoriginal, and mass-produced; addictive, poorly written, and corrupting. The enormous Minerva library, similarly, served as a focal point for societal anxieties about circulating libraries (and their patrons) in general. All the fears about fiction outlined above, in other words, attached in particular to the infamous Minerva novel; indeed, Michael Gamer has argued that the Minerva 'functioned at the turn of the nineteenth century as a synecdoche, as a way for critical writers to embody and isolate undesirable changes throughout the publishing industry'.[30]

The centrality of the rhetoric of fictional overload to this historical moment, and its ties to the Minerva Press, has been documented by many scholars of the period, particularly those working on issues of gender and literary genre. Ina Ferris, for instance, has explored how metaphors of multiplication and growth were used to condemn popular fiction by women.[31] Citing the critic John Wilson Croker's derisive reference to 'the thousand-and-one volumes with which the Minerva press inundates the shelves of circulating libraries', Ferris argues that 'over and over again, the ... novel is depicted as stamped out by machines, produced not by authors but by printing presses'.[32] She continues, 'Ordinary novels appear in "hordes", "swarms", and "shoals" – always plural and undifferentiated', pointing out that 'critical discourse responded to the ordinary novel as a signifier of potentially uncontrollable, destructive energy'.[33] The threat posed to society by the Minerva Press novel and its ilk is at once immediate and vague; these are novels that crash upon the public like a wave, exceeding demand and resisting categorization. The increasing number of women writers in the late eighteenth century, and the association between certain literary genres and women readers, plays an important role in the era's discourses of excess, as Ferris demonstrates, and as studies of reviewing – an occupation that often pitted male critics against women novelists – have shown.[34] However, concerns about literary excess and growth were by no means limited to literary pursuits perceived as 'feminine'. Novels of all types and by many different authors were characterized in this way, a conceptual approach that perpetuated the adversarial relationship between authors and reviewers, but also set the stage for later critical approaches to the novel. 'Uncontrollable' novels seem to justify ongoing attempts to control them; moreover, though, this way of thinking about fiction is often in fact a way to *avoid* thinking about (certain kinds of) fiction. Both the discourse of literary excess and its realities are in part responsible for the body of Romantic texts that, in Lee Erickson's memorable formulation, 'no one has been willing to read for a long time and ... only a few scholars today are even willing to read about'.[35] Excess offers critics a way to describe without describing and to dismiss without reading; conversely, however, as I show in this book, the dominance of the narrative that novels were self-propagating and numerous has specific effects on the ways that novels were written and received.

Inevitably, perceived problems with the Romantic novel were seen as both a product of and a threat to the habits of Romantic readers. As David Higgins argues, 'Pope's [early eighteenth-century] concern with the multiplication of bad writers became in the nineteenth century a concern with the multiplication of bad readers.'[36] It was, thus, not only the novels themselves that were conceptualized as a terrifyingly large and unruly group. Describing the expanding demand for popular fiction in this period, Emma Clery writes, 'With the tentacles of the bookselling industry now reaching into the previously untouched fastnesses of the provinces, the market for novels was made strange. Was there any limit to its appetite? How could the wishes of this prodigy be anticipated?'[37] The mutually reinforcing relationship between seemingly self-reproducing texts and uncontrollably ravenous readers – and the prodigious market created by this relationship – has long been understood as a crucial context for Gothic fiction in particular. James Watt suggests that 'the "Gothic" romances published by a press such as William Lane's generated anxiety primarily because of their quantity, their self-proclaimed commodity status, and – ultimately – their popularity'.[38] And Gamer argues that gothic writing, including that published by the Minerva Press, was 'blamed for various changes in literary production and consumption: perceived shifts from quality to quantity; originality to mass-production; and the text-as-work to the text-as-commodity'.[39]

The commercial nature of the Minerva novel was clearly an important part of the equation; in addition to offering a convenient way to deny it any artistic merit, conceiving of the novel as a 'commodity' explains how it could be understood as at once overproduced and ungovernably desired. These characterizations had broad ramifications, as Melissa Sodeman, drawing attention to the frequent unflattering comparisons between popular novels and 'mechanically produced goods', points out. She argues that quantity negatively affected the way many people thought about the novel genre itself: 'For many eighteenth-century commentators ... the sheer number of new novels – most of which were unabashedly sentimental, gothic, or some amalgamation of the two – seemed to have depleted the genre's possibilities.'[40] These perceptions have had lasting critical effects; as Deidre Lynch puts it, this is a 'literary period frequently dismissed' as a time 'when novels' numerical increase led to their qualitative decline'.[41] The inverse relationship between numbers and status is self-perpetuating: the commodified novel *must* be bad, because it is mass-produced; the numerous novel *must* be a commodity, because it is written to meet overwhelming demand. Ideas about fictional production and reception are entangled with qualitative judgements about the novel, with fundamental concerns about oversupply and uncontrollability underpinning them all.

If Romantic novels are frequently described in terms of their proliferation, the *contents* of these numerous volumes have similarly been characterized as undesirably multiplicative. Edward Jacobs has suggested, in a discussion of the ways that circulating library conventions contributed to the development of the gothic genre, that 'the commonplace complaint of eighteenth-century critics that Gothics were mere "manufacture" underscores the fact that Gothics reproduced an unusually stable set of conventions in an unprecedented number of texts'.[42] Accusations of unoriginality, derivative plots, and downright plagiarism abound in the period's criticism.[43] Elizabeth Neiman ties these critiques to the novel's proliferation, pointing to 'the idea that because they are formulaic, circulating-library novels practically self-reproduce'.[44] As Jacobs's discussion of 'manufacture', Ferris's reference to novels 'stamped out by machines', and Sodeman's 'mechanically produced goods' suggest, these claims are often governed by metaphors of automated production, which deny either talent or authorial volition to novel-writers. Aesthetic standards are subordinated in such accounts to the demands of novel-production on a massive scale.

All these discussions, in different ways, show the Romantic period's preoccupation with literary quantity, and the power the many metaphors used to characterize the age's fiction had (and indeed, still have) to diminish and dismiss the works to which they are applied. They reveal how common anxieties about reading and literature have been mapped onto ideas about growth, volume, and scale, and hint at the clear rhetorical connections between literary production and other kinds of industrial production in flux at the turn of the nineteenth century.[45] Moreover, as the examples above suggest, *all* novels in such a crowded and newly industrial milieu might potentially be deemed dangerous or superfluous, but some are much more likely to be the targets of such accusations than others. Concerns about overproduction of fiction thus often turn out, upon closer inspection, to be concerns about gender, ethics, or prestige; conversely, discussions about the aesthetic qualities or moral dangers of the Romantic novel frequently shade into debates about such works' length, size, or print run.

***

This book is an attempt to grapple seriously with the widespread, stereotypical, even formulaic critiques of the novel in the years around 1800, to understand the basis for these negative views, but also, more crucially, to explore the underlying beliefs about the novel they reveal. These shifting beliefs, as these pages demonstrate, generated new ways of writing and thinking about fiction. Rather than accepting dismissive complaints about poorly written popular fiction, women's fiction, gothic fiction, or sentimental fiction at face value, or attempting to recuperate individual works or genres through extended close reading, I develop a critical framework that re-evaluates the undesirable multiplicity and largeness of the

Romantic novel. I examine how pervasive ideas about overflowing shelves and overextended plot lines – not to mention the real (albeit often exaggerated) presence of these phenomena in readers' lives – influence the style of novels written during this period, inspire new ways of imagining the novel's temporality, and lead to an increased emphasis on the novel's physical qualities and material presence. This account does not necessarily seek to challenge the stereotype that many popular novelists of this period were at least as motivated by commercial success as by artistic idealism, but it demonstrates that the conditions in which these novels were written, published, and read did have real effects on their aesthetic qualities.

The starting point for the particular negotiations I outline is the widespread claim by contemporaries that the field of fiction is *too* large and that parameters must be set to exclude some parts of it from view.[46] But, as I also show, this persistent assertion is inseparable from a whole cluster of other debates about fiction, its value, and its legacies. To disentangle and trace these varied threads, I begin with a consideration of one key term, frequently used in contemporary discussions of fiction: excess. As I will suggest here, this term not only highlights the interrelatedness of physical and emotional, qualitative and quantitative assessments of the novel that I have outlined above, but also calls attention to the overlapping language found in both discussions of fiction and debates surrounding other economic and cultural controversies of the period. Excess, in its simplest sense, marks the fluid boundary between just enough and too much, between abundance and overload. Like the words 'trash' and 'waste' (with which it is sometimes used interchangeably), excess can be used to signal worthlessness, disposability, or repugnance, and, like these terms, it can be highly subjective.[47] Unlike these related concepts, however, excess is strongly tied to both volume and value: while trash can often be identified as such even in isolation, and waste implies a discarded by-product, 'excess' indicates that *some* part of the thing being discussed is admirable or desirable, and only the amount that exceeds desire or necessity is unwanted. In other words, the negative concept – excess – implies, even requires, the existence of a positive sufficiency. While some commentators, like Lucius from the *Universal Magazine*, were ready to relegate novels en masse to the category of 'trash', most argued that some, even many, novels were valuable and worthwhile; thus, handling their numbers was merely a matter of identifying where that line between enough and too much might fall. It is this fragile boundary that critics and supporters of the novel alike exploit, whether by identifying entire groups of novels as superfluous or consciously reframing excess as plenitude.

Outside the realm of fiction, Romantic commentators frequently used terms like 'excess' or 'excessive' in the context of ongoing debates about scarcity and worth. Thomas Malthus's 1798 treatise *An Essay on the Principle of Population*, perhaps most alarmingly, outlined the catastrophic future in store for a world in which the population outpaced global resources.[48] For Malthus, distinguishing between a sustainable sufficiency and a dangerous 'excess of population' was quite literally a matter of life and death.[49] Crucially, an overgrowth of population was portrayed as something that would gather its own momentum, reproducing out of control as soon as it passed the tipping point. The *Monthly Review*, looking back at two decades of Malthus's influence, summed up his argument: 'population ha[s] a tendency to increase much more rapidly than the means of subsistence', and 'powerful checks' are thus required to maintain equilibrium, lest more drastic measures be required.[50] The threat of unstoppable and dangerous proliferation resembles that so often invoked in contemporary discussions of novels, with critics assuming the burden of warning against and averting such growth. As we will see, fears about both self-perpetuating reproduction and competition for scarce resources were mobilized in discussions of fiction as a means of warning against fictional overproduction and justifying the necessity of measures to 'check' this growth. There are obvious limitations to the metaphorical comparison between Malthusian excess and that to be found between book covers: the life-or-death consequences of a scarcity of natural resources have no real parallel in the publishing world. Yet the hyperbole such a metaphor invited – and, as I discuss below, there was no shortage of apocalyptic metaphors when it came to novels – was clearly convenient to the commentators who warned of dangerously teetering stacks of novels, bewailed the scarcity of their limited reading time, or worried that the oversupply of novels would endanger their authorial survival by increasing the competition for increasingly scarce publishing resources. Romantic authors from William Godwin to Lord Byron (themselves both frequent commentators on the current state of publishing) engaged with and satirically cited Malthusian ideas, but the connection between his work and the literary scene is perhaps most explicitly articulated by a later scholar, P. P. Howe, who, in a 1912 *English Review* essay on 'Malthus and the Publishing Trade,' declared: 'In the present over-populated state of the book-world – which none can be found to deny and few not to deplore – it is surprising that . . . no one should have suggested that simple remedy, a repression of the natural increase of literary population.'[51] Indeed, the Romantic Age abounds with numerous examples of attempts at such 'repression', enacted most famously by reviewers but also by publishers and would-be authors themselves.

The late 1790s also saw 'excess' invoked in the financial arena, with the institution of the Bank Restriction Act in 1797.[52] Decoupling paper currency from gold and silver coinage, this measure, designed to address the financial crises brought on by the ongoing conflicts with France, raised fears about unchecked proliferation of paper banknotes, and the proportionate decrease in their value. As the *Analytical Review* wrote in September of that year, as the 'quantity of money [is] thus increased, it's [sic] value is diminished'.[53] Indeed, the article warns, the overproduction of banknotes risks their worth 'sinking almost to no value at all'.[54] As in Malthus's strictures on population, critics of this system proposed various means of restricting the growth of paper currency; checking volume is portrayed as a direct means of preserving value. The *Analytical Review* cites a proposal to 'limit the existence and circulation of this government paper' if its 'quantity became excessive'[55] and notes that paper's functionality as currency is entirely dependent on '*if it's* [sic] *quantity could be limited*'. 'This, however', the author continues, 'appears to us to be absolutely impossible.'[56] As with discussions of novels, debates like these fail to clarify how a determination of 'excessive quantity' could be made, and by whom.

Fiction too is often described in terms of an inversely proportional relationship between volume and value, with control over the former – however impossible this may be – necessary to secure the latter. Paper itself provides a symbolic link between these two debates: books and banknotes are both physically made of paper, and this specific materiality, in both realms, becomes a way of ascribing or denying value. Paper can be imbued with the ideas in a book or the worth of a banknote; as soon as belief in either system is withdrawn, however, paper abruptly transforms back into its flimsy and transient self. An accusation of superfluity or oversupply, in other words, reduces book and bill alike to their physical form, withdrawing them from the symbolic systems that grant their legitimacy.

What makes 'excess' an especially resonant term for thinking about Romantic fiction, finally, is the way that contemporary use of the word slides so easily between material and emotional meanings, between physical presence and personal behaviour. In his dictionary, Samuel Johnson's first definition for 'excess' is relatively concrete: 'more than enough;

superfluity'.[57] Such a description could be, and was, used to describe sheer numbers of authors, readers, and novels, as when a writer in the *Metropolitan* magazine, reflecting on the first decades of the nineteenth century, complained that its 'literature ... is overladen with books and with authors to a singular excess'.[58] Johnson's list of meanings for the word, however, rapidly moves to a series of definitions that concern feelings and actions rather than numbers: 'exuberance', 'intemperance', 'violence of passion', and 'transgression of due limits'. Contemporary accounts of fiction and fiction-reading reveal a similar slippage of meanings – novels aren't just physically numerous, but emotionally over-the-top; reading and writing aren't neutral processes but passionate, intemperate, and even transgressive behaviours. Novels are portrayed as emotionally overheated, overflowing with dangerous sensibility, and their physical proliferation is thus rhetorically tied to a rise in these kinds of feelings and behaviours, particularly in women.[59]

Numerous publications from this time joined the *Lady's Monthly Museum* in warning women against 'an excess of sensibility', relating cautionary examples of tragedies resulting from 'excessive sorrow' or over-weening passion.[60] These dangerous emotions were often explicitly blamed on fiction; in a particularly dramatic example from 1793, the *Weekly Entertainer* argued that 'The pernicious tendency of [novels and romances] cannot, I am afraid, be doubted.... [I]n certain situations of despair and agony, if a man or woman of sensibility, were to meet with the pathetic descriptions of fictitious writing, it might have a tendency to heighten the despair and drive them on to self-slaughter.'[61] Priscilla Wakefield, in her popular didactic text *Mental Improvement* (1794), put it clearly: condemning over-emotional language, she declared, 'Such excess of speech is to be expected from novel and romance readers, but are ill suited to a woman of good sense and propriety of manners.'[62] Gothic and sentimental novels, in particular, were associated with this kind of extreme affective response – in Stephen Ahern's phrase, 'distinguished by a penchant for emotional and rhetorical excess' – even as they were simultaneously portrayed as physically multiplicative.[63]

Emotional extremes were not limited to sentimental women, either: in the 1790s the term surfaces with alarming frequency in descriptions of the French Revolution, with the behaviour of enraged mobs described in lurid terms – 'the excesses of the most sanguinary people on earth' – by conservative commentators.[64] While these mobs, for obvious reasons, were not generally described as reading novels *while* engaged in violence, the perceived link between fiction and the spread of dangerous, revolutionary ideas has been amply established in scholarship on British responses to the French Revolution.[65] Novels spread ideas, and ideas spread feelings; if those ideas were dangerous, then towering stacks of undesirable novels easily might become crowds of ungovernable citizens, in the popular imagination at least. Novels, in other words, were not only produced in excess; they *produced* excess (of speech, of emotion, of behaviour) in others. This rhetorical slippage between physical and emotional connotations makes 'excess' an unstable critical term, but its very instability usefully reveals the conveniently overlapping accusations directed against popular fiction and those who read, wrote, and published it.

A central aim of this book, then, is to explore what happens to our picture of the Romantic novel when we focus directly on the idea of excess – or, more specifically, on the novels, genres, and publishers that this concept was so frequently used to dismiss. We can refuse, in other words, both the easy repudiation and the unexamined slippage of terms that 'excess' invites, instead considering how the material circumstances of book production in this era, and ongoing concerns about uncontrolled and uncontrollable fictions, shaped the development of fiction itself. Looking closely at the specific motivations and characteristics of many Minerva Press novels, I argue here, reveals that many, perhaps all, Romantic novels engage with similar questions of relevance and self-differentiation. Centring those novels generally accused of superfluity, instead of relegating them to the margins or the background of an argument, reveals their importance: if the period's 'innumerable' novels form a vast and overwhelming body, this body exerts a quasi-gravitational pull on everything around it – even novels that resist assimilation follow orbits shaped by the mass of their forgotten brethren.[66] In Elizabeth Neiman's new work on the Minerva Press, she explores one way this shaping process occurred, illuminating not only the 'actively collaborative model of authorship' practiced by Minerva novelists but, crucially, the influence this model had on Romantic theories of poetic genius.[67] *Romantic Fiction and Literary Excess in the Minerva Press Era* traces the press's influence in a different direction, but I am no less committed to the argument that the many, many novels associated with the Minerva Press and other popular publishers exert a powerful force on other literary works of the age.

To identify excess, as a critic, is to dismiss and to disengage. The designation itself justifies, even requires, a disdainful refusal to spend further time engaging with the details of the superfluous text. But the excesses of the Romantic novel are not so easily banished. The maligned or banished novel has a metaphorical presence, but also an actual weight and heft; those hordes and swarms threaten, I argue, because they are tied, however hyperbolically, to the actual material presence of books in the world. This exploration of overproduction and its literary repercussions is, then, ultimately an account of the ties between metaphor and material reality, between bibliographic and narrative growth, between a book-historical understanding of print production and the varied ways that authors conceptualized their place within the print marketplace. All the authors in this book, whether they wrote for Lane or a more prestigious publisher like Longman, sold well or poorly, or are now canonical or forgotten, engaged with changing beliefs about fiction through acts of resistance, re-orientation and, ultimately, acknowledgement of the polit-ical, literary, and financial possibilities presented by the novel's new prominence. It is in this sense that I think we can justifiably call the years around the turn of the nineteenth century the 'Minerva Press Era': the Minerva was far from the only publisher operational during this time, but the literary pressures and problems to which it contributed, and which it symbolically exemplified, affected *all* novel-writers and their works.

In the chapters that follow, I trace the literary effects of the novel's seemingly uncontrollable growth and influence across three main registers: materiality, temporality, and style. The novel's proliferation, clearly, is entangled with considerations about its physical form. The relationship can be seen quite literally in the development of new packaging and sales strategies designed to distinguish one text from another – or to remind a reader of the connections *between* one novel and its many fellows – but also can be seen metaphorically, in the way that the novel's materiality was conceived of in relationship to other material objects. The novel's symbolic place within the changing consumer landscape evolved in tandem with its increasing availability from circulating libraries and shops, raising ques-tions about both the labour required to produce novels and the likely fate of the piles of volumes thus created. Questions about the novel's future lead directly to the temporal dimension of fictional development I explore in this book. A sense of large or even unlimited supply and endless competition meant that the time it took to read (or write) a novel needed to be conceptualized differently, an issue complicated by multi-volume novels that circulated different parts of a single story separately. Moreover, large numbers brought questions of ongoing relevance to the fore. How long was a novel interesting or important? Ought it to be fleeting or persistent, ephemeral or eternal? Novelists, their readers, and their critics debated whether fiction was best understood in terms of its relationship to changing fashions, or whether its status, either as art or as a source of moral education, required a more timeless and enduring standard of evaluation. A sense of fictional multiplicity, finally, drove authorial experimentation with new narrative perspectives and stylistic similarities, deliberately rippling across numerous volumes, and coalescing into recognizable genres designed to appeal to broad-based readerships.

In tracing the complicated ramifications of (over)abundance in each of these three registers, I also show how interconnected they are. To take just two examples, it is impossible to understand the gothic genre – most often discussed in terms of narrative, plot, or style – or A. K. Newman's new Minerva bindings, a more strictly material or bibliographical concern, without also considering closely related issues including the timing and duration of new literary fashions and the relationship between literary genre and literary advertising. While research on Romantic novels often focuses either on their internal qualities (genre, narrative, or the development of free indirect discourse, for instance) or on their bibliographical characteristics, my analysis of fictional growth and metaphors of excess clearly shows that for contemporary commentators, production, reception, and style were crucially entwined.

***

Christina Lupton has argued compellingly that British authors of the mid-eighteenth century show 'a reiterative brand of self-consciousness for their work that points with remarkable candor to the actual conditions and materials of their writing'.[68] She offers as one example an excerpt from the preface to a 1779 novel, *Columella; or, The Distressed Anchoret*, which runs in much the same vein as my epigraphs at this introduction's beginning: 'The Public is overwhelmed already with books of every kind, but especially with tales and novels.'[69] As this quotation continues, however, it takes a more unexpected turn: 'I begin to think, that in time the world, in a literal sense, will not be able to contain the books that shall be written.'[70] Both the self-consciousness and the links between materiality and textual mediation that Lupton documents at mid-century continue to be evident in many novels well into the nineteenth century. What resonates most with my own discussion of the Romantic novel is *Columella*'s insistence on the 'overwhelm[ing]' presence of fiction in the public sphere and the characterization of this presence in a specifically material, if highly exaggerated, way. After speculating that the number of novels will soon exceed the globe's available space for them, the novelist suggests an even more apocalyptic scenario:

> a droll friend of mine imagines, that one reason why this terrestrial globe will be destroyed by fire, is, that a general conflagration will more effectually consume the infinite heaps of learned lumber (with which it was foreseen our libraries would be stored after the invention of printing) than any inundation, earthquake, or partial volcano whatsoever, could possibly do.[71]

There is a characteristic insouciance to this passage, which – even as it appears *in* the pages of a novel – invites the reader to envision the world burning, more thoroughly destroyed by 'infinite heaps' of highly flammable novels than by flood or volcano. Novels are a force to be reckoned with here; add a single match and even earthquakes and burning lava pale in comparison. (Apocalyptic visions of death-by-novel, however hyperbolic they may seem, were rather standard fare; in 1790 a reviewer claimed that novels 'cover the shelves of our circulating libraries, as locusts crowd the fields of Asia',[72] adding 'plague of locusts' to the biblically torrential or conflagratory dangers posed by the unchecked proliferation of novels.) Not all such invocations of materiality are so impressive, however, as returning to 'Lucius', the *Universal Magazine*'s correspondent from my opening paragraph, demonstrates. After complaining about the 'quantities' of 'fresh novels', he goes on:

> To produce such a number as the press every winter teems with, the principles of mechanics seem to have been resorted to, and a certain quantity of paper is filled up with as much ease, as a labourer will plough a certain number of acres, or a painter cover a certain number of square feet; with this difference, indeed, that the ground must be well opened, and the paint substantially laid on; considerations which never enter into the heads of our manufacturers of novels, to whom quantity and expedition are the only objects.[73]

Lucius's description of the press as 'teem[ing]', and his emphasis on 'quantity and expedition' over quality, are representative of the contemporary obsession with overproduction of novels, as we have seen. His criticism, however, also turns the reader's focus away from novels as vehicles of ideas or emotions and towards the novel as a physical object, produced by labour to take up space in the world. While in the first example the physical presence of novels ('learned lumber') was evoked in terms of fuel for a deadly fire, here attention to the novel's materiality ('a certain quantity of paper') embeds it in a larger system of labour and commerce. Whereas *Columella*'s novels become a firetrap, Lucius uses attention to the press, the paper, and the process of manufacture to recast the novel as a product. Both transformations, importantly, move authorial agency and artistic accomplishment out of the frame, a point that Lucius makes quite explicit in his next reflection:

> From the workman-like facility, with which modern novels are composed, and from their increasing number, it is not, perhaps, too ridiculous to suppose that . . . the operation might be performed by a machine. In our days, labour has been wonderfully abridged by the invention of an Arkwright; and . . . it is not unreasonable to foresee the time when some ingenious gentleman will apply for a patent, . . . [for] 'a Machine for making Novels, which will save the future labours of industry, and furnish the public with an article equally good, and executed in a tenth part of the time'.[74]

This argument is very much a continuation of the critical habit of characterizing popular novels as 'manufactured' or 'commodities', albeit rather more literal than most. I quote it here not simply to showcase an extreme example of this line of thinking but to call attention to Lucius's dramatic reimagining of the novel's conditions of production. As I suggest throughout this book, one perhaps unexpected outcome of the insistence that novels may be superfluous or oversupplied is the possibility such claims offer for transformation, thinking about new possibilities for understanding the novel's capacities, whether in terms of physical pages or means of sale. The assertion that novels are ubiquitous, in other words, not only continually reminds readers of how and why this seeming ubiquity occurred – presses, advertising, reviews, fashions – but easily slides into reflection on how the novel, already having saturated the market, moves forward.

While authors and reviewers often treat the qualities of literary works as self-evident – a novel is a novel and is evaluated as such – the novel in a state of over-abundance is always at risk of becoming something else: kindling or toilet paper, speaking pejoratively; a museum exhibit or treasured artifact, more optimistically. The more abstract transfigurations of the novel are even more dramatic: in these accounts, it becomes an irresistible food, an addictive drug, a fashion, a flood. A novel sold over the counter might be rhetorically indistinguishable from a bar of soap; a novel produced by a 'Spinning Jenny of Sentiment', as Lucius calls his novel-writing machine, is a workaday textile.[75] Lucius is clearly interested in transforming the novel into a machine-made product in order to denigrate it and devalue the work of authors. But many authors, as I hope my list of transformations above will suggest, see a different value in these metamorphoses. With numbers comes power, these authors argue; with efficient mass-production comes timeliness and desirability; with wide reproduction comes increased chance of survival. *Columella*'s author frames fiction's collective energies as potentially destructive, but epically massive in scope; other authors assert the novel's force in more modest ways, through claims about the breadth of their audience or the fashionable demand for their work. A novel cannot come into the world without the labour of numerous people, from author to typesetter to reader, and the metaphors of production and reproduction many authors embrace reinscribe this work, resisting and overturning the narratives of authorless books and ravenous readers levied by critics like Lucius.

***

This book traces the interlocking relationship between materiality, temporality, and style in the Romantic novel along a roughly chronological arc. Chapter 1, 'Minerva's Writers and Reviewers', lays the groundwork for the rest of the argument, tracking descriptions of and responses to literary overproduction through the two groups of people most implicated in the Romantic period's perceptions of it: reviewers and novelists themselves. Starting with the bibliographical commonplace that the end of the eighteenth century was the moment at which the number of novels published first began to exceed the annual reviewing capability of eighteenth-century reviewers, I follow the fate of the Minerva Press's novels in the pages of major and minor reviews, demonstrating how the rhetoric of excess employed by professional reviewers not only established popular beliefs about which novels were worthwhile, but actively marginalized (or identified as superfluous or dangerous) certain categories of fiction.

Authors, naturally, responded to these attacks, and I examine a range of characteristic approaches from authors in the 1780s and 1790s. In particular, Chapter 1 shows how, through paratextual materials and narrative interpolations, Minerva authors explicitly present each novel as an entrant in a crowded market, potentially overwhelmed by the competition and inevitably compared to the other works with which it appears. Some authors pre-emptively defend their works against competitors or hostile reviewers, but many humorously embrace their relative anonymity, potential unpopularity, or ephemeral success, transforming these seemingly negative attributes into selling points. Authors frequently imagine their future readers in these passages, attempting to define their audience *within* their fiction even as they were less and less able to control the audiences *of* their fiction. Through these analyses, I trace the development of several distinctive ideas about scarcity and abundance that run through the rest of the book: debates about responsibility for the age's glut of fiction; theories about the specific ties between the current crowded market and the novel form; and, finally, the relationship between excess, in its varied meanings, and literary taste.

Beginning with the Minerva novels on which so much of this discourse focused allows the subsequent chapters to expand to consider how these ideas applied to Romantic fiction more broadly. Chapter 2, 'Godwin, Bage, Parsons, and Novels as They Are', shows how the new demands of the marketplace shaped the development of 1790s political fiction. In the wake of the French revolution, the proliferation of English fiction began to strike more observers as particularly dangerous – critics feared that novels might be the vehicle of threateningly radical and immoral ideas, while many authors expressed anxieties about where and by whom their works would be read. Examining novels by writers including Eliza Parsons, William Godwin, and Robert Bage, this chapter begins to break down the divide between Minerva and non-Minerva authors, arguing that political ideas across the spectrum were often conceived and expressed as functions of multiplicity: How many readers, how many epistolary voices, how many viewpoints, how many ideological challenges could one novel handle? Focusing first on the proliferation of voices that a long novel allows, and then on concerns about the alarmingly wide and indiscriminate spread of fiction to its readers, I consider how these two ways of thinking about fiction's function tie narrative style to the decade's radical political debates. Reading across an entwined group of novels that purport to describe 'things as they are' (Godwin's *Caleb Williams*, while the most famous of the group, postdates some others by several years), I show how authors directly tie their political arguments to marketplace realities and generic constraints.

Chapter 3, 'Imitating Ann Radcliffe', maintains the focus on literary style, through a discussion of the genre most often associated with the Minerva Press: the gothic. Indeed, if the Minerva Press is the publisher most strongly associated with fictional excess, then the gothic, as so many of the scholars I have quoted above suggest, is surely excess's most representative genre. Readers decried the great length of these novels, their numerousness, their unoriginality, and the over-the-top emotions they depicted (and, it was feared, inspired in weak-minded readers). This chapter tracks the phenomenon of 'imitation' in the late eighteenth-century heyday of the gothic, first in its role as a convenient denunciation hurled at new gothic novels, and then as a broad and flexible authorial practice that, I suggest, allowed gothic novelists to capitalize on their strength in numbers and their dedicated readerships. It traces how successful Minerva Gothic novelists like Regina Maria Roche and Eliza Parsons (both of whose works famously feature in *Northanger Abbey*'s list of 'horrid novels'), as well as many others, used imitation to define and expand the norms of their genre, particularly in relation to Radcliffe, often cast as the originary gothic genius. Ultimately, I suggest, imitation allows authors to resist unsympathetic critiques by harnessing the mass energies of a newly industrial book culture.

Moving towards 1810, I trace the novel's increasing self-conceptualization as ephemeral, as fashionable, and as commercial, showing how these metaphors aligned fiction-writing with industrial production. While the physical qualities (size, appearance, accompanying ads) of novels are important to the works discussed in Chapters 2 and 3, in the second half of the book I focus in even more detail on the increasingly material characterizations of popular fiction, and particularly on the intersection of materiality and temporality. In Chapter 4, 'Hannah More's *Cœlebs* and the Novel of the Moment', I take the 1808 publication of More's unlikely best-seller, the evangelical, didactic novel *Cœlebs in Search of a Wife*, as a case study to explore the ways that authors responded to new market conditions by writing deliberately ephemeral novels – works intended not for posterity but to be read and relevant only in their contemporary moment. Within two years of *Cœlebs*' publication, other authors had produced at least six full-length response novels, which imitated, continued, parodied, or mocked the original work. For these Romantic authors, the (very) short term was far more important than any imagined future. Indeed, the potentially fleeting nature of literary relevance and success is framed, in this context, as a positive attribute, rather than an evil to be avoided: it transforms overproduction into increased opportunity. The authors of these works, I argue, embrace the idea of literary production as time-sensitive and transient: rather than fearing or fighting the phenomenon, they capitalize on the fast-paced literary culture of the time to emphasize their own works' timeliness and contemporary relevance. If there are too many books, one must read and write faster; by the same token, however, the less time on the public stage each individual book demands, the more the field is opened for even greater numbers of novels.

While Chapter 4 considers how Romantic novelists embraced speed and ephemerality as a defence against a crowded marketplace, Chapter 5, 'Fiction as Fashion from *Belinda* to Miss Byron', examines a different way that novels were envisioned as in – or out of – fashion. As industrial production ramped up in the early nineteenth century, supplying consumers with mass-produced products from Wedgewood china to pocket-watches, so too, this chapter argues, was the popular novel conceptualized as a consumer good, as an object to buy and display as much as a text to read. I begin with Maria Edgeworth's *Belinda* (1801) to explore how this work takes fashion as a topic within the novel as well as, potentially, a way to measure the novel itself. The chapter then moves forward to the 1810s, examining several novels by Minerva author 'Miss Byron', among others, to demonstrate how this discussion of novel-as-luxury could at once be used as a way to valorize the novel and to make visible the often-ignored labour of its authors. The moral and material excesses of overspending consumers become a metaphor for the glut of the literary market, while the notion of luxury as always created by someone's work – but also as essentially commodified and interchangeable – implicates the novel in a commercial system that challenges the hierarchies of strictly literary valuations.

In Chapter 6, 'Walter Scott's Industrial Antiques', I show how these increasingly material ways of valuing the novel were mobilized in the decade after 1814, as the popular novel's very ubiquity began to be portrayed as a potential justification for future literary worth. The luxuries of Chapter 5 are luxurious precisely because they are both rare (few can afford them) and numerous (in the nineteenth century's new commodity culture, there are enough quizzing-glasses and gold pocket-watches for all who can buy them). Chapter 6 shows how Walter Scott, ultimately the age's most prolific and best-selling novelist, successfully turned the era's rhetorical attacks on fiction to his own commercial ends, though not without considerable risk to his literary reputation. I begin by showing how directly and frequently Scott's novels were compared with those published by the Minerva Press in the previous two decades: Scott's defenders marked the 1814 publication of *Waverley* as the death knell of Minerva, while his detractors habitually remarked upon the parallels between his numerous, voluminous novels and those produced in equally large quantities by the Press. In readings of Scott's early novels and his self-conscious paratexts, I show how he ties the seeming historical veracity of his fiction to its market value. Scott's novels explore an antiquarian system of valuation in which even the most uninteresting document becomes valuable to posterity as soon as it is rare. In so doing, they offer a unique defence of those 'innumerable' popular novels that, as his narrators point out, churn from 'The Author of Waverley's' pen just as quickly as they had been rolling from the Minerva's in-house printing presses. The more works one produces, Scott hints, the more likely it is that least a few of them will survive to be the treasures of another age. Scott and many of the other popular novelists who wrote alongside him suggest that being truly prolific may ultimately lead to literary prestige rather than undermine it.

***

From the lofty perch of 1820, a literary commentator in *The Port-Folio* looked back on the literary developments of the previous decades, noting the novel's ubiquity, but also invoking the materiality of the circulating library and the supposed class affiliations of its patrons and contributors. The 'deluge' of novels described here is voluminous, promiscuously circu-lated, and produced by scorned scribblers:

> The path of novel-writing once laid open was imagined easy by all, and for about forty years the press was deluged with works to which we believe the literary history of no other country could produce a parallel. The milliner's prentices who had expended their furtive hours, and drenched their maud-lin fancies with tales of kneeling lords and ranting baronets at the feet of fair seamstresses … soon found it easy to stain the well-thumbed pages of a circulating library book with flimsy sentiments, and loose descriptions of their own.[76]

The portrait painted by this passage highlights problems of several differ-ent kinds, with its evocation of stereotypical plots, emotional authors, and library shelves groaning with grubby volumes. Also apparent is an obvious attempt to relegate these unpleasantries to the past, suggesting that both literature and the reading public have advanced and improved. Literary history itself is portrayed in this quotation as a kind of superfluity, con-signed wholesale to a best-forgotten closed chapter. But for all this critic's efforts, it is plain that England's age of fictional excess did not end with the fall of the Minerva Press. Burlesquing Lord Byron's burlesque *Don Juan* in 1830, a writer in *Fraser's Magazine* was still denouncing novelists as much for their sheer numerousness as for their lack of literary talent: 'But of all the classes of mediocre writers, the class of novelists beats the others hollow. They actually swarm in this department – they are like heroes, – "Every year and month sends forth a new one."'[77]

If many onlookers earlier in the eighteenth century had identified new growth across all of print culture, after the Minerva Press Era, as this satirical jab suggests, the novel retained a distinctive place as a site of specific anxieties about literary development. It is no accident that when the Victorian novelist George Eliot imagined herself as an eighteenth-century reader predicting the future of this new literary genre, it was the Minerva she saw – as she wrote in the *Westminster Magazine* in 1853, 'the Minerva press looms heavily in the distance'. The formulation is striking for the vast scale and physical size the metaphor implies, but also for the remarkable fact that Eliot viewed a single publishing house, one that had been defunct for more than thirty years at the time she wrote, as centrally significant to the novel's past and future. Amid the 'loose and baggy monsters' and ever-expanding serials of the Victorian period, the Minerva Press remained a symbol of its age, the simplest way to evoke the literary excesses of the past. To describe the Romantic period as the Minerva Press Era is a deliberately provocative re-visioning of this literary moment, a re-orientation that directs our attention to the collective rather than the singular.

CHAPTER I

Minerva's Writers and Reviewers

This is the age of scribbling; and of sentimental scribbling: and the world is already choked full of books.... —*The Scottish Review* (1809)[1]

In novels as in so many other things, excess is in the eye of the beholder. One reader's delightful plenitude may be another's crushing burden, and the novel that bores some with its length will likely please others with its profusion of successive stories. Perhaps the most challenging thing about discussing the Romantic period's abundance of fiction in retrospect, then, is teasing apart rhetoric from lived experience: dramatic claims of fictional inundation, as every chapter of this book will show, serve many useful purposes, but certainly don't always – or possibly ever – reflect historical conditions with any accuracy. As my Introduction outlines, there is clear historical evidence that numbers of novels increased dramatically towards the end of the eighteenth century. Yet the belief that this abundance constituted an *excess* – that any part of it was superfluous or undesirable – was not a foregone conclusion. In this chapter, then, I consider the two groups most affected by perceptions of increasing fictional volume but also, I suggest, most responsible for the widespread characterization of novels as over-supplied, namely, reviewers and authors themselves.

Reading what Minerva's authors and reviewers of Minerva's novels had to say about the state of fiction reveals that both groups frequently discuss novels in terms of limits and, specifically, how they exceed them: from overproduction of titles to over-prolific authors to over-digressive plots, these accounts portray a world in which fiction is thought to threaten boundaries, evade control, and overwhelm unwary readers. Whether endorsing these perspectives or defensively rebutting them, commenters return again and again to certain paradoxical claims: the novel's proliferation is either the cause or the result of contemporary tastes; the potential uncontrollability of the novel, in both physical and emotional terms, marks a turning point (for good or ill), in the development of the novel and the English reading public; and finally, the novel's growth is manifestly evident and probably unstoppable, but also necessitates action. In the pages that follow, I trace the ways these beliefs emerge across the writing of a range of contemporary commentators. Though articulated specifically about Minerva Press novels here, the later chapters of this book reveal how these interconnecting beliefs about fiction's new dominance affected the ways that the period's many other novels were written and received.

Reviewers

Anxieties about the Minerva Press's novels took a range of forms; that the books were bad (aesthetically, morally, grammatically) is a frequent refrain, but only one. Reviewers frequently describe these failures as inseparable from the market saturation achieved by these 'numerous, or, to speak with more propriety, innumerable' volumes.[2] The problem, in other words, wasn't, or wasn't only, that the Minerva Press's novels were flawed, but that there were just so many of them. There was, in the eyes of many contemporary observers, simply too much fiction flooding the market.

But too much for whom? Too many for what? Too many to read, very possibly, although for dedicated readers this was likely a good problem to have. Too many for certain modes of literary criticism, certainly, though of course the question of reading these works for purposes of scholarship was still far over the horizon at the time. Too many, at least, for one specific thing: as of the mid-1790s, there were too many novels for reviewers to review, or at least to review as they would have done thirty years before. Bibliographers and periodical scholars including Derek Roper, Peter Garside, and Antonia Forster have all pointed out this changing circumstance. Roper writes, for instance, that 'by the end of the [eighteenth] century [the ideal of comprehensive reviewing] had become impossible, if only because of the sheer volume of new publications', while Garside suggests that in the later 1780s and 1790s, the 'sudden surge in novel production ... stretched [the review] system to breaking point'.[3] The data in the *English Novel* bibliography indicate the dropping proportions of novels reviewed quite clearly; as Garside notes in the introduction to the second volume, in 1800 and 1801 'about half' of novels were reviewed in the *Critical Review*, and one quarter were reviewed in the *Monthly Review*; by 1806, only a quarter of all novels published were reviewed in the *Critical Review*, and fewer still in the *Monthly*.[4]

If anyone had a legitimate right to complain about their altered situation, then, it was reviewers – and complain they certainly did. Indeed, the
rhetoric of the overburdened reviewer is nearly as ubiquitous in the literary
culture of the 1790s and early 1800s as that of the groaning press.[5]
Reviewer Thomas Holcroft, in a typical example, irritably described 'the
young ladies who at present write novels, which none but young ladies and
we, luckless reviewers, read'.[6] (Holcroft was, of course, also a novelist
himself, but as a man he was conveniently exempt from his own critique.)[7]
Holcroft's complaint is representative of much contemporary reviewing in
its implication that women were the reviled authors and men were the
beleaguered critics. Though this dynamic is connected to some actual
shifts in publication (in particular, the greater number of women authors
entering the market), accusations of excess transcend gender stereotypes,
even as they often depend upon them. Reviewing *Emily; or, The Fatal
Promise* (1792), the *Critical Review* lamented, 'Heaven defend us from
such trash; but Reviewers must wade through the most disgusting
masses.'[8] The 'mass' – that is, the material volume – of the work in
question is an unaltering refrain in these reviews from the period's beginning to its end. A review of *The Follies of St. James Street* (1789) refers to
'the swarms of pernicious, or at best, silly volumes, that load the shelves of
a circulating library',[9] while the reviewer of the *Bristol Heiress* (1809)
describes the book as 'one of those numerous publications which issue
almost daily from the press'.[10] The output of novels is no more voluminous than the novels themselves – *The Family Party* (1791) is described as
'*Mediocre* – The attention is not sufficiently excited – and the incidents are
spun out to too great a length.'[11] And the *Critical Review* describes *Elvina*
(1792) as 'work which never rises above mediocrity, and sometimes sinks
greatly below that standard … the greater part is wire-drawn and
insipid'.[12] 'Wire-drawn' is no longer an adjective in much use, but the
obsolete definition, 'to draw or prolong to a great length; to protract
excessively', seems clearly to capture the reviewer's intended sense.[13]
There are too many books, such reviews declare – and many of them are
far too long.

As these examples suggest, critiques of fictional proliferation take many
forms. In the section that follows, I look at three types in particular that
surface most frequently: first, the idea that literary excess elicits an emotional response; second, the claim that increasing numbers necessitate the
emergence of groups and hierarchies to control and organize them; finally,
the suggestion that dangerous overgrowth can be curbed by the right kind
of criticism. Each of these often-entwined lines of thinking intersects with

one more: the suggestion that certain novels – and, specifically, novels produced by the Minerva Press – are especially problematic. These were the works most likely to be identified as superfluous, undesirable, and relegated beyond the critical pale.

Reviewers overwhelmed by new books often portray themselves as engaged in emotional management as much as aesthetic critique; reviewers must, they claim, handle their own responses to the deluge, as well as those of readers and authors. The *Critical Review* described being 'urged more by duty than by inclination' to read *Forresti* (1806), declaring heavily, 'It is our lot, we confess it with a sigh, to peruse bad and good publications.'[14] Such a duty may thicken the skin, as the reviewer of *Edmund, or The Child of the Castle* (1790) suggests, claiming that 'it is a Reviewer only, steeled by frequent practice to inflexible perseverance, who does not throw aside the work with contempt'.[15] Many reviewers describe their confusion and even sadness at being 'forced' to assess so many bad novels, taking great pains to emphasize their willingness to give a kind review – when, rarely, it is earned. As a reviewer of *Hermione, or The Orphan Sisters* (1791) puts it, 'Amidst the irksomeness of an office which imposes upon us the necessity of executing so frequently the harsher duties of criticism, we embrace with eagerness every opportunity of bestowing praise.'[16] The reviewer of *Fanny* (1792) is even more melodramatic, writing that while *Fanny* itself is acceptable, '[I]t has been our lot lately to pass sentence of death on *the first literary* attempts of many *young ladies*. We have done it not without great unwillingness, and with heavy hearts.'[17] *The Butler's Diary* (1792) elicited a more ambivalent response: 'There are many books in this species of writing, which, having read, we find ourselves entirely at a loss what sentence to inflict.'[18]

Other reviewers engaged more directly with authors, as when the *Monthly Review* observed, of *The Duchess of York* (1791), 'It has of late become a policy to elude, as may be supposed, critical strictures, by an appeal to the humanity of the reader; and by pleading personal circumstances as the motive for having recourse to the pen', the writer claims. 'When such a plea is offered in a female character, we scarcely know how to receive it, until repetition familiarizes us to it,' the piece continues, citing 'repetition' as the antidote to authorial appeals to pathos. Just one such plea might work, this formulation suggests, but when the reviewer receives *many* of them, 'then we cannot but recollect, that the public opinion of literary merit has no connection with, and will very seldom be influenced in favour of, the private motives of the writer'.[19] Reviewing is here characterized as a process of wrestling with competing demands;

authorial demands become overwhelming when presented en masse, but their very frequency can also function to inure reviewers to them.

It's no coincidence that so many of these complaints have a familiar ring: unlike most people, reviewers had a public platform from which to air their grievances. Committed to print, their perceptions had both wide distribution and staying power. If anyone is responsible for the age's perceptions of excess, then, reviewers are certainly among the guiltiest parties. For reviewers didn't only complain about the onerous burden increasing numbers of (increasingly bad) novels placed upon them; they also tried in a range of ways to rhetorically 'manage' their burden. One of the clearest strategies is the delineation of distinct classes or ranks of works, in which the unworthy many become the backdrop for the desirable few.[20] The reviewer of *Humbert Castle* (1800) used this technique to differentiate between the current generation of writings and the (presumably superior) publications of the past, writing, 'On the perusal of this novel our thoughts were carried back to the works of those who wrote in our younger days. The mode in which it is written is far superior to that of the trash which is now daily obtruded upon the public.'[21] Similarly, *Anna Melvil* (1792) was praised in terms clearly designed to distinguish it from other work: 'He is not entitled to a small degree of praise who, in the beaten path of literature, opens to the view of the beholder a perspective hitherto unseen or little noticed. Such praise belongs to the author of the novel before us, which contains incidents perfectly new.'[22] The 'beaten path of literature' suggests an over-trodden way – but a way that highlights those few books that diverge from it.

The idea that the best will rise to the top of any group sometimes grants a surprisingly positive view of the age's flourishing novel market: a few reviewers suggest (in rhetoric that would be echoed later by authors like Walter Scott) that the vast numbers of novels now being produced might ultimately result in the production of better work, by the laws of volume alone. 'Among the numerous works which issue from the prolific brains of those who seek their almost daily bread at the great manufacture in Leadenhall-street, it would be singular if there were not some that rose pre-eminently,'[23] declared the *Critical Review* in a discussion of *The Aunt and the Niece* (1804). Others, however, viewed this torrent of novels in rather less optimistic terms. The novel *Persiana* (1791), for example, receives some measure of praise from the *Critical Review*, but volume ultimately works against it, as the reviewer concludes, 'yet, perhaps, among the wretched productions that have lately issued from the press in this department, it is no very great honour to be in the first line'.[24] The very existence of these manifold other 'wretched productions' casts the merit of this work into doubt, even as they elevate it by comparison.

Whether the net effect of increased production is positive or negative, reviewers repeatedly refer to developing literary hierarchies in their efforts to categorize new work.[25] Praising *The Butler's Diary* (1792), the *Critical Review* wrote, 'There is a novelty in the style and manner ... which renders it pleasing. There is a discrimination of character also ... which seem to lift these volumes above the common rank.'[26] Sometimes the groupings had to do with content or perceived genre; *Ariana and Maud* (1803), for instance, was described as 'on the whole, amusing, but the incidents too much in the common strain to interest greatly. There is scarcely an event which we have not before witnessed, nor an escape which has not had a hundred prototypes.'[27] And a review of *First Love* (1801) refers to 'the same common-place round of a cruel father, a disappointed maiden, and a happy marriage in conclusion, which is to be found in the major part of modern novels'.[28] In other cases, however, the classification seems to be more general, and largely about status. *The Cypher; or, The World as It Goes* (1791) is said to be 'Not without merit ... This work seems entitled to a place in a circulating library.'[29] *Monimia* (1791), though 'more varied than almost any novel that we have lately read ... possesses a share of merit which will place it in a respectable station in the second rank'.[30] *Charles Henly* (1790) is predicted to 'reach the higher ranks ... not of fame, but of the library'.[31] Reviewing *Mortimer Castle* (1793), the *English Review* used comparison to address both volume and value, writing, 'As the quantity of novels with which Mr. Lane deluges the public is very large, it must be expected that some of them will be indifferent. To this class does the present tale belong. The style is not reprehensible, but the incidents have been so often repeated that they not only cease to please, but begin almost to disgust.'[32] It is overfamiliarity alone that condemns this novel, it seems; it is the repetition of too-familiar tropes across too-numerous novels, rather than anything 'reprehensible' that make this particular one so objectionable.

As these examples have already begun to suggest, reading Minerva reviews in this period reveals an emerging discourse that posits the Minerva Press itself (along with its concomitant circulating libraries and printing presses) as a kind of literary class identification. Indeed, as Megan Peiser has shown, a full 20 per cent of Minerva Press reviews in the *Monthly* and *Critical Reviews* discuss the literary 'class' of the novel.[33] Being associated with William Lane or the Minerva Press is automatically to be superfluous, generically interchangeable, and mass-produced. Even in the early 1790s, before Lane's publication numbers reached their later heights, we see reviews like that of Eliza Parsons's *Woman as She Should Be* (1793), about which the *Critical Review* declared, 'Upon the whole, we consider this lady's labours less deserving the severity of critical remark than the general run of publications from the press of Mr. Lane.'[34] The 'general run of publications' against which this one is contrasted clearly comprises works thought to be both artistically indifferent and in some way recognizable as Lane productions. Another Parsons novel, *Errors of Education* (1791), inspired a satirical riposte from the *Town and Country Magazine*, playing on the Minerva Press's unliterary location to suggest that books produced there resembled nothing more than each other: '"What's in a name? That which we call a rose by any other name would smell as sweet." – So says the great dramatic bard; and Mr. Lane might as well have named this novel *Leadenhall-Street*, as *Errors of Education*.'[35] The notion that all Minerva novels are not only the same, but identifiable with the press that made them is heightened by frequent discussions of the press as a 'manufacture' and its books as products of various kinds. *Monimia* (1791) is described as 'fabricated in one of Mr. Lane's best looms',[36] while *Baron of Manstow* (1790) inspires the declaration that 'in obedience to the mandates of fashion, the London manufacturers have, for some time past, converted their ingenuity to the fabrications of *German* novels'.[37] The textile metaphors, emphasized even more explicitly in other reviews, heighten the sense of these books – of this *class* of novels – as material objects, rather than receptacles of ideas.[38]

    If one response to reviewers' overloaded desks is to dismiss through categorization, another, more direct approach was to attempt, as it were, to address the oversupply at its source. Reviewing *Heaven's Best Gift* (1797), the *Monthly Visitor* wrote sarcastically, 'To originality [the author] may indisputably lay claim, as it is a very original thought indeed to make the hero and heroine prominent alone from their defects. We would, however, advise her, very seriously, to write no more.'[39] *Write no more* – if only more novelists would heed this plea, many reviewers lamented. But the Minerva Press and other similar publishers stand in the way of such a goal, as the *Critical Review* suggests, quoting a passage from *Edwardina* (1800) that reads in part, 'Nature gives me imagination … and the Minerva offers liberal encouragement: and I repeat, when I have too much time, and too little money, why beshrew me, but I will turn novel writer.'[40] In the face of such 'encouragement', this reviewer suggests, all criticisms will likely fall on deaf ears: 'How shall a word, issuing from the sequestered conclave of the Critical Reviewers, set aside a resolution so determinately bent on writing?' Still, 'The fair author must write her next work better, or we shall not be disposed to praise it, however liberally the Minerva may think fit to pay for the copy.'[41] Presses are pitted against reviewers in this model, with authors in the middle, being swayed to write more – or not at all. This review further suggests a more direct link between the Minerva and the age's overproduction – we know that Lane did aggressively advertise for authors, but as the accounts of poverty-stricken Minerva authors suggest, his payments may have been adequate but were hardly 'liberal'.[42]

Other authors received a more measured critique; rather than being asked to stop writing altogether, they were merely asked to reduce the *size* of their novels: Margaret Holford's reviewer, for instance, wrote in 1801, 'there is nothing reprehensible in First Impressions except its bulk ... [if the author had] compress[ed] the work into half its present size, by retrenching its superfluous garrulity, every incident might still have been narrated, and the reader would have found it not an unpleasing perfor-mance'.[43] The reviewer of *Belleville Lodge* (1793) seems to be thinking along similar lines, remarking, 'Some ingenuity seems to be exerted in filling two volumes with a meagre story – but what is impossible to a mind fraught with the rich treasures, dispensed by Lane, Hookham, and Co.'[44] As this reference to Lane's competitor Thomas Hookham reminds us, Lane was by no means alone in his novelistic ventures; he was a scapegoat, but other publishers like Hookham, Hughes, and, later, Colburn were similarly associated with popular fiction, circulating libraries, and the many-volumed productions they offered for the public's entertainment. In typical examples of such characterizations, *Independence* (1802) is described as 'at times a little too prolix',[45] and *The Family Party* (1791) 'might certainly be condensed into one volume without any injury'.[46]

Despite all these discouragements, however, Minerva Press authors continued to publish their novels each year, often in three, four, and even more volumes. The best-selling *The Beggar Girl* (1797), at seven hefty volumes, seems to deliberately defy critical strictures on prolixity.[47] Faced with examples of authorial profligacy like these, some reviewers took a different tack: extreme brevity. These reviews, which mocked the author's grandiose prose stylings with brusque summaries, model an efficient use of prose, but also seem designed as a kind of antidote to excess, balancing over-verbosity in one literary arena with understatement in another. The three-volume *Henry of Northumberland* (1800), for instance, was reduced to a single sentence: 'A desultory, ill-constructed, and uninteresting tale'.[48] Another effort, Amelia Opie's anonymously published first novel, *The Dangers of Coquetry* (1790), was similarly dismissed as 'Dull, insipid, and improbable!'[49] And T. J. Horsley Curties, author of *The Scottish Legend* (1802), found his labours summed up thus: 'We have nothing to say of this work, more than what the author has said in the title-page. *It is four volumes of* ROMANCE.'[50] Combatting narrative immoderation with deliberate, marked brevity reduces the space taken up by these novels in one sense, but ironically reproduces their multiplicity in the pages of reviews, as five or six reviews squeeze into a page that wouldn't even contain the entirety of a single longer analysis.

The trend towards compression continues even more drastically after the turn of the nineteenth century, when Minerva novels were increasingly excluded from substantive reviews in the *Monthly Review* and the *Critical Review*. Peiser's research shows that Minerva novels were relegated from the first to the less prestigious sections of major reviews: of 307 Lane or Minerva novels reviewed between 1780 and 1820, only seven ever received reviews in the main body of these journals – virtually all the reviews I've cited here appeared instead in the briefer monthly catalogue of new publications.[51] As Peiser points out, this placement would have meant that readers turning to the 'Novels' section of those catalogues would have been visually overwhelmed with Minerva titles, likely contributing to the sense that Minerva was disproportionately flooding the market.[52] As the nineteenth century wore on, however, even the briefest reviews were increasingly replaced by simple listings of titles with no commentary.

To say that reviews of Minerva Press novels become less and less visible in the pages of major reviews in the Press's second and third decade is not, however, to say that mentions of the Press disappear, nor, indeed, that its works were no longer reviewed. The complex dynamic between novelists, publishers, and reviewers continued, perhaps even more robustly, but the sites of their engagement altered. Thus, we find a curious divergence: even as actual Minerva reviews become fewer and further between, references *to* the Minerva Press become increasingly common in reviews of other novels. To some extent these usages, largely derogatory, fall in line with Emma Clery's pithy summary: 'For the following generation of Romantic writers and critics Minerva's representative status made its name synonymous with "trash".'[53] The Minerva Press is used, among other things, to symbolize the fanciful, the unrealistic, the time-wasting, in reviews of novels by other publishers, such as *Memoirs of Joan D'Arc* (1812), of which the *Critical Review* declared, 'The style in which [this work] is written deserves some notice; for, sickening as it would be even from the Minerva Press, it is absolutely intolerable as the language of sober truth and reality.'[54] A review of the *History of the Duke de Lauzun* (1808) mentions, as an aside, 'the time which [readers] now waste on the productions of the Minerva Press'.[55] But what is also striking is how many of these references refer specifically to quantity, to the very over-abundance that renders the novels themselves unreviewable. One writer, Robert Semple, was praised in 1807 for being brief, in marked contrast to other writers – Minerva Press authors – who are *not* brief: the reviewer notes that Semple tends towards straightforward summaries in his description of his travels, 'Instead of indulging his sensibility at any length', and sighs, 'Oh! that the novelists of the Minerva Press were equally forbearing!'[56] Reviewing William Godwin's play *Faulkener* (1807), the *Critical Review* wrote: 'he determined to divest himself of that ... machinery, without whose assistance the prolific ladies of the Minerva Press would be seized with a general and incurable barrenness'.[57] Several reviews mention 'the prolific ladies of the Minerva Press'[58] or expand on the reproductive metaphor's suggestion of intemperate abundance.[59] Negative descriptions of fertility and fecundity are used here to praise Godwin's originality, suggesting the myriad uses to which metaphors of overproduction could be put: not merely scarcity or brevity, but originality and genius are posited as somehow the inverse of excess. The metaphors are distinctly mixed here, of course: the kind of multiplicity implied by calling the novels the 'manufacture of Leadenhall-street', is surely of a different type than that engendered by 'prolific ladies'. But the gender and class inflections remain, in comments like 'the patrons of the Minerva press, the haberdasher and hosier readers of the day'.[60] In different ways, all these assessments deal with undesirably large quantities by establishing new hierarchies, but also by distancing those novels deemed to be superfluous from the category of the 'literary'. Just as reviews of novels that compare them to textiles diminish the novelist's intellectual accomplishment, so references to the Minerva author's uncontrolled fecundity deny her claims to brilliance or skill. These critiques in turn justify the increasing exclusion of these novels from the realm of criticism.

It is important to remember, however, that this kind of critical distancing operated in a network rather than a vacuum. When reading Minerva Press novels themselves from later years, one does not at all receive the impression of novels languishing unreviewed. In 1798, a year in which fully twenty-four of Minerva's twenty-eight novels were reviewed in either the *Critical Review*, the *Monthly Review*, or both, Mary Charlton's new novel, *Phedora*, was published with end-page ads in three of its four volumes, each announcing a new Minerva publication 'with the reviewers opinion' (see Figure 2).[61]

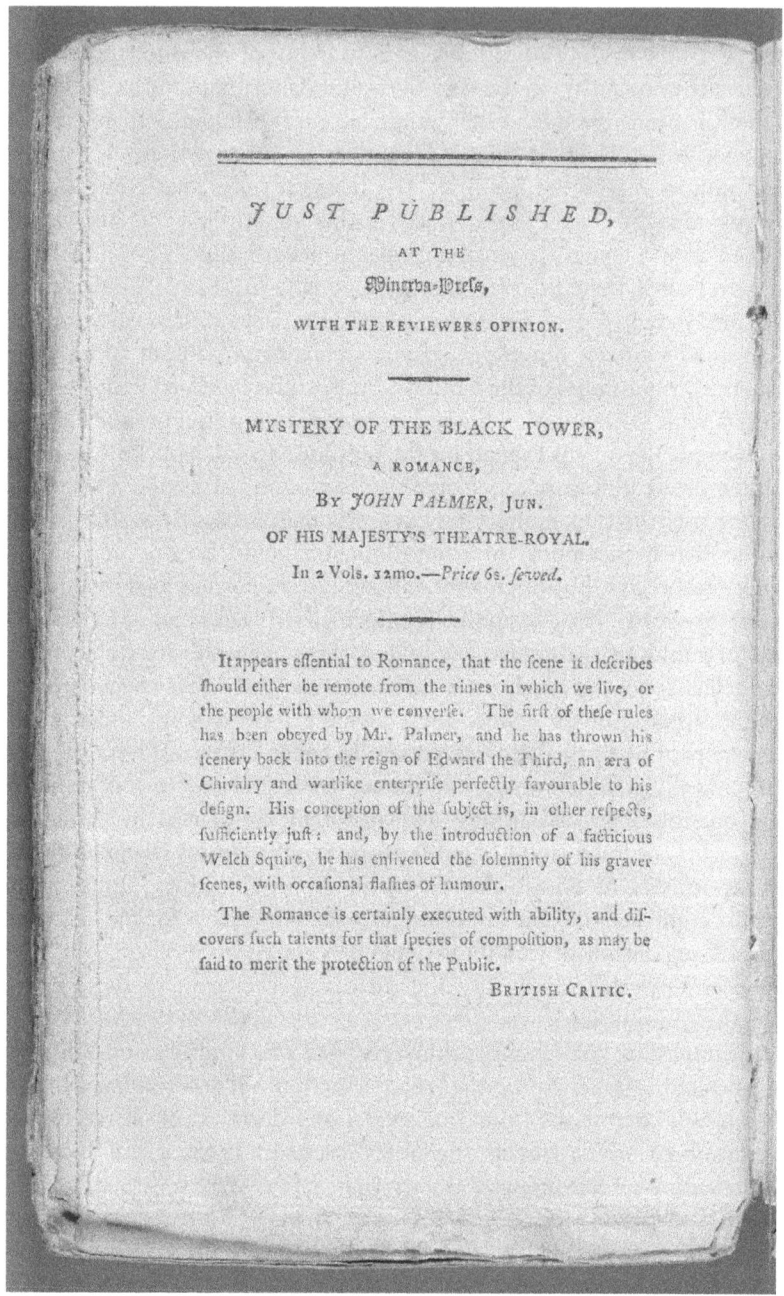

JUST PUBLISHED,

AT THE

Minerva-Press,

WITH THE REVIEWERS OPINION.

MYSTERY OF THE BLACK TOWER,

A ROMANCE,

BY *JOHN PALMER,* JUN.

OF HIS MAJESTY'S THEATRE-ROYAL.

In 2 Vols. 12mo.—*Price* 6s. *sewed.*

It appears essential to Romance, that the scene it describes should either be remote from the times in which we live, or the people with whom we converse. The first of these rules has been obeyed by Mr. Palmer, and he has thrown his scenery back into the reign of Edward the Third, an æra of Chivalry and warlike enterprise perfectly favourable to his design. His conception of the subject is, in other respects, sufficiently just: and, by the introduction of a factitious Welch Squire, he has enlivened the solemnity of his graver scenes, with occasional flashes of humour.

The Romance is certainly executed with ability, and discovers such talents for that species of composition, as may be said to merit the protection of the Public.

BRITISH CRITIC.

Figure 2 End-page advertisement, *Phedora*, vol. III, *EC8 C3818 798p. Houghton Library, Harvard University.

One of the three reproduced reviews is drawn from the *Critical Review* – apparently considered worthy of inclusion because of its source, despite its relatively lukewarm praise.[62] The other two are taken from the *British Critic*, one without even an attribution.[63] Ten years later, as we know, the reviewing scene had changed. In 1808, just one of Minerva's sixteen novels was reviewed by the *Critical* and the *Monthly*, yet when we look at novels in the years leading up to 1810, we still find plenty of glowing reviews at their end – more, in fact. In 1809, *Celia in Search of a Husband* was published with two pages' worth of Minerva Press reviews in the back of its second volume. Eleanor Sleath's the *Bristol Heiress*, also in 1809, published multiple positive reviews of Minerva novels in the back of its five volumes, and this practice is clearly standard.[64]

Strikingly, however, while both the *Bristol Heiress* and *Celia in Search of a Husband* would turn out to be among the few novels to receive notice in the *Critical Review* in 1809, something of an honour by this point, neither included reviews from that publication in the endorsements printed within them; the Minerva novel reviews excerpted are drawn from other sources, including the *British Critic*, the *Annual Review*, the *Lady's Monthly Museum*, the *Literary Journal* and *Cabinet* – in other words, periodicals that hadn't even existed before the Minerva Press was founded. The venue for reviewing Minerva's novels had changed: even as certain reviewers handled the oversupply by replacing actual reviews with concise references, letting one line do the work of hundreds of pages, the Minerva Press found many more willing critics, establishing new networks to signal their quality and popularity. Somewhat ironically, the efforts of established critics to halt the speedy fictional expansion may have in fact driven the proliferation of a different kind of texts: new review periodicals.

Authors

If reviewers decried the age's fictional abundance for increasing their workload, authors, perhaps, had even more reason to fear it – for increasing their competition. This book is full of ways authors resisted and exploited the pressure-driven marketplace in which they found themselves.[65] In this section, I focus on one particularly self-conscious and direct means of authorial engagement: the novel preface. In 1825, the novel *Burton* was prefaced with a lengthy preamble, including the declaration, 'It has become so much the custom now to write an introduction to every book, of every kind or description, before daring to submit it to the public, that it is scarcely a matter of choice.'[66] This is exaggeration, of course, but it highlights the frequency with which authors addressed their putative audiences directly, preparing them for the novels they were about to encounter with disclaimers, boasts, pleas for leniency, or explanations of the origins of their story. Whether called a 'preface', an 'introduction', or an 'address to the reader', these materials offer uniquely useful insight into the ways that authors engaged with ongoing debates about the novel's new prominence.

Some elements of prefaces are so common as to be formulaic: most familiar, perhaps, are humble (or mock-humble) apologies to prospective readers; claims for pity or leniency; and claims for the morality, if not the excellence, of the work to come. *Laurentia* (1790), one of the earliest works to appear under the Minerva imprint, offers a characteristic example of the first two categories: the authoress, signed 'Sabina', declares:

> If the Gentlemen Reviewers could know what I really feel, from the idea of the following pages passing under their eyes, they would in pity spare a simple maid (to whom the emoluments arising from the publication will be very acceptable;) and although they cannot commend, yet not too severely censure. I have no male friend, to whom I dare apply, to revise or correct, and am therefore under the necessity of sending my production into the world with all its 'imperfections on its head' . . . tremblingly anxious for the fate of my volumes, I must remain a humble petitioner for mercy.[67]

The humility, the fear of harsh reviewers – not unjustified, in light of the reviews mentioned in the previous section – and the pleas for mercy all echo again and again through the era's prefaces, as do some of Sabina's other rhetorical strategies: calling attention to her gender (and opposing it to that of reviewers, who are figured as male) and hinting at her financial need.[68] In the preface to *The Mysterious Warning* (1796), for instance, Eliza Parsons begins from a stance of deep humility, writing, 'The Author of the following Work feels herself under the necessity of apologizing to her numerous Friends, for the too frequent demands she makes on their indulgence. – Conscious of her deficiency in talents, inclination has no share in her feeble attempts to entertain the Public.'[69] This self-deprecation is so deep as to seem perhaps irredeemable, but in both her dedication and the preface that follows, Parsons suggests that her talents, or lack thereof, are less important than one other key feature: 'I have never written a line tending to corrupt the heart, sully the imagination, or mislead the judgment of my young Readers.'[70]

On the whole, the preface offers a unique opportunity to pre-empt criticisms of all kinds, to enlist readerly sympathy – or at least to prevent active enmity. Yet these gambits soon became so well-worn that, as

Burton's preface suggested, they were more rote than inspired. Nearly thirty years before *Burton*'s publication, the author of *The Haunted Castle* (1794) had voiced a very similar sentiment, with no less cynicism about the preface's purpose: 'In modern prefaces it is become a custom, not only to give some slight introduction to the work, but also the private motive for writing it; and in this, one general plan seems to be laid down, – which is, to ascribe it to a desire of doing good, and propagating virtue.'[71] Prefaces are designed, in other words, not just to contextualize the work to come, but to manipulate the reader's emotions by building sympathy for the author.

Given the prefaces' mediating function, it should not surprise us that they often engage directly with their era's discourse of ever-increasing fictional production. In Minerva prefaces, authors frequently echo reviewers in portraying novel-writing as newly common, novelists as newly prolific, and the market as newly crowded. Many authors shared reviewers' sense of a too-great profusion of novels – though they then had to find ways to exempt their own works from this overall assessment. Many more novelists, however, take a different angle on the situation: instead of complaining about how numerous, how long, or how exaggerated novels could be, they *explain* these characteristics. And still others justify the utility of modern publishing practices: even if there are too many novels, these authors suggest, the opportunities the situation provides outweigh its downsides.

One of the most frequent ways authors reference an overheated market is to consider how a surplus of similar works may have superseded their own. Sheer numerousness is a quality of novels so frequently referenced as to be taken for granted. In 1791, 'A Female Writer' prefaced her novel *Iphigenia* with a reference to her work's 'many competitors';[72] the following year, Robert Bage opened *Man as He Is* (1792) with the more sardonic admission 'There are books called novels and it is probable I am increasing the number.'[73] Like the reviewers who sought to organize novels into hierarchies or categories, authors' own self-descriptions frequently attempt to explain where their own work falls within the larger body of novels. For some, this takes the form of self-deprecation, as when the author of *Ethelwina, or The House of Fitz-Auburne* (1799) discusses ambitious authors before declaring, 'The Author of this Work soars not so high; he humbly follows the track through which superior talents have already forced a way.'[74] In claims like this, humility vies with self-justification: other talents may be 'superior', but the fact that 'the track' has already been created and well-trodden suggests its continuing popularity. The author of

Rosalind De Tracey (1799) employs the same metaphor: 'So much has, of late, been said against Novels, and so strong seems the prejudice against them, that the writer is willing to assign some cause, for travelling in a track which though generally exploded, is crowded with passengers of every capacity.'[75] Acknowledging the novel's paradoxical position – both maligned and embraced, outdated and in demand – this author too suggests that the ongoing volume of novel production is in itself an indicator of the genre's cultural relevance.

Of course, following in the footsteps of countless predecessors is not without drawbacks, not least the risk of unoriginality or superfluity. When Eliza Parsons introduced *Ellen and Julia* in 1793, she specifically referenced the changing landscape of publication, declaring,

> The following Work I submit to the Judgment of the Public with much greater diffidence and anxiety than when I first threw myself on its candour and indulgence; because the many late excellent productions of other female writers painfully convince me of my own inability and deficiencies, and at the same time lays me open to the imputation of presumption and undue vanity.[76]

Parsons's first novel had been published in 1790, just three years earlier, so her claims that *now* her work was overshadowed by others' excellence is particularly striking. Yet she too invokes the idea that popularity may be its own justification, concluding, 'But as the foil sometimes serves to give additional brilliancy to the Diamond, I may at least be pardoned for an attempt to follow, though I cannot overtake, those celebrated Ladies to whom the Public are so much obliged for their amusement.'[77] Outstanding novels, in this account, simply could not be appreciated without the many more ordinary novels that reveal their value by contrast.

Some, like the author of *Pauline* (1794), viewed the crowded field with less optimism: 'Those then, of course, who are ambitious of exercising their pens, are often much embarrassed on the choice of a subject', this author declares, 'for our novelists have not left the most trivial scene undiscribed, or the least phrase ungleaned in the fields of love, sentiment and gallantry.'[78] Ideas are finite, these metaphors suggest, and too many writers drawing upon them will simply use them up. Other authors, however, like William Linley, the author of *Forbidden Apartments* (1800), recast the situation into a call for different standards. '[T]he desire of being accounted original, especially in the construction of a Novel or a Romance, is now rarely gratified within the limits of consistency', he writes, continuing, 'The stores of ingenuity have been exhausted in illustrating, by natural fiction, the virtues and vices of mankind, improving the mind, and delighting the imagination; and if the dexterous poet can clothe his predecessor's idea in a new dress, it is as much can be reasonably expected.'[79] Originality itself is overrated, Linley hints, a theory that is perhaps supported by the indubitable success of highly formulaic gothic and sentimental novels. This claim also reveals, however, the ways that the pressures of perceived excess can generate both new discourses *and* counter-discourses: just as 'too many' novels can lead some to condemn them as unoriginal or mass-produced – thus valorizing originality in opposition – so this same pressure leads others to suggest alternate models for valuing literature.

For many novelists, wholesale endorsement of new fiction was a bridge too far, but endorsement of *some* novels is presented as especially important in the face of rising publication numbers. Anna Maria Mackenzie, for instance, in the preface to *Mysteries Elucidated* (1795), saw the current situation as a part of a larger historical trend, writing that in mid-century 'a new source of amusement was struck out, at the head of which, FIELDING and RICHARDSON stood pre-eminent; but unfortunately, their numerous copyists . . . in a great measure spoilt the designs of the excellent originals'.[80] This denouncement is, however, only laying the groundwork for a defence of some few novelists:

> That the general run of novels have this sort of tendency, I believe every subscriber to a Circulating Library can witness; (but with the sincerest admiration of their talents, let me exclude the names of Burney, Bennet, Parsons, &c. from a share in the censure, whose elegant performances will, I trust, remove much of the contempt which has fallen upon works of this denomination).[81]

The grouping of names here seems significant: Burney was a better-established and critically more applauded author, whereas Bennett and Parsons, though highly successful and more prolific, were primarily known for their Minerva Press sentimental and gothic novels. Mackenzie's modesty topos may suggest that she doesn't aspire to the lofty heights of her female peers, but the selection of these three authors is also a defence of her work, a claim that Minerva novels too can be 'elegant performances'. Mary Ann Hanway similarly decries some novels in order to defend others in the preface to *Ellinor* (1798). '[H]aving been long convinced the most baneful consequences must result to the rising generation, from reading the monstrous productions that for some years past, have issued from the press', she laments, 'let us hope, in the enlightened æra of nearly the expiration of the eighteenth century, that the *rage* for supernatural agency will soon terminate, and those hordes of ghosts that have swarmed forth from the *black forests* of the north, and taken their station on the *trembling* shelves of our circulating libraries, will soon be banished'.[82]

This banishment will not, however, mean the absence of novels altogether; rather, 'Those once disappeared, sense, wit, and nature will regain their empire' – which, Hanway suggests, means a return to fiction in the style of Richardson, Fielding, and Smollett (iv–v). In looking back to a kind of mid-century fictional golden age, these authors echoed the rhetoric of many reviewers. Though both groups frame their concern as having to do with fictional quality, *quantity* may be their real point: it's no coincidence that their nostalgia is for the period just preceding the rapid rise in fictional output at century's end.

Authors who kept their comparisons in the present were no less cognizant of the towering literary figures of their own day with whom they would inevitably be contrasted. Sarah Lansdell's *Manfredi* (1796) humbly begins by noting, 'It may be considered as presumption in a young authoress to venture her little productions abroad in the world, when there are so many works extant of Ratcliffe's, Smith's, Bennett's and Burney's, who so greatly excel in this species of composition.'[83] The next sentence, however, defends this authorial choice, explaining, 'But let it be considered that ... few persons who find in themselves an inclination to scribbling, but are willing to make one trial of their ability in that flight.'[84] Writers write simply because they cannot resist, such an explanation suggests – whether it is fame, fortune, or the mere pleasure of composition they crave, they cannot be blamed for making the attempt. As Eliza Sophia Tomlins, author of *Rosalind de Tracey* (1798), puts it, 'The very act of composition, especially where imagination is at all concerned, is so pleasing, that no author can much regret the time bestowed in it.'[85] While authors bemoaning the tired and exploded 'tracks' taken by their forebears suggest that overproduction makes originality no longer possible, those who follow *Rosalind de Tracey*'s writer tend to suggest the opposite: the endlessness of other factors – imagination, inspiration, readerly demand – is naturally, and unproblematically, reflected in the endlessness of the fiction thus inspired. Maria Hunter, in the preface to *Ella* (1798), cited the world's vast variety as a source of limitless literary inspiration: 'the great volume of human nature is an inexhaustible source of matter to the observer'.[86] William Linley, more sourly, observed that '*New* monsters, *new* devils, *new* systems, *new* conceptions, and *new* languages may every day be made to lash new vices and follies, which are multiplying every hour.'[87]

These defences easily turn from reflections on the variety of life to considerations of the variety of readers. The author of *Pauline* (1794), for instance, sees novels as useful for their social function: 'Authors are useful members of society, because twenty thousand persons live by the works, good and bad, that are published every year; and printing being a trade of importance to the state, it cannot be too far extended.'[88] Reminding readers of the vast network of labour and commerce that underpins book production grants fiction a practical importance as a part of the economy, but also emphasizes how enormous the demand for these works is. And, like novels themselves, novel-readers seemed only to multiply. Francis Lathom, in *The Unknown* (1808), notes wryly that 'Notwithstanding the censors of literature continue to inveigh as warmly as ever against novels in the aggregate, the number of novel-readers increases every day.'[89] This external circumstance, in Lathom's view, ties directly back to the question of authorial impulse: '[T]his circumstance, of course', he continues, 'spurs on the writers of such compositions to greater vigour and animation: it would be as unnatural for them to lay down their pens, as for a candidate to decline an election when the majority of the suffrages were in his favour.'[90] Successful writers want to write, this line of reasoning runs, a sentiment expressed perhaps most explicitly by the incredibly prolific Anthony Frederick Holstein, author of more than ten Minerva Press novels (as well as two more for Colburn, one of Lane's successors in the field of popular fiction) between 1808 and 1815.[91] Describing his own mental state, he dramatically declares that his brain 'at this moment has the torment of perpetual motion; I can neither analyze nor controul it, and I must e'en let it exhaust itself, and roll on the axis of thought, unless the critic would resound on my appalled ear the awful verdict of "Write no more!"'[92] Whether his echo of the *Heaven's Best Gift* review cited above is deliberate or coincidental, it represents something important: the more critics decried new novels, the more authors sought to explain and justify their own defiant production of them.

Indeed, a reading of Holstein's collected prefaces presents him as a sort of theorist of literary overload as well as a novelist. In the preface to *Bouverie* (1812) he considers his own considerable contributions to the age's fiction supply at some length, reflecting,

> I TREMBLE as I reflect on the many works which have issued from my pen within the last three years, since which my authorship has commenced!... I have a strong feeling of dread and diffidence of the fate of each [of my works], as I close a volume of fiction, lest the ordeal of

> criticism should affirm I '*write too much!*' – the most appalling verdict
> I could hear pronounced.[93]

His personal (over)production is finally justified, in this case, with the same moral arguments used by so many other authors: he concludes, 'Consider me, at least, as the friend of morality – the anxious being who seeks to amuse those vacant hours which might otherwise be filled by books from some circulating library of more exceptionable tendency.'[94] In *The Inhabitants of Earth* (1811), he again uses the rhetoric of prolific overproduction, this time in relation to the trope of authorial humility, satirically naming his publisher in the process:

> Again I wield the pen of authorship, and send forth another offspring to the world; but, alas! not like the progeny of the famed monarch of the clouds, will a Minerva issue from my far less potent head. A very *mortal* in power, I entail upon my bantlings all the errors of their father; and display, in my poor descendants, a motley volume of virtue and vice.[95]

The derogatory reproductive metaphors used by so many critics to denigrate the Minerva's ever-growing output here become a self-imposed metaphor of artistic creation, recuperating flawed texts as realistic reflections of flawed humans.

Tracking Holstein's self-conceptualization as an overproducer also reveals yet another way in which the rhetoric of authors themselves provocatively echoes (or prefigures) that of their critics. Just as reviewers called attention to the numerousness of novels, but also to their disproportionate length, so authors frequently defend the number of words, scenes, and volumes they employ to tell their story.[96] In *The Modern Kate* (1812) Holstein apologizes for 'the inaccuracies or blunders he may have committed in the *many thousand* pages of composition he has already written for the press', and in *Lady Durnevor, or My Father's Wife* (1813) he explicitly imagines his novel's reception in terms of its length: '"Near a thousand pages more!" perhaps is all the exclamation that will greet my book on a first view of it upon the counter of a circulating library.'[97] Citing the novel's subtitle, he continues his mocking self-interrogation, asking (in the guise of his putative reader), 'I wonder what "MY FATHER'S WIFE," finds to say for herself so copiously; she must be the most talkative and loquacious of her sex, and Mr. Holstein the most patient of his, to commit to paper all her voluminous nonsense.'[98] Holstein's self-conscious humour reflects a frequent refrain in other prefaces: How much story does a reader need – and how much will they tolerate? The author of *Turkish Tales* (1794) suggests that long novels may be an acquired taste, but ultimately beneficial:

It has frequently been urged as a recommendation to medicines ... that if they do no good, it is impossible that they can do any harm. On the same ground, the following Tales are offered to the Public.... To continue the analogy ... it is to be observed, that the packet ... is divided into five doses, small at first, but gradually increasing, as the strength of the reader (who if he goes thro' the whole course, may, not unaptly, be termed the patient) is able to bear them.[99]

The humour in the comparison between literature and a bitter medicine is clear, but the metaphor also seems an implied defence of lengthy fiction: the problem with a long novel may not be the author's wordiness but the unpreparedness of the reader. A five-volume novel, in this view, is not self-indulgent or reflective of an editing failure, but a kind of education, preparing the reader with each new instalment to better benefit from the next.

Authors give a variety of defences for the length of their novels in their prefaces. The art of authorial dilation, expanding a small incident into a multi-volume adventure, is sometimes cited in a tongue-in-cheek way as proof of an author's talent or work ethic. *Reginal di Torby* (1803) is said to be 'founded on a tale, told by a gentleman, for the diversion of his children'; rather sardonically, the author continues, 'The story, as I heard it related, would hardly fill ten of my pages; the reader may, therefore, imagine that I have had no slight labour to bring it to its present form and length.'[100] Holstein suggests, in contrast, that large plots simply require many pages to develop, even if the author originally intends otherwise. Upon finishing *Miseries of an Heiress* (1810), he claims,

> I had no idea, when I first began, of rendering the subject more diffuse than two volumes, and was myself deceived in the quantity I had written of manuscript, until, upon counting over the pages, I found I had already entered upon the third volume; nor, even then, left sufficient space to develop the plot.... I was thus induced to commence a fourth, which, I confess, was contrary to my inclinations; for I think three volumes should be the extent of any Novel or Romance of this description.[101]

Given the number of novels Holstein wrote, we may take his self-proclaimed length limitations with more than a grain of salt. Yet he reflects the rhetoric of many other authors when he suggests that it is the sheer interest and complexity of his story that demands so many volumes, and emphasizes his own heroic labour in complying with the plot's oversized demands – at the novel's completion, he claims, 'The pen dropped from my almost-paralyzed hand, after an incessant scribbling of many wearying hours!'[102] The extended time it takes to write a long novel (prefiguring the time it will take to *read* it) is tied to the material conditions of the writing process, which in turn ties back to the novel's plot and narrative style: temporal, material, and stylistic dimensions are interlinked.

Others offered more cynical interpretations for authorial prolixity. *Something Odd!* (1804), though attributed to a woman, Mary Meeke, begins with a lengthy satirical 'Dialogue between the Author and His Pen', which suggests that (male?) authors simply lack self-restraint; when the Author declares his 'hope for a favourable fiat' from reviewers, the Pen responds, 'Hope away, my dear director; *I* am not quite so sanguine. I anticipate a *deadly* trimming for you; and, to be candid, I have run headlong over words, sentences, sentiments, passages, and pages, which, without any the least subtraction from the *value* of your work, you might have omitted.'[103] And William Linley, in *Forbidden Apartments* (1800), suggests that even the stars of the current literary firmament (the female ones, at least) are guilty of unnecessary narrative dilation. 'When I mention the names of a Smith, a D'Arblay, an Inchbald, a Radcliffe, and a Lee', he declares, 'it is not without the highest respect for their talents; but at the same time, I cannot help lamenting that one or two of these ingenious writers have so spun out their narratives, that a story has been made to drag through six volumes, which might have been related with much greater satisfaction to the reader in one.'[104] Linley suggests that such lengthiness harms readerly understanding and thus a novel's reputation, writing,

> I will only venture to observe that a tale is more likely to become popular, and to preserve a lasting reputation, that is permitted to glide smoothly on without the constant introduction of new characters and incidents, uncon-nected with the main subject.... It is impossible for the memory, however retentive, to preserve such a chain of occurrences; and nothing injures the interest and moral effect of any literary production so much as a perpetual reference to what has gone before.[105]

Even if the failure to understand or enjoy a novel is ultimately the reader's fault, in other words, Linley argues, authors would be wise to take their predilections into account.

The respective reputations of the prolix women writers above and Linley may suggest that his reading of public taste was more polemical than accurate, but he was far from alone in critiquing the authors of supposedly overlong novels in order to endorse his own. Joseph Moser, author of the two-volume *The Hermit of the Caucusus* (1796), offers brevity as an endorsement of his novel, declaring that while 'some critic may observe, that with a touch of my pen, I have shrunk the *immense Caucausus* to a *molehill* ... I had taken space enough into my canvas, whether we consider it historically or perspectively, for the scene which is there represented' (vi). He adds, 'To crowd a picture or book with too many objects, is more likely to produce confusion, than either *elegance* or *effect*' (vii). Moser concludes that 'after my solitary excursion upon the mountain, I was happy to revisit the busy haunts of men, which the reader, whose *patience* is unexhausted, will find that I do in the last volume'.[106] The author of *Melbourne* (1798) too suggests that readers may easily weary of novels that go on interminably; comparing reading to a stagecoach, she writes that 'whenever [readers] become disgusted or tired, the door may be opened, and they have only to step out'.[107] The author of *Horrid Mysteries* (1796) praises himself for keeping 'the mysterious events occurring in the subsequent volumes' from being 'elucidated with that tiresome minuteness which renders many of our modern novels rather tedious than interesting'.[108] And 'The Authoress' of *Concealment* (1801) declares that while 'She is conscious the monotonous complainings of Matilda will weary many listless high-bred readers ... they have one consolation – *The Book is short.*'[109]

As quotations like this one show, the question of whether it was possible to have too much writing *within* a novel was just as hotly debated as whether there were too many novels to start with. Long novels might be so because they simply had to be, in response to pressures of readerly expectation, plot requirements, or authorial exuberance; conversely, they might be seen as unnecessarily long, lengthy only because of lack of self-control, too much ambition, or unnecessary digression. Though most prefatory discussions of length hinge primarily on aesthetic or artistic criteria, the preface to *De Willenberg; or, The Talisman* (1821) by 'I. M. H. Hales, Esq'., suggests another, underlying motivation for very long narratives. 'Be it as it may, my book has been read, and (shall I say?) praised', Hales declares, before continuing,

> Oh, vanity, vanity, that is too much! Well then I will only say, that had I been as learned an 'Astrologer' as Osmin the monk [a character from his last book], I should have foreseen his reception, and carried him through *six* good-sized volumes instead of three; thus doubling the profits to the bookseller and myself, like many shrewd and sensible authors of the present day.[110]

Imagining the unnecessarily enlarged size of novels as directly tied to the business of publication challenges any claims for the intrinsic necessity of length, but also suggests that length is an inevitable outcome of contemporary publishing norms.

Considering novel-writing in this broader sense, within a larger ecosystem of publication, circulation, and readerly demand, opens the scope of discourse out again beyond the bounds of each individual novel. A final strand of discussion found in many prefaces ties novel (over)production to liberty, suggesting that a large number should always be thought of as plenitude rather than an excess: with numbers come choice, and with choice comes freedom. If readers *or* critics are displeased with the book they are perusing, these authors suggest, they have only themselves to blame; they are welcome to choose a different novel at any time, and all of society benefits in the process. In the introduction to *Bungay Castle* (1796), Elizabeth Bonhote writes,

> Gentle reader, we will now enter upon a story.... If any, who sit down to read it ... should find a temporary relief from misery or languor, the Author will consider it as a luxuriant reward for her employment. If, on the contrary, they should be disappointed, or dissatisfied, she sincerely wishes they may meet a more agreeable entertainment from the next publication thrown in their way.[111]

Francis Lathom takes a more oblique approach to the same idea, declaring, in the preface to *London; or, Truth without Treason* (1809), 'With regard to the characters contained in my volumes, I have worked like an army tailor, who makes a multitude of suits, without having taken measure of any individual, and leaves it to every member of the regiment to select for himself the one which fits him best.'[112] The derogatory valences of critical metaphors comparing fiction and textiles are here transformed into a defence of variety: variety and industry are the author's responsibilities in this model; selecting pleasing reading material falls to the reader.

While authors like Latham rebutted critical claims about an 'excess' of novels, still others used their prefaces, and similar rhetorics of variety and free choice, to attack their critics themselves. Responding to critics who found it useful to categorize and dismiss large groups of novels on the grounds of similarity, authors mock reviewers for their apparent inability to distinguish between the many fictional choices on offer. Henry Siddons remarks, 'It has been very much the fashion, of late, to decry all Novels and Romances as sad trash and contemptible stuff. When once a common cant has got abroad it is very difficult to stop it', before complaining that 'really it is hard to condemn us in a *lump* for the wild imaginations of a few'.[113] The preface to *Leopold Warndorf* (1800), more pointedly, uses *Hamlet* to satirize the critical tendency to lump unlike works together, overlooking distinctions in the haste to identify new works as adherents of any new fad. 'I know the prejudices arising from comparison', he warns, before quoting:

HAMLET.   Methinks it is like a weasel.
POLONIUS.   It is back'd like a weasel.
HAMLET.   Or, like a whale?
POLONIUS.   Very like a whale.

'Some of the inconsistencies of the Danish Courtier may be found in the ingenious critics of the eighteenth century', Somersett concludes.[114]

Regina Maria Roche, in contrast, finds comfort in the wide array of other available novels, expressing hope that they will distract critics from focusing on her own work. 'To you, Oh ye critics!... I implore you to disregard this humble TALE', she writes. 'Permit it, I entreat you, to pass by in unheeded insignificance, and reserve your sagacious animadversions for those stupendous works that, like the Pyramids of Egypt, rise successively above each other, and provoke, by their pretensions to fame, an enquiry into the nature of their structure, and the basis of their elevation.'[115] Numerousness might provide grounds for dismissal, but it could also shelter some novels (especially those lacking in 'pretensions') from critical appraisal, Roche's plea humorously suggests.

If prefaces are a crucial site for theorizing fictional quantity and quality, they are also, ironically, sites of contestation about these theories; while many authors of the *Burton* school declare the modern necessity of prefacing their work, other authors suggest that prefaces themselves are intrinsically superfluous, a tipping point between a sufficiency (the novel itself) and unnecessary, ego-boosting verbosity. Quintin Poynet, Esq., declares that 'prefatory matter (especially by readers of romances and novels) is much more frequently considered an encumbrance, or at best as a piece of surplussage'.[116] And James MacHenry claims, 'I know that prefaces to such works are seldom or never read' in order to explain why he is 'not prefixing to this book, according to custom, half a dozen pages of useless matter'.[117] The author of *Beatrice* (1824) remarks, 'Prefaces are so seldom read, that I have very little encouragement to write one', and Anna Maria Mackenzie calls them 'useless decorations'.[118] But what is unnecessary to the reader may still be desirable to the author; Helen Craik's *Henry of Northumberland* (1800) features a prefatory conversation with an unnamed 'friend', who tells the author, 'yes, by all means, let us have a Preface; every Novel writer furnishes one; 'tis the Author's best possible mode of indulging in a little agreeable egotism'.[119] Introducing *The*

Mysterious Freebooter (1806), Francis Lathom suggests that he has been forced to include a preface because of hostile reviewers:

> After the daily instances which we have of this species of composition [novels] meeting with the greatest success, I should have deemed it quite superfluous to have written a line of defence for one more added to the number, were I not aware that *some* of the reviewers are like hornets, looking out for a hole in a man's jerkin, through which they may drive their stings.[120]

But it is Henry Siddons who provides perhaps the most ironic use of the preface to comment on one common outcome of novel-writing in the Romantic age in his novel *Reginal di Torby* (1803). He dedicates the work: 'To oblivion, who has always been so kind as to take care of the works of the numerous tribe of my brother authors, and has shewn the same indulgence to some of my productions, the present one is inscribed, with respect and gratitude, by the author'.[121] To write is to offer one's work to the world, but the presence of 'a numerous tribe' of other writers ensures, for better or worse, that many or most such works will be overlooked or soon forgotten.

Variety and the Romantic Reader

Romantic authors and reviewers, however rhetorically inconsistent or varied in approach, provide satisfyingly concrete evidence of their attitudes towards the Minerva novel, in the form of the hundreds of reviews and prefaces analysed here. Although their approaches differ widely, as a group these paratexts oscillate between rejection, defensiveness, grudging acceptance, and hopeful enthusiasm for the changing literary norms they describe. While authors and reviewers are the best-documented commentators, and arguably the most materially concerned with debates about changing literary norms, I conclude this chapter with a reminder of a third – and by far the largest – group of stakeholders in this debate: readers. With their numbers expanding every year, Romantic readers, as reception scholars like William St Clair and Heather Jackson have shown, are even more numerous and heterogeneous than any of the groups – or indeed, works – already discussed here.[122] Yet, as I suggested at this chapter's beginning, they were probably the least likely to view the age's literary proliferations with concern. Under no obligation to read every new title, and with no need to worry about competitors, readers surely had the most reason to regard the age's new variety of books with optimism.

Like *Northanger Abbey*'s fictional Isabella Thorpe, delighted at the range of 'all horrible' novels available to her and her friend, increased selection and increased supply are gifts to the already-eager reader and offer access to more would-be readers than before. Some readers have left marginal traces of their attitudes towards specific novels, while others have their tastes recorded in surviving circulating-library catalogues.[123] We can sometimes infer projected readerships or successful sales from print runs and multiple editions, and large-scale projects like the *Reading Experience Database* are in the process of collating a fuller picture of the range of ways that people read, and thought about reading.[124] Certainly, some readers kept detailed accounts of their reading, in journals or letters, but those that have been preserved, remain publicly available, and focus on popular novels tend to belong to readers who are famous for other literary accomplishments – generally, writing or reviewing novels – and thus are also part of the other groups I have analysed here.[125]

In other words, however ubiquitous those claims of 'too many' and 'too much' may seem when we peruse sources from the period, it is likely these perspectives are far more the exception than the rule. The haste of reviewers and authors to make claims about what 'readers' prefer, or what 'many readers' demand, documented throughout this book, makes readers an inseparable part of the ongoing debate about overproduction, but historically, it is far more probable that an individual Romantic reader would have had access to too few books than too many. Reviewers and writers, too, whose very occupations would potentially cease to exist were the excesses they decry truly curbed, likely benefit far more than they lose by the deluge. Talking about fiction in terms of excess is a rhetorical strategy rather than an accurate description of literary reality or a helpful characterization of lived experience for Romantic readers; acknowledging this, while also recognizing the astonishingly widespread use of precisely this rhetoric, can help us begin to trace its effects on the literary works that were produced and shaped by it.

CHAPTER 2

Godwin, Bage, Parsons, and Novels as They Are

How say you, critic Gods, and you below;
Are you all friends? – or here – and there – a foe?
Come to protect your literary trade,
Which Mrs. Scribble dares again invade –
But know you not – in all the fair ones do,
'Tis not to please themselves alone – but you.
—Elizabeth Inchbald, *Such Things Are* (1787)

Attentive readers of the *Analytical Review* in 1789 would have seen a brief and unremarkable review of a new novel, *The Vicar of Lansdowne*, by an unknown female novelist. The reviewer, none too impressed by the work, urged the young writer to abandon her new profession in a tone that, while kind, is undeniably patronizing: 'As we imagine the author must be a *very* young lady, and deeply read in poetry and novels, we forbear to censure in a sarcastic style; . . . If she will listen to the warning voice of experience, we advise her to throw aside her pen, and not attempt to enter *the road of glory*, as she fancifully calls publishing a novel.'[1] The piece, like most of the contents of the *Analytical Review*, was anonymous, not even bearing the single initial with which many contributors signaled their identities.[2] It is doubtful that the review made much of an impression on anyone (except perhaps the fledgling author herself), given its brevity, its lukewarm praise – 'There is certainly nothing immoral to be found in the volumes' – and its general air of benevolent censure towards that misguided creature, so common by the late eighteenth century, the young lady novelist.

As I will argue in this chapter, however, this brief notice deserves our attention, both as a singular interaction between two women who would soon rise to prominence in two very different aspects of London letters, and for the entry it provides into a series of complex and interconnected issues: literary style, politics, popularity, and prestige.[3] The reviewer has been identified as Mary Wollstonecraft, who had already published her own attempt at 'entering the road of glory', in the form of *Mary: A Fiction* in 1788, and the novelist was Regina Maria Dalton, later Roche, an Irishwoman who eventually became one of the best-selling authors of the 1790s, publishing more than a dozen widely popular 'Romances', 'Tales', and 'Novels'.[4] Wollstonecraft, of course, would go on to write more controversial and high-profile works in different genres – most famously, her *Vindication of the Rights of Woman* (1792) – before her untimely death in 1798; Roche, for her part, continued her novel-writing career for nearly thirty years.[5]

Some five years before Dalton's first novel made its appearance, in 1784, a rather different work had made a similarly unremarkable entrance onto the London literary scene. Entitled *Imogen*, this fiction was subtitled 'A Pastoral Romance: From the Ancient British' and purported to be a translation from an ancient Welsh original.[6] Explicitly influenced by Milton's *Comus*, the novel extols the power of virtuous innocence, embodied in this case in the persons of both the titular heroine and her noble lover and rescuer, Edwin. That *Imogen* was published before Mary Wollstonecraft began to write for the *Analytical Review* is unfortunate, at least for those who would love to see how Wollstonecraft's sharp pen would have handled the novel's wilting heroine. Other reviewers did offer some criticism in this vein, however, hinting significantly that a romance 'should not be turgid and extravagant' and offering only tepid approbation for *Imogen*'s 'chaste and virtuous tendency'.[7] The author of this anonymously published fiction, rather surprisingly, was the philosopher William Godwin, now much better known for his controversial treatise *Enquiry Concerning Political Justice* (1794) and his best-selling novel, *Caleb Williams* (1794), which denounced the English justice system in no uncertain terms.

Even more surprising, for those familiar with the reputations of 1780s publishers, are these two novels' respective places of publication: *Imogen* was one of dozens of novels published by William Lane from the same Leadenhall Street premises that, beginning in the 1790s would house his newly titled Minerva Press. Regina Roche, née Dalton, ultimately had a far more extensive connection with Lane: she went on to become one of Minerva's most successful and recognizable authors. Her first novel, however, the one Wollstonecraft reviewed, was not published by William Lane; instead, *The Vicar of Lansdowne* was published by Joseph Johnson, Mary Wollstonecraft's employer at the *Analytical Review* and the publisher of radical political-philosophical works including Thomas Paine's *Rights of Man* (1791) and Godwin's *Political Justice*. William Lane explicitly acknowledged Roche's importance to the publishing house in 1798, listing her as one of Minerva's 'particular and favorite Authors' in the Minerva Press Prospectus of that year;[8] Godwin, in contrast, deliberately distanced himself from *Imogen* and the Minerva Press in the 1790s and 1800s, explaining that he had written the work in a matter of months, and only because 'Lane gave me ten pounds' for it.[9] In retrospect, he described this period of his life as a time when he merely tried 'to meet [his] expenses, while writing different things of obscure note, the names of which . . . I am rather inclined to suppress'.[10] And although William Godwin and Mary Wollstonecraft had not yet met at the time of either of these anecdotes, they married within the decade.[11]

These two interlocking scenes of publication remind us, then, of some of the less-visible connections between very different groups of literary professionals publishing in London in the 1780s and 1790s. Writers like Wollstonecraft and Godwin are now widely studied and highly regarded for their political and intellectual work, while Roche and other Minerva authors like her are largely known, if they are known at all, for their authorship of anodyne and unimpressive popular gothic novels. Politically and personally, the so-called English Jacobins seem to have little in common with Minerva Press novelists like Roche. Considering these moments of intersection shows us the porosity between these seemingly distinct categories; more importantly, I would suggest, it allows us to see an example of how the complex negotiations surrounding the new mass production of novels played out among a group of novelists who engaged with politically charged topics.

This chapter takes up two threads of the ongoing discussions about fiction introduced in the previous chapter – characters and plots proliferating *within* the over-long novel, and the promiscuous spread and wide circulation of novels themselves – and traces how these concerns intersect, and sometimes collide, with contemporary discourses about politics and literature. The entwined anecdotes above, for instance, certainly have something to do with prestige; Wollstonecraft's advice to Roche may have been well-meant, but it also seems designed to discourage future publication – at once reinforcing the idea that only a few novels can be worthy of praise and eliminating a possible competitor. Godwin's abandonment of *Imogen*, conversely, seems designed to establish a hierarchy within his own work. By disavowing his early and more sentimental novels, he was able to make a stronger claim for his newer work's exceptionality, its right to stand out above the common crowd. The publisher Johnson, in his turn, by having his publications reviewed in his own periodical, ensured that they would not languish unreviewed and thus, perhaps, unread. As I will suggest here, these processes of differentiation are connected with the way Romantic authors thought about fiction's potential for political change and commercial success. Turning our attention specifically to the period's pre-occupations with fictional proliferation shows us that the radical authors of the 1790s had more in common with Minerva Press authors than just the odd pointed review or deniable early novel, and reveals how this framework inflects the ways authors discuss politically charged material, from the rights of woman to legal reform. Even as oft-repeated concerns about the ways that novels were simply too much, or too many, to control shaped the way authors envisioned their own reception, so we can see different authors responding in different ways to the novel's potential for social disruption. The traces of these debates remain in authors' reflections on their own works' impact, but also in the style and content of their narratives.

My discussion focuses on a group of novels written during the early and mid-1790s, at a peak of political unrest and Revolutionary uneasiness in England, all of which purport to intervene directly in contemporary events, by either proscriptively mirroring them or prescriptively offering ways to improve them. The connection between them, and their explicit attempt to critique contemporary mores, is apparent from their titles: Robert Bage's *Man as He Is* (1792) and *Hermsprong; or, Man as He Is Not* (1796); Eliza Parsons's *Woman as She Should Be* (1793) and *Women as They Are* (1796); and William Godwin's *Things as They Are; or, Caleb Williams* (1794). These novels represent the central moment of a publication trend, possibly inaugurated by Inchbald's *Such Things Are* (1787) (the source of my epigraph), which continued with later works like *Ellinor; or, The World as It Is* (1798),[12] highlighting a late eighteenth-century preoccupation with fiction's relationship to reality. They also represent a series of entangled aims, associations, and reputations that mirror those in my opening anecdotes. Bage and Parsons were Minerva authors, both listed alongside Roche on that 1798 prospectus of Minerva's best-sellers; Bage and Godwin have often been grouped together with other authors like Wollstonecraft, Mary Hays, and Thomas Holcroft, known for their radical politics.[13] And at least four of Eliza Parsons's numerous novels were reviewed in the pages of Johnson's *Analytical Review*, possibly by Mary Wollstonecraft herself;[14] certainly, Wollstonecraft reviewed Bage in that publication.[15] These novels differ from each other in substantial ways, but they have two important things in common besides their titles: all of them manipulate narrative in order to explore the novel form's potential for portraying dissenting perspectives, and all of them appear to consider readers – their numbers, their understanding, their spending power, their varying beliefs – as an essential factor in the way their political critiques are handled. Indeed, examining these novels and their reception suggests that these novelists saw these two unruly groups as two sides of the same coin: dissenting voices within the novel, strategically deployed, might mirror or foreclose dissenting voices from its readership.[16] The 'overlong' novels so often decried in Chapter 1 become, for some authors, an opportunity for multiple stories and perspectives to coexist and conflict within a single work of fiction. As Inchbald reminded would-be critics in *Such Things Are*, authors – perhaps particularly those who are directly concerned with real-life interventions – write not for themselves alone, but for their varied and unruly audiences.

Recent scholars including Jon Mee, Mark Philp, and John Barrell have explored the impact of revolutionary ideas on London authors and reformers in the 1790s, revealing the rich and complicated setting into which these novels made their debut. Their accounts call attention to the ways that radical discourse crossed many genres; as Mark Philp asks, 'What are the boundaries for what has been best described as "the revolution controversy" (does it include canonical works of literature at one end, and handbills and chalked slogans on walls at the other?)?'[17] Novels, in this context, are hardly surprising vehicles for political debate; despite the well-documented suspicion of the form as an appropriate outlet for political engagement, they nonetheless clearly participate, alongside other texts ranging from philosophical treatises to popular songs and caricatures.[18] This variation characterizes even the group of novels that do explicitly handle political topics, and it can be difficult to divide them into opposing political camps. While M. O. Grenby argues that 'many novels were regarded as either Jacobin or anti-Jacobin when they were first produced', the complex gradations of status, prestige, and intellectual aspiration create areas of overlap and varied subgroups among the novels on each side.[19] Moreover, scholarship on 1790s reformers demonstrates that not only was the divide between 'radical' and 'loyalist' not always straightforward in political terms, but each of these two groups was made up of many more internal factions or schools of thought. Mee reminds us of the 'lack of coherence in [radicalism's] arguments for reform'; as Grenby succinctly puts it, 'Much has been written about radicalism in Britain in the 1790s, but this is not to say that a congruous ideology of radicalism has ever been discerned.'[20] The analysis in this chapter confirms both the difficulty in drawing a firm line between the supposedly conservative and supposedly radical author and the variation even among authors who are theoretically writing from the same perspective. Most striking of all, however, are the areas of overlap between the way contemporaries discussed the role of print in disseminating political ideas and the simultaneous discussions of fiction's growth and social value. The stylistic innovations of Bage, Parsons, and Godwin reflect conflicting discourses about print's role in the growth and spread of ideas, which might be viewed one way in the context of discussions about reform, and quite another way in debates about popular fiction.

Jon Mee uses the term 'print magic' to describe a specific radical attitude towards print during the 1790s: the 'faith that print could liberate mankind simply by bringing ideas into printed circulation'.[21] In his discussion of the features of this belief, Mee describes the appeal of 'an electric immediacy of communication', quoting the radical organizer John Thelwall's idea of 'a glowing energy that may ... fly from breast to breast like that electrical principle which is perhaps the true soul of the physical universe'.[22] Such a conception of radical ideas might be either alluring or terrifying, as Mee points out, contrasting Thelwall's formulation with the anti-revolutionary warnings of Burke: '[Thelwall's idea] was the positive version of the 'electrick communication every where' feared by Edmund Burke, promising or threatening, depending on one's point of view, to jump across all channels of 'transmission'.[23] In both its potential duality and its invocation of unstoppable proliferation, this way of imagining how ideas are shared also bears a strong resemblance to contemporary descriptions of fiction's spread. Mee's portrait of Thelwall demonstrates the latter's belief in the press as an unstoppable force: Thelwall asserts that 'Fortunately for mankind the press *cannot* be silenced ... wherever the press has once been established on a broad foundation, liberty must ultimately triumph. It is easier to sweep the whole human race from the surface of the earth than to stop the torrent of information and political improvement, when the art of printing has attained its present height.'[24] This imagery of apocalyptic destruction – outmatched by the 'torrent' of printed matter – is reminiscent of the world-ending, novel-fueled fire described in this book's introduction. While the former is glorified for its power, and the latter is used to comment on the oversupply of books, both link the concepts of human survival or destruction with the new production of vast reams of print.

Mary Fairclough's account of the Romantic crowd has made it clear that not all reformers were as enthused as Thelwall by the prospect of an untrammeled 'electric' communication between mass groups of people, but she demonstrates how authors like Wollstonecraft and Godwin were nonetheless invested in the prospect of recuperating 'sympathetic communication' as a path to radical action.[25] While Fairclough's account is focused more specifically on conceptions of 'sympathy' than on print, her observation that 'Wollstonecraft's and Godwin's descriptions of sympathetic communication are characterised by a repeated slippage from a discussion of instinctive action to one of pathology ... both tend to characterise the actions of collectives as prompted by a pernicious, unthinking contagion of influence'[26] nonetheless should remind us of the ways that, in discussions of the novel, large numbers (of readers or novels) are rhetorically transformed into something more dangerous, as agency is occluded and reading assumes a self-reproducing power of its own.

We can examine the work of 1790s novelists like Bage, Parsons, and Godwin in light of the overlaps and conflicts between these two discourses, literary and political: on the one hand, these authors wrote at a time when, as they well knew, fiction was frequently perceived and described in terms of overabundance; with every word they potentially added to the pre-existing superfluity. Simultaneously, however, they wrote in a context in which many were animated by a belief in the transformative power of print and the press's (potentially) unlimited power to effect change. In both spheres, volume and spread might be seen as powerful or pernicious, and 'success' in one realm might result in dangerous loss of control in the other. A shared vocabulary often blurs the boundaries between positive and negative, political and literary representations of mass readership; in another example, Paul Keen cites Wollstonecraft's approving description of the 'rapidly multiplied copies of the productions of genius ... bringing them within the reach of all ranks of men'.[27] While Wollstonecraft is obviously in support of 'rapid multiplication' in this particular instance, in others, her depictions of fiction and popular readership sound much closer to the derogatory reproductive metaphors directed against women writers and their ever-reproducing novels. When it comes to proliferation, in other words, context is everything: a barrage of text might enlighten or overwhelm, pass a spark of inspiration or spread like a contagion.

While I will return to the broader question of multiplying copies and numerous readers at the end of this chapter, my argument about Bage and Parsons begins with the ways that these novelists' contemporaries discussed the novel's ever-increasing *length*. Like the references to 'torrents' and 'multiplication' of print, which might shift meaning across different literary and political realms, so discussions of fiction that mention its length interpret this quality differently for different purposes. Some critics of over-long novels, as we have seen, seemed to object largely on grounds of readerly boredom. A columnist in the January 1787 issue of the *Lady's Magazine*, writing 'On the Epistolary Mode of Novel-Writing', seems at first to fall into this category. According to this writer, works 'written in the epistolary manner necessarily appear prolix and redundant'.[28] As the article continues, however, the writer expands the scope of concern: 'To sustain, with propriety, all the different personages, to think, to act in their peculiar characters through a whole life … requires a truly dramatic genius', a later passage reads, with obvious scepticism that most contemporary novels met this bar.[29] The largeness, the scale and scope of the novel form, are painted here as potential obstacles in themselves; unlike the dramatist, the writer reminds us, the novelist 'supports a character through life … he observes probability in the transactions, possibly, of half a century … he must rouse the passions, and engage the attention through a variety of unconnected incidents'.[30] The sheer number of 'transactions' and 'incidents' involved in portraying a whole life, as well as the diversity of 'different personages' to be encountered, poses a challenge that, this writer thought, most authors could not meet. In other words, length is closely related to style; certain stylistic and narrative choices are facilitated by the precondition of length.

While this argument is largely aesthetic, Paul Keen points out that both 'size' and 'style' were also invoked as factors in determining a book's likely political impact. Quoting the conservative *British Critic*, he points out that 'it suggested that Godwin's *Political Justice* might escape prosecution because it was written in a style that was not likely to attract the attention of the most dangerous sectors of the reading public'.[31] And when it came to fiction, length specifically, as Keen shows, was given as the reason why Thomas Holcroft's novel *Hugh Trevor* was not seen as a threat by the same journal: 'the length of the tale (for these three volumes are only the beginning of Trevor's sorrows) is the only chance it has of not rendering its writer answerable for a great deal of mischief'.[32] What interests me about both the *Lady's Magazine*'s complaint and the *British Critic*'s backhanded compliment are how they target the very fictional features – length, duration of reading time, proliferation of events – upon which novelists like Bage and Parsons capitalize. As I will suggest in the next section, the variety of characters in a novel and the great length at which events can unfold and these characters change become, for some authors, a crucial means of navigating some of the day's most controversial topics.

Proliferating Narratives and the Pleasures of Suspense

In most ways, Robert Bage (1730–1801) and Eliza Parsons (1740–1811) would seem to have little in common. He was a middle-aged paper manufacturer from rural Tamworth, near Birmingham, best-known for his progressive views on class and an ongoing affiliation with the Birmingham Lunar Society; she, a decade-younger matron, was raised in self-described 'affluence' but, conditioned by poverty and family tragedy, apparently dedicated herself in adulthood to the conservative cultural virtues of thrift, strict morality, and parentally sanctioned marriage.[33] Neither makes a likely literary star, and their respective biographies, as they have come down to us, certainly do not paint them as participants in a shared literary circle – no evidence suggests that they ever exchanged even a word.[34] Yet even if the two authors never met, their novels certainly spoke to each other. In this section, I examine their four novels dealing with men and woman as they are – or should be – to show how their narrative choices allow them to strategically engage with topical political issues. Both, I suggest, cleverly exploit the novel's controversial elements, transforming the form's baggy capaciousness and its dangerously over-broad audience into narrative energy.

As one might expect from two novels with titles as opinionated as *Woman as She Should Be* and *Man as He Is*, both Parsons and Bage begin their works with a maxim, which, they claim, their respective novels will demonstrate.[35] Parsons declares that she intends 'to delineate a noble mind, that can submit to temporal evils, rather than forfeit its dignity and integrity of heart' (I:7), while Bage writes that he will illustrate the adage that 'any deviation from virtue is a deviation from happiness' (I:[viii]). Both novels fulfil their didactic claims on some level; as I will suggest here, however, to read them as straightforward exemplars of a particular perspective is to miss the complex ways they use the novel's multifariousness to highlight conflictory, and highly politicized, points of view.[36] These conflicts, in turn, are used to generate suspense in the plot. Both the need to state a moral and the deviation of a text from that moral are potential targets for criticism, as a review of a different novel, *The Spirit of the Elbe* (1799), reminds us. Of that work, the reviewer sarcastically remarks, 'it would not have been easy to discover what moral truth was meant to be inculcated, had not the author said, in the dedication . . . "that Heaven is the proper champion of the injured, is what I would incul-cate"'.[37] The observation seems to imply both an aesthetic and a moral criticism – a failure of clarity is a failure of style as well as substance – but the work of Bage and Parsons suggests an altogether different reason why an immediately perceptible and consistent philosophical or moral stance might not be the most successful approach for a popular novelist.

A brief overview of the plot of *Woman as She Should Be* appears to align with Parsons's stated plan for the novel. The heroine, Miss Oswald, obeys her father and marries the wealthy Mr Menville rather than her first love, the poor Mr Harley; the marriage goes sour as Mr Menville takes up with another woman and subjects his wife to increasingly terrible indignities (imprisoning her, reclaiming her annual settlement, and so forth), which she endures with perfect wifely patience. Ultimately, after having been confined to a convent in France, Mrs Menville hastens to her dying husband's side, where he repents, deeply impressed with her forgiveness and generosity. Admired by all, the widowed Mrs Menville returns to England and eventually marries the equally virtuous Mr Harley, to live happily ever after. Yet a closer examination reveals considerably more ambiguity in this text than such a simplistic summary suggests. Indeed, perhaps the most striking thing about *Woman as She Should Be* as a 'moral' work is how profoundly conflicted the morals in the work appear. While the larger arc of the plot conforms to recognizable conservative mores, particularly those endorsing feminine obedience and docility, as well as to Parsons's stated aim for the text (showing how a mind can remain virtuous even under the worse circumstances), it is beset from within with strikingly persistent dissenting voices. It, like Parsons's earlier novels, is epistolary, but this form – already near its final stages by the 1790s – is pressed into service in a way that seems designed to push the novel's capaciousness, its numerous 'different personages', as the *Lady's Magazine* writer complained, to its fullest extent.[38]

The multitude of individual voices, often in disagreement, that can be aired in an epistolary format is, of course, often used to humorous or dramatic effect in eighteenth-century novels. In *Woman as She Should Be*, however, this potential is taken a step further: the views expressed by some of the characters are so compelling, and so much more persuasive than the (supposed) stance of the author or main character, that the reader is left with a genuine feeling of suspense, uncertain whether the stated moral parameters of the novel are serious or satirical. This suspense translates into actual plot suspense, as we begin to wonder what this 'virtuous' character will actually do in the name of virtue, and thus what the plot's resolution will be. The ostensible lessons of the text are clear, both in the preface and in the priorities of the main character, Mrs Menville: women ought to be obedient and loyal to the men in their lives, should be tolerant of any treatment that doesn't directly force them to live 'immorally', and, particularly in the matter of marriage, must be guided by their parents rather than exercising choice on their own. Yet Parsons undercuts each of these morals effectively, through both her plotting and her characterization. In this way, the contemporary debates about marriage, social class, and the right of women to dignity and intellectual autonomy that seem to have been firmly excluded from the novel at the start in fact resurface throughout it.

This dynamic is first apparent in the situation that opens the whole novel. Although Emily Oswald is betrothed to the upstanding Mr Harley, with her father's full consent, he soon changes his mind when a wealthier candidate, Mr Menville, arrives on the scene. Emily is distraught at the turn of events, but follows her late mother's instructions and obeys her father unquestioningly, declaring, 'I do not hesitate, dispose of me as you please, I must ever find my own felicity in promoting yours' (I:44). As Emily's marriage to Menville deteriorates, she is then repeatedly forced to lie to her father when he asks whether she is happy (II:104; II:136). If the moral of the story is that obedience to one's parents is a universal virtue, this descent into falsehood seems very poor evidence for it. While Mrs Menville never so much as hints that her father might have been in the wrong, her friends freely articulate it in their letters, when they accuse her father, though 'a worthy man', of 'break[ing] his word, and tak[ing] advantage of his child's love and filial duty' (II:118). These letters challenge the very patriarchal structures of authority that the heroine is dedicated to upholding, and they do so in a way that seems deliberately designed to call the reader's attention to their internal inconsistencies.

As Mr Menville's actions grow increasingly outrageous, this narrative strategy continues. Mrs Menville never complains, but her friends – and eventually even her slight acquaintances – certainly do; they freely critique his cruelties and upbraid her for the passivity of her acquiescence, calling her, for example, *'too submissive'* (II:224) and pointing out that her husband's excuses are merely 'trifling pretences' (II:143). Given the patent truth of these observations, we are left to feel either that the narrator, who continues to endorse Mrs Menville's obedience, is fatally out of touch with reality or that she does in fact intend us to agree with Mrs Menville's friends rather than Mrs Menville herself. Indeed, Mr Menville's horrifying behaviour seems designed to push the reader past the point of acceptance: it's amazing that his wife can keep her patience – but should she?

Most striking of all is the turn the novel takes after the eventual death of Mr Menville. His widow now declares her determination to retreat to the countryside with her little daughter and her female companion, and to live in peace and solitude there. As she writes firmly to the still-hovering Mr Harley:

> I never shall marry again, 'tis a fixed resolution; I have many strong reasons for my determination, and I flatter myself you are so well acquainted with my principles, that when I have told you I have made up my mind, and devote my life to the care of my child *only* . . . I trust you will acquiesce with the propriety of my resolution on this subject, and give up every idea which may militate against it. (IV:158)

This plan seems logical, even ideal, after all that Mrs Menville has suffered from the institution of marriage. Menville's death leaves her financially secure; she has a lovely cottage of her own, to replace the grim estate at which he imprisoned her, and rather than having to raise her daughter on her own, as she did during her marriage, she now has a companion, Louisa, a former nun who now vows to stay with her and help to care for Emily: 'Call me your Louisa . . . let me be your sister, your friend!' (IV:168).[39] Similar scenarios, in which women respond to mistreatment and exploitation by men by rejecting marriage and forming their own domestic circle, are found in novels ranging from Sarah Scott's *Millenium Hall* (1762) to Wollstonecraft's novels *Mary* (1789) and *Maria* (1798). In aligning with works like this, Parsons leads readers to sympathize with a radical rejection of the world as it currently is.

This is, perhaps, exactly why the novel's competing voices now come to the fore in a shockingly sudden manner. When Mrs Menville's dear friends – the very same ones who have long documented the many miseries of her marriage – realize that she is absolutely serious about maintaining an independent life, they turn on her with surprising viciousness, demanding that she marry Mr Harley and denying that she has any right to decline his offers: 'Consider what you owe to an affection like his . . . had he not a right to have insisted upon that engagement taking place?' (IV:175–176). Despite having just spent some 400 pages urging Mrs Menville to be more assertive, one friend now sarcastically attacks her for being so: 'But go on; live for *yourself* only; persevere in those false delicacies which are to destroy the happiness of your friends . . . be no more than a common woman, fond of power, triumphing in the pangs of a worthy man, and gratified in pursuing fastidious notions that are to make others unhappy!' (IV:177). This seems deeply unfair, not to mention unexpected, and Mrs Menville responds, 'Your severity has almost broken my heart' (IV:187). As it turns out, peer pressure has the desired effect; Mrs Menville – in a move Mary Wollstonecraft surely would not have applauded – soon decides to relinquish her own agency once more, declaring, 'I will write to [Captain Harley]; *he* shall decide for me' (IV:189). He naturally decides that she should marry him, but the wedding bells that ensue are not sufficiently joyful to expunge our memory of Mrs Menville's ruined idyll.

Before returning to the central question of what Parsons is trying to accomplish with this narrative technique, I turn first to an analysis of Robert Bage's novel of the previous year. While *Man as He Is* is not an epistolary novel (it does occasionally use interpolated letters), Bage uses its third-person narration to create a very similar sense of multiple, potentially irreconcilable, viewpoints, developing in turn over the novel's substantial four-volume length. The plot of the story, in brief, is as follows: the youthful Sir George inherits his title and fortune after the unfortunate demise of his father and two older brothers. As part of his resistance to the social snobbery of his mother and the political machinations of his uncle, he claims the right to 'think for himself' and takes a tutor, Mr Lindsay, known more for his rectitude and adherence to moral principle than for either wealth or elegance. These two travel the country and soon encounter two attractive ladies in unfortunate financial circumstances. Sir George immediately falls in love with one, Miss Colerain, while Lindsay (though we don't learn this until much later) develops a tendre for her spritely companion, Miss Carlill.

The path of true love does not run smooth, however: the combination of misunderstanding, carelessness, and Sir George's restlessness send the two pairs of friends in separate ways, with Miss Colerain suspicious that Sir George's generosity to her had a less-than-gentlemanly purpose. To Sir George's credit, this suspicion is unfounded; less flattering to his character, however, are his juvenile capers following the separation. Ignoring Mr Lindsay's advice at every turn, he gradually acquires a number of bad habits: gaming, womanizing, and general hedonism. The downhill slide culminates in Paris (some 500 pages later), when his mistress turns out to be the ex-wife of a friend, his so-called friends swindle him and leave him in prison, and Miss Colerain happens to show up just in time to witness the whole debacle. Although it takes several hundred more pages for the situation to resolve itself – there is much soul-searching and backsliding on Sir George's part, and an implausibly large number of encounters with Miss Colerain at awkward and damning moments – Sir George ultimately marries his upstanding lady.

Just as with Parsons's novel, however, to relate the plot in this summary manner is to omit nearly all of the characteristics that make the reading of *Man as He Is* such an interesting experience. In this novel it is similarly

difficult to locate either the political or the moral compass of the characters. Certainly one cannot say that the novel espouses a radical viewpoint
in any straightforward way. This difficulty stems, as in *Woman as She
Should Be*, from the large number of characters who offer their conflicting
opinions, opinions that, moreover, seem sometimes to align with the
projected opinion of the reader, sometimes with the (apparent) opinion
of the author or narrator, and sometimes defy both of these perspectives.
The reader, attempting to discern which viewpoint represents the novel's
'true' moral, and thus its likely ending, is constantly left in uncertainty.

When the protagonist, Sir George, first appears in the text, for example,
he seems to be a model of good sense and admirable sentiment. He is not
reconciled to the death of his father and brothers by the money he inherits
(as the narrator implies other members of his family would have been), and
he even maintains affection for his terrible mother, while resisting the
pressures she exerts on him. Certainly the reader finds it much easier to be
in sympathy with Sir George than with any of the other characters, and it
seems that the narrator admires him as well. Soon, however, Sir George
begins to reveal some slightly more problematic attributes; not coincidentally, this change occurs at about the same time that his advisor, Mr
Lindsay, enters the plot. Whereas Sir George initially seems compassionate, reasonable, and relatively wise, comparison with his older mentor
begins to reveal him in a rather more frivolous light. When explaining
his reasons for wanting to hire Lindsay as a tutor, Sir George suggests that
he wants Lindsay's wisdom without going through any of the suffering by
which he gained it: he seeks 'prudence, temperance, and fortitude' and
declares that 'these I have much inclination to learn, but none to go into
your school [the school of adversity]' (I:22). Mr Lindsay's role as sober
guide grows increasingly clear as his young charge falls rapidly in love with
Miss Colerain. Lindsay's warnings against too-hasty action, coupled with
his firmly ethical rebuttal of Sir George's Uncle Auschamp (who first
rejects him for his lowly origins and then seeks to recruit him as a Tory
propagandist), win the reader's trust. He may be somewhat sterner and less
affable than Sir George, but as the younger man repeatedly shows poor
judgment and acts rashly, it is Lindsay who can be counted upon to
provide the sympathetic voice of reason in the novel. Rejecting the values
of the wealthy Tory Auschamp, Lindsay seems committed to the power of
individual rationality, and the reader is led to agree.

Yet Lindsay in his turn is likewise supplanted. Miss Colerain and Miss
Carlill are both decidedly moral characters, and they both exhibit a
strength of will and an ability to voice their opinions clearly that quickly

make them as attractive to the reader as they are to the men. Further, while Lindsay tends toward the ponderous, and Sir George toward the frivolous, Miss Carlill in particular manages to combine good sense with wit in a way that enlivens each scene she enters. Her scathing commentaries on the foolishness of men frequently put the male characters in their place, but her remarks are invariably so accurate, in the context of the plot, that the reader can't help but agree with her assessment. The humour of many of these scenes further draws attention, making Lindsay's moral commitments seem, by comparison, boring and irrelevant.

As Sir George grows more and more misguided, Lindsay drops out of the text altogether for a time. Just as the reader despairs of anyone with any common sense remaining in the novel, Sir George comes across the eccentric Mr Bardoe, whose acerbic indictments of the young man's foolishness become the new guiding force of the narrative. As the unstable and shifting sympathies of the narrator disallow any single interpretation of the novel's ultimate meaning, so too do they disrupt the work's apparent political allegiances and the reader's certainty about its ending. Bage's characters do voice radical sentiments from time to time, just as Parsons's characters often espouse more traditional ones. But in the former case, as in the latter, the narrative consistently undercuts these statements, leaving the reader uncertain as to what is admirable and what the butt of satire. When Mr Lindsay defends Sir George's decision to take a mistress by declaring that if 'temporary contracts between men and women' were legal then no one would criticize him (III:195), his logic foreshadows William Godwin's famous arguments against the institution of marriage in *Political Justice*, published the following year.[40] But the context of Lindsay's defence makes it clear that this rationale should be seen as morally and philosophically unpersuasive – even ridiculous.

Similarly, when Sir George, having just met a group of politically motivated Parisian intellectuals, vows to turn his hitherto scattered attention away from women and gambling and towards more serious pursuits, the narrator mockingly questions his seriousness. Sir George's new friends clearly espouse ideas like those associated with Godwin and Thomas Paine: 'Never before had Sir Geo[rge] heard the science of government so freely canvassed; the rights of men so deeply appreciated' (III:118). Yet, in a satirical scene that, despite the apparent differences in the authors' politics, directly echoes many examples offered by M. O. Grenby in *The Anti-Jacobin Novel*, these ideals not only fail to capture the young man's attention for long, but are presented in a way which undermines their seriousness:

never before had he felt so highly the dignity of his nature ... Of specu-
lations so sublime, it is impossible a man should ever grow weary; and Sir
George determined to indulge himself till the hour of repose. He dined....
After this he began to resume his sublime ideas. They were in rebellion. He
stretched, yawned, and at last found it absolutely necessary to get up
and walk. (III:125)

This is an indictment of Sir George's character, but also, within the
context of the whole novel, in which commitment to *any* political or
moral position is fleeting, it seems a challenge to the idea of radicalism
itself. If 'man as he is' can't sustain attention to any cause for more than a
few pages, then the very concept of the novel of ideas as an agent of change
is thrown into doubt.

Women as They Are and *Hermsprong; or, Man as He Is Not*, Parsons's and
Bage's next works in this grouping (Parsons published several other novels
in different genres in the interim) follow very similar patterns, although
I will not analyse them here at such length. The former work features two
sisters, a supposedly admirable one, whose grimly moralistic prosing
alienates the reader along with the novel's other characters, and another,
theoretically the work's cautionary tale, but also its primary source of
interest and plot advancement: if the older sister succeeded in converting
the younger, as the novel insists she ought to, the plot would come to an
abrupt halt. *Hermsprong* features, among other things, an apparently
revolutionary hero who refuses to kowtow to wealth or titles – the force
of this message, however, is rather diminished when he ultimately reveals
himself to be the most wealthy man of all, his moral authority under-
pinned by material power after all. (In another example of the overlap
between apparently radical authors like Bage and avowedly loyalist ones,
Grenby discusses a scene from *Hermsprong* when the hero quells a
working-class uprising as an example of the characteristic anti-Jacobin
opposition to revolution, however justifiable.)[41] Both novels feature countless small incidents in which seemingly clear positions on morality, human
rights, or authority are challenged or reversed.

If Bage and Parsons repeatedly raise politically topical issues, then throw
their stances on them into doubt, what does this accomplish for their
fiction? Rather than fearing the variety provided by their many personages,
I would suggest, these novelists embrace them for a very practical purpose.
The length and episodic nature of their works allow both authors to
explore different perspectives on current debates, but also to contain them.
Raised but never fully resolved, important questions about human rights
and an ordered society remain active within each text – but also safely

neutralized for the reader.[42] In other words, we might say, these authors write in anticipation of their own popularity, reflecting the widely varied and conflictory opinions held by their potential *audience* in their varied characters, and transmuting potentially troublesome controversy to universally enjoyable plot suspense. It's certainly possible to read such a choice as artistic (or political) capitulation to merely financial concerns. As Grenby argues, both political and financial concerns, deliberately or not, were always entangled with the novelist's aesthetic choices; it can sometimes be difficult to distinguish between them.[43] But I would argue we should also consider this kind of anticipatory plotting as a crucial aspect of writing in a marketplace in which the unruly masses of one's audience are always looming. In both of these works, Bage and Parsons create plots that can be interpreted in a range of ways by a widely various audience, emphasizing readerly pleasure over authorial or critical control, and underscoring the reality that to achieve success in the world 'as it is' requires cognizance of that world's parameters. In a practical sense, allowing one's novel to display multiple viewpoints with equal sympathy provides a sort of plausible deniability: while novelists may have been relatively safe from the government prosecutions faced by political authors in other genres, they were all the more susceptible to the fickleness of a reading audience that could reject works they found unpalatable. More abstractly, this kind of ambiguity and fragmentation is a kind of test of fiction's capacities: if reviewers complained of novels being too numerous, too long, and filled with too many characters, some authors clearly saw narrative opportunity in these observations, and adjusted their style accordingly.

Radical Fiction as Crowd Control

Of her first short novel, *Mary: A Fiction*, Mary Wollstonecraft wrote to a friend, 'I have lately written, a fiction which I intend to give to the world; it is a tale, to illustrate an opinion of mine, that a genius will educate itself.'[44] This formulation – 'a tale, to illustrate an opinion' – is striking for its explicit linkage between fiction and real life, between authorial intention and artistic outcome. Although Wollstonecraft later came to believe that she had fallen short of her own goals with this first novel – she told her sister in 1797 that she now 'consider[ed] it as a crude production' – the idea that theory and practice were uniquely united in the form of the political novel of the 1790s is one that has become deeply rooted in the critical imagination.[45] Gary Kelly's influential description of the Jacobin novel's 'unity of purpose' is one important component of this belief; another is the persistence of the idea that the female novelists of the era, in particular, showed an unprecedented level of autobiographical revelation in their fictional work.[46] To some extent these authors seem to have deliberately courted these comparisons: Mary Hays did use actual letters from her correspondence with William Frend and William Godwin in her novel *Memoirs of Emma Courtney* (1796); Mary Wollstonecraft titled both of her fictions with variants of her own name; Elizabeth Inchbald sent her heroine to a costume ball dressed in a costume like one she had notoriously worn herself.[47] As I will argue in this section, this singular focus can be understood as a form of response to the decade's insistence on the power and danger of print in the hands of a crowd.

While authors like Bage and Parsons exploit the novel's capacity for multitudinous voices, others, including William Godwin, write in ways that deliberately and repeatedly foreclose that capacity. The constantly looming claims about the popular novel, in other words, with all their evocations of dangerous growth and uncontrollable response, catalyse a narrative style that emphasizes univocality and tight control over potential interpretations. The 'unity' that Godwin cites in his later reflections on *Caleb Williams* is, I propose, also a way of controlling the novel's dangerous excesses. While Bage and Parsons use the novel's potentially enervating length as a starting point for a narrative that engages with, but also neutralizes, contemporary controversies, Godwin addresses a different danger: given fiction's ability to easily carry ideas to a wide audience, he structures his plot in a way that seeks to maintain control over how those ideas will be received. This difference may have something to do with practical considerations (we know that Parsons, for instance, was desperately in need of money and could likely not afford to alienate potential readers in a largely conservative climate).[48] While Godwin also was in need of funds at many points in his career, as both his early publication of *Imogen* and his later pleas for financial support from Percy Shelley suggest, his attitudes here seem primarily reflective of radical beliefs about print, that 'print magic' described by Mee. A strong conviction that print can indeed bring about social change is energizing and compelling, but also potentially terrifying: if the novel can and should bring about change in the real world, then the stakes of ensuring what that change will be are considerably higher. Whereas Bage and Parsons follow the popular authorial maxim that because readers demand books, those books should be written (and written to their tastes, even when those tastes are highly varied), Godwin takes up the inverse position: books, once written, may be read – but the variety of their potential readers might also mean a dangerous variety in their responses to the text.

Clearly, Godwin both hoped and intended that his novel would indeed influence his readers, claiming, 'I was excited to write [*Things as They Are; or, Caleb Williams*] by a strong idea occurring to my mind, which I conceived, if worked up into a story ... was capable of a powerful effect.'[49] The notion of a *single* strong idea, which might have 'a powerful effect' if properly elucidated, is a seductive one, uniting the power of revolutionary thought with the broad appeal of the popular story. Indeed, as M. O. Grenby notes, anti-Jacobin commentators spe-cifically critiqued Godwin because they knew, and feared, fiction's power to engage the emotions. Novelist Robert Bisset complained, of *Caleb Williams*, 'Subtle sophistry alone could hardly establish the inutility of criminal justice, but an affecting fable setting forth the punishment of innocence, and escape of guilt, strongly interests the feelings; and the emotions of the heart are mistaken for the conclusions of the head.'[50] Yet these emotions, by their very strength, might do harm, and not only the harm that Bisset envisioned. By reining in the prolixity, eliminating redundancy, silencing competing narrative voices, and framing the entire novel as an elaboration on a single theme, Godwin creates a compelling and suspenseful tale. He also pre-empts many of the critiques of the novel levied by his contemporaries and, most importantly, reduces the potential for dangerously varied (mis)interpretations of his central mes-sage. Representing his novel as the direct outgrowth of the author's single-minded idea, Godwin rhetorically saps the power of its unruly readership.

Godwin makes it clear that fiction's accessibility and broad appeal are why he has chosen this genre. He wants, he declares, his central claims 'to be communicated to persons whom books of philosophy and science are never likely to reach' – novel-readers, in other words.[51] And in referring to fiction as 'the vehicle he has chosen' for the enterprise, he expresses appreciation for the novel's ability to engage the emotions as well as the intellect, the 'interest and passion' that a well-told story excites (312). His novel fulfils this promise, but it also does something else: through its focus on a deceptively individual 'fervour' it suppresses and compresses the multitudes of potential voices and stories that comprise it.

Caleb Williams's narrative voice is solipsistic from the first paragraph, which uses the words 'my', 'me', and 'I' no fewer than twenty-one times in only eleven sentences. The insistent repetition of 'my life', 'my enemy', 'my ... prospects', 'my name', and 'my story' fills the reader's eye and ear with a single perspective, precluding even the possibility of others. If, as Caleb Williams suggests in the novel's striking first line, his 'life has for several years been a theatre of calamity', it is a theatre with room for only one player on the stage. While Williams is using the term in a different sense, the implication of spectacle in the phrase seems nonetheless deliberate: this is a pose, Godwin reminds us, with the deliberately singular voice an illusion, a performance, rather than the straightforward reflection of reality it purports to be. Williams early declares that his 'story will at least appear to have ... consistency', an oddly lukewarm adjective for one's own life, until we realize that consistency is, for this narrator, a – perhaps *the* – infallible sign of 'truth' (3). That sameness, repetition, lack of change should be signs of truth seems less self-evident than Williams makes out, but the strangeness of the assertion passes unnoticed, and Godwin soon provides numerous illustrations of what he means by 'consistency'. Caleb Williams identifies one single trait as his governing characteristic, suggesting that not only his entire personality but the entire course of his life unspool neatly from this one cause: 'The spring of action which, perhaps more than any other, characterised the whole train of my life, was curiosity.... I was desirous of tracing the variety of effects which might be produced from given causes' (314), he declares in Godwin's revised version of the novel. From the first, then, readers are assured that the whole of the novel to come will be 'consistent', will be, in a sense, already known to them, just as it is already known to Caleb Williams at the time of his retrospective narration.

Foreshadowing so explicit as to hardly merit the name ensures that the denouement of the novel will not surprise the reader with deviations from this pattern; it is only a few pages in that Williams declares, 'I little suspected that the gaiety and lightness of heart I had hitherto enjoyed were upon the point of leaving me for ever, and that the rest of my days were devoted to misery and alarm' (5). Together, all this 'consistency' creates a marked effect: the novel has, and will have, only one voice, only one perspective, and only one possible interpretation of events. If one of the strengths of the novel form in general is its ability (in the words of a *European Magazine* correspondent) to show not 'only the *effects* of the passions, the follies, the virtues, and the vices of mankind', as the drama does, 'But ... the *causes* also', Godwin takes care to rein in those causes too.[52] *Things as They Are* renders the multiple singular: each story has not many causes and effects, but one.

The extent to which this governs the novel's structure becomes apparent as the story continues and Caleb Williams uncovers a secret about his employer's past, thus earning his enmity and vindictive legal prosecution. Not only does the narrator offer sustained pieces of evidence to support his early claims – providing frequent instances of his 'curiosity' to demonstrate its pervasiveness, for instance – but he also maintains almost fanatically tight narrative control. When Williams has the chance to hear about his mysterious employer's back story from another character, Mr Collins, many novels of this era would allow Collins to take the stage, usurping the first-person perspective for the duration of the tale. Williams, however, explicitly disallows this, explaining, 'I shall join to Mr. Collins's story various information which I afterwards received from other quarters,' and Godwin later revised the passage to add 'To avoid confusion in my narrative, I shall drop the person of Collins, and assume to be myself the historian of our patron' (8–9, 314). All of the novel's stories, even those to which Williams could not possibly be privy himself, are thus subsumed into his singular narrative. As he 'drop[s] the person of Collins', so he assimilates all the novel's experiences into his own, continuing, 'To the reader it may appear at first sight as if this detail of the preceding life of Mr. Falkland were foreign to my history. Alas, I know from bitter experience that it is otherwise. My heart bleeds at the recollection of his misfortunes as if they were my own' (9). By converging all the novel's voices and viewpoints into one, ostensibly to avoid readerly 'confusion', Williams also claims all the work's emotional knowledge; no perspective (that this novel will provide) is *not* his own, he insists.

As the novel's scenes of paranoia and persecution unfold, the narrator maintains this self-centred focus. The arcs of secondary characters, like Mr Falkland, are similarly reduced to a straightforward, seemingly inevitable conclusion: 'All I have farther to state of [Falkland's] history is the unin-terrupted persecution of a malignant destiny, a series of adventures that seemed to take their rise in various accidents, but pointing to one termi-nation' (15), Williams remarks. Yet the pressures of the novel's many stories threaten to shatter Williams's hard-won illusion of control. 'I do not pretend to warrant the authenticity of any part of these memoirs except so much as fell under my own knowledge', he concedes, a consid-erable admission given that precisely none of the lengthy story he has just told could possibly have been from his own experience (103). At another point he reminds the reader of the patched-together nature of his seem-ingly unified narrative: 'It will . . . most probably happen, while I am thus employed in collecting together the scattered incidents of my history, that I shall upon some occasions annex to appearances an explanation, which I was far from possessing at the time, and was only suggested to me through the medium of subsequent events' (115). Indeed, the labour and uncertainty in gathering knowledge, organizing and shaping it, and telling it as one's own surfaces repeatedly; although Caleb Williams insists to the very end that this novel is his own history, a story over which he, and he alone, has control, the irrepressible sense of many stories and perspectives, barely contained, builds as the narrative goes on. Narratives, in this model, just as in the novels of Bage and Parsons, are at once personal and unreliable, true reflections of reality and free-floating narratives subject to scepticism and misuse. The dangers of fiction – its power to emotionally manipulate or deceive, its distance from reason – compete with its possibilities for sharing truth and inspiring change.

The uncontrollable nature of the published story reaches a culminating point in *Things as they Are* after Caleb Williams, as a fugitive, is suddenly exposed in print:

> Here you have the Most Wonderful and Surprising History and Miraculous Adventures of Caleb Williams! you are informed how he first robbed, and then brought false accusations against his master; as also of his attempting divers times to break out of prison, till at last he effected his escape in the most wonderful and uncredible manner … All for the price of one halfpenny. (258)

The print-cultural sphere has ultimately defeated Williams' attempts to keep control over his own narrative; the 'hawker … bawling his wares' (258) cares about profit rather than truth, and the countless readers of the broadsheet, motivated by both entertainment and the promised reward, will draw their own conclusions as to its veracity. Williams ultimately – perhaps – wrenches the story back with his grim first-person narration, but his reflections on justice, truth, and society are permanently inflected by the sense that competing narratives and uncontrolled readership are dangerous. Political fiction, by this model, *must* be unified, to prevent misinterpretation or belief in the 'wrong' story.

The Popular Is Political; or, The Despotism of Bad Readers

In this chapter so far, I have primarily considered the novel's internal qualities, particularly its length and potentially cacophonous range of narratorial voices. But as has likely been clear all along, and as the closing example of *Caleb Williams* particularly reminds us, writers' exploitation or refusal of these fictional possibilities is also tied to their own perceptions of an external group: the real readers who might buy, read, scorn, or misinterpret their work. While it is far more difficult to track literacy rates with the relative precision we can (now) use for novel publication numbers, the numbers we do have suggest that literacy across social classes was rising during this period.[53] With the initial hopes and ensuing anxieties of the French Revolution running high and the ever-present threat of government censorship hovering over acts of publication, it's unsurprising that worries about prospective readers – a potentially large and terrifyingly uncontrollable group – would inflect politically engaged works during this time.

When the *European Magazine* remarked in 1819 on 'The almost universal habit of novel reading',[54] it inadvertently echoed one of Robert Bage's characters from thirty years before: as Miss Lamounde in *James Wallace* (1788) declares, nowadays 'all people read'.[55] The reality of universal literacy aside, the rhetorical effect of such claims is clear: reading, and reading fiction in particular, is not only trendy but ubiquitous.[56] Hypothetically, such a scenario is an ideal setting for political fiction to thrive – quite obviously, publishing ideas as fiction means that a single person's idea can now easily be shared among many people; the more readers there are, the wider the purchase the idea might have. Authors like Bage and Parsons, who, as we have seen, allowed multiple viewpoints and voices to play out in their plots, unsurprisingly tend to focus on the benefits of such a broad reception, suggesting that authors must cater to readers' disparate tastes if they wish to achieve broad popularity.

An anecdote about a principled, but unsuccessful, bookseller in one of Bage's early novels, *Barham Downs* (1784), underscores the interdependency of readerly taste and commercial production: 'Of the manuscripts offered to him for sale', readers are told, 'he chose invariably those which taught something worthy to be learnt … [a]s invariably he rejected the lewd, the factious, and personally malignant. Unfortunately the public judged differently.'[57] Literary production is here portrayed as inseparable from the demands of the marketplace, with public taste both shaping and shaped by the financial constraints of the publishers who supply them with their reading material. Books do have the power to stir controversy and alter real-life events in this model, as another early Bage novel suggests; in his first novel, *Mount Henneth* (1782), a character uses a new printing office in Boston to produce and distribute a book that 'boldly denied witchcraft ever to have existed', after which his book is burnt for 'impiety'.[58] This condemnation naturally arouses public interest – '[i]t run immediately thro' twelve editions' – and this in turn effects a change in the laws concerning witchcraft, completing a cycle in which ideas, mediated through the press and, crucially, the public, actually change 'things as they are'.[59] Though this example, like so many of Bage's anecdotes, is clearly tongue-in-cheek, Bage does seem to be seriously suggesting that reader response, more than abstract ideas, engenders social change. In some cases, a too-extreme stance, one that alienates or bores readers, may ultimately be of less political utility than one that simply raises multiple thought-provoking possibilities in an entertaining way.

In catering unabashedly to public tastes, authors like Bage and Parsons may have achieved greater financial success than they otherwise would have (their place on the Minerva prospectus of best-sellers suggests as much). However, they very possibly also harmed their literary reputations. To conclude this chapter, I return to one of the issues raised at its beginning: the development of literary hierarchy. The idea of broad readership in this period is explicitly tied to notions of literary merit – in readers, just as in novels, the excellence of the few is ultimately revealed by the mediocrity of the many. Robert Bage uses precisely this terminology when he rejects such a hierarchical notion of merit in the preface to *Man as He Is*, declaring, 'For fame is fame; whether it arise from the delicate whisper of the well-judging few, or the loud roar of the many' (I:iv–v). It's easy to imagine a public figure (or government censor) in the 1790s feeling a twinge of apprehension at that phrase the 'roar of the many', with its evocation of a rising populace. But radical novelists too clearly felt the anxiety of the unruly masses. As Jon Mee has argued, '[p]rint made it possible for radicals to imagine themselves addressing a potentially limitless category of "the people" and for their readers to imagine themselves as subjects within this category.'[60] There was great power in such a vision, but as we have so frequently seen, the response to anything limitless is often (and certainly in the literary realm) an anxious urge to impose limits.

The violence in France presented one cautionary tale about the dangerous potential of 'the people' en masse; these authors also wrote under the shadow of what John Barrell describes as a pervasive 'atmosphere of suspicion', in which any activity might be surveilled and 'everything had suddenly been or could suddenly become politicized'.[61] Though authors like Godwin were deliberately and explicitly political in their writing, the effects of a potentially 'limitless' readership – any one of whom might misinterpret, fail to understand, or respond with hostility to the ideas contained in their work – are visible in their conflicted response to the idea of writing for a 'popular' audience. Mary Fairclough has demonstrated how radical authors including Godwin, Wollstonecraft, and Thelwall understood revolutionary action through the lens of sympathy, arguing in particular that the 'instantaneous, instinctive, far-reaching, and obscure' action of sympathy within a revolutionary crowd resulted in '[a]nxieties about crowd behavior' and suggesting that '[a]n implicit element of this common discomfort about collective action is a broader anxiety about democratic politics, which is evident even in the work of reformist writers.'[62] The greater the faith in fiction's power to move a populace, the greater the risk of such writing became; thus, while authors like Bage and Parsons embrace the crowd, novelists like Godwin and Wollstonecraft invoke an excellence that is defined by the very existence of a readership too broad and indiscriminating to appreciate it. In this sense, the idea of the ungovernable reader not only influences narrative style, but feeds into emerging categories of aesthetic and intellectual accomplishment.

Caleb Williams makes an interesting test case, as it is clearly the best-seller among all the novels discussed in this chapter, both widely read and critically acclaimed.[63] While Godwin could not have anticipated the scope of his future success, he certainly did intend for his work to be, in multiple senses of the word, popular. Yet gaining an enormous audience seems to have posed challenges of its own. His acknowledgement of the public's 'unusual degree of favour' for *Caleb Williams* in his introduction to *Fleetwood* ends on an anxious note: 'And when I had done all, what had I done? Written a book to amuse boys and girls in their vacant hours, a story to be hastily gobbled up by them, swallowed in a pusillanimous and unanimated mood, without chewing and digestion.'[64] There are several striking critiques packed into the answer to this short rhetorical question: first, and most obviously, the implied criticism of unprepared readers, the 'pusillanimous' and 'unanimated' 'boys and girls' who, Godwin fears, may devour his work without understanding or caring about it. The particular adjectives he uses, moreover, seem designed to emphasize the possibility that his readers may be merely consumers, too cowardly or unenergetic to *act* on the new ideas they've imbibed. Yet Godwin's fear clearly encompasses his own work, as well. If it is only 'written . . . to amuse', is it even possible that it (a mere fiction) could do more – that is, educate or galvanize an audience? His metaphor of eating, as familiar in the eighteenth century as it is today as a means of characterizing a particular kind of gluttonous and useless textual consumption, mirrors the one used in a much earlier remark by Mary Wollstonecraft.[65] In a letter to her sister in 1797, Wollstonecraft wrote:

> Your description of the females, of your happy family, makes me hug myself in the solitude of my fireside ... the contents of the dozen novels, they devour in a week, whirled round my head till it ached again. In short ... you have contrive [*sic*] to give me an idea of a party destitute of sentiment, fancy or feeling, taste is, of course, out of the question.[66]

While her letter certainly suggests a general distaste for her sister's companions, it is striking that one of the only pieces of information Wollstonecraft offers to illustrate their complete lack of 'taste' is that they 'devour' a 'dozen novels ... in a week'. Is this an indictment of the readers or the books? As in Godwin's lament, both seem to be in doubt. In Wollstonecraft's and Godwin's writings, it is possible to perceive an emergent sense of anxious ambivalence about the popularity of their own work. The ideas they most wanted to promulgate could be spread effectively by a best-selling work, as they were clearly aware; yet there is a constant refrain that at once ties their own novels to their 'mass' counterparts and seeks to differentiate the two groups.[67] In her account of Godwin and Wollstonecraft's efforts to distinguish between a rational basis for collective action and a more emotional, unthinking crowd response, Mary Fairclough argues that the 'instinctive qualities of sympathetic communication' are problematic for both Wollstonecraft and Godwin because 'instinctive reactions resist the control of the rational faculties', and this same suspicion of 'instinctive' response is visible in the way both authors talk about their readers.[68] Bodily metaphors of contagion, gluttony, passion (all the same metaphors associated with the spread and consumption of the popular novel) imply unthinkingness, a response to fiction that overrides choice or reason – just as dangerous in the political realm as the literary one. And just as many of the authors and critics in the previous chapter invoked exclusivity or individual genius as a means of distinguishing specific works from the larger group of their peers, so Godwin, Wollstonecraft, and other radical authors often make claims for a selective, rational readership to elevate the aesthetic qualities of their own fiction. By emphasizing their own accomplishments in the light of exclusivity rather than popularity, they resist both the political dangers of uncontrolled emotion and the closely linked accusations of dangerous proliferation that attach to popular novels.

If Godwin's unease about his own best-selling status was simply rooted in a concern about whether or not his ideas would prove to be lasting, one would think that the passage of time would serve to allay his fears. On the contrary, however, as his retrospective refrain – 'what had I done?' – makes plain, the uneasy status of his novel grew increasingly worrisome over time.

In other words, recognition, in the form of critical praise, numerous reprintings, and canonization (as represented, for example, by the inclusion of *Caleb Williams* in Bentley's 'Standard Novels' series), was not enough to dispel the lingering associations between Godwin's production and its much-maligned double, the 'popular' novel. Neither is the doubt merely authorial neurosis; indeed, later reviews of *Caleb Williams* not only keep up the polarizing emphasis on the novel's popularity, but increase the intensity of their focus on this aspect of Godwin's work. In what could be a direct response to the *Monthly Review*'s claim (in 1794) that Godwin's novel would never languish on the 'loaded shelves of some circulating libraries', there is the *Edinburgh Review*'s confirmation in 1815 that, indeed, various translations of *Caleb Williams* were so widely read across Europe that '[t]here is scarcely a continental circulating library in which it is not one of the books which most quickly require to be replaced.'[69] Godwin's own fear that his novel might be devoured by unthinking 'boys and girls' would not necessarily have been allayed by the same publication's assurance that *Caleb Williams* is 'one of those very few books ... which delight every reader from the philosopher to the child'.[70]

It is striking, in light of this observation, how many contemporary reviewers of *Caleb Williams* focus not just on the plot and style of the book itself, or on the politics (for good or ill) of its author, but on the *breadth* of the audience which they saw as eager to receive this novel. Positive reviewers were pleased by its potentially wide circulation, and negative reviewers dismayed. The *Critical Review* believed that 'so very interesting and entertaining a book must soon come to ... a future edition'; and the *Monthly Review* observed that 'it is not difficult to perceive that [Godwin's object] has been to give an easy passport, and general circulation, to some of his favourite opinions', focusing the reader's attention on the prospect of more books, and more readers, in the future.[71] The prospect of future editions and wide circulation is, in contrast, expressly displeasing to the conservative *British Critic*, which, unsurprisingly, printed two of the most scathing critiques of the novel's ideological basis. It deplored it most of all for its potential to disseminate these ideas widely, writing, 'When a work is so directly pointed at every band which connects society, and at every principle which renders it amiable, its very merits become noxious as they tend to cause its *being known in a wider circle*.'[72] Even the novel's champions, however, show a surprising investment in differentiating *Caleb Williams* from other works with similarly numerous readers. The *Critical Review*'s writer's praise focuses on *Caleb Williams*' uniqueness; while it will surely be popular, the reviewer claims, he hastens to emphasize that 'this work ranks greatly above the *whole mass of publications* which bear the name of novels'.[73] The fears and hopes of the reviewers – in particular this apparently troubling dichotomy between popularity and some of its most potent signifiers in the late eighteenth century, namely, mass production and wide circulation, seem mirror images of Godwin's own thoughts on his novel. Fairclough argues that, for 'Godwin, the "mindless uniformity of the mob" is the nadir of instinctive action'.[74] Reading his thoughts on *Caleb Williams*'s success shows us how this political stance intersects with contemporary discourses about fiction: the very qualities that give novels their broad appeal and emotional power might also foster worries about ungovernable mass response; conversely, limiting reader response and interpretation can be framed as distinguishing a novel from its undifferentiated mass peers.

Godwin and Wollstonecraft were not alone in their anxiety about the potential scope (and response) of their audience. Mary Hays opened her novel, *Memoirs of Emma Courtney*, with this pronouncement: 'I am not sanguine respecting the success of this little publication.. . . To the feeling and the thinking few, this production of an active mind . . . is presented.'[75] The polar opposite of Bage's declaration that 'the well-judging few' or the 'roar of the many' are equally capable of bestowing fame, Hays's rhetoric reads as both a kind of modesty topos (or, more cynically, pre-emptive sour grapes) and a claim for intellectual superiority. The ideas in the book are too rarefied, the emotions too deep, to appeal to an ordinary reader, or to every reader. M. O. Grenby's reminder that, despite the prominence of radical novelists in Romantic scholarship today, public attitudes in the late 1790s were much more uniformly loyalist, suggests that Hays's defensive prediction of her work's small readership may have been simply realistic.[76] But, like Godwin's disclaimers, her insistence on a tightly controlled readership ties political efficacy to a broader idea of literary prestige. Godwin, in the process of reflecting on the success of *Things as They Are* and explaining his disavowal of earlier and more commercial works like *Imogen*, suggests that his singular focus after *Political Justice* has an inherent prestige attached. 'The tone of my mind, both during the period in which I was engaged in the work, and afterwards, acquired a certain elevation, and made me now unwilling to stoop to what was insignificant', he explains.[77] The would-be political novelist, threatened, on the one hand, by her ideological opponents and, on the other, by those who condemned her genre itself on aesthetic, moral, or intellectual terms, had to make her own decisions about what comprises insignificance; the novel's length, many voices, and wide circulation might be a route to significance and success, or a primary threat to it. An author's stylistic choices can be a way of signalling literary affiliation and marking value, but exploiting the potential ties between fictional perspectives and actual readers also provides authors with a means of conceptualizing the relationship between their novels and the real world in which they tried to intervene. In the fraught 1790s, debates surrounding key political issues made their way into novels just as they appeared in countless other media forms. As the novels in this chapter demonstrate, authors approached the complex interactions between the competing but overlapping discourses surrounding fictional proliferation and print politics in different ways, but both their style and their words about their own work show how deeply enmeshed their novels were with the questions of scope, volume, and spread that informed their literary moment.

CHAPTER 3

Imitating Ann Radcliffe

> Not far from her place of residence, through a dark, dismal, and
> apparently impenetrable forest, appeared the turrets of an ancient and
> gothic structure, whose solitary grandeur seemed to frown on the
> rushing and discolored torrents, that had for ages dashed against its
> cold rocky basis; where, oft-times, as legends record, did malignant and
> dangerous spirits resort; and many a frighted peasant, trembling, told
> his dreadful tale, 'of strange noises and of stranger sights'. —'A Tale
> Addressed to the Novel Readers of the Present Day' (1794)

Like so many gothic stories of the 1790s, the 'Tale' excerpted above
oscillates between rhapsodic descriptions of nature and accounts of 'trembling' terror; all events, of course, revolve around an atmospheric and
appropriately decrepit gothic castle. Unlike other such scenes, however,
this one is not a part of a longer novel, nor was it printed as a chapbook or
serialized in a magazine. Instead, this passage is taken from a pamphlet-
length advertisement for the Minerva Press: written by William Lane
himself (or at least attributed to him), it takes the form of a short story
and showcases the titles of Minerva Press novels, thirty-eight of which are
woven into the narrative[1] (see Figure 3).

The main character is 'ELLEN, COUNTESS OF CASTLE HOWELL'
(1794), and her gothic adventures and misadventures comprise a patch-
work of references, as the quotation below illustrates:

> The Castle was governed by a most dangerous NECROMANCER, well skilled
> in the black and magical enchantments, which are recorded in the TURKISH
> TALES. – Many a Knight (the most distinguished of whom were EDWARD
> DE COURCY and COUNT RODERICK from The CASTLE ZITTAW,) had been
> conquered by his diabolical powers, and many a beautiful lady, who had
> refused submission to his will, were confined in the dreadful and dreary
> dungeons of his Castle.[2]

The small capitals indicate titles of contemporary Minerva novels;[3] should
this connection have been in doubt to any reader, the goddess 'Minerva'

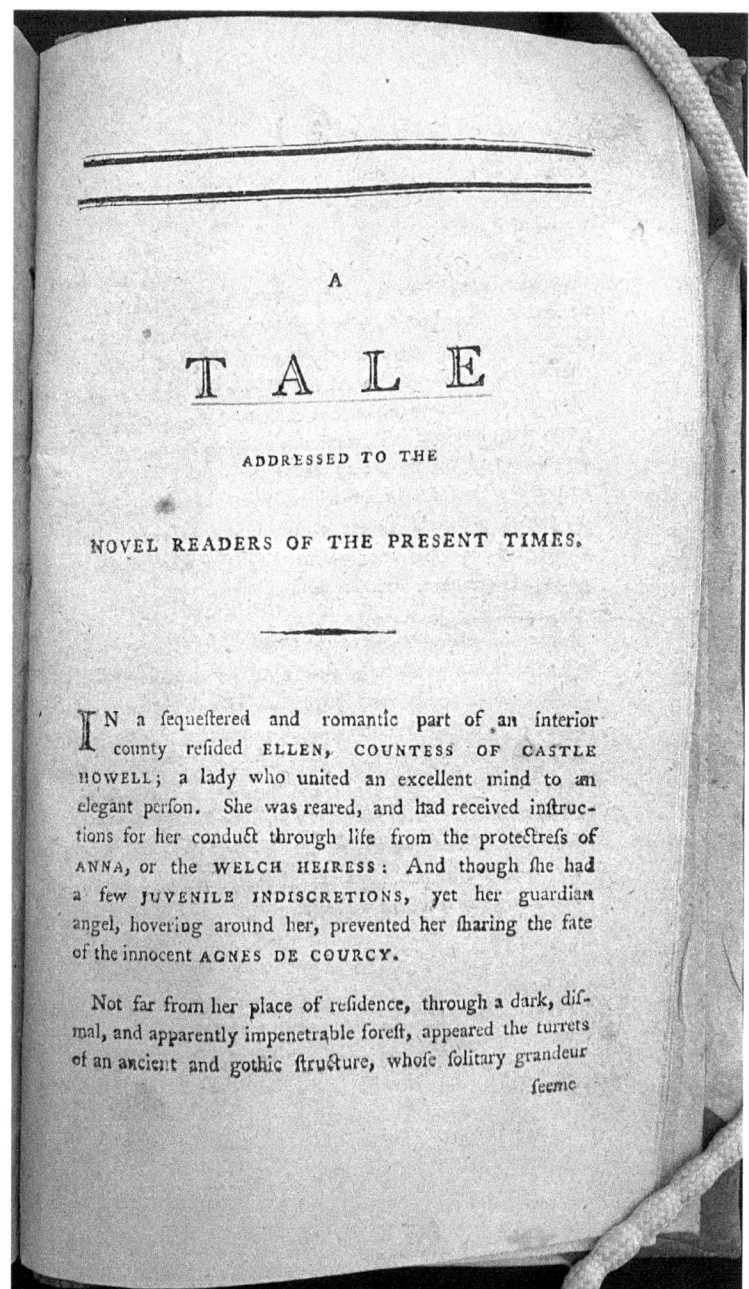

Figure 3   First page of [William Lane], 'A Tale Addressed to the Novel Readers of the Present Day' (image cropped), courtesy of the New York Society Library.

appears by the second page, in the form of an alabaster statue with 'the mystical power to fortify and guard the human mind against the power of temptations and machinations of the wicked' (2).[4] This remarkable document is thus at once advertisement and defence, luring readers with familiar tropes and well-known titles, presenting newer titles perhaps not yet known, and rebutting critiques of novels and circulating libraries in general (and the Minerva Press in particular). Introducing dozens of novels in a format deliberately designed to resemble them, the pamphlet reminds us of the deliberate and extensive nature of Lane's advertising strategies, but also raises interesting questions about the likenesses between his many novels.[5] An advertisement like this gives no details about each novel beyond its title; moreover, the gothic genre of the story implies that all the novels mentioned within it are gothic, which is not in fact the case. The list of 'Just Published' and 'In the Press' novels that follows the tale adds little more information – it provides the format, number of volumes, and price of each of the mentioned titles, but does not include author names or any further description of the titles that might help a reader to select one. How should we understand this curious advertisement, which depends so heavily on the press's vast fictional production, yet makes so little effort to distinguish between its numerous offerings?

In this chapter, I explore how the questions of multiplicity and generic resemblance raised by this pamphlet are central to our understanding of how gothic novels were read, written, and sold in the 1790s. Considering the points of connection between the gothic stereotypes so effectively used here by Lane and the strategies of critics encountering countless novels with apparently little to distinguish between them, I develop the idea of 'imitation' as literary practice, particularly in relation to the pre-eminent gothic novelist of the day, Ann Radcliffe. Examining 'imitation' allows us to see how novelists used their characters and narrative choices, particularly the deployment of recognizable genre tropes like those in the epigraph, to establish literary authority and retain a distinctive position within the market.

In a passage near the end of *Northanger Abbey*, in what may well now be the most famous literary characterization of the Minerva Press gothic, Jane Austen refers to the 'charming' works of Mrs Radcliffe and 'all her imitators'.[6] Radcliffe's novels, in particular *The Mysteries of Udolpho* (1794), are discussed throughout Austen's tale, but *Northanger Abbey*'s premise also depends on our awareness of a much larger body of texts – those 'imitators', among them the 'hundreds and hundreds' of novels that Catherine's suitor Henry Tiley claims to have read, as well as the group of seven 'all horrid' novels recommended to Catherine by her friend Isabella

Thorpe.[7] Although Austen only periodically mentions specific titles of contemporary novels, and never emphasizes a particular publisher as their source, her readers would no doubt have recognized the Minerva Press – the publishing house behind six of the seven 'horrid' novels (several of which feature in Lane's gothic 'Tale') – in her satirical depiction of the recent rage for popular fiction.

Austen's reference to Radcliffe and 'all her imitators' can thus be seen, from a modern scholar's perspective, both as a satirical characterization of an often-dismissed group of novels and as a record of a historical mode of describing those same texts. For although her iteration of it is probably the best known to a twenty-first-century reader, Austen was not the coiner of this phrase, and she was far from the last to use it. This chapter reconsiders and reorients the seemingly familiar language of 'imitation' as it has been used to describe the gothic novel of the 1790s, arguing that the notion of 'imitation', so dependent on the distinction between the admirably singular and the excessively multiple, should be understood both as a key way authors and critics positioned themselves vis-à-vis the new fictional status quo and, more broadly, as a crucial fulcrum in the ongoing Romantic debate over the literary status of the novel. For 'imitation' is a double-edged sword, often wielded against the popular novelist but also deliberately employed by her (and her publisher). Pressing on the critical language of 'imitation' to reveal its presuppositions – resemblance, repetition, similarity, predictability – allows us both to understand the utility of the term as a categorical dismissal *and* to see how the idea of imitation, applied to the emergent gothic genre, could be both productive and empowering for authors, readers, and book publishers. 'Imitation' connotes inferiority, critique, and dismissal, but it also confers authority, creates familiarity, and allows for meaningful variation. To put this another way, imitation might be a cause of the Romantic period's fictional excess, but it is also one of its most significant outcomes.

Recent scholarship on book history, popular fiction, and the gothic has already begun to re-evaluate many of the novels so frequently dismissed, then and now, as 'mere' imitations, suggesting that the interconnected and replicative nature of much popular fiction of the 1790s and early 1800s may be a part of its interest rather than a reason to dismiss it. Elizabeth Neiman, for instance, has recently described Minerva Press novelists as 'develop[ing] their own model of collective authorship', in which they '[link] their work to the codes and conventions of formula' and 'connect their writings to seminal literary and philosophical texts'.[8] Edward Jacobs has argued that circulating 'libraries gave readers an unprecedented material basis for recognizing intertextual relationships, and for identifying generic conventions',[9] while Deidre Lynch has noted the gothic's affinity for literary referentiality, writing that these novels 'are remarkable ... for the density of their intertextual allusions'.[10] And Edward Copeland describes Romantic novel production as a 'conversation among women' and connects this intertextual conversation to the real-life economic pre-occupations that he argues structure much of the period's fiction.[11]

Gothic scholarship in particular has explored the formulaic and dupli-cative qualities of popular gothic novels, and the relationship between these novels and their readers, in some detail. Emma Clery, for instance, has suggested that much of the appeal of the Minerva Press's gothic novels was precisely their predictability – they were 'a dependable commodity to the regular consumer'.[12] Michael Gamer argues that the Gothic was in part 'extremely attractive' to authors and readers 'because it is so conspicuous', signalling its generic affiliations with recognizable, clichéd plots and dis-tinctive bindings and library placement.[13] These aspects of the novels attracted much critical ire, but, as James Watt has shown, 'while many works were attacked for their formulaic depiction of supernatural agency ... such criticism was always informed by larger concerns about the production and reception of escapist fiction in general'.[14] Indeed, while the connective models just described are largely narrative, they are inseparable from the replicative modes of production, the material and economic conditions, that enable their publication.[15] Here I examine this interconnectedness across and between novels and their contexts specifi-cally in terms of 'imitation': showing the range of ways that 'imitation' was used, as both a discourse and a practice, to conceptualize popular fiction in this period. As I argue in this chapter, these are all facets of imitation, and all serve specific purposes in Romantic literary culture. 'Imitation' func-tions to develop and reinforce literary hierarchies in an increasingly crowded market, and provides readers, authors, and publishers with ways to build upon the new energies of industrial book culture.

'Imitators of Radcliffe'

The connection between the Minerva Press, Ann Radcliffe, and gothic imitation has much to do with William Lane's timing. By the late 1780s reviewers were beginning to identify novelists whom they saw as following in the footsteps of gothic innovators like Horace Walpole, Clara Reeve, and A. L. Aikin (later Barbauld).[16] Ann Radcliffe published her first novel, *Castles of Athlin and Dunbayne*, in 1789, rapidly following with *A Sicilian*

Romance, which appeared in 1790, the same year that Lane founded the Minerva imprint. Radcliffe's very successful *Romance of the Forest* (1791) appeared soon after, and she reached a peak of popularity with the publication of her best-known works, *The Mysteries of Udolpho* (1794) and *The Italian* (1796).[17] During the very same years that the Minerva Press grew from fledgling press to a publishing behemoth, then, single-handedly capturing fully one quarter of the increasing market for novels, Radcliffe's fame and the popularity of the gothic novel also sharply increased.[18] Many observers saw these developments as directly related; as a writer in the *Monthly Visitor* declared in 1797; 'Since the appearance of Mrs. RADCLIFFE, ghosts and descriptions, descriptions and ghosts, have alarmed and astonished the simple of mankind.'[19]

There is no question that Radcliffe's works inspired a wide variety of direct responses of numerous kinds, stage adaptations and poems as well as novels,[20] and, given her indubitably massive success, it is perhaps unsurprising that she came to be seen as the lone original among a horde of inferior imitators.[21] As Rictor Norton memorably puts it, 'The list of derivative adaptations and anonymous plagiarisms could be continued indefinitely: Ann Radcliffe's hideous progeny is enormous.'[22] This wonderfully vivid image captures the sense of unchecked literary reproduction underlying much of the anti-novel rhetoric surrounding the gothic in the 1790s. For, of course, dismissing an undefined – but large – number of novels as 'hideous progeny' is an aesthetic judgment, but also a critical tactic; whether or not we admire the novels thus spurned (and some of them make this task admittedly difficult), such a formulation is less a factual descriptor than a rhetorical mode of capturing a moment of fictional proliferation.

This chapter's purpose is not, then, to determine the relative hideousness of any particularly gothic novel, nor to ascertain how nearly specific novels resemble (or don't resemble) Radcliffe's, though I am certainly in agreement with recent scholars who have pointed out that such comparisons tend to be erroneously over-general.[23] Rather, I am interested in the critical work that the theory and practice of imitation carries out in this period, and how its fundamental assumption of likeness allows participants in Romantic literary culture to navigate its challenges in different ways. The discourse of 'imitation' delineates the emergence of a genre, in the case of the gothic, but it simultaneously marks the boundaries of that genre as porous and protean, necessarily manipulable by critics seeking to distinguish worthy entrants from unworthy, but also navigable by authors who use affinities across texts for commercial, political, and artistic ends.[24]

If there are, as I contend, many sides to the story of gothic imitation, then the most familiar one is surely that espoused by scornful critics and ironically echoed by Austen. Examples abound in the mid-1790s: *The Abbey of St. Asaph* (1795), declared *The Critical Review*, was composed 'In humble imitation of the well-known novels of Mrs. Radcliffe'.[25] While, as Yael Shapira has shown, this summary of *The Abbey of St. Asaph* is dependent on a partial and oversimplified reading of the novel, many reviewers seemed uninterested in such nuances.[26] 'One successful literary adventurer commonly attracts a numerous train of followers', noted the *Analytical Review* the following year, continuing, 'Mrs. Radcliffe's "Mysteries of Udolpho" have given birth to several humble imitations, which have resembled the original in nothing, but in attempting to excite surprise and terrour.'[27] A critic at the *Monthly Review* called *Santa Maria; or, The Mysterious Pregnancy* 'A very poor and evident imitation of the style and character of Mrs. Radcliffe's romances',[28] and by 1797, a reviewer at *The Monthly Visitor* would write of a particularly unfortunate novel, 'This work, as an imitation of Ann Radcliffe, is perhaps one of the most despicable performances that ever appeared.'[29] Even more straightfor-wardly pejorative was *The Critical Review*'s claim that it was a severe 'penance' to be forced to review 'such vapid and servile imitations as the Orphan of the Rhine, and other recent romances'.[30] Such uses of 'imita-tion' clearly function to place the 'imitations' in a subordinate literary position relative to a more valorised 'original', but the novels in question are also being identified, increasingly, as members of a particular literary class or kind – that is, as an identifiable genre, and one that is growing uncontrollably.[31]

The act of imitation is sometimes portrayed as a deliberate authorial choice rather than a reflection of intrinsic ability; as the *Monthly Visitor* lamented in 1797, 'Assuredly, it is a matter of regret, that writers of merit should lose that merit in imitation.'[32] Authors chose to imitate, reviewers hint, for practical reasons. Calling Mary Robinson's novel *Hubert de Sevrac* 'an imitation of Mrs. Radcliffe's romances', the *Critical Review* declared, 'it may be necessary to apprise novel-writers, in general, that [the present taste for romances] is declining, and that real life and manners will soon assert their claims'.[33] A change in the marketability of gothic texts would, this formulation suggests, soon lead 'writers of merit' to direct their talents elsewhere. At other moments, however, the difference between an imitator and an original is portrayed as inherent rather than elective. The *Monthly Visitor* continued, 'If a Radcliffe were no more, her successors would yet suffer by comparison: while she lives, there is little hope for the mimic or the copyist.'[34] Of the novel *Dusseldorf; or The Fratricide*, one reviewer opined, 'With regard to the incidents of this romance, the writer imitates those of Mrs. Radcliffe; but she is far from being equal to that lady in this branch of composition.'[35] And the *Critical Review* exempted *only* Radcliffe from its blanket dismissal of gothic novels and their authors: 'In truth, we are almost weary of Gothic castles.... The tale of shrieking spectres, and bloody murders, has been repeated till it palls upon the sense. It requires the genius of a Radcliffe to harrow up our souls with these visionary terrors.'[36]

Radcliffe's distinction was not merely aesthetic, but also political; in her discussion of the gothic and the French Revolution, Angela Wright points to the connections many commentators saw between the gothic and political unrest; for these readers, 'Gothic romance posed a particular threat to the constitution of England.'[37] Though Wright demonstrates that Radcliffe's engagement with the issues surrounding the Revolution in France was in fact far more significant than previous scholarship has acknowledged, she also highlights how Radcliffe's canny handling of these topics 'exonerated her from the charges of literary sedition that many of her "Gothic" contemporaries attracted', maintaining a uniquely 'unblemished' reputation in the early and mid-1790s.[38] However, Radcliffe's perceived innocence did not serve as a defence of her fellow gothic authors; quite the reverse. As Wright puts it, 'reviewers complained vigorously about her imitators'.[39] Political judgements were often very difficult to separate from aesthetic judgements; in Radcliffe's case, it appears that both the literary qualities of her work and her apparent political inoffensiveness united to exempt her from the similarly tautological critiques of other authors, whose works were widely assumed to be at once ethically dubious and aesthetically reprehensible.

Critics were by no means unaware of their own dependence on formula in these critiques. 'Since Mrs. Radcliffe's justly admired and successful romances, the press has teemed with stories of haunted castles and visionary terrors; the incidents of which are so little diversified, that criticism is at a loss to vary its remarks', wrote one reviewer in *The Critical Review* in 1796.[40] Although this now-famous remark is often read as a straightforward indictment of the fiction of the age, for the purposes of my argument, it is the reviewer's comments about *critical* unoriginality – what Wright, with reference to this review, calls 'the plagiaristic tendencies of criticism' – that are particularly interesting.[41] We can see in all these references to Radcliffe's imitators that a genre-specific identification of a literary fashion was clearly also functioning as a convenient catch-all phrase, designed to dismiss the works discussed as 'imitations' and to effectively exclude them from the realm of literary criticism. Reliance on this formula could be a shorthand through which critics – with ever-increasing numbers of new novels taxing their review capacity – could categorize and dismiss at least one substantial group of them.[42]

Indeed, although Radcliffe published no more novels in her lifetime, the critical habit of identifying new novels as 'imitations' of her work showed few signs of lessening. In 1805, some eight years after the publication of *The Italian*, the *Critical Review* identified the novel *Valombrosa* specifically as an imitation of *Udolpho*, and proceeded to use the word in various forms no fewer than four times in one short paragraph:

> Amongst the numerous, or, to speak with more propriety, innumerable, *imitations* of 'the Mysteries of Udolpho,' with which the press has groaned, we must rank the present production.... We should have paused to observe, that the author is sometimes an agreeable and not unsuccessful *imitator*, – ... had not [his fancy] too often presented pictures which ought not to be exhibited, and [his language] been made the vehicle of ideas the most impure. Here then the *imitation* ceases: we cannot congratulate this gentleman ... on the slightest ambition to *imitate* that delicacy which is one of the many beauties so profusely scattered over the writings of Mrs. Radcliffe.[43]

Such a passage highlights the range of critical functions that this term could serve and shows that it remained a legible marker of the gothic well after the mid-1790s. But the reviewer's concession that 'the author is sometimes an agreeable and not unsuccessful imitator', a claim that may surprise us after the litanies of insults explored so far, hints at another aspect of gothic imitation, one that, as the next sections will show, is both historically grounded and newly relevant in the Romantic period.

Imitation's Authority

When we read countless 1790s reviewers disparaging gothic imitators, or note how frequently contemporary critics have adopted this dismissive terminology to describe the decade's popular gothic novels by less famous authors, it may be easy to disconnect this use of the term from the eighteenth century's longer history of literary imitation.[44] To do so is, however, to take overwhelmed reviewers too much at their word; it is also to miss the ways that gothic novelists use the rhetoric of imitation to bolster, not to undermine, their own authority. The *English Short-Title Catalog* currently shows more than 600 results for English works with 'imitation' in their title between 1700 and 1800; in other words, large numbers of works throughout the century identify *themselves* as imitations.[45] In the earlier eighteenth century, the titular words 'imitation', 'imitate', and 'imitator' are used most frequently in a Neoclassical, religious, or didactic context, describing, for instance, author David Crauford's 1703 publication *Ovidius Britannicus; or, Love Epistles. In Imitation of Ovid* or, the following year, *Divine Hymns and Poems on Several Occasions . . . In Imitation of Mr. Milton*. Illustrious English authors (Shakespeare, Spenser, Milton) are frequently identified alongside classical works as the objects of imitation. 'Imitation' is explicitly used in these cases to identify a work's genre and to tie it to authors, works, and ideas that have already achieved acclaim or cultural importance.

This is not, of course, to suggest that the practice of imitation was perceived as entirely admirable or elevated prior to the 1790s – as Samuel Johnson records in his *Dictionary* under the entry for 'imitator', citing Dryden's seventeenth-century remark: '*Imitators* are but a servile kind of cattle.' But what we do see throughout the century is a robust practice of authors identifying their works as imitations in a bid for increased respectability or generic legibility. The ability to identify an author (an Ovid, a Livy, a Shakespeare, a Milton) *worthy* of imitation is in this sense a form of demonstrating one's literary knowledge, and the ability to actually produce said imitation is a vindication of skill and talent. While the majority of these titles were not novels, at mid-century, some novelists did identify their works as 'imitations': perhaps most famously, Henry Fielding described his first novel *Joseph Andrews* as 'Written in Imitation of the Manner of Cervantes'. By the 1790s, when the output of novels had risen dramatically, one might expect to see a corresponding rise in novels titled, for example, 'in imitation of Fielding', but, while many novelists clearly were imitating Fielding's plots, this doesn't tend to be indicated on the title page. Instead, the explicit discourse of imitation, as it applies to fiction, migrates into periodical discussions. But authors still invoke it in their paratexts and in their plots; gothic imitations, like the century's earlier imitations, use literary lineage as a way to identify themselves and signal generic allegiances.

It is unsurprising, then, that gothic fiction from this period is full of explicit references to Ann Radcliffe. Writing the preface to her 1804 gothic novella, *The Castle of Kolmeras*, for instance, Stéphanie-Félicité de Genlis openly acknowledged the perceived relationship between the genre in which she was writing and Radcliffe. As soon as *Kolmeras* was published, de Genlis's narrator declares,

> I shall speedily publish another under the title of *The Castle of Bentheim* ...
> [which] I found ready to my hands, and all in a fine state of ruin, on the
> road from Hamburgh.... As I went over it, I thanked heaven that Mrs.
> Radcliffe had not been there before me; for she could not have failed to take
> possession of so fine a groundwork for a Romance.[46]

This light-hearted acknowledgement seems designed to forestall a
reviewer's dismissal of the work as an 'imitation' of Radcliffe – of course
this is Radcliffean! It proclaims. Rather than defensively argue for her own
work's uniqueness, de Genlis seizes control of the narrative, using
Radcliffe's acknowledged fame to locate her own efforts within the genre.
As Angela Wright has shown, the relationship between de Genlis and
Radcliffe was by no means one-sided; Wright argues that de Genlis's work,
particularly her thinking on education and self-love, was highly influential
to Radcliffe's gothic novels.[47] In writing a tale about a stereotypically
ruined castle, however, de Genlis, rather mockingly, suggests a flow of
influence that runs the other way: *all* gothic tales, in a sense, belong
to Radcliffe.

Introducing one's own work with a reference to Radcliffe is a technique
frequently employed by gothic authors in this era, with varying degrees of
apparent sincerity. In 1801, the Gothic novelist T. J. Horsley Curties
completed his second novel, *Ancient Records, or, The Abbey of Saint
Oswyth*, with a preface that quite openly proclaimed it to be the work of
a 'shadow' of the great Ann Radcliffe. Emerging from the anonymity that
had veiled his first literary attempt, Curties wrote:

> Encouraged by that reception with which his first essay was accepted by the
> Public, the Author of Ancient Records again entrusts his Work to their
> hands.... Its mysteries – its terrific illusions – its very errors must be
> attributed to a love of Romance, caught from an enthusiastic admiration
> of Udolpho's unrivalled Foundress. – He follows her through all the
> venerable gloom of horrors, not as a kindred spirit, but contented, as a
> shadow, in attending her footsteps.[48]

It is not at all clear that the reception of *Ancient Records* was in fact quite as
encouraging as Curties's optimistic preface suggests;[49] most interesting,
however, is that an author so preoccupied with establishing his own
authorial legitimacy, and so explicitly concerned elsewhere in this preface
with denigrating the work of his female gothic competitors in order to
defend his own, would choose to declare himself an inferior acolyte of
Radcliffe.[50] Even more abject is the prefatory appeal of the young author
of *Eloise de Montblanc* (1796), who invokes not just Radcliffe but a whole
pantheon of female novelists to express the fear that 'the female Pen of

Seventeen' feels as 'she...recollects the perfect Pen of a Burney, a Radcliffe, a Bennet, or a Smith, [and] shrinks at meeting the scrutinizing Eye of Criticism'.[51] In all these cases, we might read the pose of humility as a ploy to gain reviewers' sympathy, and reviewers often interpret it as such (not always sympathetically). But de Genlis, Curties, *Eloise*'s anonymous young author, and the many other authors who employ this technique are also working to legitimize the form and genre in which they write by comparing their own work to that of the gothic novel's most successful practitioners.[52] (The author of *Eloise* makes it plain that imitation, not just adulation, underlies her comparative choices by including Minerva author Anna Maria Bennett, a best-seller but by no means as acclaimed as Burney and Radcliffe, in her list. If Burney isn't truly within her reach, perhaps Bennett will serve the purpose.)

The English gothic novelist may not have an Ovid, a Shakespeare, or a Milton to imitate, but repeatedly citing Radcliffe grants her a similar authority, an authority that may, in turn, transfer to other adherents of the writing style she practices. Miss Hutchison, the author of *Exhibitions of the Heart* (1799), uses a similar technique intra- rather than paratextually in her novel, which features a heroine who, 'turning over page after page, volume after volume ... found nothing to attach her attention, which required something more ... more than *Pope* has left; more than *Dryden* ever thought; more than *Fielding* could display; more than *Radcliffe* can invent; more than genius could impart'.[53] Moving from poets to novelists, and from male authors to a woman writer, this list not only elevates Radcliffe to canonical status, but makes room for a female novelist – like the author of this novel – in the literary ranks.

Passages like these remind us that for all Radcliffe's acclaim, as a female author and an author of gothic novels, her literary status was still, from a certain perspective, precarious. The prolific novelist Francis Lathom (his works include *The Midnight Bell*, another of Austen's 'horrid novels') reproduces an example of the anti-novel discourse directed at Radcliffe and her peers in his *Men and Manners* (1799), using dialogue between characters to mock the pretensions of those who refuse to acknowledge the value of novels. A young female novel-reader debates her male companion, who pompously proclaims:

> '... the English are most excellent in their fictitious writings ...'
> 'You admire Udolpho then, sir, I dare say?'
> 'I am not versed in Italian.'
> 'Oh, Udolpho is English; it is the name of the book; a romance by the incomparable Mrs. Radcliffe.'

'I never read such insignificant works as romances', he replied.

'I thought you spoke in praise of fictious [*sic*] writings, just now, sir.'

'The fictions of Homer, Sophocles, Virgil, Shakespeare, and Pope, are not novels.'[54]

The heroine rebuts her interlocuter's perspective by remarking that many of the above works are 'ten times more insignificant, and out of the way, than any novel you can point out to me in the language'; he ('well read in books, without knowing much of men') comes off much the worse in the debate, suggesting that Lathom, like Hutchison, is ultimately using a defence of Radcliffe as a defence of his own work.[55] For these authors, to 'imitate' Radcliffe is to attach their reputation to that of someone with more fame, but it is also to throw their weight on the pro-novel side of the scales alongside her. While critics may have wearied of the 'numerous, or to speak with more propriety, innumerable, imitations of Radcliffe' they were tasked with reading, many authors clearly concluded that more novels meant more publicity, which might in turn lead to greater success for all.[56]

To say that gothic authors invoke Radcliffe to legitimate their own work or to make its genre legible to readers, however, doesn't quite capture all the complexities of this imitative practice. To compare oneself to Radcliffe is also, in various places, to poke fun at the standards of the genre, to suggest that Radcliffe is no less subject to its more ludicrous constraints or its derivative qualities than any other author, and, finally, to hint that some of the genre's most praised qualities may be more worthy of interrogation than acclaim. In other words, imitation invokes authority, but also challenges it. Edward Du Bois suggests as much when, mid-text in *St. Godwin* (1800), his narrator interjects, 'A dreadful storm came on, the awful thunder rolled over the vast expanse of heaven, and the vivid lightning in refulgent corruscations darted from – from – (I wish I had Ann Radcliffe by me, for I am at a stand; I know this is the place for description, but I cannot get on.)'[57] Du Bois's comic pose echoes the humility of passages like the preface to *Eloise de Montblanc*, acknowledging that Radcliffe is the reigning expert in this type of writing and suggesting that this author cannot hope to live up to her example. However, the overheated melodrama of the prose in this passage suggests gentle mockery of Radcliffe's style rather than sincere veneration, and the reference to a 'place for description' surely pokes fun at Radcliffe's extended landscape descriptions.

Returning to the preface to *The Castle of Kolmeras*, we can see how de Genlis's mock-competitive comparison ('As I went over [the ruin],

I thanked heaven that Mrs. Radcliffe had not been there before me') also functions as a kind of challenge to Radcliffe's singular and unique imaginative genius. Here, literary inspiration (the ruined castle, the 'groundwork for a Romance') is not only physically concrete; it is also characterized as accessible by any one of a network of authors, each familiar with the tropes their novels share, and equally capable of capitalizing on a new source of inspiration. Playfully referencing the castle's ready-to-hand 'machinery' – 'It was besieged in 1794, its walls are battered with cannon, several of its apartments are yet stained with blood, its courts are full of human bones, &c.' (4) – de Genlis invites amused recognition of these well-known motifs, but also suggests that Radcliffe herself is no less dependent on them than any other gothic writer. The date of the siege, moreover, poses a different kind of challenge to Radcliffe's authority: as a Frenchwoman who was exiled from France during the Revolution, de Genlis's satiric tone in this passage seems calculated to highlight the difference between Radcliffe's 'terrors' and the Terror, with the former appearing rather less authentic (not to mention ethically questionable as a source of entertainment) by the comparison.[58] Imitation, then, however positive, rarely takes the form of straightforward praise; when the narrator declares, 'As to Castles ... I fear no rivals' it is both an ironic reminder of just how many gothic novelists are competing for readership and acclaim and an assertion that, even or especially within the constraints of genre, each work stands to benefit from the successes of its peers.

Gothic Machinery and Generic Expectations

Imitation is clearly about authorial identity, about signalling (as either a criticism or a sign of allegiance) affinities to a particular author, genre, or canon. But the substance of such an affinity is primarily textual. Whether authors self-identified as writers in a Radcliffean vein or were dismissively categorized as such by reviewers, such claims nearly always hinge on the use and reuse of recognizable gothic formulae. *The Abbey of St. Asaph* (1795) was said to be 'duly equipped with all the appurtenances of ruined towers, falling battlements, moats, draw-bridges, Gothic porches, tombs, vaults, and apparitions',[59] and another novel, *Dusseldorf; or, The Fratricide* (1798), was summed up with the remark: 'It seems to be agreed that those who write on the horrific plan must employ the same instruments – cruel German counts, each with two wives – old castles – private doors – sliding pannels – banditti – assassins – ghosts, &c.'[60] When discussing *The Wanderer of the Alps* (1797), the *Critical Review* referred to 'the hackneyed

and borrowed machinery of *haunted castles, skeletons, banditti,* &c.'[61]
'[T]he concomitant circumstances of ghosts, murders, midnight bells,
&c. are introduced with the usual mysterious apparatus',[62] remarked a
reviewer of Francis Lathom's *Midnight Bell*. Whether characterized as
'appurtenances', 'apparatus', 'ingredients', or 'machinery', descriptions like
these reinforce the idea that the gothic novel depends on certain highly
predictable topoi.[63] What such a formulation leaves out entirely, however,
is the potential that such set elements provide for creative variation.[64]
Precisely because certain 'ingredients' of these gothic fictions are so predictable, authors were able to meaningfully alter and destabilize them to
create a range of effects. Predicating their experiments on an assumed
readership intimately familiar with the 'norms' of the genre, Minerva's
authors undermine and repurpose the gothic conventions they employ,
using the imitative mode to capitalize on the narrative possibilities
of genre.

If castles, banditti, and ghosts create the mandatory backdrop for a
gothic tale, the unfortunate young women who encounter them are no less
central – and no less stereotyped. Marilyn Butler sums up the situation
thus: 'The commonest of all plots of the eighteenth-century Gothic novel
involves a frail protagonist in terrible danger. She . . . is placed in a hostile,
threatening, mysterious environment, usually so prodigiously large that it
dwarfs her; she is made prisoner; she is threatened by individuals who
should protect her.'[65] Unsurprisingly, then, given the trends I have outlined, Minerva authors frequently use their heroines to play up, and to
question, gothic stereotypes. This pattern is evident in three best-selling
gothic novels by two of the Minerva Press's best-known gothic novelists:
The Castle of Wolfenbach (1793) and *Lucy* (1794) by Eliza Parsons, and
Clermont (1798) by Regina Maria Roche.[66] In all three novels, the narratives use their young heroines to call attention to the very predictability of
the 'machinery' that operates their tales. These narrative ruptures can be
brief and humorous, as when the young heroine of *Lucy*, immured in a
ruin with her adoptive parents, wonders, '[B]y what means did we come to
this ugly old castle?',[67] echoing the thoughts of many a reader bewildered
by the oversupply of ruined castles in the gothic landscape. Occasionally,
they seem to call the centrality of the gothic setting into question; in
Clermont, for example, Madeline's new romantic prospects are accompanied by a complete revolution in her feelings from one day to the next:

> How light was the step – how bright was the eye – how gay was the smile of
> Madeline when she descended the next morning to the breakfast parlour . . .

the appearance of every thing seemed changed, the awful gloom which had
so long pervaded the apartments, was banished; and in the landscape before
the windows Madeline now discovered beauties which had before escaped
her notice.[68]

This change is so dramatic that it throws even the actual gloominess of the
setting into doubt, suggesting that, packed as this novel is with terrifying
generic set-pieces, it is ultimately the protagonist's emotions – that is, her
potentially unexpected responses to expected narrative stereotypes – that
form much of its interest for the reader.

On other occasions, novels contain narrative interjections or tonal
inconsistencies that throw the status of the entire novel – its seriousness,
its intended effect, its likely outcome – into question. When Matilda, the
heroine of *The Castle of Wolfenbach*, finally penetrates the hidden room
in the castle where a Countess has been cruelly imprisoned, for example,
we are told that she finds lines of poetry cut into the window with a
diamond, and that these writings are 'expressive of misery, though not of
poetical talents'.[69] Given that the reader has already been alerted that
these lines are one of the most terrifying aspects of the castle – Matilda is
warned before visiting that it contains '[in]scriptions . . . on the windows,
to make a body's hair stand on end' (4) – it is difficult to know how to
respond to this sudden cool appraisal. Taking the statement as a joke
undermines the whole premise of the novel as terrifying; to interpret
Matilda's words as seriously meant, however, places her in the role of
jaded critic rather than compassionate heroine. Lines like this should
certainly be understood in part as what Horner and Zloznik have
identified as gothic's 'comic turn', that is, the potential for comedy that,
they argue, 'is intrinsic to a mode of writing that has been hybrid since its
very inception'.[70] But I would also suggest that Matilda's comment is
most resonant only when it is read in context, that is, against a backdrop
of dozens of other gothic novels in which characters compose poetry of
questionable merit at every opportunity.[71] (While the quality of gothic
poetry is of course a matter of subjective judgement, it is tempting to
read this line as faint mockery of Radcliffe, whose heroines' poetic flights
are often cited as evidence of her genius.) Similarly, *Lucy*'s narrator
remarks at one point that the eponymous heroine (while exploring a
deserted underground passage) is 'entirely unacquainted with any stories
of ghosts and apparitions' and thus 'apprehend[s] no danger' and is not
'sensible of the hazards she run[s]' (I:76). The necessity for an explanation of this kind, of course, only stems from the sure awareness of a
projected reader who will know exactly what kind of 'story' Lucy is in,

and what kinds of 'hazards' she is sure to face in it. In all of these cases, the novels' genre becomes their subject.

Although examples of this kind could be gathered endlessly, I will conclude this discussion with one more cluster of references from *Lucy*, which illustrates the potential range of purposes to which such meta-commentary could be put. At the stage of the novel at which the heroine seems not yet to have recognized her gothic status, the narrator suggests that her lack of generic self-identification – that is, her failure to act as the heroine of a gothic romance should do – may stem from a similar failure on the part of her guardians, given their unseemly (for the gothic) dependence on the prosaic needs of life. Upon first settling in the 'ugly old castle' that Lucy wonders at, their first act is 'planting potatoes' (I:4), and potatoes make cameo appearances surprisingly often thereafter. It is 'while roasting a few potatoes' that the couple hears the fateful footsteps of the horseman who abandons the infant Lucy (I:9), and it is hunger that then motivates the young Lucy to rouse her mother from her stupor of grief after her father's death: 'I am very hungry', she remarks, 'must we all die together?' (I:21). Left alone in the castle some years later, Lucy makes a stab at typical gothic-heroine exploration, but finding that the path to the subterranean passages she hopes to explore is 'walled up, and she could go no farther', she goes home instead, 'to boil her potatoes' (I:30). And after the death of her foster-mother, when Lucy is left to fend for herself once and for all, her embarkation on the path of an orphan heroine is marked by her romantic refusal of all life's necessities: 'She returned to her room, alas! how gloomy, how frightful its appearance! No gentle friend to speak the words of kindness; no mother to instruct or amuse her ... she lighted no fire, boiled no potatoes, made no bed' (I:43).

While my aim here is not to attempt an extended close reading of the Gothic Potato, I dwell on this detail at some length because of its potential to illustrate some of the instabilities characteristic of Minerva's imitative fiction. All the potatoes might be read, for example, as simply clumsy writing, too-frequent reuse of an unfortunate image. They might also be taken as a spoof on dainty gothic heroines, who are seldom seen eating, and would, we imagine, scorn a meal so unglamorous as a home-grown potato. (*The Mysteries of Udolpho*, for instance, contains the word 'hunger' only three times, once in an abstract reference to hunger and exhaustion, and twice in scenes that mock Emily's maidservant Annette for her focus on food, which both characters and narrator treat as clearly crass and unladylike.[72] 'Potato', naturally, appears not at all.) There is likely some truth in both the careless and the parodic explanations, but I would also like to suggest a third: Lucy's potatoes remind readers of the real risks of hunger and of the importance assumed by food in situations in which it is scarce. This last reading may seem the furthest-fetched, given the very brief summary I offered above, but in fact the novel offers a great deal of evidence for it. Poverty is a constant threat, and the novel's characters repeatedly take a pointed interest in explaining to Lucy that she will have to work to earn her living and to have enough to eat. In other words, the persistence of that out-of-place gothic potato uses the collective aesthetics of this 'horrifying' genre to remind readers of the genuine (and much more common) horrors of hunger and poverty.[73] The frequently precarious financial status of Minerva authors including Parsons, as Jennie Batchelor and Edward Copeland have shown, directly influences the conditions of their literary production; as Copeland points out, in Parsons's last novel, she 'rebuke[s] Radcliffe ... implicitly for what she perceives as Radcliffe's inadequate account of the miseries of women's economic isolation'.[74] Passages like this one from *Lucy* show us clearly that the conventions of genre can be, and were, used to reflect upon class-based life experiences.[75]

Imitation and Intertextuality

Different forms of gothic imitation allowed authors to capitalize on their own positionality in a crowded market, maximizing the benefits – the recognition, the publicity, the appeal – of writing in a familiar genre, and exploiting that seeming familiarity in order to highlight critiques or revisions of the genre itself. Mary Charlton's *Rosella, or Modern Occurrences* (1799), provides a final case study in the ways that imitation appeals directly to readers through manipulation of genre norms and direct connection to other recognizable popular works. *Rosella*, like many Minerva Press novels, is difficult to categorize. It could fairly be called a parody; we might also read it as a satirical send-up of female readers. It also, however, reads for long stretches as a persuasively didactic sentimental novel, and in others could very easily be taken for a thoroughly gothic one. *Rosella* borrows from recognizable genre tropes, but also reflects upon the material conditions of its own production. Both the physical realities of novel-reading and the crowded marketplace into which such books necessarily entered become parts of the plot.[76] Thus *Rosella* provides a representative example of a Minerva author's imitative and intertextual relationship with other authors, readers, and texts. Not only does the imitative mode allow authors to import plots, characters, and even the identities of other authors into their own works; it renders the intertextual project explicit. The devoted readers who are merely implied in many other gothic fictions here make their way right into the text, transforming the potentially overwhelming number of novels in circulation into a network of familiar references, a community rather than a crowd.

Miss Sophia Beauclerc, at the novel's opening, is immediately identified as a female quixote, foolishly addicted to contemporary novels.[77] The opening scenes of *Rosella* predate the eponymous heroine's birth; as we soon discover, Miss Beauclerc is in the midst of a fiction-inspired and friend-abetted elopement with an unsuitable lover. (Both Sophia and her friend, the equally novel-addicted Selina, derive immense enjoyment from imagining themselves to be gothic heroines.) Charlton plays up the humour of their heroic self-perception, but she also grounds the satire in the mechanisms of popular readership. Looking in the mirror, Sophia enjoys the 'elevated pleasure of beholding *in propria persona* a heroine in the bloom of youth, emerging into those delightful, mysterious, and sentimental situations which so agreeably occupy the imagination, when viewed within the inclosure of a tremendous breadth of margin, and cased in a surtout of marbled paper, extremely soiled by the devotion of the curious' (I:9). In its ironic emphasis on the materiality of the popular circulating-library novel, *Rosella* invokes the fictions it mocks and whose conditions of production it in fact shared. If some onlookers found the supply of novels unnecessarily large (and the reference to 'tremendous breadth of margin' clearly suggests that at least some of this volume was a deliberate printing strategy), this passage also reminds us of the countless others who eagerly awaited each new volume.

No reader familiar with the quixotic tradition will be surprised to learn that Sophia's youthful escapade does not go smoothly – her love affair with the feckless and indebted Raymond ends in his death and her own pregnancy. Both her impending motherhood and the fact of her brief marriage are hastily hushed up by her concerned parents. The child – Rosella – is shipped off for fostering, and Selina and Sophia both return home, somewhat chastened but, as we soon learn, no wiser for the experience. If the story ended here, *Rosella* would be an entertaining and relatively simple rewriting of the female quixote trope. As the title suggests, however, this tidy plot – which fills only the first hundred pages or so – is merely the prelude to the central story of the novel. As the action begins to unfold, we find ourselves in what seems to be a parody of a parodic novel (or perhaps, to put it in the terms I have thus far been using, an imitation of an imitation): now it is the innocent Rosella (innocent of moral error as well as of excessive novel reading) who is the heroine, and Selina and Sophia, grown up into Mrs Ellinger and Miss Beauclerc, who are the 'authors' of her melodramatic escapades.[78] Charlton misses no opportunity to reiterate gothic and sentimental stereotypes through the musings of Selina and Sophia, but she also repeatedly emphasizes the active, writerly role these two women take in creating their own novelistic tale, as Sophia recounts Rosella's adventures in lengthy letters to her friend. Where Rosella's natural inclinations and experiences, like Lucy's in Parsons's earlier novel, do not align with her status as heroine, her guardians do their best to alter them, a process that necessitates such steps as the purchase of a harp, voice lessons, and removal to a country estate: 'her progress in celebrity and heroism . . . [was] not to be attained in the odious metropolis' (I:124). The humour of such scenes depends on familiarity with genre tropes, and the plot device itself suggests that readers' expectations push novels to conform with pre-existing standards.

Authors in this model are not, however, portrayed as blind adherents to formula. Like Parsons, Charlton uses her metafiction to trouble the notion of a genteel or morally pure terror (of the kind that critics often praised in Radcliffe's works) with frequent references to the horrors of poverty, illness, and social inequality. In these moments, Miss Beauclerc's novel addiction is not problematic so much for its silliness as for its tendency to make her, for example, dismiss the tragedy of a peasant woman left widowed and penniless, when it turns out that her father 'instead of being the ennobled Lord of a fine old castle, containing a fine old skeleton, and a fine old mysterious manuscript, was no other than a wretched fisherman who caught and cured herrings' (III:41). Poor children here are ragged and dirty rather than beautiful and politely mannered; underpaid clerks gaze out of their 'very dirty grim window' onto 'a marvellous foul cinder heap, which the elevated notions of the lady of the mansion prevented her from observing' (I:155); and landlords offer chivalrous assistance only when they are confident that they will be well recompensed for their pains. Even more than *Lucy*, *Rosella* uses genre standards to reinsert concrete financial concerns into fictional scenes. Social critique thus intersects directly with humorous revision of genre norms; the dependence of the critique on the familiar stereotypes of popular fiction, however, means that without knowledge of the latter, the point of the former is likely to be missed. Imitation is about genre critique, but it can also be about social critique, and the distance some literary characters appear to have from the necessities of everyday survival becomes yet another theme to rewrite.

That this rewriting is both deliberate and dependent on the author's sense of the countless other novels with which the reader of *Rosella* is doubtless familiar becomes increasingly evident when we pay attention to Charlton's numerous intertextual references. Throughout *Rosella*, Miss Beauclerc discusses specific plot points, characters, and incidents from other novels she has read, in order to compare them with the situation at hand. The scenes are often stereotypical or comically melodramatic, as one might expect; what might not be so immediately apparent, however, is that they are also often referencing actual contemporary novels. When Miss Beauclerc describes the 'captivating heroine . . . who made a pedestrian tour on the Continent of more than eight hundred miles, in pursuance of the dictates of "Plain Sense"' (II:173–174),[79] readers would surely have caught the reference to the best-selling Minerva Press novel *Plain Sense* (1795), which reached at least three editions in the 1790s. Similarly, when we are told that in Miss Beauclerc's favourite reading spot she 'relished more particularly the descriptive progress of the loves of all the Ethelindas, the Jemimas, the Fredericas, and the Georgianas, with all their panics, their castles, and their visions' (I:125), we may not now recognize that these names refer specifically to heroines in different popular novels published in the 1790s.[80] When Miss Beauclerc asks Rosella, '[I]n the charming new novel we lately read, did not a very amiable, honest, and moral man introduce a very lovely young stranger to his wife and daughters, as their niece and cousin'?, she is not merely justifying her own point of view; this description (and the entire page-long plot summary that follows it) also serves as a hint to all of *Rosella*'s readers who have also read the novel in question, *The Beggar Girl* (1797), by Anna Maria Bennett (II:244) – the same author cited as a Radcliffean exemplar by the author of *Eloise de Montblanc*.[81]

Further allusions of this kind fill the novel; when Miss Beauclerc demands that she and her protégée traipse alone along a pitch-dark path in order to uncover the 'mystery' of a strange man they've met, for example, Rosella 'had no objection to the proposition, but she wished to *elucidate the mystery* in a less heroic manner – that is, she would have made her present peregrination at a more convenient hour, when the sun might have illuminated her on the way' (II:86, emphasis added). While the reference is less explicit, it's hard to think it coincidental that a few years earlier, another Minerva gothic author, Anna Maria Mackenzie, had published an equally knowing pseudo-satire of gothic fiction called *Mysteries Elucidated*.[82]

As Deidre Lynch has argued, 'Gothic fictions . . . produced a nation of knowing readers. . . . This knowingness bespoke the repeatability of this fiction's formulae.'[83] Just what did those knowing readers know? As the novels I have examined in this chapter suggest, one of the most salient characteristics of the Romantic-era novel is a hyper-consciousness of other novels. The ramifications of imitation, then, extend far beyond issues of plot: they invoke the authority of a large body of fellow texts, signalling either legitimacy or dismissive familiarity, but they also evoke large numbers of fellow *readers*, using reader demand to justify the novels' very existence and making reading itself a collective pleasure rather than a private activity.

Invoking implied readers obviously necessitates a certain speculative leap; no matter how persuasive the evidence may be, the structures of a novel itself can never tell us for certain how its actual readers received it. In *Rosella*'s case, however, the patterns so provocatively suggested by the novel's narrative are also substantiated by the material form of one of its surviving copies. In the British Library's copy of *Rosella*, at least one real reader has left notes and annotations throughout, many of which explicitly respond to the novel's intertextual references, identifying authors, novel titles, or plot details alluded to by the characters and helpfully inscribing them in the margins.[84]

Returning for a moment to the advertisement with which this chapter began, we can see that in many ways this reader is reading as the Minerva Press trained her to read – and, from a different perspective, Charlton is writing as the Minerva Press expected her to write. Whether or not reader or author ever read Lane's 'Tale', there is a clear likeness between the many passages in *Rosella* that simultaneously advertise other Minerva novels and invite readers to recognize them and the allusive, insider appeal of a paragraph like this one from Lane's short story:

> [Ellen's] companions were PAULINE, A VICTIM OF THE HEART, and MADELINE, of the HOUSE OF MONTGOMERY. Her attendants LUCY, with the twins ELLEN AND JULIA, having been reared in the CASTLE OF WOLFENBACH, were, from some ERRORS OF EDUCATION, not the WOMEN THEY SHOULD BE; and as such, were constantly stopt by the dragons, till the Countess returned from her pious visits.[85]

As this passage makes clear, allusion and recognition *can* be about genre – as with the many gothic stereotypes evoked above – but it is clearly not only about a strictly defined subgenre. Just as *Rosella* moves between explicitly gothic moments and sections that are far more sentimental, didactic, or satirical, so Lane's advertisement uses gothic language to highlight a whole range of the Minerva's fiction. This is, of course, expedient for his business purposes, but should remind us that 'imitation' has many different registers: the sameness of being published by a single press, for instance, or obtained from the same circulating library, or issued with a recognizably formulaic title, may have more significance to the reader than the stricter parameter of genre laid out by caricaturing reviewers.

Imitators Everywhere

The culture of imitation that pervaded gothic fiction production in the 1790s is perhaps most easily understood in relation to the popular, and often critically maligned, novels published by the Minerva Press and others. But the pervasiveness of imitation, and its importance to literary history in this period, extends well beyond these novels.[86] Indeed, no gothic author, however high their profile, was completely exempt from its terms; everyone, from a certain perspective, was an imitator. Matthew Lewis, for instance, was criticized for his play *Castle Spectre*'s failure to live up to the emotional standards of 'Mr. L's great exemplar, Mrs. Radcliffe';[87] his best-known work, *The Monk*, was likewise described by the *Monthly Review* in terms meant to emphasize the essentially imitative nature of the gothic:

> The outline of the monk Ambrosio's story was suggested by that of the *Santon Barsisa*, in the Guardian: the form of temptation is borrowed from the *Devil in Love* of Cazotte; and the catastrophe is taken from *the Sorceror*. The adventures of Raymond and Agnes are less obviously imitations; yet the forest-scene near Strasburgh brings to mind an incident in Smollet's Ferdinand Count Fathom: the bleeding Nun is described by the author as a popular tale of the Germans; and the convent-prison resembles the inflictions of Mrs. Radcliffe.[88]

These comparisons to Radcliffe and accusations of imitativeness are unlikely to surprise us much by this point; more unexpected, and perhaps most telling of all, are reviews of Radcliffe's own works that employ precisely the same critiques and comparisons.[89] Reviewing her novel *The Romance of the Forest*, the *English Review* declared that 'we cannot accuse the fair author of the slightest tendency to the crime of plagiarism',[90] but the review's selected quotation begins with Radcliffe's second chapter epigraph, a passage from Walpole's *Otranto*. Radcliffe's selection of this epigraph is clearly a way of borrowing authority via imitation; her first chapter's epigraph is taken from Shakespeare, so she is at once elevating the status of the Walpolean gothic novel through the comparison and, implicitly, defending her own work by the inclusion of its gothic predecessor.[91] The *English Review*'s choice of this particular passage to excerpt, and the reproduction of the epigraph in full, makes it clear that they understood this rhetorical move, and clearly locates Radcliffe as an author writing within a recognizable generic tradition. Other reviews illustrate this point, showing that Radcliffe's works, however admired, were perceived in terms of recognizable narrative formulae just as other gothic novels were. Describing the plot of *The Castles of Athlin and Dunbayne*, for instance, the *Monthly Review* noted that 'By means of trap-doors, false pannels, subterranean passages, &c. &c. [Radcliffe's] purpose is effected.'[92] Reviewing *A Sicilian Romance* in 1791, the *Critical Review* similarly remarked upon Radcliffe's (over)use of this familiar machinery, writing, 'We would advise her not to introduce so many caverns with such peculiar concealments, or so many spring-locks which open only on one side.'[93]

These remarks were made relatively early in Radcliffe's writing career, but she was, if anything, even more susceptible to the rhetoric of imitation by its end. By the publication of *The Italian*, as we have seen, countless new authors had been compared with Radcliffe, largely to their detriment. How fitting, then, that the *British Critic* found her newest novel too an unsatisfactory imitation – of her own former work: 'In comparing this work [*The Italian*] with the most popular productions of Mrs. R. we are not quite convinced that we should do it any essential service. Authors are not always advanced in fame by being compared with themselves.'[94] And the *Critical Review* went even further, claiming that one of the novel's scenes, 'the court of inquisition', 'is so improbable, that we should rather have attributed it to one of Mrs. Radcliffe's numerous imitators'.[95] Scholarship on Radcliffe reveals her to have been, in Dale Townshend and Angela Wright's words, 'a writer who ... defended her literary reputation with considerable gusto and energy' and was invested in differentiating her own work from that of her fellow authors, so comparisons of this kind were no doubt painfully ironic.[96] (Indeed, as Townshend and Wright note, some contemporary commentators attributed her disappearance from the publishing world after the publication of *The Italian* to her chagrin at the many 'imitations of her style and manner' and 'the flippant use of the term "Radcliffe school"'.)[97] However counter to her own intentions such comparisons may have been, however – and it should be reiterated that critiques of this type were balanced, and ultimately likely drowned out, by praise for her originality and genius – it is clear that the generic contours of Radcliffe's work were subject to continual re-evaluation and could be interpreted in varied ways. Returning to the *Critical Review*'s critique of *The Italian*: if Radcliffe's apparent failure to successfully imitate *herself* tells us something about the essential emptiness of the 'imitation' signifier, it also ought to bring home its incredible usefulness. Authors imitate, and reviewers accuse them of imitation, because such activities allow them to successfully navigate a crowded marketplace, to sift through unprecedented numbers of novels on a desk, or to situate their own novel among its potential peers. Perhaps more than anyone else, publishers and booksellers had an interest in perpetuating the discourse and practice of imitation because it offered a justification for producing more books as well as a means of making those new books legible to the reading public. If the culture of gothic imitation was, as I have contended here, a crucial part of the writing, reading, and reviewing experience of the 1790s, this was in no small part due to the promotional efforts of book industry professionals, who fostered the ideas of similarity, plenitude, and inter-referentiality upon which the discourse of imitation depends.

Edward Jacobs has shown that circulating libraries played a key role in the development of the gothic genre, arguing that 'the specific conventions of gothic romances and mysteries discursively co-operated with the phys-ical ways in which circulating libraries stimulated readers' sensitivity to the generic skeletons of individual books'.[98] Indeed, the physical structures of novels do often echo (or prefigure) their imitative contents. When Joseph Fox's *Tancred: A Tale of Ancient Times* was published in 1791, to take one example, the *English Review* described it as a gothic novel and – typically – phrased this explicitly in terms of imitation: 'This novel is written in imitation of the *Old English Baron* and the *Castle of Otranto*.'[99] Its imitative qualities are not limited to its narrative, however; the physical novel itself, too, plays on the notion of likeness and replication. The distinctive black-letter typeface used to identify nearly all books published under the Minerva imprint begins, on the title page, to remind readers of the distinctive commodity they now hold in their hands.[100] And the points of comparison grow more specific in the advertisements at the end of the second volume, which offer two pages of 'Lane's new and entertaining novels, tales, adventures, &c. published this season'.[101] The selection of Minerva titles offered here spans genres, reflecting the breadth of the catalogue, but begins with the two titles most similar to Fox's own work: *The Countess of Hennebon* is described as 'An Historical Novel' and the *Duke of Exeter* as 'An Historical Romance', cuing readers who enjoy fiction set in 'Ancient Times' to other works that might fit the bill (see Figure 4). The key qualities that identify a particular novel are thus signalled through advertisement as well as in the substance of the novel itself.

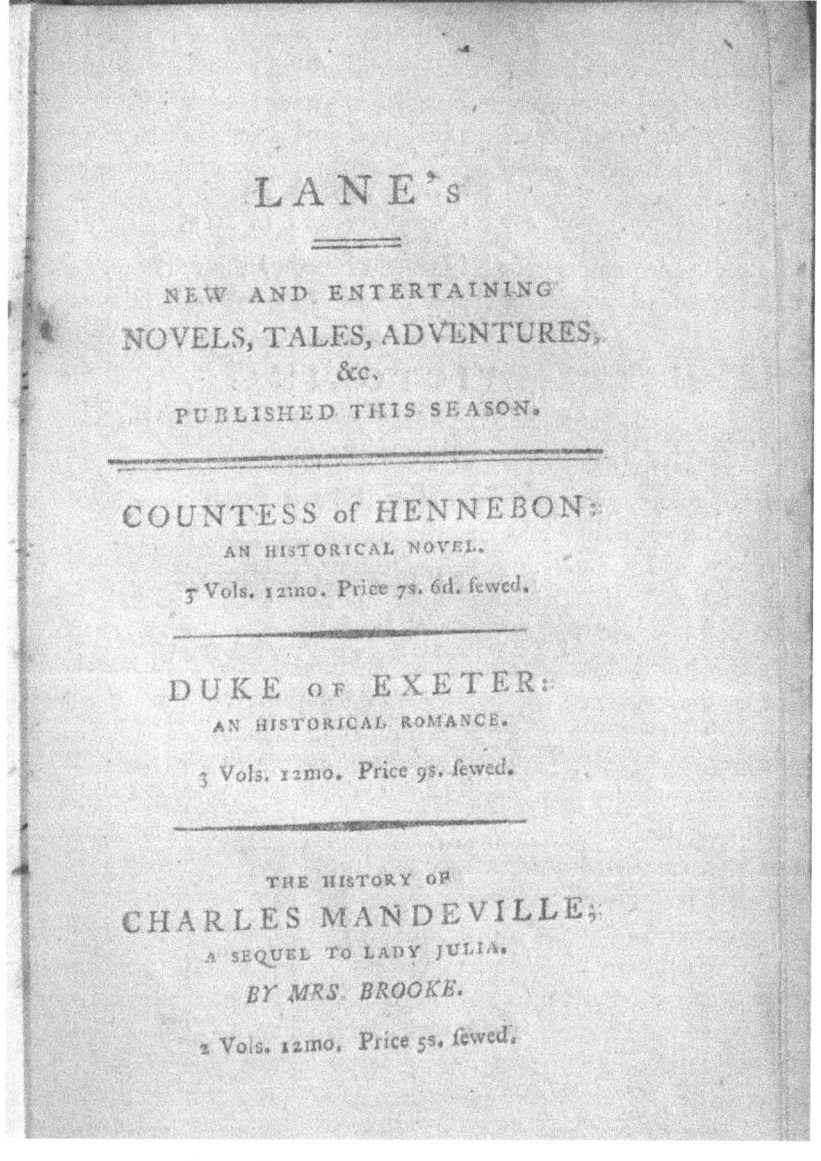

Figure 4   End-page advertisement, *Tancred*, vol. II, courtesy of the Beinecke Rare Book and Manuscript Library, Yale University.

Not all Minerva novels include these advertisements (and some have likely lost them in the binding or rebinding process), and not all advertisements list titles in an identifiable genre grouping, but as a body these works clearly remind us that similarity and, to some degree, predictability are as important to establishing a brand as a genre. Thus T. J. Horsley Curties's first novel, *Ethelwina* (1799) was published with an ad for Isabella Kelly's *Abbey of St. Asaph* (1795) in its third volume, meaning that a work once reviewed as having been written '[i]n humble imitation of the well-known novels of Mrs. Radcliffe'[102] was advertised in the back of another work, by Curties, the same author who would soon declare his 'enthusiastic admiration of Udolpho's unrivalled Foundress'.[103] It's hard to say whether the original accusation of imitation might have inspired the inclusion of this ad in the later work, or whether Curties's declaration of himself as an imitator was based on the success of earlier 'imitations' like Kelly's. But the circularity of these references clearly suggests the potential benefits of comparison – or, to use JoEllen DeLucia's formulation, the construction of a 'corporate Radcliffe' – for all parties.[104]

Minerva novels, unsurprisingly, tended to advertise other works published by Lane, so connections to Radcliffe in these works, however multi-layered, remain third-hand; her own publishers, however, had no such difficulty.[105] Although Fox published *Tancred* with Lane, another of his novels with a different publisher, *The Bastard of Normandy* (1793), appeared with a list of other 'Books Printed by Hookham and Carpenter'. The first three titles? The *Romance of the Forest*, *Sicilian Romance*, and *The Castle of Athelen* [*sic*] *and Dunbayne*, all by 'Mrs. Radcliffe', and all published by Hookham.[106] Another Hookham novel, the anonymous *Edelfrida* (1792), contains a longer list of advertised novels, but begins with the same three Radcliffe titles, suggesting the benefits to a publisher of reminding readers of best-selling and familiar works when publishing new works in a similar vein.[107]

For a publisher, in other words, signalling that a new novelist was an 'imitator of Radcliffe' through this kind of advertising could draw readers to the new work.[108] Further afield, J. Connor, of a Dublin circulating library, was less constrained by original publisher affiliation when printing novels previously published elsewhere: *The Cavern of Death: A Moral Tale* was followed in its third edition (1795) by an advertisement featuring, among other titles, three Radcliffe novels (by two different publishers, presumably all carried by Connor's library) and *Ellen, Countess Howel* (1794), a Minerva Press novel by Anna Maria Bennett (the author of *The Beggar Girl*, discussed above).[109] George Justice has argued that 'paraliterary discourses, reviews and book advertisements both depend upon and enable the emergence of the literary culture that they represent as commodities', a claim that these examples clearly illustrate: the patterns of intertextuality and imitation that are visible within the novels are also embedded in their presentation and reflected in the language of their reception.[110]

Such systems of reference are both straightforwardly promotional and thematically recursive: 'original' novels are re-marketed through sales of 'imitations' of them; authors who declare themselves imitators of one author are vehicles for the promotion of another's work; textual and paratextual references overlap. Each novel produced is one of many, conceived and received as a text accompanied by a huge number of similar texts. Gothic novels, long, formulaic, numerous, and melodramatic, epitomize the cluster of ideas contemporaries summed up with charges of excess; this is, perhaps, why gothic imitation, with its blurring of commercial and literary motivations, and its simultaneous ability to simplify (through categorization) and complicate (through variation), became such a predominant literary mode in the 1790s.

Returning a final time to Lane's gothic advertisement, we see a similar overlapping of text and paratext: the story highlights the novels, which are listed again, with prices, at the story's end. The British Library's copy goes still further, incorporating 'An Address to the Public, on Circulating Libraries, &c.' and signed by Lane, in the final pages of the pamphlet. The self-conscious metaphor of the tale itself becomes explicit when, in a Chaucerian conclusion, all the novel-characters prepare 'to recount a Tale' of the 'variety of adventures' they have undergone: Minerva then 'descend [s] from her throne, with information, that she would take them all under her patronage, and [that they] should, in the course of the year, be presented to the shrine of public approbation'.[111] As characters in the short story transmute back into the novels they originally were, the tale closes by reminding interested readers where these fuller stories can be acquired: they are directed to make 'application to [Minerva's] Temple – where, for their Entertainment, all these MYSTERIES will be ELUCIDATED' (see Figure 5).[112] The story, and the listed titles themselves, are positioned as tempting hints, invitations to further engagement.

While Lane clearly intended this pamphlet to be an entry point into the riches of the Minerva Library, his audience seems (unsurprisingly) to have had a more cynical view of its function. The *Lady & Gentleman's Pocket Magazine of Literary and Polite Amusement* reprinted the story, with a slightly altered title and Lane listed explicitly as the author, in November 1796; the short editor's note that preceded the story, however, made it

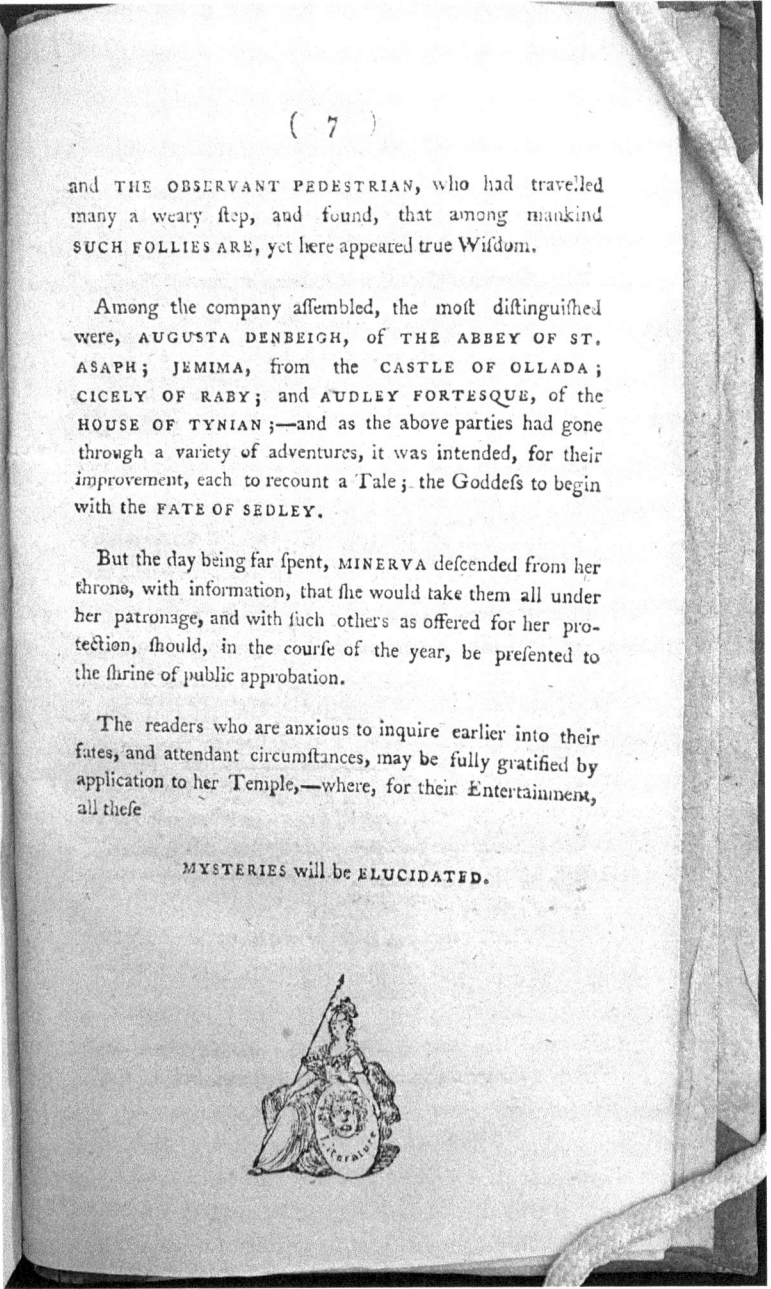

(7)

and THE OBSERVANT PEDESTRIAN, who had travelled many a weary ftep, and found, that among mankind SUCH FOLLIES ARE, yet here appeared true Wifdom.

Among the company affembled, the moft diftinguifhed were, AUGUSTA DENBEIGH, of THE ABBEY OF ST. ASAPH; JEMIMA, from the CASTLE OF OLLADA; CICELY OF RABY; and AUDLEY FORTESQUE, of the HOUSE OF TYNIAN;—and as the above parties had gone through a variety of adventures, it was intended, for their improvement, each to recount a Tale; the Goddefs to begin with the FATE OF SEDLEY.

But the day being far fpent, MINERVA defcended from her throne, with information, that fhe would take them all under her patronage, and with fuch others as offered for her pro-tection, fhould, in the courfe of the year, be prefented to the fhrine of public approbation.

The readers who are anxious to inquire earlier into their fates, and attendant circumftances, may be fully gratified by application to her Temple,—where, for their Entertainment, all thefe

MYSTERIES will be ELUCIDATED.

Figure 5   Last page of [William Lane], 'A Tale Addressed to the Novel Readers of the Present Day' (image cropped), courtesy of the New York Society Library.

clear that their own aims in reprinting it did not necessarily align with Lane's.[113] The brief introduction begins on a satirical note: 'The Editors presume their readers will fully appreciate the merits of the following important TALE', the first line reads. The next sentences take a fascinating turn: rather than suggesting that readers who enjoy this tale might (as Lane obviously intended) want to seek out the many titles it introduces, the editors reverse the equation. Just as critics used the idea of gothic 'imitation' as a shorthand means of summing up and dismissing lengthy gothic works, so these editors suggest that Lane's story serves a similar summarizing function. 'They anticipate,' the piece continues,

> that [the perusal of this tale] will supercede the necessity of wading through voluminous works, the expence, and sum total of which is here reduced to a narrow compass; by which means the mind, not being long kept in a state of insulting suspense, must reflect with a considerable degree of satisfaction, upon having escaped the fatigue and anxiety to which it would otherwise have been liable.[114]

The ironies in this claim are layered, from the sarcastic 'important' and the mocking small caps of 'TALE' in the first sentence, which mirror those used to indicate novel titles in the story itself. Even more fascinating, however, is the way the editors' framing of Lane's tale mirrors the complex of ideas explored in this chapter on imitation: using genre tropes to evoke recognition; blurring the boundaries between story and advertisement, brand and genre; and questioning the role of originality in building suspense. Lane positions his novels as a series of 'mysteries' that can be solved only by reading; the editors, on the other hand, point to the time and trouble of reading lengthy novels, suggesting that – since there are clearly too many of them – readers will be grateful to read a simple summary instead.

To claim that a list of novels is equivalent, or even superior, to the actual novels themselves, however tongue-in-cheek such a suggestion may be, is of course an insult to the novels in question. It implies, further, that the style of the writing is irrelevant; only the content (formulaic and easily condensed) matters, and this can be summed up by any clichéd gothic story. But in a sense this logic is the same as that employed by Lane and his authors, albeit to different purpose: while critics suggested that many gothic novels all told a single story, allusive novels like *Rosella*, like Lane's pamphlet, suggest that each single story actually might 'contain' – or reference – many gothic novels and that, moreover, this is where a large part of such a work's value inheres. Just as circulating-library proprietors tended to inflate the number of volumes they held in order to attract readers, Lane's Tale is an ostentatious reminder of the size of the Minerva catalogue.[115] It is also, explicitly, a defence of large libraries, an invitation to authors who might want to publish their books with Minerva, and a suggestion that the publisher's novels are more significant as a body than individually. The negating charge of imitation, which uses resemblance and collectivity to dismiss, in other words, is here reversed. Lane takes little trouble to distinguish one of his titles from another because he doesn't need to: the sociality of the novels, which (in their incarnation as characters) cluster together and interact is portrayed as much of their appeal. Whether Lane sought to cultivate this ideal among his authors or follow their lead in this advertisement, the importance of drawing connections between numerous novels and their readers is reflected in both the extreme recognizability of gothic style and the material forms of the publications in which these tales appeared.

CHAPTER 4

Hannah More's Cœlebs *and the Novel*
of the Moment

Novels, however, though generally read, and though it is now the
practice to make them the vehicles of new opinions, do not make so
permanent an impression on the mind as their authors may imagine.
—Review of Mary Wollstonecraft's *Posthumous Works* (1798)[1]

'Cœlebs', for a little period, superseded all other productions of the
press. —John Laurens Bicknell, *Original Miscellanies* (1820)[2]

Near the end of 1808, the Evangelical author and educator Hannah More
tried a new tactic in her ongoing project of showing the English public the
error of its ways: she wrote a novel. Entitled *Cœlebs in Search of a Wife*, this
work narrated the lengthy search of the eponymous hero for an appropriately devout and suitable wife. Aesthetically speaking, the novel has its
flaws – contemporary reviewers tended to praise its morality but question
its execution – but it clearly spoke to its cultural moment: within a year it
was in its twelfth edition and was widely reviewed and discussed.[3]
Unsurprisingly, given More's background – she had previously been
best-known for her educational and religious works, including the hugely
popular pamphlets known as the *Cheap Repository Tracts* (1795–1817) –
she was somewhat ambivalent about *Cœlebs'* status as a novel, and the work
reflects this uncertainty. The *Monthly Review* summed up More's intentions in writing it thus: 'By the usual furniture of circulating libraries,
deceptive views of life, a false taste, and pernicious principles, have been
disseminated; and it is the commendable object of the writer of the
volumes before us to counteract the poison of novels by something which
assumes the form of a novel.'[4] The ends justified the form, in other words;
as More herself later wrote, with the publication of *Cœlebs* and its entry
into the contemporary literary marketplace, she had intended to 'to raise
the tone of that mart of mischief, and to counteract its corruptions'.[5]

But her willingness to participate in contemporary trends by writing
fiction had another ironic consequence: *Cœlebs* immediately gave rise to a

whole host of response novels, which explicitly imitated, continued, parodied, or mocked the original work.[6] Before the end of 1809, works including *Nubilia in Search of a Husband* (1809), *Celia in Search of a Husband* (1809), *Cœlebs Suited* (1809), and *Coelibia Choosing a Husband* (1809) vied for their share of the market; by 1810, at least seven novels had been published, including *Cœlebs in Search of a Mistress* (1810), *Lindamira; or, An Old Maid in Search of a Husband* (1810) and *Celia Suited* (1810); and novels such as *Sequel to Cœlebs* (1812), *Cœlebs Married* (1814), and *Cœlebs Deceived* (1817) continued to appear throughout the following decade. Of necessity, these works were written and published in haste: in order to capitalize on a literary trend, one must publish while the trend is still in progress. Perhaps the most interesting thing about these novels, however, is the emphasis that they place on their contemporaneous nature. These authors frame their writing as a filling a particular cultural need, created by *Cœlebs* and fulfillable only by their own speedy action.

Such a spate of responses to a best-selling work is by no means unprecedented; indeed, this mode of profitable enthusiasm accompanied the novel from the start. Defoe's *Robinson Crusoe* (1719), to take perhaps the most famous example, inspired sequels and imitations so widespread as to have their own collective name – the Robinsonade – and these responses were still being produced nearly a century later.[7] In the 1740s, Samuel Richardson's *Pamela* (1740) similarly inaugurated what William Warner has called 'the *Pamela* media event', with satirical responses like *Shamela* (1741) and *Anti-Pamela* (1741) appearing within a year of the original.[8] And, as Chapter 3 documents, numerous gothic authors in the 1790s seriously or ironically cited Ann Radcliffe's work, particularly *The Mysteries of Udolpho*, as the inspiration for the genre in which they wrote. These are only a few of the most prominent examples, but they clearly indicate that the numerous novelists who hastened to respond to *Cœlebs* were not outliers, but adherents of a long novelistic tradition. Yet the *Cœlebs* example has several distinctive features, which not only set it apart from these predecessors, but firmly locate it in its own literary moment. Robinsonade authors generally were responding to the primary plot of the story: their fiction concerns an individual surviving in a remote location. *Pamela* respondents, in contrast, tended to directly attack Richardson and his pretensions, through their responses to his text. The high profile of some of his interlocutors made these responses as much a sparring match between authors as a specific response to the novel in question. And Radcliffe's 'imitators' most often followed the broad contours of genre – terrorized heroines in gothic settings – rather than directly attacking her or engaging with her specific characters.

Cœlebs respondents differ from all of these. While they do tend to emulate the general theme of the original novel (young person seeking suitable spouse), they very frequently include direct references to characters, or rewritings of key messages, making for more direct engagement with More's work. These authors are uniformly less famous than More, and many of the responses were published anonymously or pseudonymously, assuring that they would be received in textual, rather than authorial, terms. They are specific enough to form a group rather than a genre; most importantly, as I will suggest here, they are *about* what they *represent*: collectively, the *Cœlebs* novels interrogate a system of literary value that prioritizes lasting fame over of-the-moment pertinence, and they explore the relationship between the novel's claim to novelty and its contested moral status. While literary scholars are familiar with discourses of value that dismiss ephemeral works and valorise lasting fame, this chapter highlights a counter-narrative that characterizes much Romantic fiction. For many novels of this era the short term – sometimes the very short term – was of paramount importance.

In the works I explore here, the potentially fleeting nature of literary relevance and success is framed as a cause of anxiety but also, more surprisingly, as empowering: being truly of-the-moment, these authors suggest, grants their novels a form of authority that they might otherwise lack, as pointed and ever-evolving commentators on current events. This is not to say that the authors I discuss here were not motivated by commercial concerns: speedy publication is a practical strategy as much as anything else. However, these writers repeatedly suggest that authority and monetary motivations are not opposed: if their work is commercially successful, they suggest, it is *because* it offers something – timeliness – that is of particular cultural value. Whereas much of the age's literary criticism emphasized the importance of taste, judgement, and disinterested critique in assessing new fiction, increasingly suggesting that few novels merited praise (and few readers were capable of accurately identifying excellence), this emphasis on timeliness granted a much broader swathe of the literary public a different standard by which to assess literature, more closely tied to personal experience and knowledge of current fashion than to external standards of excellence. This reframing also positioned the novel itself as a uniquely timely form, in tandem with, or even superseding, the quintessentially timely periodical. Not coincidentally, such an insistence on the value of novelty in fiction also served a practical function: it effectively and continually cleared the literary decks, managing the increasingly unmanageable number of new publications by sweeping older works into obscurity, month after month. While arguments for the social value and importance of timely writing should be taken with some scepticism – authors obviously had a strong motivation for adopting this rhetorical stance – the pervasiveness of justifications for writing to the moment invites serious critical engagement.

The authors of the *Cœlebs* novels use their prefaces, in particular, to embrace the idea of literary production as time-sensitive and transient: rather than fearing or fighting the phenomenon, they capitalize on the fast-paced literary culture of the time to emphasize their own works' timeliness and contemporary relevance. Reviewers of these novels too reference a culture of speed and ephemerality in their understanding of *Cœlebs* and its successor novels. These para- and extra-textual discourses can help the reader to understand the contradictory messages explored in the novels themselves; collectively and individually, these works explore what it means to be timely, timeless, or too late, as each text considers its own temporal positioning and moral authority. Considering, in particular, the central tension between *Cœlebs* as a champion of 'ageless' values and its role as an initiator of extremely time-sensitive and fleeting literature (and, indeed, as a highly timely participant in the fashion for popular didactic fiction) reveals the connections between the fictional abundance of the Romantic period, ephemerality, and the moral possibilities of the novel.

Prefacing 'the New *Cœlebs*'

Even a reader wholly oblivious to the success of *Cœlebs* would be hard-pressed to miss the connection between that work and its sequels. The self-conscious prefaces with which many of these novels begin call attention to their relationship to *Cœlebs*, deliberately heightening the reader's awareness of just how quickly each work was written. *Cœlebs* itself set a precedent for these claims to speed; its preface (signed 'Cœlebs', rather than More) begins: 'When I quitted home ... in the spring of this present year 1808, a thought struck me, which I began to put into immediate execution.'[9] This plan, 'to commit to paper' all his circumstances and conversations on 'important' subjects, was carried out at once, the character-as-author reports, and 'in the autumn of *this same year*, it was my amusement ... to look over and arrange these papers' (37, emphasis added). Cœlebs' self-declared speediness seems to have dual narrative purposes; it makes it clear that the world he is about to describe is very much the contemporary world, but also supports his later derogatory claims (and More's own ambivalence) about the novel as a genre – writing quickly, here, suggests that his own account is a reliable factual record rather than a carefully crafted fiction.

The idea that there might be something particularly true or relevant about writing produced in the moment is reminiscent of the claims of the sentimental epistolary novel, in which letter-writers bare their souls in tear-filled letters; here, it takes on an additional moral valence. Cœlebs writes to the world to record his important thoughts in a truthful and accurate manner, for the immediate edification of others; moreover, More's intent to 'counteract the corruptions' of the world with her fiction depends on the appearance of her work at a moment and in a milieu where those specific corruptions will be recognizable enough to combat. More herself, as this comparison suggests, was as committed to speed as her narratorial avatar; she prepared the text for the second edition of Cœlebs all of two weeks after the publication of the first.[10] The preface thus prepares us for the paradoxical claims about literary value that the Cœlebs novels later explore: while Coelebs positions itself as not-quite-a-novel, and explicitly decries the fleeting, ephemeral nature of most fiction, contrasting trivial 'fashions' with eternal 'truths', More was in fact participating in a literary fashion in a quite deliberate manner.

While, as scholars including Ian Haywood and M. O. Grenby have shown, More's relationship to conservatism in the 1790s and early 1800s was complex, due to her championing of working-class literacy initiatives, her eventual embrace of the novel as an effective means of rebutting immoral or radical ideas was characteristic of the fad for anti-Jacobin fiction around 1800.[11] As Grenby puts it, 'even Hannah More, the form's greatest foe, came round'[12] and willingly capitalized on the appetite for fiction espousing conservative mores. Moreover, the timing of Coelebs, published on the heels of a decade of fervent Evangelical religious activity and debate following the Methodist schism with the Church of England in 1795,[13] and More's own brush with accusations of Methodism around 1800, was itself a part of a long history of Evangelicalism's strategic use of media. Brett McInelly argues, for instance, that 'Methodists relied on the press not merely to serve the devotional needs of its members, but to publicize the revival to a wider audience.'[14] Andrew Winckles, more broadly, has argued that 'evangelicalism was fundamentally a *media* revolution', with transformative effects on broader literary and cultural discourses, and in the case of the Cœlebs novels we can clearly see how closely religion and print culture are entwined.[15] While More clearly sought to distance herself from both the moral danger of the novel form in general and the enthusiasm of Methodist writings more specifically, her novel's enormous success was clearly tied to its timing vis-à-vis both of these literary trends. While this chapter focuses on the responses to her novel primarily in terms of their reception and temporal self-positioning, both *Cœlebs* and all the subsequent publications engaging with it were equally a part of other ongoing debates about religious devotion, education, and orthodoxy.

The earliest-published response titles, *Nubilia in Search of a Husband* (1809) and *Celia in Search of a Husband* (1809), follow *Cœlebs'* lead in emphasizing their very speedy composition, though with rather different purpose. 'A Modern Antique', the pseudonymous author of *Celia in Search of a Husband*, begins her preface on a defensive note: 'The title-page prefixed to this book bears a strong appearance of *presumption*; and the reader of these pages may, in the *conclusion*, pronounce the author both *vain* and futile. The *only* apology she has to offer may probably lead her yet deeper into error; yet she cannot resist saying something of herself, or rather of her motives.'[16] The presumption inheres, of course, in the titular reference to the best-selling *Cœlebs*, though the author leaves it to the reader to determine whether it is that work's popularity or its morality that is most presumptuous to emulate. In either case, she hastens to defend herself, by declaring 'Cœlebs had appeared – it *would* be *answered*; but it must be answered *directly*' (I:i). We may wonder at this supposed necessity, and indeed the Modern Antique anticipates just such skepticism: 'The reader very naturally asks, *why* answer it at all?' (I:ii). She offers two answers: first, her novel will be informed by a bit more 'worldly knowledge' than her predecessor's; second, time was of the essence: 'the *garreteers* had taken scent – goose-quills and crow-quills were immersed; but the pen that writes quickest will suit the town best; for expectation is excited, and though it should be disappointed, we all know that "Anticipation loads the wings of time"'.[17] The book must be written now, in other words, because readers are eagerly waiting for it – and other writers are working on responses that might reach them first. Moreover, this novel will, theoretically, provide readers with a particular kind of knowledge that they currently lack.

While such a justification is clearly rhetorical (and not a little tautological – readers learn to await books that are written only because they are waiting), it is also true in a more literal sense, as the nearly simultaneous appearance of so many other response novels suggests. Such language echoes the haste-laden discourse surrounding other forms of consumer production during this same period, during which '[b]oth commercial activity and the consumer response to it were feverish'.[18] But the language laid out by the Modern Antique also suggests a specific way that her novel and others use temporal language to respond to their literary moment. Writing quickly – striking while the iron is hot, beating competitors, capitalizing on reader interest – is a crucial skill in a such a market; moreover, though, endorsing such a credo of speed is a way of making room for new work, as older works are constantly shifted to the metaphorical scrapheap as outdated. The prefaces to the *Cœlebs* novels are explicit about this balancing act to varying degrees, but all must navigate the central problem of commemorating an inspirational original text (one that has, in one way or another, created the occasion for the production of one's own) while also conveying the impression that this original is, of necessity, already relegated to the past.

William Mudford, the author of *Nubilia*, declares even more bluntly that '[i]t is not to deprecate criticism that it is told, the following work was commenced on the 10th of May, 1809, and finished on the 3d of June following.'[19] Mudford offers no alternate reason for sharing this timetable with the reader, but in the context of the other prefaces, it seems clear that this piece of information – an indicator of the author's speed and the book's timeliness – is meant to be both a pre-emptive apologia (despite Mudford's claim to the contrary) and a selling point in itself. An author's agility in rising to meet readers' interests with adequate haste is, it seems, an essential literary skill. *Cœlebs Suited*, another 1809 entry into the race, takes this angle as well, but demonstrates its own timeliness in a slightly different way. It purports to be the story of 'Sir George Rover', who sails to England to join his friend 'Caleb Cœlebs'. He begins his narrative in 1808, and notes that Caleb is 'a distant relation of a gentleman of the same name, who has *lately* made a great noise'.[20] Recasting Cœlebs the character as Cœlebs the recent celebrity entertainingly inverts the logic of More's novel, which, as some scholars have argued, could be read as a roman à clef, satirizing the behaviour of well-known figures such as the Duchess of Devonshire.[21] It also imagines the novel as a form specifically designed to respond to, or intervene in, current events – the Cœlebs 'who has lately made a great noise' is less an enduring artistic creation than a creature of his moment.

Moreover, by calling his own hero 'Caleb Cœlebs', the author seems to be tapping into a satirical vein of contemporary commentary on the title of More's work. Jane Austen, for instance, wrote to her sister Cassandra (after erroneously referring to the novel as *Caleb* in a previous letter) that 'the only merit [More's novel] could have, was in the name of Caleb, which has an honest, unpretending sound; but in Cœlebs, there is pedantry & affectation'.[22] Whether recording facts before they are forgotten, responding to reader demand, or entering into current debates, novelists must act fast, these works proclaim; in so doing, authors simultaneously justify their own existence and hint that, by their own appearance, their predecessors' works have been revealed as incomplete or out of date.

Celia Suited, with a preface dated 'Nov. the 9th, 1809' to emphasize its timeliness, achieves the latter goal in several stages.[23] Like the 'Modern Antique', the author directly acknowledges, with apparent humility, that her work is written 'in the manner of that celebrated work, called "Cœlebs in Search of a Wife"'.[24] But a note of irony soon emerges, as the author notes that she 'professes to have read [*Cœlebs*] with sentiments of admiration it would be difficult to do justice to'. This might be taken for sincerity, but becomes clearly satirical: the author has written her own novel because 'the generality of novel readers ... will never benefit by that inestimable work [*Cœlebs*], for this plain reason, because they will not *read it*'.[25] *Cœlebs* is dull, in other words, and all the references to its morality, virtue, and excellence that fill the rest of the preface do little to dispel this central critique. The author '*professes* to have read' *Cœlebs* – but, the reader now realizes, this isn't precisely the same as saying she *has* read it.

This not-so-subtle disparagement clearly reveals the connection between timeliness and morality: the 'celebrated work' has created the occasion for this new work, and it has *also* revealed its necessity: a reader who acknowledges the moral force of More's message, accepting her belief that the novel can indeed serve as moral guidance, must surely also acknowledge the benefit of such a work *being read by more readers*. As we have already seen, some of More's respondents took this moral duty rather more seriously than others (or claimed to do so) but they consistently employ the rhetoric of moral obligation to consider the place of the novel in contemporary society. Indeed, the author of *Celia Suited* directly claims that a novel's effect on its readers should be weighed more heavily than other considerations (such as originality), writing that 'there is, perhaps, more useful merit in treading the steps of those who have enlightened the world by their productions, than in the vain attempt of becoming original at the expense of morality and virtue'.[26] The decoupling of originality and newness here is especially interesting: whereas 'novelty' is often taken to indicate that something is 'new' in terms of time as well as content, the *Cœlebs* novels clearly show that these two kinds of newness need not overlap.

Even by 1814, not a great deal later in terms of the time it (usually) takes to write a novel, the author of *Cœlebs Married* continued to insist that it was thoughts of waiting readers – the Modern Antique's 'expectation . . . excited' – that motivated this new publication: 'It was the abrupt manner in which Cœlebs terminates, that suggested the scheme of this work, it appearing a desire common to every reader to know when and where he was married. To gratify the general curiosity, which appeared raised, but not satisfied . . . was one motive for this undertaking.'[27] And just as the Modern Antique insisted that this 'expectation' outweighed other criteria for literary judgement, so the anonymous author of *Cœlebs Married* suggests that unsatisfied curiosity is the best metric for gauging a work's importance. This preface, like the preface to More's own work, is written in the first person by the character of Cœlebs himself, and the author uses his changed state (now, as the title suggests, Cœlebs is married) to account for the fact '[t]hat the language and arrangements of this volume are inferior to the original work, in a very visible degree'.[28] Such a claim skates between mock-humility and moral challenge: Is it possible that Cœlebs' marriage, that much-desired state, has not improved him in all ways? And, perhaps even more to the point, is it possible that meeting 'general curiosity' is a more powerful defense of a novel than its aesthetic qualities? This author certainly suggests as much.

Cœlebs Deceived (1817), perhaps because it is the most belated of the group, has some of the most explicit references to its expected readers and their demands.[29] In an advertisement preceding the preface, the author suggests not just that readers of *Cœlebs* are eagerly awaiting this new work, but that this novel itself, already published in serial form, has a ready-made and eager audience. 'The favourable notice which this little work has already received, first from the Editors of the Christian Miscellany, and next from the numerous readers of their valuable publication, has induced the Author to venture on a wider circulation', it reads in part.[30] But the author's primary purpose is clearly a satirical portrait of contemporary readers and their motivations; the author supports 'wider circulation', and the persons who will comprise the readership are conveniently described in the preface in a series of humorous vignettes. For some, a reflection of their personal life is the draw: '"Cœlebs Deceived," exclaims a Bachelor, just verging on his seventieth year. "I like that title, a satire on the female world no doubt. Yes, yes, deceived in women; I will purchase, for I have been deceived too."'[31] Others hope for curative properties: 'by all means purchase the new book for Mr. —,' recommends 'a grave physician', 'it may prolong his existence'.[32] And a 'young Attorney' wonders whether 'this new book' may 'treat of any new methods of deception'.[33] Readers see what they want to see in any text, these examples suggest, and its reception will have more to do with their expectations than any intrinsic qualities. But their responses are also shaped by something else: whether or not a new novel will meet the expectations raised by its predecessor. Previous impressions might help *or* harm, as one of the vignettes makes clear:

> 'Nor, pray Papa, don't order that new book', cries Miss —, just returned from school, 'for indeed, I thought the last Cœlebs so dull and grave, that he gave me the vapours, and I only finished reading him because you desired me.' 'You grieve me, my dear child, by your remark; but, indeed, I must order the book for the sake of the name, for liking the elder Cœlebs so well, I wish to invite the younger from respect.'[34]

While the father counts on likeness, the daughter fears it, in an illustration of the response novel's central paradox. Do readers hope for more of the same or something quite different? The time-sensitive novel always offers an answer to this question, but most often the answer is: both. The Captain who asks his 'inamorata' what she is reading receives a cynical answer: 'I was so curious to know whether it was the same moral monster re-entering, that I lost no time in sending for the book', she declares.[35] And when 'the village Curate' asks his wife to 'send for the new Cœlebs', it is because she 'transcribed so much matter from the last Cœlebs, as served [him] for three months' as fodder for his sermons.[36] This reader wants more of the same – but the phrase 'the new Cœlebs' also reminds us of the fundamental displacement this kind of continuation entails. The 'old' Cœlebs has been mined and exhausted, and its exhaustion, as these last two examples hint, offers the hope of either a rejuvenation of old ideas or a new path entirely.

Thus the proliferation of Cœlebiana around 1810 must be understood in part as a means of establishing a specific path to literary legitimacy: by citing inspiration, by insisting on readerly demand for more of the same, and then *by dismissing* that inspiration as already passé. Whether suggesting that no one actually read *Cœlebs*, inventing readers who call the novel 'dull and grave' and its hero a 'moral monster', or simply remarking pointedly that '[t]he business of life is not transacted in pompous language, nor the speeches of *all* lovers made in verse', these novelists each model the process of displacement that their own works are designed to enact.[37] If *Cœlebs* is known, then their works will also be known, but each subsequent act of publishing automatically confers the stamp of novelty, making the newest work more relevant, more fashionable, and more desirable. This ongoing process of challenge was not merely literary, of course – while some of Cœlebs' respondents took a decidedly satirical approach, declining to espouse serious religious views in their novels at all, others used their works as a place to hash out the ongoing theological and social debates surrounding Evangelicalism (and More specifically) at this time. Reviews reveal, however, that such concerns were in many ways inseparable from more general claims about literary merit – as with the political novel of the 1790s, literary and moral admiration were often deployed interchangeably. M. O. Grenby's observation, of the former genre, that '[c]learly, it was the political content of these novels that won them such acclaim, and yet ... their political correctness was endorsed in terms of congratulation for their apparently discernible *literary* merit' seems equally applicable here.[38] Very different from discussions of the cluster of political novels examined in Chapter 2, however, is the strong emphasis here on timeliness, alongside concerns about morality and literary quality.

The drive to displace an original is risky, of course: if an author fails to convince readers that his new text indeed replaces its more-renowned predecessor, the comparison can only be odious. William Mudford, the author of *Nubilia in Search of a Husband*, seems to have found this to be the case; somewhat comically, in the preface to the second edition, he decries any connection to *Cœlebs*, despite their manifest resemblances, writing, 'It seems to have been impossible to avoid a comparison between *Cœlebs* and *Nubilia*. They are in no respect similar. They were never meant to be so. The merits of *Cœlebs* (and very eminent merits it certainly has) cannot detract, by comparison, from those of *Nubilia*).' This new preface is dated 15 August 1809, meaning it was written only three months after the completion of the *first* edition, an undeniably speedy update. This time, however, Mudford makes no reference to his quickness or timeliness – such an approach is only useful, one might infer, when supplanting an older work is the goal. Should that effort fail, however, insisting on a fundamental difference between the works may be the more effective tactic.

Periodical Discourse and Literary Fashion

Among the many satirical characters depicted in the Preface to *Cœlebs Deceived* is a 'learned Reviewer', who awaits the new *Cœlebs* novel with something less than unmixed enthusiasm. Upon 'read[ing] the title-page', he irritably declares, '"Was ever any thing so provoking ... we exhausted all our critical venom on the last Cœlebs, where shall we find more to pour upon this?"[39] "Take comfort," replies a brother Critic ... "a book unread does not preclude hope; perhaps there is less religion about the new Cœlebs.'"[40] This exchange echoes the many scenes of pre-emptive prefatorial criticism discussed in Chapter 1, in which authors defang prospective critics by anticipating their objections. It also, however, accurately portrays the ways that many actual critics engaged with the moral and temporal dimensions of the *Cœlebs* phenomenon. If the novelists responding to *Cœlebs* insisted that timeliness was a crucial part of understanding their works, professional critics seemed quite ready to take them at their word.

Periodical reviews, whether of *Cœlebs* itself or its successors, were of course frequently informed by the religious perspective of each publication or individual reviewer: theological disagreement could fuel critique, while agreement upon religious principles might result in praise – there is no way to wholly separate aesthetic judgements from moral ones. Further, though, periodical reception of these novels directly contributed to the cycle of novelty and displacement referenced in so many of them. The feedback loop between novel and periodical springs into focus when we consider how the speedy responses to speedily written novels both reinforced the authors' claims for contemporary relevance and prepared the ground for still more responses. While many reviewers viewed the novelists' claimed accomplishments with scepticism, in other words, the rhetoric of haste and missed opportunities put forth in the prefaces is both echoed by and drawn from the language of the reviewers. Both the *Critical Review* and the *Monthly Review*, for example, took note of William Mudford's claim to have written *Nubilia* in a matter of weeks, specifically repeating Mudford's claim for quick composition and acknowledging, if not endorsing, the necessity of timeliness for this kind of literary production. The *Critical Review* noted, 'The novel of Cœlebs has experienced such a rapid and extensive sale that numerous authors seem to have been seized with a desire if not to rival the fame, at least to partake of the emoluments.'[41] The *Monthly Review* concurred, remarking , 'If one writer sends a gentleman in pursuit of a wife, another is sure to take the hint, and to exhibit a lady in search of a husband. Modern book-makers avail themselves of every opportunity of putting their pens in motion, and the success which *Cœlebs* has obtained presented a temptation not to be resisted.'[42] Both reviewers place the primary responsibility for the trend with authors, rather than readers, implicitly criticizing those authors with their mentions of financial incentives, but both also paint a picture of an eminently competitive marketplace, in which novels follow novels in rapid succession and the tardy author will be forgotten.

The *Critical Review* refers to a 'parturition of less than one month' when describing *Nubilia*, and the *Monthly Review* exactly repeats the timetable given by Mudford: 'we find that on the 10th of May 1809 the author of the present work began his undertaking; and so intent was he on bringing it out in time while *Cœlebs* was in course of reading, that by the 3d of June following he had completed it'.[43] There certainly seems to be an element of mockery in highlighting the speed of the composition, as when the aptly named publication *The Satirist* called it 'really a proof of somewhat more than common insolence, for [Mudford] to stand up and assure the world, that he scribbled as fast as he could lay fist to paper, 456 pages in twenty-four days; i.e. *nineteen pages per day*'.[44] But the precision of the repeated dates, like the claim that this timing was essential for the new novel to appear 'while *Cœlebs* was in course of reading', also emphasizes the importance of a specifically delimited temporality for the success of a new work.

Other periodicals go further to explore the relationship between new publications and the time in which they appear. The *Universal Magazine* historicizes the phenomenon, looking back to the seventeenth century for comparison and reminding readers that time-sensitive literary fads have a long history: 'When Don Quixote appeared in Spain, the field of literature immediately after swarmed with Dons of all descriptions, who, like the knight of La Mancha, sallied forth in quest of adventures.'[45] But the conclusions the writer draws from this analogy suggest that the timetable of such fashions is ever-accelerating, so that in the present situation, *Nubilia* 'trod so close on the heels of its prototype, that they may almost be called beings of the same day'. This diurnal metaphor, which the author plays out at some length, suggests, even more explicitly than the prefaces did, that the goal of all this haste is not mere imitation, but displacement: 'it appears, that when a star of a particular magnitude appears in the zenith of literature, it is quickly followed by others, which attempt to vie with it in splendour, and, if possible, to eclipse it'.[46] And while the reviewer is not willing to concede that *Nubilia* has totally succeeded in effecting such an eclipse (he insists that 'both ... have their respective merits'), the astronomical comparison clearly implies an overshadowing effect: 'Cœlebs had run but a very limited part of his course, when in the same hemisphere Nubilia burst upon our gaze, her splendour not so dazzling, but not less pleasing.'[47]

If the *Universal Magazine* envisioned the competitive relationship between old and new work as a gentle casting into shade, however, the *Satirist* viewed the scenario as outright theft, referring to 'a spirit yet meaner, if possible; one, that unblushingly steals the mechanism from the patentee, and, disguising the theft so as to elude penalties, applies it without hesitation or remorse to any dirty purpose'.[48] There is less room for coexistence in this metaphor, which at once suggests that a 'mechanism' once stolen will work just as well for another, and strongly hints that subsequent works in a particular vein do not just add to the fame of the original, but take something from it. These accounts consider, in other words, what 'firstness' means but also what responses – described as near-inevitable – mean for the ongoing life or death of the original.

Reviews of *Celia in Search of a Husband* are no less frank about the work's temporal relationship to *Cœlebs*, and they use their reflections to upend assumptions about the relationship between haste and value. The *British Critic* piece begins, 'After reading, in the Preface to this Novel, a kind of confession that it was written in haste, in order to be first in the market, after the impression made by Cœlebs, we were not a little surprised to find it a production of so much merit.'[49] The *Critical Review* engages even more directly with the Modern Antique's rhetoric, quoting her phrase: '"Cœlebs" she says "had appeared; *it would be answered*; but it must be answered *directly*."'[50] While at first the reviewer seems mocking, writing, 'A Snarler would, perhaps say to the lady, "Where is the necessity?"' the review ultimately concludes that *Celia* actually outdoes its predecessor. Decrying *Cœlebs'* smug over-piety, the reviewer praises the greater humility of the Modern Antique, concluding, 'we are of opinion that "Celia in search of a Husband" is direct evidence that a life, not we imagine, very long, nor yet blessed with any great superiority of endowments, is sufficient to produce a work whose *intrinsic* worth sets it very far above the said performance [*Cœlebs'*]'. Whereas temporal brevity – of life or of composition time – may raise doubts about merit, these reviewers make it clear that an inverse relationship between the two should not be taken as automatic. Indeed, both reviews obliquely suggest that speed offers benefits of its own, in freshness, interest, and timeliness.

Perhaps nothing endorses the sense of urgency expressed by authors like Mudford and the Modern Antique more than the rapid decline in periodical coverage of *Cœlebs* responses after the publication of their works. While both *Celia* and *Nubilia*, the first on the scene, were reviewed in multiple outlets, and *Nubilia* was the subject of a months-long critical debate in the pages of the *Universal Magazine*, entrants published even a month or two later were hardly reviewed at all.[51] Only *Sequel to Cœlebs* (1812) and *Cœlebs Deceived* (1817) received substantive reviews, and these were primarily focused on their religious merits (or lack thereof) rather than in terms of their relationship to other *Cœlebs* novels. The lively engagement with – and then rapid abandonment of – the *Cœlebs* responses in the day's print media demonstrates that the emphasis on haste insisted upon by so many novelists was neither strictly imaginary nor a phenomenon of fiction-writing alone. Periodicals participated in, and in many ways created, that sense of excited expectation the Modern Antique cites as the reason for her composition. And they did this in a variety of ways: the periodical press – particularly reviews but also magazines, newspapers, and other forms of contemporary print media – not only fostered the culture of speed by reviewing and discussing response novels in terms that emphasize their timeliness; it also prepared the way for more of these novels through advertising, fostering controversy, notices from correspondents, and anticipatory literary coverage. The *Anti-Jacobin* magazine, for instance, informed readers of the Correspondence section that '[a] *new* edition of Nubilia, we understand, is in the Press, which we shall notice; in the mean time we may observe, that its merits and *defects*, we think, have been more *impartially* estimated in the Antijacobin, than in any other work which we have yet seen.'[52] A notice like this serves at least three purposes: it informs readers of a coming publication; it calls attention to the newness of *Nubilia*, not only published soon after *Cœlebs*, but appearing in still another new edition within months; and, of course, it stakes a claim for the ongoing importance of the magazine itself in mediating readers' relationship to this literature.

In this sense, periodical publication is inseparably tied to the production and reception of new time-sensitive novels: if a novel is (theoretically) meant to endure, periodicals (again, theoretically) are meant to be ephemeral, produced for the moment, and each issue rapidly superseded by the next. Just as recent work in periodical studies has complicated this temporality, however, so fiction scholarship must embrace different visions of the temporalities with which novels were conceived and received.[53] In the case of the *Cœlebs* responses, periodicals certainly responded to novel publication. But they also pre-empted, or paved the way for, such publication, as when *Cœlebs Deceived* was initially published in the *Christian Miscellany*, or *La Belle Assemblée* published *Hymenæa in Search of a Husband*, a novel in the form of a lengthy letter to the editor, which ran in each month's issue for more than three years, between March 1809 and November 1812.[54] Even as they comment upon the desires of readers or motivations of authors, they add momentum to these trends by advertising 'a *new* edition' or, as the *Gentleman's Magazine* did in October of 1809, letting readers know that 'A Companion to Miss BYRON's "Celia", intituled, "Celia Suited", will speedily appear.'[55] The author of *Nubilia* used periodicals as a site to fan the controversies surrounding his book after its publication, writing to contest claims made in reviews and debate the morality and aesthetic qualities of his own novel.[56] And the time-sensitive relationship between novels and periodicals comes full circle when, as we have seen, publishers reprint reviews of novels in the back of new novels, a practice that is both a convenient publicity mechanism and a means of ensuring that the newest works meet the public eye.

Fictions of the Moment

When the *Critical Review* expressed its preference for *Celia in Search of a Husband* over *Cœlebs in Search of a Wife*, it did so in words that closely tie the two novels' morality to their temporality. The reviewer is 'far from thinking that the pious book [*Cœlebs*] mentioned above is a specimen of . . . transcendent genius', he writes.[57] What the reviewer seems to most dislike about the novel, indeed, is its pretence of being above earthly concerns. The more human, humble scale of *Celia* is preferable, the reviewer plainly states, praising the Modern Antique's 'christian humility and christian charity'.[58] The distinction between these two approaches, however, has to do not just with scale but with *time*. Decrying *Cœlebs'* pretensions to piety and moral superiority, the reviewer invokes, again and again, words having to do with duration. The Modern Antique is better than More, by this calculus, because the former 'does not impiously pretend to be so far favoured with a knowledge of the inscrutable designs of Providence as to point out with certainty the objects of *future* indignation and mercy'; further, 'She neither arrogates to herself an undoubted election to *eternal* happiness, nor . . . denounces *everlasting* damnation.'[59] The reviewer's critique of *Cœlebs'* theological position may seem far removed from the discussions of hasty writing examined so far, but, as this section will suggest, they are closely interrelated. The speedy responses to *Cœlebs*, in this light, are neither coincidental nor counterintuitive; rather, it is precisely *Cœlebs'* moral claims, and particularly its self-positioning as a text of eternal, timeless truths, rather than a timely fiction, that invite response texts engaging with questions of the novel's moral and temporal status. *Cœlebs'* paradoxical status as an eminently fashionable work (one of many to take advantage of the contemporary popularity of didactic fiction) that consistently espouses disdain for rapidly changing fashions, in other words, opens a dialogue among novelists about the novel's value and temporal scale.

  Although these novels vary widely in content, length, and tone (those that comically satirize *Cœlebs* and those that seriously expand upon or repudiate it, in particular, are quite distinct from each other), they all explore questions of morality and timing, and the role of print culture in mediating these concepts. In *Celia in Search of a Husband*, the author's pseudonym itself already hints at a set of concerns about time, objects, and relevance that foreshadow and configure the themes that motivate the novels. 'A Modern Antique' creates an interesting tension between new and old – the faintly derogatory associations of 'antique' suggest the author poking fun at herself for her old-fashioned views, yet also hint that these views are classic and enduring. At the novel's end, in mock-apology for any failings the reader may have perceived, she declares that critics may call her 'a *ridiculous antique*' (II:305); this indictment, though, is immediately turned around by her claim for the fashionable nature of antiquity: 'Now, you know, your *tastes* lean that *way*, that *antiques* are the rage' (II:305).[60] Antique and Modern at once, she is, in a sense, doubly fashionable. The author plays on her ambiguous status in the preface as well, claiming, on the one hand, to write of the world 'without *mixing* in its haunts' (I:ii) and, on the other, to be depicting the world accurately as it is: 'The novel-writer is engaged in portraits, in which every one knows the original, and can detect any deviation from exactness of resemblance' (I:iv).[61] This tension is a central concern of all the *Cœlebs* novels, which figure themselves both as (timeless) commentaries on modern circumstances and (timely) participants in contemporary culture.

The 'Modern Antique' misses no opportunity to follow up on the broad hints dropped in the preface about the importance of the propitious moment: though author and protagonist are inclined to be critical of over-strict adherence to fashion, the novel nonetheless demonstrates familiarity with all manner of up-to-date trends. The novel presents itself as an accurate mirror of fashionable life, and the Modern Antique delights in describing new habits, systems, and fads. These fashions, ranging from new diet and exercise routines to the trend of upper-class ladies making their own shoes, are cited both to establish the novel's bona fides as an accurate representation of modern life and as a way of satirizing such faddish trends.[62] Like the Modern Antique's pseudonym, then, there is an inherent doubleness to this portrayal of fashion, which at once mocks a foolish addiction to novelty and clearly anticipates the importance of accuracy and timeliness in portraying it.

Mentions of time-sensitive trends, and particularly of the fickleness of fashion, are scattered through the other novels, directly following the discourse established by More's original novel, in which Cœlebs frequently speaks disparagingly of the 'passion for novelty' that motivates many of the people he encounters in society. His description of the ever-changing landscape of fashionable London directly foreshadows the later counterpoints set up by More's successors. 'This successive abundance of fresh supply gives an ephemeral importance to every thing, and a lasting importance to nothing', Cœlebs declares in one conversation. 'What was old, however momentous, was rejected as dull, what was new, however insignificant, was thought interesting. Events of the past week were placed with those beyond the flood' (279). Cœlebs' claim that it is timing alone, not intrinsic merit, that determines the value contemporary society grants to anything echoes through the later works. In *Cœlebs Married*, for instance, a storekeeper, Mr Thompson, laments that '[t]he public, always voracious after novelty, first went to the new shops', going on to denounce '[t]his fickleness of the public, or rather thirst for something new' (101). Other novels apply this logic not just to consumerism but to life itself, as when *Nubilia* repeatedly criticizes characters who place too much importance on the present moment. Discussing some fashionable characters, for instance, Nubilia's father remarks, 'The conduct of such persons appears to be, and in fact is, capricious and fantastical. They are creatures of the moment' (32).

The complaints of all these characters not only are ironic, coming as they do in novels explicitly designed to meet the public's 'thirst for something new', but present a reflection in miniature of the contemporary novelist's dilemma. Timeliness is of the utmost importance, as authors, characters, and reviewers alike make clear; yet, fully accepting the importance of novelty relegates one's own work to oblivion as soon as a new competitor arises. Cœlebs' complaints take on a rather different valence in this larger context: while he claims to be talking about the world at large, perhaps it is the novel *in which he appears* that he (accurately) anticipates will be found 'dull'; perhaps it is the response novels, 'however insignificant', soon to eclipse his own that he resents. Indeed, he says as much in the preface, declaring that the indeterminate genre of the work to come may pose challenges for readers: 'The Novel reader will reject it as dull; the religious may throw it aside as frivolous' (38). While this opening gambit frames readers' responses in terms of qualitative experience, however, the context of the novel as a whole reveals the dilemma to be largely temporal rather than moral or aesthetic.

The constant query, 'How should we value literature?' is thus rewritten in these works as a different question: 'How long does it last?' The ethical assessment of ever-changing fashions offered by the *Cœlebs* novels can also, then, be understood as a debate between two conflicting views of literary value, the one predicated on an unchanging (if often ill-defined) notion of aesthetic or moral excellence and the other reflective of the constant flux of readers' interests and cultural demands. Many of the novelists make this connection explicit, with 'Modern literature' a favourite topic of conversation and trends in literature directly compared with other fleeting fads. As the narrator of *Lindamira* puts it at one point, 'Short chapters at the end of long works, and abrupt conclusions to tedious compositions, are all the fashion, I am told. I always had a strong predilection for being in the fashion.'[63]

In using references to literary works to explore questions of value and relevance, as in so much else, the *Cœlebs* novels follow their predecessor. As Patricia Demers writes, '[t]he scene in *Cœlebs* is one of conversation and literary allusion' (10). However, all allusions are not created equal, as Demers points out; circulating-library novels appear as 'a satirized subset of reading choices' and there 'are no excerpts from . . . [More's] Romantic contemporaries. More's intertextual references reach back at least one generation, and often much further' (11). Cœlebs himself prefers the 'classic' works of Milton to more contemporary fare, and More decries the rapidly changing field of literature through other characters too. Ruminating on the lost popularity of Akenside's *Pleasures of the Imagination*, one of them wonders, 'Is it . . . the rage for novelty, or a real degeneracy of taste, that we now so seldom hear of a poet, who, when I was a boy, was the admiration of every man who had a relish for true genius?' (80). Literary status here is a function of taste but also a function of time.

Yet, just as More reviled the novel genre but acknowledged its utility for sending a message she wished many people to receive, so *Cœlebs* itself participates in the 'rage of novelty' it decries, implicitly acknowledging through its allusions that the reading public holds very different values than the protagonist does. Two sisters with whom Cœlebs talks in an early chapter, for instance, are nonplussed by a question about Virgil, but readily share their preferred reading material: 'she had read Tears of Sensibility, and Rosa Matilda, and Sympathy of Souls, and Too Civil by Half, and the Sorrows of Werter, and the Stranger, and the Orphans of Snowdon. "Yes, Sir", joined in the younger sister . . . "and we have read Perfidy Punished, and Jemmy and Jenny Jessamy, and the Fortunate Footman, and the Illustrious Chambermaid"' (57). While Cœlebs, naturally, scorns this selection of relatively recent novels and plays, *readers* of *Cœlebs* would certainly have recognized these titles.[64] And based on the speed with which Lane's competitor J. F. Hughes, for example, published

Cœlebia Choosing a Husband (1809) and *Lindamira* (1810), he must have anticipated that some of the readers of novels like *Confessions of the Nun of St. Omer* (written by the above-mentioned 'Rosa Matilda', in 1805), published by his press a few years before, would enjoy both that novel and the responses to *Cœlebs*.[65]

Celia in Search of a Husband explores the connection between literary value and time at some length. The novel's initial epigraph is from Milton, and quotations from Shakespeare and other already-canonical English authors make their way into the text throughout, but the author is particularly interested in the kinds of print culture that are uniquely of the moment, particularly novels, as well as the periodicals and advertisements that heralded the rapidly cycling London fashions and, as such, were an essential component of the fashions themselves.[66] Celia's zealous guardian (the most evangelical character in the novel, whose views are consistently portrayed as slightly ridiculous), bans these kinds of publications from her home. Even she, however, can't do without some periodical updates, however infrequently she may accept them: 'Celia was a stranger to the *diurnal* prints, Mrs. Mansfield being content to receive all *current news* and *opinions* through the medium of a weekly paper. "This will suffice", said this excellent woman. "There is little to *instruct* in these pages, and much to *deplore*. The less we see of them the better"' (I:37).

The newness and ephemerality of these publications is a key aspect of their questionable moral status, as Mrs Mansfield's compromise – weekly papers *only* – rather comically suggests. Other forms of literature, too, are often discussed, with Mrs Mansfield largely opposed to most, the sheltered Celia unfamiliar with them – 'I am a stranger to modern literature', said Celia; 'excepting the elegant "Minstrel", and some few others' (I:155) – and the other characters falling at various places along the spectrum. Celia's familiarity with Walter Scott's contemporary and wildly popular poem *The Lay of the Last Minstrel* (1805) proves her interest in certain literary fashions to be wholly active, even as it reinforces the divide between 'respectable' poets and novelists, all of whom were at risk of disreputability by their genre alone. Milton and Shakespeare are frequently referenced, but, just as in *Cœlebs*, readers are also certainly expected to catch the reference to Walter Scott, and to understand the significance of describing a character who 'stands confest a *convert* to the *Rights of Woman*' (I:226). The reader of *Cœlibia Choosing a Husband*, likewise, is clearly expected to comprehend, if not to identify with, an unfortunate character ruined by novel-reading when she describes '[t]he delight I experienced from the first novel I read, which happened to be the "Old Manor House" [a novel by Charlotte Smith] . . . My whole soul was absorbed' (I:51).[67]

Scott, Charlotte Smith, and Mary Wollstonecraft, all well-known 'modern' authors, are dropped into texts to trigger reader recognition and mark the contemporary nature of the scenes they depict; they are also presented to contrast with older and more respectable works, although the boundary between moral and immoral, improving and dangerous, is always shifting. Scott is praised by Celia with apparent sincerity (while both Wollstonecraft and Smith are clearly represented as pernicious), and the Cœlebs of *Cœlebs Married* echoes her in viewing Scott as an exceptionally timeless contemporary author. On a book-shopping expedition, he remarks, 'as the first of modern poets, I did not forget the works of Walter Scott. His imagery and descriptions are far beyond any thing of the present age, and we fancy ourselves carried back into the times of old' (111). Yet Scott's narratives have danger too; in their seductive power, they are compared to those novels that Mary in *Cœlibia Choosing a Husband* finds so entrancing. Mary describes 'an uncontroulable longing to taste the forbidden fruit' of fiction, just as Cœlebs (in *Cœlebs Married*) worries 'however the mind may be enchanted by the wild witchery of the bard [Scott], I fear, that in common with our best prose romances, much mischief to our Protestant church is produced' (111). Scott's poetry may be dangerous, in other words, because it is both too good and too much like a novel. It is at once out of time, 'far beyond any thing of the present age', and alarmingly like the most contemporary of genres. The slippage between affective impact and moral value draws attention to the varying standards by which literary works are judged: a simplistic division between old and new works is no more universally valid than one between moral and immoral literatures, these scenes collectively suggest.

The purpose in drawing attention to the temporality of the novel is particularly clear when we examine the many instances in which *Cœlebs* itself is the intertext used to interrogate the moral status of 'modern literature'. It is the silliest characters in *Celia in Search of a Husband*, for instance, who love *Cœlebs*, and their efforts to take that novel's didacticism to heart are invariably mocked.[68] Careful adherence to *Cœlebs'* precepts is itself presented as the folly of over-sensitivity to fashionable trends, as when the ridiculous Lady Desmond declares that since she read *Cœlebs*, 'nothing but the Stanley's has run in my brain . . . I have discharged my housekeeper, because she was a fine lady, and have engaged the most complete piece of antiquity you ever beheld; and, to complete my satisfaction, her name is *Nonfit,* instead of *Comfit* [the name of the housekeeper in More's work]' (166–167). Other response novels take similar liberties with their characters' relationships to the original novel, generally in ways that, even if nominally admiring, function to relegate that text to one of the two poles of literary oblivion: too fashionable, or too old-fashioned.

Lindamira, or An Old Maid in Search of a Husband too refers directly to *Cœlebs* – and its responses – as examples of 'modern literature'. It opens with a classic female quixote character, Miss Betty Gubbins, who, we are told, 'not only exhausted all the treasures of every circulating library within the circle of ten miles' but also 'indulged her taste for reading … by purchasing … popular publications of the novel kind' (I:2–3). One imagines Hannah More's mixed feelings at learning that 'Cœlebs had lately enriched her private collection, and she had read with delight' (I:3) Miss Gubbins is even more delighted, we learn on the next page, when 'unpacking a parcel of new books sent her by her attentive bookseller in London, her eagle eye first caught the following charming titles. "Celia in search of a *Husband.*" "Nubilia in Search of a *Husband*"' (I:4). This timely discovery sets Miss Gubbins off on a quest to find a husband of her own, but it also aligns her with the reader, who is similarly enjoying literature that has been produced 'lately'. Here, contemporaneity is used to deny *Cœlebs* any special status – Miss Gubbins enjoyed it, but indiscriminately, and is even more taken with the newer texts that will soon supplant it. *Lindamira* marks its own newness by the inclusion of *Celia* and *Nubilia,* both published only a matter of months earlier, in the plot, and the protagonist's subtitular status as an 'Old Maid in Search of a Husband' underscores the importance of timeliness: while Cœlebs, Celia, Nubilia, and the rest are young people seeking to marry at the proper time, Miss Gubbins (like *Cœlebs* itself) is portrayed as fundamentally past it, already out of date and out of fashion.

In this way, the respondents to *Cœlebs* manoeuvre their predecessor into a perfect double-bind. *Cœlebs* is at once outdated and *too* fashionable; discussed by all but also relegated, like the Modern Antique, to the old-fashioned status of moral improver. *Celia's* Lady Bab confesses ironically that she might someday benefit from *Cœlebs'* moral message, 'but I am as yet little advanced in its pages: I always *reserve* it for *Sunday reading*' (II:168). More old-fashioned sermon than modern novel, *Cœlebs'* position, however hallowed, is hardly in competition with other fashionable works.

A Modern Antique makes this point in more detail at the end of *Celia in Search of a Husband*:

> The dramas of Shakespeare *live*, and will *live,* while a *taste* for genius exists. The plays of *modern* days perish, and – I say nothing. Now I, with an humility for which I *feel* I deserve *praise*, sincerely *wish* my *book* may share the *fate* of a *modern play*, first allowing me to get my *nine nights*, not *nine editions*. (II:302–303)

Her claim to 'humility' is unsurprising in the context of other novelists' modest apologies for lack of genius, yet her claims for the necessity of haste in the preface suggest that we might be wise to take this claim rather more literally: to be a sensation for 'nine nights' may after all be the more significant accomplishment, in fashionable – and, potentially, financial – terms. Rather than capturing an audience's attention for years or centuries after one's own death, in other words, a nine-night sensation captures a particular moment, with the living author's ability to tap into more ephemeral trends and audience expectations. This is a different kind of artistic accomplishment than the one we more traditionally espouse, but not, as the Modern Antique so often hints, one without its own standards and merits.

The question of literary fashion, and particularly the passage of older works into fame or obscurity, is repeatedly raised by characters in these novels, with lengthy meditations on changing trends. In *Cœlebs Married*, the newlywed Cœlebs ruminates:

> Lucilla and I soon completed our purchases: I could not avoid remarking the rapid changes of fashion even in literature; and my bookseller informed me, that every few months, there was a current demand for all books of a similar tendency, and which perhaps, had been heretofore neglected and given up to the worms. When I first visited London ... romances were all the rage, and tales of horror were in the hands of every lady. Now, I found that a thirst for caricature and personal allusions had become so predominant, that ... the title and the advertisement, to attract, must be drawn up to rouse expectation in search of the secret memoirs of some public or notorious personage.[69]

The shift from gothic novel to society roman à clef described here corresponds loosely with actual changes in literary fashion in this period; in emphasizing its causes Cœlebs seems to be reviving the same argument given by so many authors in their prefaces: new demand even for books that had been 'given up to the worms' shifts emphasis away from sheer novelty and towards reader tastes. It is more important that a book's 'tendency' matches up with 'current demand' than that it be new – but new books written to order are certainly more likely to meet that demand.

In *Nubilia*, a Mr Vaughan reflects on the volumes in a library with even more explicit thoughts on the passage of time:

> The sight of so much mortality ... as loads the shelves, awakens in me reflections of a serious nature. When I look upon the names of the authors, and recollect that they were eminent in their time; that they were loved and honoured, or neglected and despised, by the age in which they lived; that the mind which conceived, and the hand which wrote, those exquisite productions which have formed the solace of my life are gone and perished; when I see the poet, and his critic of after ages, side by side ... and when I call to memory, that the dust of those illustrious beings, could it be gathered together from distant regions, would be in nothing distinguishable from the common earth we tread upon, I am filled with awe.[70]

While some few books may be rediscovered and recirculated at fashion's whim, *Nubilia* reminds readers that the passage of time is generally much more inexorable. However moved Mr Vaughan may be at the thought of past geniuses, they are gone. The 'exquisite productions' he praises survive their authors – for now – but the blurred lines between the lost bodies of authors and the physical forms of the books that outlast them, as reminders of mortality, suggest a similar fate for both. All these scenes emphasize the changing tides of fashion and the unavoidable passage of some works into obscurity; moreover, however, they proffer a kind of literary levelling theory, in which original merit is less important than suitedness to current trends, and where the dust of a Shakespeare is indistinguishable from that of his obscurer (and less brilliant?) counterpart. If time is the great leveller, reducing all to dust, then so too might fashion be seen as an equalizer of sorts, raising everything that fits a new trend to the heights of success. The appeal of such a theory is easy to see for the authors of novels bound to be dismissed as trendy imitations.

The preface of *Cœlebs Deceived* grapples most explicitly with the competing values of timelessness and trendiness, and the role of the novel in mediating them. In it, a 'good old gentleman in spectacles', reading the 'Philanthropic Gazette', complains that 'here is another of these religious Novels advertised. Ah, what would our pious forefathers of the sixteenth century have said to the levity of this age? Shame on the public taste to encourage thus the vain sallies of imagination. Such works deserve *to be burnt by the common hang-man*.'[71] His grandson, overhearing his complaint, calls his bluff, making as if to cast one of his books into the fire. '"I am only, Sir," replied the youth, "going to sacrifice old John Bunyan, as the ring-leader of this set of authors." "Thou art a shrewd lad," cries the

Old Gentleman, "let John Bunyan alone; and here take the purchase-money for the new book."[72] At once conflating the works of John Bunyan with newly trendy 'religious novels' and pointing out the hypocrisy of a reader who would value one and dismiss the other, this anecdote denies explicitly religious or moral texts (like Bunyan's or, indeed, *Cœlebs* itself) a special exemption from the levelling rules of time.

In tracing the contours of timeliness, belatedness, and morality, the response novels follow – but often resist – the theological debates of *Cœlebs*; in which, at one point, a young heroine is reminded 'we do not go to church to hear news. Christianity is no novelty' (193). Earlier in the same scene, we learn that a character 'does not approve of the habit of criticizing the sermon', as it will lead to 'a display, not of Christian temper, but of critical skill' (192). As a religious and morally improving text, by this logic, *Cœlebs* should not be subject to the pressures of either novelty or aesthetic criticism. As its many respondents make clear, however, this is not an exemption they are willing to grant. Christianity may not be a novelty, but novels *about* it very much are. And as all the *Cœlebs* authors frequently remind us, this can be a good thing. When the Modern Antique declares, 'if the Ladies, for whom I write, if *they* should give me a *patient* reading, not put me on the *shelf* from *Sunday* to *Sunday*, I shall be grateful', she is modelling humility, but also seems to be implicitly comparing the work of More, her predecessor, to a Bible – admirable, morally unassailable, certainly important and influential, but apt to remain 'on the shelf' until piety requires its removal.[73] To be 'timeless', the Modern Antique suggests, may also mean being poorly suited to everyday reading.

Cœlebiana and the Culture of Speed

When *Northanger Abbey* was finally published at the end of 1817, more than a decade after Jane Austen first submitted it for publication, it began with a disclaimer, in the form of an 'Advertisement, by the Authoress': 'The public are entreated to bear in mind', Austen wrote, 'that thirteen years have passed since [this novel] was finished, many more since it was begun, and that during that period, places, manners, books, and opinions have undergone considerable changes.'[74] Accordingly, she felt it necessary to state, 'some observation is necessary upon those parts of the work which thirteen years have made comparatively obsolete'.[75]

How long is thirteen years? Given the longevity of Austen's work, her anxiety about the fate of her novel after only thirteen years may seem, from our present point of view, overblown, or at least, as Timothy Campbell suggests, to have a 'falsely modest tone' about it.[76] Certainly, this open acknowledgement of her work's locatedness in a particular, distinctive cultural moment presents a strong contrast with the attitudes of some other Romantic authors, many of whom characterized writing as precisely that which would – or, if done well, should – survive the passing of time and the vagaries of fashion. In the company of the novels I have examined in this chapter, however, Austen's explicit worry that her work may have grown obsolete in such a short span of time takes on a different resonance. Especially given the preponderance of printed materials flooding the market around the turn of the nineteenth century, many authors besides Austen wondered: What prospects for long-term survival and relevance did their works have? Would a poem or novel from 1810 or 1820 still speak to readers even a decade later, let alone a generation or two along?

In the first part of this chapter I have looked closely at one distinctive group of novels written between 1808 and 1817 – in other words, during some of the same years during which *Northanger Abbey*, in its first incarnation, was languishing in the publisher Crosby and Co.'s filing cabinet, despite Austen's efforts to retrieve it. Austen's experience with Crosby and Co. (who were behind only Minerva, Hughes, and Longman in numbers of novels published between 1800 and 1810) reminds us that despite the rhetoric of indiscriminate publication and insatiable publishers, novels weren't necessarily published as soon as they were written, or at all; authors still faced obstacles and publishers could be gatekeepers even as they invited and fostered new talent.[77] Looking at the *Cœlebs* novels contextualizes Austen's concern with the question of her work's ongoing cultural legibility and offers a window into an alternate model of Romantic authorship, one preoccupied with timeliness and changing tastes. Campbell describes *Northanger Abbey* as 'present[ing] itself as a self-conscious chronicle of fashion' which is particularly attentive to 'the peculiar kinds of change that grow visible within a narrower span of time'.[78] In this closing section, I explore the aftermath of the *Cœlebs* phenomenon, looking at the continuing significance of this particular fleeting fashion in other novels over the next decade.

It is hard to overstate the familiarity with which *Cœlebs* and its many successors are invoked in Romantic popular fiction. 'Cœlebs' is widely used as a shorthand for an unmarried man in novels through the 1810s and 1820s, often in contexts that drastically alter the spirit of More's original. Sarah Green's *Scotch Novel Reading* (1824) refers to 'the Cœlebs-like search [a character] was making', and an advice-giver in Innes Hoole's *Scenes at Brighton* (1821) encourages young ladies to draw the eye of the fashionable world, as 'it will make you doubly sought after by the *Cœlebs* that surround you'.[79] And in Anthony Frederick Holstein's *The Discontented Man* (1815), one character's 'gay associates laughingly affirmed him another Cœlebs in search of a wife'.[80] Women too are described in these terms, in a conscious echo of the gender-reversed response novels starring Nubilia, Celia, and others. In Mary Meeke's *Strategems Defeated* (1811) a young woman is said to be possibly 'doomed to a life of celibacy, as she will never leave home in "Search of a Husband", nor *unsought be won*' (54); on the very next page, 'our hero' declares that another character is 'bent upon sending him, like Cœlebs, in search of a wife'.[81] Even Byron, in *Don Juan*, includes a reference to *Cœlebs* in his litany of contemporary literary types; his satirical take clearly follows in the vein of the response novels:

> In short, she was a walking calculation,
> Miss Edgeworth's novels stepping from their covers,
> Or Mrs. Trimmer's books on education,
> Or 'Cœlebs' Wife' set out in quest of lovers.[82]

While works like these simply borrow the character-as-type, other novels more explicitly engage with the reception of *Cœlebs* and all its successors within their own plots. Many characters are described as reading one or more of the *Cœlebs* novels; a bachelor in *Happiness* (1821) asks his companions, 'You have all, I suppose, heard of "Cœlebs in search of a Wife"? this was once my character; but I have long since renounced it. I am a bachelor at forty; and a bachelor I intend to continue.'[83] Elsewhere in *Strategems Defeated*, we are told that '[t]he ladies were of his opinion, both having read "Celia in search of a Husband," which they pronounced to be an inimitable picture of high life.'[84] Such scenes clearly testify to the continuing familiarity of *Cœlebs* to the reading public, but they also permit authors a shorthand for continued engagement with the standards of haste and speed the *Cœlebs* novels represent, and particularly the way that discourses of speed can be used to help other works jockey for position. In *Mortimer Hall* (1811), two characters debate *Nubilia* in terms that closely echo the language used in both prefaces and reviews of the period: '"Well, Damer, pray tell me what you think of the book I gave you to read?"', asks one character; '"how do you like Miss Nubilia?"'

> 'I think it', replied Mr. Damer, 'one of those ephemeral productions which ought never to have appeared before the public. The haste with which the author professes to have written it, is no excuse for the laxity of principle it exhibits.'[85]

It seems unlikely to be coincidental that both *Mortimer Hall* and *Strategems Defeated* were, like *Celia in Search of a Husband*, published by the Minerva Press: thus we find *Celia* praised and her most direct competitor, *Nubilia* (published by Ridgeway, Sherwood, Neely and Jones, one of Minerva's more prolific rivals in the 1810s), maligned in their pages.[86] Beyond this, though, we can see in these debates the tension between the admirably fashionable and the pointlessly ephemeral. Mudford, *Nubilia*'s author, claimed – and indeed managed – to write for the moment; the 'time for consideration' Mr Damer wishes he had taken is precisely what would have precluded him from joining in the conversation altogether.

Tales of a Tourist (1823), published by A. K. Newman more than a decade later, engages in the same push-and-pull publicity, reminding readers of the *Cœlebs* fad as if it is still going on, but simultaneously using humour to dismiss *Cœlebs* itself. Mrs Sanderson, a character mocked for her literary pretensions (she wants to go to the '*libery*' because, she declares, 'I do love reading, it is such a gentlewomanlike employment'), takes her daughters to their nearby circulating library where 'Eliza Sanderson asked for Celia in Search of a Husband. Gone that morning to Torpington Castle . . .. Mrs. Sanderson now pushed forward and, in spite of her daughter Jane's hints and admonitions, intrepidly demanded – "Cyclops in Search of a Wife".'[87] Mrs Sanderson's malapropism is humour at her expense, but *Cœlebs* itself, described by another character in the next line as 'the greatest compendium of commonplaces that ever prosed itself into popularity . . . with the sour-visaged rigour of puritanism', is perhaps even more the target.[88] Falling ever-further into the past, its moral promises remain unfulfilled.

Earlier in *Happiness*, one character asks another, '[D]oes not your new associate belong to the tribe of sentimental sermonising female authors, who lounge at Hatchard's, and talk theology with the solemn decent gentlemen in black, who spend their mornings there? She is not quite old enough to be the methodistical writer of Cœlebs.'[89] The mention of More's age, a thinly veiled insult, turns out also to be a proxy for the outdatedness of her book. *Cœlebs*, according to this character, 'notwithstanding the noise it made at first, is now almost forgotten in the fashionable world. The truth is, it does not suit our meridian. I took up the last volume the other day, but I began to feel *ennui*; by the way, I never *begin* any book except a *real* novel' (67). While More and some of her cohort of authors, like Mudford, rejected the 'novel' designation for its immoral connotations, this author uses it to reject *Cœlebs* as boring and passé. The 'noise it made' at the time of publication seems almost a precondition of its disappearance from public memory. The clear untruth of this assertion – obviously, *Cœlebs* was still quite well remembered enough to be cited without explanation in numerous novels even more than a decade later – reminds us that the rhetorical stance is not so much about what is actually forgotten, but about an idea of a literary world in which old works are always sinking out of sight, making room for newcomers.

Authors publishing during the original *Cœlebs* fad were, perhaps unsurprisingly, even more explicit about positioning themselves in relation to it. The author of *Ferdinand and Ordinella* (1810), the possibly pseudonymous Priscilla Parlante, dedicates a lengthy preface largely to disparaging *Cœlebs*, of which, she declares: 'neither the perusal of master Cœlebs' adventures, nor the character of that youthful and pious spark (who displays all the scrupulous exactness of an antiquated vestal, in his diligent search for a consistent help-mate) delights or amuses me'.[90] The adjective 'antiquated' echoes both the pseudonym of *Celia*'s author and the overall project of rendering *Cœlebs* (all of eighteen months old at this point) obsolete. Indeed, this author declares a few pages later, 'For abate (as time will soon abate) that sort of curiosity excited by the alluring title, and ... no individual who is not infected by the contagion of methodism, will have patience to wade through any of [Cœlebs'] sermonizing dialogues.'[91] Scholars including Misty Anderson and Andrew Winckles have explored the relationship between Methodism and literature in the eighteenth century; here, the author uses it satirically to explain *Cœlebs*' otherwise unjustifiable (she hints) success. If religion does indeed allow some works to stand the test of time, Parlante pointedly suggests, this is no testament either to their quality or the discernment of their readers, but rather to the 'contagiousness' of the ideas contained.

Anthony Frederick Holstein, in a lengthy preface to his 1810 novel *Miseries of an Heiress*, offers the most lengthy and explicit engagement with the *Cœlebs* novels, providing in the process corroboration of the time-sensitive and competitive literary culture cited by so many of the novelists I've already examined. His preface begins in terms that clearly place it in time and in relation to the other novels it cites:

> Some few weeks before 'Cœlebs in Search of a Wife' was spoken of as in the press, a friend suggested to me a similar idea for the foundation of a Work, which, however, was not intended to have been in the same style as the very religious, serious production, which has issued from the far more competent powers of Miss More. I hesitated between a Gentleman in search of a Wife, or a Lady in search of a Husband; but, being then engaged in the construction of another Novel, I determined to embrace the hint of my friend at my leisure.[92]

Leisure, as the other *Cœlebs* responses make abundantly clear, is precisely what an author trying to break in to the market at this literary moment cannot afford. Holstein describes himself first as stymied by More's publication: 'Meanwhile my purpose was stayed by the publication of "CŒLEBS"; and I wholly relinquished the design.'[93] But soon, he claims, he had a new idea: 'it occurred to me, that a *Latinized* Bachelor in search of a Wife, might be answered by an *Italianized* Maiden in search of a Husband: I therefore, under the appropriate name of ZITELLA, sought to display this female'.[94] Unfortunately, however, this idea too had come too late, a fact affirmed, according to Holstein, both by his publisher (the Minerva Press) and by the reading public itself, which he feared would be tired of the topic: 'I offered Mr. Newman to finish it within a given period, if he would engage to purchase the Work when completed: his reply was, that one of a similarly descriptive title, "CELIA," was then in his hands, and consequently my proposal was declined.'[95] Nor was his defeat yet complete; he continues: 'On also finding that Nubilia and Cœlibia had set out on the same hunt, I thought the subject would be literally overdone, and I therefore forebore the hackneyed theme.'[96]

This remarkable account, whatever its literal truth, provides a fascinating counterpoint to the narratives of haste provided by the authors who *did* follow in *Cœlebs'* footsteps. It suggests that their claims for speedy writing were neither overblown nor purely rhetorical: 'the pen that writes quickest', as the Modern Antique put it, got the publishing contract. Holstein's claim that A. K. Newman declined to publish his work because *Celia* was already forthcoming also reminds us that authors weren't playing the game of speed in a vacuum: publishers too had to strike a balance between capitalizing on a literary fashion and not undercutting their own profits with competing titles. Given that multiple other authors did succeed in publishing *Cœlebs* responses well after *Celia*, *Nubilia*, and *Cœlebia*, the market clearly wasn't as thoroughly 'overdone' as Holstein feared; on the other hand, though, the lack of reviews of these later texts makes it clear that none received the attention of the first two. Indeed, only two of the nine responses were published by the same publisher, J. F. Hughes, suggesting that literary titles in the same vein were not always figured as mutually reinforcing, as gothic fictions tended to be, but might instead be competitors for market share.[97]

The rhetoric of speed – writing quickly and with specifically contemporary relevance – is a crucial strategy for handling such a market, and *Cœlebs* authors were not the only ones to deploy it. Sydney Owenson, for instance, the highly popular author of novels including *The Wild Irish Girl* (1806), made exactly this move in the preface to *Woman; or, Ida of Athens* (1809), in which she declares, 'I have already written almost as many volumes as I have years', and includes a footnote that specifies 'The "Wild Irish Girl" was written in six weeks; the "Sketches" in one; and "Woman", though I had long revolved its plan and tendency in my mind . . . was not begun until the 20th of last July.. . . It was finished on the 18th of October, and is now printed from the first copy.'[98] She claims not to be using this information 'to excuse [her] errors', and her tone is hardly apologetic; rather, her claims that 'I have been necessitated to compose with great rapidity' seem rather proud. Her youth and her speed are linked, both testifying to her ability to write to the moment. Indeed, *The Satirist*, when reviewing *Nubilia*, viewed this rhetoric of speed itself as a literary fashion, calling Mudford's listing of his own dates of composition '*à-la-mode de Mademoiselle Owenson*'.[99] Jane Austen herself, her personal concerns about timely publication notwithstanding, treated Owenson's rhetoric of haste with her customary wit, writing to her sister Cassandra, 'To set against your new Novel, of which nobody ever heard before & perhaps never may again, We have got "Ida of Athens" by Miss Owenson; which must be very clever, because it was written as the Authoress says, in three months.'[100]

Returning to *Nubilia* one final time brings us back to one more scathing review. The *Literary Panorama*, like so many other publications, seized on the detailed dates of Mudford's hasty writing process, declaring, 'A production so rapid can hardly expect to maintain itself long in the world.'[101] This pronouncement has largely proved true; but this, I think, is exactly the point. The *Cœlebs* novels and their spreading influence show us that many Romantic-era novels not only engaged directly with the question of their own longevity, but also deliberately wrote for the present moment, rather than for posterity. In order to survive, compete, and justify their own existence in a crowded market, novelists used the rhetoric of novelty, of speed, and of timeliness to glorify the newest thing and relegate all older productions to the past. While Cœlebs claimed to espouse a timeless morality that eschewed fashion and contemporary events, the novel in which he featured, and the many more he inspired, recognized the importance of timing to continued success. In so doing, these works also offer a vision of literary influence that is predicated not on long-lasting appeal but rather on direct and speedy engagement with contemporaries. While (fittingly) this model has had less staying power than ones that emphasize enduring excellence, recognizing its dominance allows us to better understand many of the ephemeral novels of the early nineteenth century, written for their own age, and no other.

CHAPTER 5

Fiction as Fashion from Belinda *to Miss Byron*

Novels, like all other popular objects, have their fashion. —*Asmodeus; or, The Devil in London* (1808)[1]

Readers of the 'Domestic Intelligence' section of the *European Magazine* in June of 1802 were treated to descriptions of a wide array of events, from an unfortunate drowning and a castle fire to a 'splendid Gala' boasting lavish decorations and a 'grand entertainment at Ranelagh'.[2] This last event, hosted by 'The Gentlemen of Boodle's Club', featured a drawing in which the winners collected a tempting array of small, portable industrial goods: 'The prizes consisted of shawls, parasols, handkerchiefs, quizzing glasses, &c. and the drawing occasioned great mirth.'[3] The microcosm of the early nineteenth-century world offered in these brief glimpses emphasizes fashion and luxury as forms of entertainment; readers are assured of the aforementioned Gala that 'the anxiety of the fashionable world to arrive in time was so great, that every avenue to Cumberland-house was completely blocked up before midnight ... All that the inventive taste of luxury could devise was combined in the dresses and metamorphoses of the company.'[4] Such glamorous scenes seem distant from the busy printing presses of Leadenhall Street, the much-thumbed circulating-library volumes produced there, and the struggling authors who penned them. Yet, as this chapter suggests, the 'inventive taste of luxury', particularly as it related to the sale and circulation of status-marking commodities from dresses to quizzing-glasses, is in fact a central discourse that early nineteenth-century popular novelists used to theorize and defend their work. Through readings of novels from Maria Edgeworth's *Belinda* (1801) to Minerva author Miss Byron's *The Alderman and the Peer; or, The Ancient Castle and Modern Villa* (1810), this chapter shows how these works unsettle assumptions about literary prestige with their portrayal of the relationship between literature and fashion. Novels serve a dual function in the works I examine here. They portray a culture in which characters read about, discuss, and buy the latest trends, whether hats or horses, but they also are themselves presented as fashionable *objects*, texts to be consumed, displayed, and shared by those in search of the next new thing. Being in fashion is about timeliness and novelty, as the previous chapter explored at some length; it is also, however, about being an active part of the buying, selling, acquisition, and display of material goods. Both ways of thinking about 'fashionable' novels are also ways of conceptualizing and managing the problems (and opportunities) created by fictional plenitude, but they engender quite different ways of thinking about the novel's value.

Historians of English consumer culture have highlighted the rise, over the course of the eighteenth century, of mass-produced products, available by 1800 to broad swathes of the public in previously unthinkable quantities and speeds. New cycles of consumption depended on following ever-changing-styles; Maxine Berg points to the specific importance of 'fashion' in driving consumer purchases of new items: 'What made these goods desirable above all else was fashion.... Fashion, soon attaching itself to all kinds of ornamental and even everyday articles, was what shoppers sought.'[5] As Neil McKendrick describes it, 'In fashion novelty became an irresistible drug. In possessions for the home, new fashions were insisted on – in pottery, furniture, fabrics, cutlery, even wallpaper.'[6] Production of all sorts of goods escalated with industrial growth over these years, and the English populace, particularly in urban areas such as London, purchased these goods on an unprecedented scale.[7] Though scholars have disagreed on the impetus for this growth (did desire drive production, or production foster desire?)[8] the increase is undisputed: by the end of the nineteenth century's first decade, when Edgeworth, Byron, and the other authors discussed in this chapter were publishing, consumable items from clocks to clothes to carriages were readily available in the streets and shops of London, and the purchase and display of these items comprised an important part of social status. Jan de Vries begins his account of European industrialization and consumer culture with a persuasive claim for the essential interconnectedness of supply and demand: '[C]onsumer aspirations have a history', he argues; 'they are not simply the second-order consequences of other, more fundamental forces, nor are they autonomous acts of creative individuality.'[9] The fiction of the period reflects both an overall attentiveness to fashion and the idea that consumer desire at once drives and is stoked by external circumstances including advertisements and shopping districts.[10] Consumption – particularly of luxury goods, but also many smaller and more trivial purchases – features largely in many novel plots.[11] Indeed, as Edward Copeland has argued, '[w]omen's fiction between 1790 and 1820 turned its attention to the "meaning" of consumption ... as a concern of defining importance.'[12]

Some early nineteenth-century novels feature characters whose elaborate adornments are described in painstaking detail. Miss Wantonley, of *Hardenbrass and Haverill* (1817), wears 'a flaxen wig', and that's only the beginning: she has also donned 'a comb richly studded with emeralds', 'a fine lace cap, adorned with a faded artificial rose in front', a 'three-coiled twist of pearls', 'an emerald necklace and cross', 'a sprig of artificial myrtle', 'a lace tucker, with an emerald broach', emerald 'ear-rings and bracelets', 'a richly ornamented gold quizzing-glass appended to a triple gold chain', 'a superb watch and seals', and 'many rings'.[13] Women are not uniquely susceptible to the vanities of over-adornment; a young man in *Paired Not Matched* (1815) is described as wearing, simultaneously, 'a brimstone-coloured coat', a 'blue satin waistcoat and white kerseymeres', 'two or three collars of different colours', 'a frill of great breadth ... on each side [of] his bosom', 'two broaches of different devices, and different though brilliant materials', and 'a very glittering chain' that 'support[s] a quizzing glass'.[14] While most characters, however dedicated to fashion, never reach quite such ridiculous levels of adornment, it is hard to find a novel from this period without at least a few scenes of shopping or descriptions of luxurious accessories.[15] Famously, the Bennet sisters in *Pride and Prejudice* (1813) are 'usually tempted [to nearby Meryton] three or four times a week, to pay their duty to their aunt and to a milliner's shop just over the way'.[16] And 'nothing less than a very smart bonnet indeed, or a really new muslin in a shop window', can distract Kitty and Lydia from ogling the soldiers of the visiting regiment.[17]

Few examples from the period remain as familiar as Austen's, but her memorable scenes, with their focus on conspicuous consumption and portable goods for purchase, are highly representative of a whole group of novels that appeared around the same years. In their preoccupation with the specific accoutrements of fashionable London life, many of these now-forgotten novels prefigure their better-known successors, the 'Silver Fork' novels of the 1820s and 1830s, which have attracted growing critical interest in recent years.[18] Indeed, as Cheryl A. Wilson points out, the Silver Fork novelists themselves were clearly aware that their chosen genre had earlier iterations; she notes the 'self-consciousness on the part of silver-fork novels to distance their works from the negative reputation of the Minerva Press, even as they benefited from the Minerva tradition'.[19] The connection between fiction and consumer culture is more than thematic, however. As the earlier chapters of this book have outlined, books too were published on an ever-growing scale at the turn of the nineteenth century, and McKendrick's 'irrestistible drug', novelty, seemed as addictive when it came to the printed word as to any other kind of consumable object. Reading material was as fashionable (or unfashionable) as anything else, and novels could both perpetuate this system by portraying it and partic-ipate *in* it, as objects to be acquired and displayed along with other status symbols.

In a certain sense, this booming consumer culture was ideal for novels: there were more of them than ever to buy or borrow, and their narrative function meant they could exploit or explode new fashions, keeping readers informed. As James Raven has argued, 'Print not only stimulated the fashion-booms of consumer products spreading across the nation ... but was itself used to sustain consumer interest in the literary product and to refashion the sales techniques of publishing and bookselling'.[20] The capitalist rhetoric of free choice, supply and demand, supported the increase in novels as long as there were readers to consume them, though, as the previous chapter suggests, the fickle tide of fashion also carried the constant threat of obsolescence. But novels also resist their associations with fashion. All the works examined in this chapter critique over-the-top consumer culture and unthinking adherence to trends, and their heroes and heroines are usually those who are able to resist the siren song of novel luxury. An extreme interest in fashion is equally contemptible whether it is displayed by a 'Miss Wantonley' or Kitty and Lydia Bennet. 'A Modern Antique' summarizes this viewpoint succinctly in *The English Exposé* (1814) when she refers to 'Fashion' as 'that most idiot-like of all princi-ples'.[21] However, there is a real ambiguity in how all these novels treat their objects: they are supposedly superfluous, base, and meant to be transcended; but they are still seductive, still deliberately appealing to the reader.[22] Raven points out that 'in defining the vulgar and condemning the purely fashionable, popular publishers faced an embarrassing dilemma' in that '[l]iterature itself was part of the fashion industry.'[23] This dilemma is passed along to the reader of novels that glamorize luxury goods: we may join with a narrator in mocking the spoilt wife who spends her husband's money on new dresses and redecorating fads, but we are likely no less susceptible to the allure of these objects.

Ultimately, novels use this productive tension to explore the problems of plenitude. Excess – having more than you need, or even more than you want – can be a luxury in itself, but it confounds other markers of value: scarcity, originality, costliness. Authors of popular novels, widely viewed as over-supplied, unoriginal, and cheaply available from the circulating library, certainly had little access to these particular status markers for their own work. Accordingly, they shift the register, insisting that skill, labour, and appropriate payment are primary ways to think about literary value and thus transforming their treatment of luxury goods into a way of defending their own work. Serena Dyer, Chloe Wigston Smith, and others have recently called attention to the wide variety of ways women participated in the creation of material objects as 'professional and amateur makers', work in which they consciously 'resist the temptation to set material literacy against reading practices' – reading and making, they argue, were often connected.[24] As Jennie Batchelor has shown, writing and 'making' of different kinds were often connected under the larger umbrella of women's work, and 'work is crucial to many female authors' self-construction'.[25] In the novels I examine here I explore the connection between reading, writing, and 'making' in a different way, using the popular novel's depiction of consumer objects as a means of exploring how these novels themselves functioned as made objects within the market. In refusing to wholly relinquish – and indeed, through investment with symbolic significance, by valorising – the material objects they depict, the novels of the early nineteenth century defend their own material presence, making visible the labour involved in producing and selling a newly purchased shiny pocket-watch or a crisp new book, and suggesting that recognition of this labour gives value to objects of *all* kinds, especially those otherwise perceived as superfluous, over-the-top, or even immoral.

Given the widespread denigration of the Minerva Press's novels in the popular press, and the criticisms that associated the press's readers with lower-class status, there is something ironic, even touching, about this particular narrative strategy, which paints even the least successful novel as the coveted equal of a luxurious gold locket or a finely handcrafted piece of lace. But there is also a certain logic to it: though criticized by moral arbiters or defenders of aesthetic standards, consumers wanted fine jewellery and new furniture – and, manifestly, they also wanted novels. The very voracious readers bemoaned by reviewers as tragically ignorant are recast, then, as fashionable shoppers. Blurring the boundaries between different kinds of status objects – a dress is a book is a coach – as these didactic tales tend to do, takes the focus off the individual attributes of each item, reminding readers instead of what they all have in common: they were all produced through labour, marketed to the public, and they all have a price.

The centrality of luxury and consumption to these novels means that complex ideas of space and time are often represented in their pages through depictions of commercial, status-marking objects.[26] Their characters, like the attendees of the Ranelagh entertainment described by the *European Magazine*, are marked by their golden watches and ornamental quizzing-glasses, and their streets are populated by shoppers, sellers, and craftspeople. The novels themselves are likewise located within this system of commerce, in the double role of objective social critics and implicated participants. As such, they speak directly to the vexed relationship between writing and other kinds of work.[27] Putting the focus on labour also allows novelists to grapple with the apparent conflict between originality and multiplicity at the heart of debates about the popular novel. The very idea of a mass market, of industrial production, elides the individual labourers who produce the goods – something made in a factory and sold in a shop (or printed in a printing press and circulated from a library) doesn't show its labour in uniqueness like a handcrafted piece of lace or a handwritten letter. These novels point out over and over again, however, that even the labour that goes into a unique, singular, handcrafted item is made invisible if the consumer refuses to pay for it. Upper-class characters who refuse to pay for their goods abound in these works, and they are invariably rebuked or punished by the turns of the plot. If we view these novels as primarily didactic, the downfall of these object-obsessed characters seems the plot's main purpose. I would suggest, however, that turning our attention to the other side of the equation – the unpaid-for objects themselves and the working people who provide them – allows us to see how these vignettes also function as a way to explore the question: How do we value the novel? One explanation for the curious persistence of glamorous status objects in texts that claim to abjure them lies in the corollary to this question: How do we value the *novelist* if we do not value the novels she writes? By insisting that neither object nor creator fall from sight, these novelists propose a system of valuation that, unlike the prevailing literary-critical mode, might value these novels as work, even if they aren't valued as literature.

Belinda's Indulgences

Maria Edgeworth's 1801 novel *Belinda* has often been read as an exploration of the outcomes of good – or bad – education for women, and certainly the novel, like so many other works around 1800, *is* highly concerned with this question. This chapter, however, approaches *Belinda* from a different angle: as a depiction of 'inventive luxury' and an investigation of the ways two discourses of fashion intersected in the early nineteenth century. The words 'fashion' and 'fashionable' are ubiquitous, appearing on nearly every page of the novel, sometimes multiple times; characters feel pressure to keep up with fashion's vagaries, and perhaps the most important way they do so is through the status provided by the right consumer goods. To read Edgeworth's novels for their engagement with fashion is, it should be said, to read against the grain: as a review of her *Tales of Fashionable Life* (1809 and 1812) put it, 'There is a moral purpose so evident in all the writings which this lady hath given to the world ... that the most indifferent observer cannot fail to derive benefit.'[28] And Edgeworth's 'moral purpose' in her work is manifestly to satirize fashion, not to endorse it.[29] Yet, as I will argue here, looking closely at the ways Edgeworth deals with 'fashion' in her texts – that is, the specific items that represent 'fashion' to her characters – suggests that Edgeworth is also using her critique of the fashionable world to consider the symbolic power of objects in fictional character development. Moreover, her work explores how the discourse of industrial luxury sets the register of value for labour in a way that applies to novels as well as fashionable shoes.

If the pages of *Belinda* are filled with mentions of fashion, so too are they replete with the items that determine whether one is in – or out – of fashion. Dresses, bracelets, hoop skirts, and diamonds casually drop into conversations, and the interpersonal dramas unfold against a backdrop of dropped combs, china vases, glass goldfish bowls, and newly painted carriages. When the young Belinda Portman comes to London to stay with the highly fashionable Lady Delacour, the advice her aunt gives her in her very first letter has to do with shopping and spending: 'To know how and when to lay out money, is highly commendable', she writes.[30] Lady Delacour certainly seems to live by this credo: 'The newspapers were full of lady Delacour's parties, and lady Delacour's dresses, and lady Delacour's bon mots: every thing, that her ladyship said, was repeated as witty; every thing, that her ladyship wore, was imitated as fashionable' (10). As Belinda soon discovers, however, Lady Delacour's profligate lifestyle is no route to happiness; indeed, her insistence on 'the new carriage [she has] bespoke' (12) and her preoccupation with superficial discussions of 'fashionable bracelets' and wigs (14) has clearly alienated her from her husband's affections. The romance plots that unfold (will Lady Delacour and her husband be reconciled? which of her wealthy suitors will Belinda choose?) all revolve around financial issues to some degree, and although readers are clearly supposed to take away the twin ideas that fashion is foolish and money isn't everything, the novel also contains a clear counter-plot, one considerably more ambivalent about the role of fashionable objects *and* the importance of money.

Most objects, on their own, have little symbolic power. In order to imbue them with the force that makes them irresistible, something else is needed; in *Belinda*, this force comes from two sources: fashion and advertising.[31] Although the two are of course closely related – fashionable items might be advertised, and a successful advertisement might create a fashion – in the novel they are treated as relatively separate. Fashion is propagated primarily by competition with other upper-class people; advertisement is employed by tradespeople or shopkeepers to persuade people to buy their wares. The culture of advertising is pervasive, and almost anything, even animals, can be thus promoted (161). Important plot points hinge on mentions of advertising; the revelation, for instance, that Belinda's suitor Clarence Hervey may have a secret mistress begins with a description of a possible ad. Just back from buying birdseed, Lady Delacour's maid Marriott relates that 'wrapped round it, as it were, [was] a printed handbill, as it might be, or advertisement, which I threw off, disregardingly, taking it for granted, it might have been some of those advertisements for lozenges or razor-straps, that meet one wherever one goes' (326). This 'advertisement' is a red herring – it's not a commercial ad at all – and the only narrative purpose in making Marriott mistake it for one is to remind us that the characters live in a world in which commercialism is so omnipresent as to be taken for granted.

It is unsurprising, then, that the literal advertisements like those described here bleed over into the novel's metaphorical language. Pronouncements like 'I used to see multitudes of silly girls, seemingly all cut out upon the same pattern' (8), suggest that mass production, and the problems with sameness it engenders, affect the world of people as much as the world of things. Women are repeatedly discussed as if they are luxury objects; two women wearing hoops are described as 'like two decanters in a bottle-coaster – with such magnificent diamond labels round their necks!' (74). And if they are objects, they are also advertisements, as with another character said to be 'Overdressed like a true city dame! [in] her bale of gold muslin, and conscious of her bulse of diamonds! "Worth, if I'm worth a farthing, five hundred thousand pounds Bank currency!" she says, or seems to say, whenever she comes into the room' (169). Chloe Wigston Smith, in an analysis of Frances Burney's later novels, points to the ways that consumer culture, and particularly shops and shopping, 'presented social and corporeal risks to women'; the space of the shop, she argues, 'made available instances of consumer agency and sociability, while trafficking in the perceived associations between commerce and promiscuity, shopping and circulation'.[32] *Belinda*'s scenes of shopping aren't primarily depicted in actual shops, but the novel depends nonetheless on the complicated relationship between buying, selling, and women's power and value (or lack thereof). For Belinda, the problems with this objectifying discourse come into sharp focus in the line used for the epigraph of this section, when she overhears Clarence Hervey and his friends gossiping about her: 'Belinda Portman, and her accomplishments, I'll swear, were as well advertised, as Packwood's razor strops' (25). The insult in this comment is multi-layered: a razor strop is of course an unpleasantly workaday thing to be compared with, common and cheap, neither rare nor beautiful. But to be advertised *at all* is also problematic, suggesting a grasping and shameless display that is both insufficiently aristocratic and insufficiently moral. That there is something inherently shameless (and thus shameful) about advertising is clear from Belinda's horrified response. This scene isn't isolated, either; the accusation, and the specific mention of razor strops, is raised twice more, as Clarence Hervey slowly backs away from his accusation, first reflecting that Belinda 'seems to have too much dignity to advertise herself' (73) and then begging Lady Delacour to tell Belinda he was mistaken in his comments: 'I am much concerned about that foolish razor-strop dialogue, which she overheard' (77).

Paradoxically, Hervey's decision that Belinda is not being advertised is an assertion of her value: 'I am convinced, that . . . she has dignity of mind, and simplicity of character' (77). Throughout the novel, renunciation of monetary gifts (objects that specifically measure the value of a life or relationship) is highlighted as a sign of good sense. Lady Delacour, who spends most of the work seeking new dresses, new carriages, and new pleasures, demonstrates emotional growth by acknowledging to Belinda that status isn't everything:

> As she pronounced the word 'coronet', she pointed to a coronet set in diamonds on her watch-case, which lay on the table. Then suddenly seizing the watch, she dashed it upon the marble hearth with all her force, 'Vile bauble!' cried she, 'must I lose my only friend for such a thing as you? Oh, Belinda! do not you see that a coronet cannot confer happiness?' (206–207)

And after she and her husband regain their marital happiness through Belinda's efforts, she no longer wishes him to express his feelings for her with the diamond ring she had previously coveted, declaring:

'My taste for diamonds now is o'er,
The sparkling baubles please no more.
If you wish to do me a kindness, I will tell you what I should like
much better than diamonds.' (291)

Yet for all this renunciation, this repeated claim that value lies in personal morality and interpersonal harmony alone, the novel relentlessly suggests that all people – indeed, all living things, including plants and animals – do have their price. Flowers, birds, and horses are bought and sold, sought and displayed both for pleasure and status. Indeed, it is in the slippage between the value of the object and the value of the being that I will suggest the novel's ultimate argument lies, the argument that would be picked up in the later Minerva Press novels discussed here. When Lady Delacour tells her husband she doesn't need the diamond ring, the favour she asks him for instead is monetary: she wants him to pay off the debt she owes to an old gardener, who raised a valuable and rare aloe plant that she bought from him for less than its worth, in order to outshine a fellow socialite at a gala through the aloe's display. The imbrication of the living plant into the system of prized but inanimate objects with which Lady Delacour and her friends vie for social status reinforces the idea that everything has a value.

But this scene has a further significance. The plant itself may have intrinsic value (or did at one time), but what Lady Delacour acknowledges in this scene is the previously invisible value of something else – the old gardener's labour. It's no accident that this scene takes place at a major turning point in Lady Delacour's character development. If the plot of *Belinda* is full of luxurious objects, it is similarly full of the workers who make, sell, or maintain them. The relationship between the wealthy and the 'trades-people' who support their tastes is laid out, in fact, in Belinda's aunt's initial letter, right alongside her advice on spending money. 'You will, of course, have credit with all her ladyship's trades-people, if you manage properly', she writes, concluding, 'people judge of what one can afford by what one actually spends' (9). The thrust of this advice is clear: fashionable spending often does *not* align with 'what one can afford'; hence, of course, the need for credit.

While most of the actual labour (the emotional labour of Lady Delacour's maid excepted) takes place behind the scenes, the novel's workers themselves are unexpectedly visible. By the third chapter, 'Mrs Franks, the milliner', has appeared to discuss 'the crape petticoat' of Lady

Delacour's 'birthnight dress' (34). Lady Delacour treats the milliner with the casual disregard that we soon find typifies her character, demanding, on her departure, 'Mrs Franks, let [Belinda's] dress, for Heaven's sake, be something that will make a fine paragraph. I give you four and twenty hours to think of it' (35). Her priorities, with gossip column placement superseding any thought of Mrs Franks's schedule or workload, are clear, but most telling is the narrator's aside that (after the characters discuss decorating the gown with golden flowers) 'lady Delacour, who was afraid that the milliner's imagination, now that it had once touched upon gold, might be led to the vulgar idea of *ready money*, suddenly broke up the conference' (35). Lady Delacour, in other words, owes Mrs Franks money, and does not wish to pay her. This ethical lapse is wholly consistent with Lady Delacour's other shortcomings at this stage of the novel, but it is also highly characteristic of the work's pervasive concern with advertising, labour, responsibility, and fair compensation.

Interactions with tradespeople fill the novel. Mrs Franks visits several times, crafting beautiful dresses for Lady Delacour and Belinda, and attempting to adhere to instructions like 'So Mrs Franks let this [Belinda's dress] be finished first, as fast as you can' (72). But, as in their first scene together, the question of payment is always present and always fraught. When Belinda decides not to spend the money to buy a 'birthnight' dress after all (after Lady Delacour has encumbered her with a debt she is anxious to repay), Belinda pays Mrs Franks to sell her dress to someone else – 'ten guineas made everything possible' (84). Explaining her failure to pay Clarence Hervey back the money she owes *him* for a new coach bought under false pretences, Lady Delacour declares that he 'could wait for his money better than a poor devil of a coachmaker, so I paid the coachmaker' (87). And when Lady Delacour falls out with her maid Marriott, she sends Belinda 'to pay you every thing that is due to you' (160). Even the quack who has been treating Lady Delacour's medical condition 'is yet to be paid and dismissed. That should have been done long ago, but I had not money both for him and Mrs Franks the milliner' (293–294). Lines of credit notwithstanding, no one's funds are unlimited, and any shortfall has consequences for those whose labour makes the novel's desirable lifestyles possible.

Lady Delacour uses the rhetoric of advertising to obliquely defend her frequent non-payment of tradespeople when, early in the novel, she explains her unhappy marriage to Belinda in terms of overwhelming commercial choice:

> any girl who is not used to have a parcel of admirers, would think it the easiest thing in the world to make her choice; but let her judge by what she feels when a dexterous mercer or linen-draper produces pretty thing after pretty thing – and this is so becoming, and this will wear for ever – as he swears; but then that's so fashionable – the novice stands in a charming perplexity, and after examining, and doubting, and tossing over half the goods in the shop, it's ten to one, when it begins to get late, the young lady, in a hurry, pitches upon the very ugliest and worst thing that she has seen. (36)

Too much choice is as bad as too little, this anecdote claims; there is another subtext too, suggesting that the mercer and the linen-draper, through over-zealous presentation of their goods, are in some way responsible for the girl's poor selection – and thus, perhaps, deserve the non-payment they are likely to receive. This unease with advertisement is also an unease with plenitude – the girl in this metaphor is overwhelmed with options, led to choose poorly because of her inability to appropriately assess 'pretty thing after pretty thing'. After Lady Delacour's reform, when she no longer views her marriage as a hasty and erroneous choice – and no longer rationalizes away her ill-treatment of her tradespeople – her attitudes towards excess change as well, and her shifting registers of value are reflected, in part, in the novel's attitude towards literature.

Edgeworth takes great pains to distinguish between literature and fashion throughout the novel: indeed, in its first pages, we learn that '[Belinda's] taste for literature declined in proportion to her intercourse with the fashionable world' (10), placing the two worlds (and value systems) in direct opposition. But, as in so many novels of this period, mentions of literary works of various kinds pepper the text, presuming the reader's familiarity with them. Lady Delacour and Clarence Hervey quote Shakespeare in their first scene together; Lady Delacour describes Hervey's travels as a 'Radcliffean tour'; and references to works including Sterne's *Sentimental Journey* and Fordyce's *Sermons* (271–272) drop into casual conversation. Indeed, even the wisest and most admirable characters seem to have quite a working familiarity with the literary fashions of the day. The exemplary Dr. X—, reformer of Clarence Hervey, praises Belinda's level-headedness specifically by contrasting her with a heroine of a popular novel: 'a romance called the Mysterious Boudoir, of nine volumes at least, might be written on this subject, if you would only condescend to act like almost all other heroines, that is to say, without common sense' (132–133).

Pointing out the contrast between the sensible Belinda and her counterparts in other novels is an endorsement of Belinda the character and

Belinda the novel. But it also suggests a way that fashions in the literary world echo those in the world of high society: both are tempting and easily recognizable, and both can lead to bad judgement by overwhelming potential adherents with choice or volume. 'Nine volumes at least' caricatures a novel about to overpower a reader with narrative (not to mention sheer size), just as a reference to 'all other heroines' hints at the countless characters sharing similar stereotypical traits. In the end, *Belinda* suggests that the way to navigate excess, whether in literature or in life, is not ignorance, haste, or impulse, nor through avoidance, but by a thoughtful and thorough appraisal of value.

Miss Byron's Object Lessons

Eight years after the publication of *Belinda*, Minerva Press author 'Miss Byron' published her second novel, *Hours of Affluence, and Days of Indigence* (1809).[33] The novel opens with a scene that encapsulates the entwined themes of time and fashion that bind together the disparate topics of the work: '"Harriet", said Lord Querulous, to his young and blooming wife, as he entered her boudoir, and presented a watch of brilliant external appearance to her, "I thought this bauble would please you."'[34] At a stroke, this opening vignette presents the main characters of the first two volumes, foregrounds the novel's preoccupation with material goods – giving them, keeping them, evaluating them – and renders the characters' obsession with time in a concrete form. This watch, to which the 'young and blooming' Harriet often refers as she rapidly grows less young and less blooming, represents the wealthy and fashion-obsessed world she has married into, and self-consciously ticks off the minutes, hours, and days of the novel's title, reminding both characters and readers that time is passing. The novel's overarching themes are represented through this material object. The pervasiveness of such items in novels like this one, and of the buying, selling, shopping, and making activities that surround them, reveals the same ambivalence towards luxury displayed in *Belinda*: explicitly, the novels tell us, these items shouldn't be valued, but their centrality to the plot suggests that rising above the world of objects is more easily said than done. And indeed, as I argue later in this chapter, the fashionable novel of the 1810s doesn't ultimately endorse a break with commercial culture. Instead, these works suggest that entanglement with systems of production and commerce is inevitable, whatever one's position – and that ensuring fair compensation and appreciation of labour is as important for novelists as it is for weavers or watchmakers.

Hours of Affluence, and Days of Indigence reflects a fashion in titling that reached its peak in the early nineteenth century. These twinned opposite titles, probably most familiar to many readers in the works *Pride and Prejudice* (1813) and *Sense and Sensibility* (1811), proliferated in the years around 1810, with works like *Virtue and Vice* (1806), *Riches and Poverty* (1808), and *Family Pride and Humble Merit* (1810),[35] and Byron herself took up the style again the following year, with *The Alderman and the Peer; or Ancient Castle and Modern Villa* (1809).[36] Byron's two works are particularly fascinating for this discussion of luxury objects because, unlike the other novels listed here, their double titles actually represent double *novels* – two separate stories in one. Volumes 1 and 2 have one plot, setting, and set of characters, and volumes 3 and 4 (in *Alderman and Peer*, which is only three volumes long, the break happens mid-volume 2) have an entirely different set, and a completely unrelated story,[37] with no overlap whatsoever between the two. In both novels, however, one continuity holds the two halves together: a focus on specific commercial objects, which serve as a metaphorical representation of each novel's main didactic theme. As their respective titles suggest, *Hours of Affluence, and Days of Indigence* is interested in time, while *The Alderman and the Peer* explores social class. In the former work, time's fleeting nature is marked, indeed, defined, by the physical objects that keep it: the watch that runs through the first two volumes is joined by a clock that chimes the hours, the 'Horse Guards' (a prominent London clock in the building of the same name), a second watch, and an hourglass that the two heroines of the second half often consult. The second novel is more concerned with visual markers of social status, most frequently represented in the section I analyse here by the quizzing-glass.

Early in *The Alderman and the Peer*, the author apostrophizes, 'Great Britain, mart of the world, proud treasurer of all that art and luxury requires' (I:14), and London, in particular, seems throughout the work to be little more than a massive 'mart'. Indeed, scholarship suggests that this was not a particularly exaggerated conceptualization; over the course of the eighteenth century, Londoners themselves, and, even more markedly, visitors from abroad, were stunned by the multitude of things to be bought and sold in London's crowded streets.[38] Maxine Berg has described how London, along with Great Britain's other industrial cities, became increasingly oriented around commerce and the purchase of goods: 'The streets were new public spaces with paving and shops. They provided a stage for inventing, buying, and displaying novelties.'[39] The *Alderman and the Peer* offers this perspective through the eyes of the character Conway

Burlington, who comes to London from his country home to stay with his fashionable and upper-class aunt and uncle, the Chesterfords. Lady Chesterford in particular represents all that Burlington has been taught to despise about the peerage; consumerist, snobbish, and socially narrow-minded, she buys all the newest goods merely for the purposes of display, and refuses to associate with people or neighbourhoods she views as unfashionable. When Burlington falls in love with the daughter of a wealthy alderman, Elverton – and Elverton's son becomes involved with Lady Chesterford – the classes and their attitudes towards commerce collide. When Lady Chesterton declares (just before buying a new, third, carriage), 'Pshaw! it is not what one has, but what others have, in these cases' (I:188), she sums up the views of the majority of the characters, who delight in consuming goods, and competitively displaying their purchases to prove that they have done so.

And what goods there are: along with the carriages and quizzing-glasses that consume Lady Chesterton's borrowed income, the pages are filled with clothing, books, baubles, swings, and wheelbarrows, designed for the pleasure of the upper classes. The author takes pains, however, to indicate that the pursuit of new goods is not purely an upper-class habit – this spending has changed daily life for people of all classes. Lord Chesterford, criticizing the desire to keep up with trends, remarks, 'Lord Barrymore's brass harness, or Mr. Anybody's plated trappings – Colonel Thornton's land-boat, or the *Brewer's* dog-basket – these are the toys of contention, for which the sons of honest men become jockies, coachmen, *bon vivants*, and, ultimately, villains, to attain' (I:48–49).

This too aligns with our historical understanding of changing consumer habits in this period. As Berg puts it, 'Britain's new luxuries [conveyed] modernity, refinement, and pleasure, not just among the elites, but among the middling classes' (4). Evident in this passage from *Alderman and Peer*, however, is scepticism about the poor and middling classes' new partici-pation in the luxury economy. Byron clearly expresses concern in this novel that consumer culture led many people, not merely the rich, to spend more than they could afford, or possibly repay.[40] Some accounts of the rise of consumer culture focus on the optimistic sides of this narrative of development – economic growth, rising standards of living – while moralizing critics of the period also saw the drawbacks – debt, wasteful luxury, consumers bankrupting themselves. While *Belinda* clearly falls into the latter category, it focuses primarily on the ethical problems of upper-class consumers; Miss Byron's works, on the other hand, reveal this concern as affecting a much larger swathe of society – coachmen as well as counts may be led to spend beyond their means. At the same time, her novels pull back from the fuller critique of consumerism that at least some of *Belinda*'s characters voice: buying and selling in these works are necessities, to be cautiously applauded, rather than castigated.

In the Byron novels I explore here, specific, commercially produced objects – quizzing-glass, pocket-watch, hour-glass, globe – become governing symbols, used to reveal the emotional state of the characters and uniting the novels' bipartite narratives with their themes. In this way, despite repeatedly condemning the characters' interest in fashion and dependence on purchased objects, the novels suggest the absolute centrality of industry to modern life. In *Hours of Affluence*, for instance, as soon as Harriet receives the watch from Querulous, it becomes a symbol of social difference and is intimately tied to her sufferings. Querulous upbraids her for not praising its luxuriousness sufficiently, but then, in a neat pivot, reproaches her for being *too* impressed by it, and thereby displaying her humble origins: 'do not express your opinion so rapturously ... for the world ... would immediately discover, that ornaments of such superior value were new to your family' (I:3). The watch remains her constant companion throughout the novel until, as her death approaches, its symbolic function becomes increasingly overt. '"Time wears, my father", said the resigned sufferer, referring to her "*watch*". She took the splendid bauble from her side.... "The retrospect", said she, "for one so young, is gloomy"' (II:225). The shortness of her life and the length of her suffering contrast with the costly splendour of the object; the lesson is heavy-handed but nonetheless ambiguous in its competing visions of speeding and slowing time. Harriet's demise too is related in terms of this persistent time-piece: 'The "*watch*" yet beat; but the heart of its lovely owner had ceased *for ever*' (II:227).

The Alderman and the Peer is a less melancholy work, but no less mediated by objects. If the gold pocket-watch encapsulates the main ideas of the first half of *Hours of Affluence*, the quizzing-glass – an ornamental, single-lensed vision aid – is central to *The Alderman*.[41] Quizzing-glasses surface in scene after scene. They serve a range of purposes, from the most simplistic (enabling clearer vision) to the socially laden (indicating class by imposing hierarchies of power on social interactions and providing a means of displaying wealth on one's person). The obvious metaphorical potential of the glasses is often played up in the satirical asides that cast doubt on the clear-seeing abilities of fashion's sillier members.

The novel's many scenes of social engagement focus on the markers of class and status and are also, with the aid of the ubiquitous quizzing-glasses, scenes of seeing. At one of the first events, Lady Chesterford is described as 'using her eye-glass, to help her brilliant hazel eyes' (I:23). When she sees the handsome Mr Elverton for the first time, the future entanglement between the two fashionables is presaged as an exchange of glass-assisted gazes: '"Who is that elegant young man?" continued her Ladyship, again using her glass.... Mr. Elverton, equally fashionable as her ladyship, was quizzing the party in every direction' (I:25). Even the soldiers loitering in the streets 'in amiable trios' are 'marshalling their quizzing-glasses' (I:47). Conway Burlington's entrance into society is heralded with the glitter of glasses: 'Half a dozen glasses were pointed to Mr. Burlington, as he entered the drawing-room. He was new, and it is the fashion to take a good look' (I:49). Later, Lady Fenton calls him '"divinely handsome", using her eye-glass, to take a correct observation' (I:97).

The intersection between quizzing-glass as luxury object and as moral viewpoint reaches its most interesting moment at the narrative climax of volume 1. The ongoing relationship between Henry Elverton and Lady Chesterford has progressed to a morally untenable point (at least in Burlington's view), and when the tensions reach their breaking point, it is the quizzing-glass that serves as their focus. 'Henry was quizzing the few remaining stragglers through her Ladyship's eye-glass. The familiarity was odious to Burlington; he looked sternly on his kinswoman' (I:156). The intimacy of this shared gaze offends Burlington's moral sense, as much for the joint participation in affected luxury as for the physical closeness implied by the sharing of the glass. The offence moves him to his only act of physical violence in the novel (even when he is challenged to a duel, he shoots in the air):

> 'It always appeared a superfluous, not to say ridiculous, appendage here', said Conway, passing the long chain over the head of her Ladyship; 'but since it has so far deceived your sight, as to blind your affections, to say nothing of duty, it must be defective'; and he crushed the glass beneath his foot, and calmly put the chain into his pocket. (I:157)

The significance of the glass does not end here, however, though it drops out of the story for thirty pages or so. When the topic comes up again, it serves to emphasize the glass's status as a luxury in a newly marked way. Now, more than simply an accessory carried by the wealthy, it is revealed as a valuable object to be purchased. After Burlington has drawn on his own funds to extricate his aunt from the worst of her financial difficulties without alerting his uncle, she seizes on her newly solvent status as an opportunity to replace her favourite status symbol. Directing them to Bond Street, she proceeds to shop with enthusiasm:

> A number of elegant baubles were presented for the decision of her Ladyship; after much silly admiration, and variety of opinion, she chose a very highly-ornamented glass and chain, paid a sum for it that actually made Conway shudder; and then, with a *sang froid* perfectly in character with her present flow of spirits, sat quizzing her *primitive* nephew, as she termed him. (I:189)

This scene of commercialism is a natural fit for a novel that dwells at length on the buying, selling, and production-related activities that constitute fashionable London in this period. But if the novel is tied to fashion, so too does 'fashion' encompass the novel. In *Hours of Affluence, Days of Indigence*, for instance, we see the consummate consumer Lauriston buying baubles – but also books. Encouraging his friend Taunton to peruse them, he declares, '"Read, Charles; give me an order – you know the extent of my library. What shall I send you?" The major smiled; the idea of a merchant's library was novel' (III:13). As this small scene suggests, social class is no less important to the world of books than the world of things, and ownership is always tied to social status.

Luxury, Labour, and the Invisible Novelist

In *Hours of Affluence and Days of Indigence* and *The Alderman and the Peer*, just as in *Belinda*, everything ties back to buying and selling. Objects, animals, and people all have a value, and all are enmeshed in a competitive and crowded economic system. Whereas Edgeworth's approach to this reality was to set her own work apart from that of competitors by calling *Belinda* 'A Moral Tale' rather than a novel, Miss Byron takes a different approach.[42] By describing key concepts in terms of objects, Byron continually reminds readers that fashion is dependent on much larger social and moral economy. Further, rather than condemning this economy, Miss Byron repeatedly shows her characters trying to enter into it; in so doing, she figures the work of literary production, and the written book, a saleable object, as all of a piece with the other endeavours that mark the efforts of the characters to participate in the fashionable system.[43] This observation aligns with Edward Copeland's argument that 'Minerva novelists wield a double-edged sword' when it comes to depictions of commerce and wealth: 'one side of the blade for promoting the dignity of commercial station, the other for exacting revenge on "upstart wealth"'.[44] Attending more directly to the connection between novel publication and other types of commercial activity, however, also allows us to see the importance of materiality to contemporary representations of fiction; attention to the novel's material qualities, moreover (how it is made, by whom produced, where sold) is one way that novelists like Byron underscore connections between their work and commerce at large.

While wealthy Lauriston enjoys buying books, in another section of *Hours of Affluence* Byron describes poor Emily Annesley struggling to *write* one to earn money: '[Emily] was alone, devoting the energies of a mind attenuated by sorrow to the most painful of all exertions – a literary attempt' (III:115).[45] That failing, she is reduced to selling a book already in the family's possession, which results in a different kind of pain:

> Emily looked around her – they possessed no valuables; at last, a folio, of trinsic [*sic*] worth, was fixed on as the only means; and in the evening, our trembling child of poverty, wrapped in a coat, that disguised her real appearance effectually, issued forth to offer the book for sale. The night was dark, and the shopkeepers were beginning to dismantle their windows. Emily perceived there was no time to lose, and she turned into a book-seller's in Parliament-street. (III:131–132)

The humiliation that ensues as the bookseller refuses to give her a fair price, taking advantage of her penury, exactly mirrors the difficulties she faces when, attempting to sell embroidery patterns instead, she is refused work by a successful tailor, who is suspicious of her because of her low asking price, which he deems 'a mere *bagatelle*', implying her amateur status (III:33). The obvious parallels are made even more explicit when we consider Emily's experience, walking through streets of lighted shop windows, some filled with elaborately displayed books, others, just as elaborate, offering gloves and dresses. The author suggests that watching the changing of the windows, the crowds that flow before them, and the characters who frequent them is much of London's primary occupation: 'And every body, that is the world of fashion, is gratified hourly by this exhibition' (III:161). Books, whether appearing as cultural signifiers, potential sources of revenue, or simply valuable objects, figure into the commercial network alongside all the other items being produced and sold. Rather than attempts to differentiate her novel from other novels – or, more generally, novels from other objects – Miss Byron uses her work to make connections between labour and its material fruits.[46]

As Byron repeatedly reminds the reader, the luxury items sported by the wealthy on the London streets do not spring from nowhere; indeed, she takes pains both to show the skill and work required to make these objects and to reprimand those who fail to acknowledge this fact. Fashionable patrons (like Lady Delacour) who fail to pay their bills are the especial bane of the novelist, and the moral failings of characters are handily summed up in litanies of the unpaid workers who supplied them with their finery: as Lady Chesterford's maid recites, 'There was the jeweller, and the fan and ribbon-man, and the green-grocer, and the flower-man, and the music-man, who as good as said you had cheated him' (I:12). This general criticism takes on a more personal aspect near the end of the first volume of *The Alderman and the Peer*, when Burlington encounters the unfortunate seamstress Mrs Shannon and her child, and learns that though it is her handiwork that has kept Lady Chesterton in fashionable veils, the lady has long since ceased to pay her. Burlington forces the issue, and the ensuing conversation with his aunt is wonderfully telling. Ingenuously complimenting her on her veil, he asks her from whence it came.

> 'Oh, you love to trace things to their source', said Lady Chesterford, with a smile half satirical. 'Well, now, my dear Burlington, in the first place, the silkworms spun the silk, it was bleached and woven into this delicate shade, which at once heightens and conceals our irresistible charms.'
>
> 'You have passed over the most interesting part of the process, the needle-work,' said Conway.
>
> 'Oh, that one can always get done in London', and a tinge, something like a blush, mixed in her artificial bloom. (I:184)

Lady Chesterford's desire to elide the handiwork that went into creating her veil stands in broadly for all the kinds of invisible labour that permit her day-to-day life to continue, and (again like Lady Delacour) it is an index of her personal moral reform, as the novel proceeds, that she begins to pay back all of her debts to the craftspeople who outfit her. Even the grammatical construction of this passage emphasizes the threat – the elision of labour – posed by her wilful blindness: while even the silkworms apparently spin with agency, as soon as human work enters the equation, the voice becomes passive ('it was bleached and woven') and the individuals involved in making and consuming vanish.

The author's outrage on behalf of all the Mrs Shannons of London is palpable, and becomes more comprehensible when we understand that her novel itself is being figured as one of the objects produced for, and consumed by, the often uncaring citizens of London. Novels are explicitly included in the descriptions of fashionable life; one character, the wealthy young Miss Bermuda, declares herself to have recently read the novel *The Wild Irish Girl* (1806), and Henry and Lady Chesterford are discovered together 'reading a popular and well-written production of modern date, in which a boy is made the lover of a married woman' (I:144). Even the upright Burlington, when accused of not being a novel-reader, denies it plainly: 'You mistake me, I assure you.... I look into most of the publications of the day' (I:146). Miss Byron clearly sees herself and her fellow novelists as catering to these ever-changing tastes; when she describes herself, for instance, as a 'female scribbler', with 'a duty incumbent on her to be as concise as possible' (I:83), she places herself among the other craftspeople depicted in her novels who labour to meet the expectations of their customers. The financial necessity that impels this constant production is clear in authorial asides like this one: 'for the creature who rhymes for a living, and he who publishes on *vellum* in calf, are as distinct as their emblems, *poverty* and *affluence*' (I:120). Minerva Press novels in this period, of course, were not published 'on vellum in calf', but rather on paper in inexpensive, library-ready boards, and if Miss Byron and her fellow authors wrote prose rather than poetry, they were no less 'rhyming for a living' than any struggling poet.[47]

Even *The Alderman and the Peer*'s description of different London spaces underscores the connection between class and commerce. Mr Burlington's introduction to London life is enumerated as a list of fashionable streets – he 'paraded Bond-street, St. James's, and Pall-Mall' (I:47) – that inversely mirror Lady Chesterford's recital of places she'd never consider visiting. Urged to attend an event at the Elverton's villa, she declares, 'Provoking creature! . . . you know I have a terror of these sort of people; and if one goes to their rural fetes, they will be so unconscionable, as to think we ought to call in Rood-lane, Leadenhall-street, or Finsbury-square' – in other words, the commercial districts where 'these sort of people' earn their money (I:5). Leadenhall Street, the location of the Minerva Press and its massive circulating library, seems a particularly pointed inclusion on this list.

What comes across clearly in *The Alderman and the Peer* is Miss Byron's conception of the novel as a commodity, produced by poorer (and usually female) people in 'undesirable' and scorned parts of the city, only to be consumed in great numbers, and without much appreciation, by the richer inhabitants of London. Indeed, though this critique is distinctly London-focused, there are clear hints that the problem as she sees it may be a global one: the appearance of characters like the nabob 'Mr. Java' and the heiress 'Miss Bermuda' hint that the power differential should be understood to extend on an imperial scale, an interpretation underscored by a scene where Miss Bermuda and the young Elverton ladies study a globe, yet another luxury object, laden with dual commercial and symbolic significance. Lady Chesterford's caustic singling out of Leadenhall Street – which housed the East India Company as well as the Minerva Press – makes it easy to see the novel's titular 'affluence' as a construct that depends on a world-wide network of unacknowledged labourers.

Obviously, Byron's novel is very critical of fashion and of unnecessary and unthinking spending on luxury goods. But it is important to note that, despite its claims to defend simplicity, it does not seem actually to be critical of either money or consumer culture. The wealthy, respectable, and responsible alderman is firmly defended throughout the novel, and the work also constitutes an impassioned plea on behalf of all the makers and sellers of the objects the characters consume. Luxury per se is not the problem the author decries, then – if there were no market for delicate embroidery or ornate quizzing-glasses, the novel's logic seems to run, then the skilled artisans who make them would be even poorer. It is failure to pay for goods received that is reprehensible: some people ought to be rich, apparently, as long as they don't gamble their money, spend over-frivolously, or fail to pay their craftspeople. Indeed, the story's happy resolution depends entirely on the enormous wealth of the alderman, which he uses (to the tune of 4,000 pounds) to extricate Lady Chesterford from her financial problems.[48] It is work, and perhaps especially women's work, that is often ignored, yet makes the fashionable world run.

Novel Commerce

The Enchantress (1801), which appeared anonymously from the Minerva Press in the year of *Belinda*'s publication, engages directly with the era's commercial language from the very first page. 'In the most fashionable newspapers in the month of March, 17—, appeared, for several successive days, the following advertisement', the novel's first lines read.[49] The language of the notice follows, making it clear that not all nineteenth-century characters were as averse as Belinda to advancing their love lives through advertisement: 'A MAN wants a wife. If any woman of sense, virtue, and spirit, will venture to answer this notice to Q——. at the ——— Coffee-house, ———-street, she shall have no reason to repent her condescension.'[50]

Indeed, as this chapter has suggested, more nineteenth-century novels follow *Belinda* the novel than Belinda the character in their attitudes toward commercial enterprise. Advertising and industry are, in many popular works, not something to be shunned or shamefully concealed, but are, rather, foregrounded as central components of modern life.[51] *The Enchantress* is far from the only novel to feature advertising or shopping on the first page or as central plot points, and in many works, like Miss Byron's, these shops are depicted not only as sites of recreational luxury but as sources of livelihood. Barbara Hofland's *A Father as He Should Be* (1815)[52] begins with a damsel in distress encountered, unglamorously, in a fishmonger's shop; Mrs Thomson's *The Pride of Ancestry* (1804)[53] follows a character who has risen through the ranks after a humble beginning as a shopkeeper; Miriam Malden's *Jessica Mandaville* (1804) too engages with the merchant class.[54] The first chapter opens, 'Frederic Mandaville, the youngest son of an ancient and honorable family . . . was, at the early age of twenty-two, taken as partner into the very respectable firm of Burnt, Fiefield, and Co. merchants in London';[55] volume three, similarly, begins, 'Mr. Figgins was an eminent retail grocer.'[56] The plot of Mary Meeke's *Conscience* (1814)[57] revolves around an apothecary's shop, and *Beauty and Ugliness* (1819), the second of two tales published by Elizabeth Bennet in a single four-volume collection, focuses on a small village shop from the first page, which begins

> In an obscure village . . . was a small dwelling, whose outward attractions were an awkward bow-window, in which was exhibited a variety of articles for sale . . . and under [the window] a long red board . . . on whose dingy surface was yet visible, in large white letters, "*Christopher Owen, Dealer in Tea, Sugar, and Tobacco;*" and in the lower window was seen, on a dirty piece of once-white paper, badly written "*A Good Price given for Rags.*"[58]

As these examples show, fictional depictions of industry are as frequently focused on its workaday manifestations as on the glittering shop-fronts of Pall Mall. These very different representations have a connection, however, and it is their emphasis on labour. Just as glamourous, bejewelled, and silk-clad socialites are revealed in works like *Belinda* and *The Alderman and Peer* to be made possible only by the (often unacknowledged) labour of countless tradespeople, so the *work* it takes to run a dusty shop or a busy apothecary reminds readers that the modern era's bounteous goods don't come into the world unmediated. And it is in this constant reminder of labour that the novel constantly relocates itself into the word of fashion and, more broadly, into the world of commerce.

When we consider the circumstances of book circulation in England in this period it is little surprise that books should be easily conceptualized along other kinds of consumer goods. As Richard Altick reminds us, in the eighteenth century, 'Except in London, Edinburgh and a few other towns, there were no shops devoted exclusively to books.'[59] And David Allan points out that 'the sale of books was frequently only one aspect, and not necessarily even the most visible or most lucrative part, of [booksellers'] retail enterprise'.[60] Books were often sold, then, alongside a variety of other goods, creating connections between books and other objects that may be invisible to today's reader, but were clearly taken for granted in literature of this period.[61] Allan offers a range of striking examples of the overlap between bookselling, library circulation, and the sale (and, indeed, production) of other items, noting that 'the sale of insurance and the supply of medicines' were two of 'the most common accompaniments' to book sales.[62] One proprietor 'us[ed] his circulating library catalogue to remind his customers that he also supplied "patent and public medicines", while others sold memorably-named remedies including "American Soothing Syrup" and "Barclay's Asthmatic Candy"'.[63] As Christopher Skelton-Foord argues, 'Circulating-library proprietors . . . were required above all to be adaptable, skilful and enterprising in what was a variable and also relatively new form of commercial business.'[64] Outlets for buying or borrowing books continued to increase over the course of the century, but scene after scene in early nineteenth-century novels – set both in and out of London – directly connect bookstores and circulating libraries with other kinds of shopping, reminding us that, while literary criticism understandably tends to analyse novels in isolation, for many eighteenth- and nineteenth-century readers acquiring a novel would have been more akin to a trip to the pharmacy than a rarefied intellectual experience. Books hold no special status in these accounts – for all the efforts of many Romantic authors to emphasize the intellectual and creative sides of their work, numerous novelists clearly make a point of de-emphasizing the distinction between books and other commercial products. Circulating libraries are but one of many sites of acquisition; books pass over counters right along with stockings and soap.

The distinctively titled *Says She to Her Neighbour, What?* (1812) includes the circulating library in a list of the local commercial establishments, remarking (of a rumour) that 'the only wonder in the business is, how such an immense story should move with the amazing celerity it did, from the blacksmith's to the baker's, the town-pump, and the manglehouse; thence to the hairdresser's, the milliner's, and the circulating-library'.[65] A description of a small town in *George the Third* (1807) runs through a similar list to demonstrate the village's lack of urbanity: it 'possessed neither magistrate, post-office, milliner's shop, nor circulating library'.[66] This description goes on to further blur the lines between library and other places of business:

The latter ingredient [a circulating library] in the composition of a town was, I allow, a disputed point . . . because Mrs. Strap, the barber's wife, did assert that she kept one; and notified the same to the public by the following inscription over the door . . . 'Abigail Strap Lic^d to sel sope candles forrin sperits, Tobacquo snuf; hard wear; oatmeale stockings; &c. buys olde rags; Childeren tote, and N. B. Boocks lent to read.' Now though I have been often in the shop, I never could discern any specimens of literature.[67]

These books – conceptualized as objects rather than 'literature' – are offered right alongside 'forrin sperits' and 'oatmeale stockings' for consumers to select.

Mrs Strap's vision of a shop-library is fully realized in other novels, where the line between book- and object-sellers vanishes altogether, reflecting the blurriness between these categories in many real establishments. In *Nobility Run Mad* (1802) the narrator recounts

Stepping into a circulating library one Saturday evening with a friend, where the mistress, as is generally the case every where but in London, dealt in a variety of articles in the perfumery and stationary line, as well as in Romances, Tales, and Novels, I was near expressing my wonder at the degeneracy of the age, upon finding her shop or literary repository absolutely crowded with females of every denomination waiting to have their marble covered, half bound love tales changed. My friend, who had drawn me there, merely wanted a cake of Windsor Soap.[68]

A novel or a bar of soap – both were mass-produced amenities of modern life, both available over the counter at this circulating library, both prone to problems of oversupply (historian Tammy C. Whitlock tells the story of a failed merchant who, when his bazaar went out of business in 1834, 'was left with over 1,000 packages of Windsor soap').[69] This narrator suggests that this blending of books and commerce happens 'every where but in London', and certainly it seems likely that, as Paul Keen argues, many 'provincial bookstores were forced by their more limited market to offer books as one of the many products they stocked'.[70] Yet as other contemporary novels show, works set in the metropolis often highlight the same connections between fashion and literature, shop and library. George Jones's *Supreme Bon Ton and Bon Ton by Profession* (1820) features characters who walk some of London's most famous shopping streets to visit the circulating library: 'As Inis had expressed a wish to read some of the modern publications, Mrs. Fletchingly, as they walked up Pall Mall, entered a large and handsome shop, in the front of which "Circulating Library" appeared in legible characters, to put down their names as subscribers.'[71] The use of 'shop' to describe this establishment mirrors the overlap a few pages later when the pair visit Bond Street, famous as a shopping district, but also as a centre of the book trade: 'Inis could not help expressing her wonder that a street so very inferior to many in London should become the focus of fashion.'[72] In other words, Bond Street is simultaneously the 'headquarters of the circulating libraries', as a later historian of Bond Street described it, and 'the focus of fashion'.[73] Shops and libraries, literature and fashion, are tied together at sites of consumption like these just as novels and other manufactured objects are portrayed as linked by their means of production.

Indeed, in the satirical *Asmodeus; or, The Devil in London* (1808), the titular devil escorts his innocent charge to Bond Street specifically to visit not one, but two circulating libraries. One, it is darkly hinted, serves a purpose other than reading, but the other is for book-lovers who wish to see and be seen: '"This" – pointing to a large Library, as they floated over Bond-street – "is the fashionable lounge for readers."'[74] The two proceed directly from this library to an auction house, where 'the frothy declamation of a fashionable auctioneer' serves to encourage the purchase of 'a glittering profusion of costly ornaments, unique gems, foreign china, pictures by the best masters, terra cotta models, bronzes, and a thousand objects'.[75] Books are as much a part of this shopping district as any other item.

Whether peering through a quizzing-glass, browsing the beautifully lit and richly stocked shop windows of London, or donning luxurious and fashionable garments, the characters in the early nineteenth century's popular novels participate whole-heartedly in the consumer revolution described by so many scholars of the period. They also, however, focus on the risks, dangers, and challenges inherent in this commercial system, exposing the ways that fashionable consumption exploits workers and ruins consumers even as they celebrate the fast pace of fashion itself. Somewhat ironically, many of the novels that focus most on unattainable luxuries – diamonds, coaches, gold-embroidered gowns – also focus the most on the unglamourous work, whether it be weaving or keeping a shop, needed to make these items available. In using their plots to bring attention to labour, the novelists of this period remind us of their *own* labour, often invisible and poorly compensated. The proliferation of items, whether 'marble-covered, half bound love tales' or 'costly objects', gives the modern consumer a proliferation of choices – a desirable, if dangerous, luxury, these novelists insist. To keep this plenitude, however, requires continued investment in the system of labour that produces it, or the work – and the value – will be lost. As Mary Meeke, one of the Minerva Press's best-selling authors, puts it in her preface to *Midnight Weddings* (1802): An author ought to 'consult the taste of her publisher. Indeed to secure their approbation is rather the general aim; for should you fail of meeting with a purchaser, that labour you hope will immortalize you is absolutely lost.'[76] A novel without a purchaser, rather like a thousand cakes of Windsor soap, will languish unsold; more importantly, though, the work of the author will remain invisible and unappreciated. Studying the ways popular fiction discusses fashion allows us to see how novels themselves used changing trends as a means of navigating their competitive marketplace. By tying novels to other kinds of goods available in newly swelling numbers, novelists recast wasteful or dangerous excess as consumer opportunity; by drawing attention to labour, they at once maintain a moral high ground and insist on the value and uniqueness of each work, however mass-produced it may be.

CHAPTER 6

Walter Scott's Industrial Antiques

The astonishing popularity and well-earned success of the class of fictions called *par excellence* 'the Scottish novels' ... are rare singularities in the history of our light literature. It is also worth remarking, how silently, and how rapidly, the whole brood of compositions which by courtesy had been suffered to usurp the name of novels, the countless, nameless equivocal things that crawled into languid, ephemeral life from the Minerva press and other equally respectable repositories of amusements, – have, since the dawning of the Waverley luminary, flitted away ... into the unsubstantial vapour which gave them birth. —Review of Walter Scott's *Walladmor* (1825)[1]

Although the Minerva Press produced books through the end of 1820 – and, absent its distinctive name, continued to do so into the 1830s – many readers have located its demise much earlier, in 1814, when Walter Scott's anonymously published novel *Waverley* hit the bookshops. Looking back on the fateful day from a decade or two later, onlookers like the one above, writing in the *Eclectic Review* in 1825, described the event as a fundamental change in the literary order. While the Minerva Press had previously dominated the market for popular novels ('light literature'), formulations like this imply, Scott now reigned supreme, with profound repercussions for the novel's quality and status. This narrative has survived the ups and downs of Scott's reputation to the present day, when Scott's importance to the history of the novel is once more widely acknowledged.[2] Though the Minerva's fall into relative obscurity over the intervening centuries means that it is now less frequently identified explicitly as the source of the fiction Scott superseded, the identification of *Waverley*'s publication as a significant turning point between bad and good, illegitimate and legitimate fictions, remains. This chapter resituates Scott within the literary marketplace of the 1810s and 1820s to show how the publication of *Waverley* might fruitfully be regarded not as a break with past fictions but as a continuation of popular trends.[3] Ina Ferris's influential research compellingly explores the

168

changing reputations of prominent woman authors including Radcliffe and
Frances Burney in light of Scott's new prominence; more recently, scholars
including Anne Stevens and Fiona Price have located Scott's work within a
longer tradition of the British historical novel.[4] In this chapter, I highlight a
third literary category against which Scott was continually and meaningfully
contrasted: the Minerva novel. Scott's novels can be better understood,
I argue here, when we see them as participants in the same overheated
market as the Minerva Press's novels, and addressing it in many similar
ways. His self-conscious historical fiction is, in this sense, a way of both
resisting that culture's critiques and potentially transforming its discourses
of abundance and scarcity into a mode of rehabilitation for the contemporary industrial novel.

In 1814, when Scott entered the ranks of popular British novelists, he
was moving into a field that had been shaped for nearly a quarter century
by the immensely popular and productive Minerva Press, as the previous
chapters of this book have shown. Scott too was an unprecedented
marketing phenomenon; his works had first-run printings of 10,000
copies within three years of *Waverley*, and his novels regularly ran into
more than three editions.[5] Recent work in book history often notes the
proximity of these two dominant groups of fictions, but tends to separate
them in a way that suggests that Scott's appearance immediately displaced
the Minerva novel. Anthony Mandal writes, for example, that '[i]n the
post-Scottian 1820s ... [Minerva] failed to sustain the dominance of
earlier years', later arguing that 'Scott's pivotal role in transfiguring this
market from the female circulating library to the male private library is
without question.'[6] William St Clair hints at a similar displacement when,
after describing the Minerva Press's immense circulating library business
in the 1790s and 1810s, he goes on to say, 'After 1814, what subscribers
to circulating libraries read most were Waverley novels.... The demand
for borrowing so outran supply that we hear of circulating libraries
splitting volumes in half, to make six volumes per title instead of three.'[7]
More recently, Megan Peiser has documented how Walter Scott's later
biographers perpetuated the divide between Scott's work and previous
novels (especially Minerva Press novels by women authors).[8] The arrival
of the 'Author of Waverley' forever changed the contours of the popular
novel market, certainly. But the Minerva Press – or, more precisely, what
it had come to represent – was by no means thoroughly vanquished by
Waverley's publication. Indeed, as I will argue here, the Minerva Press was
and remained a yardstick against which Scott's Waverley novels were
measured; and despite the Scottian turn of fiction after 1814, their

coexistence was extended, uneasy and complex. The Minerva novel was the 'other' over which, in these accounts, Scott's novels triumphed, and against which their excellencies were displayed. It was also, however, a persistent threat to the Waverley novel, in that the precise strategies that made Scott's fictions so popular also identified them with their reviled – but successful – predecessors. Ina Ferris persuasively argues that the harsh critiques of Scott made by later nineteenth- and early twentieth-century critics were 'made possible by the very terms in which the Author of Waverley was canonized by his first readers';[9] while she locates the beginning of this turn against Scott at the end of the 1830s, with an essay by Carlyle in the *London and Westminster Review*, my reading suggests that the terms of the critique were active much earlier, and indeed, were inherent in Scott's cultural position as a popular, commercially successful novelist from the very beginning.[10]

Scott's contemporaries often explicity compared and contrasted Scott's novels with the Minerva Press's fictions. Whether jealously defending Scott's oeuvre from Minerva Press associations or accusing Scott of taking a leaf from the Minerva's plot-book, nineteenth-century onlookers perceived these two bodies of works as interrelated in a way that has often been overlooked in scholarly accounts of Scott. Scott's defenders, as the accounts above suggest, marked the 1814 publication of *Waverley* as the death knell of Minerva, while his detractors habitually remarked upon the parallels between his numerous, voluminous novels and those produced in equally large quantities by the Press. (James Raven points to a different 1814 event, the first time an issue of the *Times* was printed by the newly invented steam-press, as a key turning point in literary history. While, as he reminds us, the transition to this more industrial mode of book publication was gradual, Scott's rhetorical references to the mass production enabled by this new technology ironically link his work all the more firmly to the old over-producer: the Minerva.)[11] In readings of Scott's early novels and his self-conscious paratexts, I show how he ties the supposed historical veracity of his fiction to its market value and suggests that his own 'rare' attention to unique historical details lends his novels a seriousness and a validity not found in other popular fiction – even as he openly acknowledges that his novels prioritize a plot-serving ideal of history over strict accuracy. Scott's works, like many of the Minerva novels analysed in the previous chapter, turn the reader's attention to the novel's material qualities, inviting consideration of books' physical presence and means of production. Rather than imagining them as leisure or luxury objects, however, Scott's novels explore (and satirically expose) an antiquarian system of valuation in which even the most uninteresting document becomes valuable to posterity as soon as it's rare. In so doing, they offer a unique defence of those 'innumerable' popular novels that, as his narrators point out, churn from the Author of Waverley's pen just as quickly as they had been rolling from the Minerva's in-house printing presses. As Scott and the Minerva Press authors who (despite the dire predictions of Scott's fans) continued to write alongside him well after 1814 suggest, prolificity may ultimately lead to literary prestige rather than undermine it.

Minerva's Readers, Scott's Novels

In the fall of 1832, a writer for the *Gentleman's Magazine* surveyed the state of nineteenth-century fiction in terms that emphasized the cyclical nature of literary fashion. The piece began with what seemed to be an encomium to Walter Scott: 'It is now about twenty years since the appearance of "Waverley" produced an absolute revolution in the manufacture of Novels.' As the writer's account continued, however, this unqualified praise for Scott's genius became rather more complicated.

> Previous to that period ... the Minerva-Press manufacturers could do little else than vamp up their old materials in apparently new forms.... Scarcely, however, had Sir Walter Scott begun to attract customers to his new concern, when rivals started up in every quarter ... insomuch that after the comparatively short period of twenty years we are brought back to the point from whence we started ... [T]he ground ... has been worked so unmercifully, that ... even Scott himself has been compelled to be content with a stray bit of ore, found in the very mine he was first to lay open.[12]

There is no doubt that Walter Scott's novels were astonishingly popular, and there are a number of ways in which the first assertion of the *Gentleman's Magazine* – that 'Waverley produced an absolute revolution in the manufacture of Novels' – might be said to be true. Clearly, other contemporaries endorsed this view, also expressed in the epigraph to this chapter; *Fraser's Magazine*, for example, just a few years later, asked: '[W]hat has been the effect of the manly and masterful novels of Sir Walter Scott? The whole trash [the novel genre], even with the Minerva press to boot, have perished from off the face of the earth, and the booksellers' counters.'[13] In this chapter, however, I focus on a different aspect of the analysis in the *Gentleman's Magazine*, one that has more to do with the ways that Scott, Scott's readers, and Scott's critics *didn't* break with the past. When the writer of this review needed something against which to contrast Scott, the innovative and groundbreaking novelist, and his work, he chose neither a washed-up writer of fiction nor an outmoded genre from the last century, but a press: the Minerva Press. This choice has to do with both the Press's general function as a shorthand for popular – but bad – fiction and its strong associations with literary overproduction, which would also come to characterize many discussions of Walter Scott.

From the first, the Minerva Press, and the popular, critically maligned circulating-library novels with which it was associated, offered Scott's champions a way to talk about the *Waverley* phenomenon, highlighting the new novels' strengths by emphasizing what kinds of fiction they were *not*. Scott's friend John Morritt – one of the very few to be officially let into the secret of the Author of Waverley's identity – wrote to him in July 1814, after reading the first volume,

> I can assure you it has already entertained us beyond belief. Your manner of narrating . . . cannot, I think, fail to strike anybody who knows what stile is, though amongst the gentle class of readers, who swallow every blue-backed book in a circulating library for the sake of the story, I should fear that half the knowledge of nature it contains and all the Humour would be thrown away.[14]

The mental image of thousands of circulating-library readers must have stayed with Morritt, for just a week later he was writing on the topic again. Urging Scott to acknowledge his authorship of the forthcoming novel, Morritt argued that 'your name would procure the readers who with[ou]t it are justly averse to opening a bluebacked book after the thousand & one annual abortions of the circulating library have terrified them at unknown authors'.[15] Scott resisted this argument, as we know, and it soon became evident that Morritt's fears were misplaced – everyone, it seemed, was reading the anonymous *Waverley*, circulating-library fiction aficionados and defenders of more serious literature alike.

Morritt was not, however, the only contemporary observer concerned about the relationship between the vast readership primed to read the Minerva's circulating-library novels and Scott's new breed of fiction. While Scott's friend suggested that the humour and knowledge of *Waverley* would fly straight over the heads of most novel-readers (thereby implying that they probably would read it, just not with full appreciation), other onlookers predicted that the revolution in novel-writing would result in a completely divided readership for novels: Scott's works were so different, and so superior, they suggested, that readers accustomed to the Minerva Press's style would not even find them appealing. *The Scourge* wrote in October of 1814 that *Waverley* 'will please the man of taste and of feeling, but will not be likely to obtain an extensive popularity among the readers of circulating libraries. It abounds too little with nonsense, affectation, and romance, to be acceptable to the masters and misses who command a market for the annual productions of the Minerva press.'[16]

As passages like this one suggest, even critiques that supposedly focused on the book's contents had a tendency to veer again and again into the question of the reader. What would a nation reared on Minerva Press fiction think of *Waverley*? As the book went into its second, third, and, within a year, its fifth edition, and was rapidly followed by its successors *Guy Mannering* (1815) and *The Antiquary* (1815), claims for the exclusivity of the *Waverley* franchise died away. However, this success was a double-edged sword: the more popular and prolific the author of *Waverley* became, the closer his novels edged to becoming indistinguishable from the very Minerva fictions against which they had been so dramatically contrasted. The Minerva Press and its authors had long been accused of flooding the market with wordy and derivative novels; Scott's incredible productivity as a novelist, and his perpetuation of a distinctive fictional genre under a recognizable authorial 'brand', soon opened him up to similar charges.

By the early 1820s these comparisons began to fly fast and thick. The Waverley novels had succeeded in gathering a vast readership, including, undoubtedly, very many readers who had been – or remained – fans of the Minerva Press's fiction. What had once seemed like an unlikely conjunction now came to sound increasingly suspicious: What if the Waverley novels, which continued to churn from the press at an alarming rate, were attracting so many readers not because of their differences from previous fictions, but because of their similarity to them?[17] Some critics who raised this possibility chose to use it as a further defence of the universal genius of Scott's fiction. The *Literary Speculum* claimed, in 1822, that '[s]uch a writer could scarcely fail becoming popular, even had his first effusions emanated from the Minerva Press, and been doomed to appeal for appreciation to ... the lady patronesses of that far famed emporium.'[18] In other words, even such bad readers as the fans of the Minerva Press were assumed to be couldn't help but appreciate the greatness of Scott.

Other readers, however, were straightforwardly harsh in their judgements and invoked the Minerva Press to show just how bad Scott's new fictions were. Complaining about the 'stiff, stilted language' in Scott's novels set in England, the *London Magazine* asked, '[W]hy those inversions of language, which had, we thought, gone out of vogue for ever with the Minerva Press breed of romances'?[19] *Kaleidoscope* quoted a complaint about *Redgauntlet* (1824): 'We are sadly disappointed with this novel.... Take away a few pages, and it would do no credit to the Minerva Press.'[20] The *Monthly Review* argued that *Woodstock* (1826) was wildly implausible and ridiculous, concluding, 'To the whole of this machinery we object.... It lengthens out the story unnecessarily, and forms a combination of that species of pseudo-horrors, which have been hitherto confined to the Minerva press.'[21] And the *Westminster Review* went one step further, sighing, '[T]he admirers of the Scotch novels will, for some space, read such performances ... without discovering that they are perusing books of the stamp and order of the "Minerva Press", and that the genius of the author of Waverley has degenerated to the ordinary slip-slop of the circulating library'.[22] William Hazlitt, later in Scott's career, thought much the same (though for him the gender and education level of readers did play a role): he declared, 'If put to the vote of all the milliners' girls in London, *Old Mortality*, or even the *Heart of Mid Lothian*, would not carry the day, (or, at least, not very triumphantly), over a common Minerva-press novel.'[23]

If Scott's novels were indeed now 'of the stamp and order' of the very Press whose degeneracies he was supposed to have rescued English readers from, critics needed somewhere to lay the blame, preferably somewhere that didn't render their own earlier praises of Scott's genius ridiculous. Fortunately, there were thousands of scapegoats ready to hand – those unreliable readers. Two reviews of Scott's novel *Woodstock*, both written in 1826, reassess Scott's oeuvre in ways that criticize Scott's authorship, but place the actual blame at the feet of an undiscriminating readership. *The London Magazine* wrote, 'Sir Walter Scott ... renovates (we believe that is the phrase) his old thread-bare stories, fresh binds them, and palm[s] them on us as new ... but so long as the public consent to be deceived and amused by it, we cannot blame the author for practising it.'[24] Scott's work is being critiqued here, certainly, but it is the 'public' who are portrayed as the impetus for his tired renovations. In the words of the *Westminster Review*, 'The mystery of sir Frederick Vernon, in Rob Roy, the intrigues of Donald Lean, in Waverley, the mistakes about identity in the Abbot, the machinations of Fenella in Peveril of the Peak, and the Glenallan story in the Antiquary, are all so many compliances with a taste perverted by the Minerva Press and similar manufactories of fiction.'[25] In these critiques we see one of the same rhetorical moves so frequently explored in the previous chapters of this book. If too many novels are proliferating, one must create a hierarchy to separate the good ones from the bad; one also might, however, achieve these aims by creating a hierarchy of *readers*, distinguishing those discerning few – whether they be the 'feeling and the thinking' souls imagined by Mary Hays in Chapter 2 or the cadre of reviewers who lamented their increasingly onerous reading responsibilities in Chapter 1 – from the ignorant many. In the 1780s and 1790s some observers talked about the novel fad as if it were temporary and might die away, if the gothic, or the Minerva Press, or the circulating library would only disappear. By the 1820s it must have been rather more clear to everyone that this state of affairs was permanent and that the number of novels was likely only to increase. It is in this sense that all the references to the Minerva Press in Scott's reviews are so understandable: the Minerva Press represented a literary era that critics hoped would soon pass away; when it did not, the Press could be blamed for a permanent corruption of readerly taste.

However, just as authors in previous chapters found ways to harness the energies of critical complaint, transforming weakness into rhetorical strength, so too Scott and many other popular novelists of the decade managed to turn this supposed horde of demanding and relentless readers into impetus for ever-increasing literary production. Drawing together already-developed threads of fictional discourse that reimagined the mass-produced novel in terms of time, originality, and physical presence, Scott and his peers reminded would-be critics that readers and judgments pass away, and literary standards can change.

Antiquarian Realisms

> I strolled onwards in that labyrinth of small dark rooms, or *crypts*, to speak our own antiquarian language, which form the extensive back-settlements of that celebrated publishing-house. Yet, as I proceeded from one obscure recess to another, filled, some of them with old volumes, some with such as ... I suspected to be the less saleable modern books of the concern, I could not help feeling a holy horror creep upon me.... Still, however, the irresistible impulse of an undefined curiosity drove me on through this succession of darksome chambers, till ... I at length reached a vaulted room, dedicated to secrecy and silence, and beheld ... the Author of Waverley! —Walter Scott, Preface to *The Fortunes of Nigel*[26]

Scott's distinctive blend of the prosaic and the fantastic is handily illustrated in this epigraph, taken from the preface to *Fortunes of Nigel*. The *Fortunes of Nigel* and *Peveril of the Peak*, both published in 1822, begin with mock letters exchanged between the 'Reverend Doctor Driasdust of York' and 'Captain Clutterbuck',[27] and hinge on the characters' metafictional interactions with 'the Author of Waverley'.[28] Here, Clutterbuck's introduction to the hidden sides of 'that celebrated publishing house', safely past the 'unrespective shop-lad[s]' who guard its outer reaches and witness to the back rooms in which the 'less saleable' volumes are piled away, is also very obviously characterized as an initiation into a realm of gothic secrets. Antiquarian language, as the narrator observes, opens the door to this version of modernity, in which shabby, mercantile back rooms are reinterpreted as '*crypts*' filled with 'old volumes', inspiring both 'holy horror' and 'irresistible ... curiosity'. Age and darkness create an air of mystery, sending Clutterbuck on a quest as quixotic as that of any gothic heroine. But what he finds when he finally penetrates the inner sanctum is neither a terrifying skeleton nor a terrified captive, but the (self-satisfied and well-fed) 'Author of Waverley'.[29] The seeming contradictions in this anecdote are highly characteristic of Scott's work overall: from his earliest novels, he plays on the tension between rote daily commerce and romantic adventure, the new and the old, and, most importantly, the common and the rare. For Scott, setting his novels apart from 'the countless, nameless equivocal things' (namely, other novels) with which he was competing depended on a strategy that valorised historical content and antiquarian objects – but ultimately revealed both to be commercially fuelled projections of readerly desire.

Deidre Lynch has observed that Scott's Northumbrian aristocrats and landholders fallen on hard times tend to mark both their longevity and their poverty with large libraries filled with mouldering, though still attractive, tomes.[30] Characters like Jonathan Oldbuck, Scott's eponymous Antiquary, dramatize and satirize the author's own bibliophilia, not only collecting rare volumes but consulting them for insight into the plot's various mysteries. But Scott's books are not, in the end, really antiquarian artifacts. Instead, as this section's epigraph suggests, Scott uses books within his novels as a go-between to bridge the world of gentlemanly historiography and knowledge and the working world of modern industrial publishing.[31] Emphasizing the materiality of books – books as created objects – allows him to use them to evoke 'respectable' models for book ownership (the gentleman-collector, the scholar-antiquarian). *Rob Roy* (1818) and *The Antiquary* (1816) treat these themes in two quite different ways; both books, however, set up contrasts between history and modernity, popularity and exclusivity, that centre on the physical presence and provenance of the texts that circulate within them. Books, especially old books, may initially appear to be detached from the spheres of commerce and contemporary trends, but Scott's works ultimately suggest that such a separation is merely illusory.

The Antiquary's Jonathan Oldbuck lives at home, against a backdrop of literary overload. His dusty apartment overwhelms the protagonist, Lovel, on his first visit, with its abundance of objects:

> One end was entirely occupied by book-shelves, greatly too limited in space for the number of volumes placed upon them, which were, therefore, drawn up in ranks of two or three files deep, while numberless others littered the floor and the tables, amid a chaos of maps, engravings, scraps of parchment, bundles of papers, pieces of old armour, swords, dirks, helmets, and Highland targets.[32]

Paper objects – volumes, scraps, pictures – mingle indiscriminately with other sorts of historical curiosities. The mixing exemplifies the ambiguous role of books in the text. Placing them cheek-by-jowl with other wildly varying ancient artifacts historicizes them, removing them from the world of commerce to locate them instead in the gentlemanly realm of historical pursuit. Unlike the fashionable novels of Chapter 4, these works of fiction do not inspire thoughts of Bond Street or bustling shops. That antiquarianism turns out to be the common interest of Oldbuck and the local aristocrat, Sir Arthur Wardour, emphasizes the manly, civilized nature of the pursuit; women, servants, and working-class people are excluded from this realm of discourse, as they are from Oldbuck's 'sanctum sanctorum' (31). Scott's incorporation of snippets of old songs, real historical figures, and descriptions of actual buildings might be said to serve a similar function in his novels, offering a legitimizing, masculinizing patina of 'truth' to the disrespected and feminized novel genre. Scholars including Ina Ferris and Mike Goode have explored the ways that Scott's use of history in his fictions was tied to gendered ideas about both novel-reading and history. Ferris, for instance, calls attention to *Waverley's* reception, noting that nineteenth-century reviewers emphasized the novel's '"variety" of mode, scene and characterization' as well as 'the "fact" and "accuracy" of its depiction of historical event and cultural life', in order to argue that it had 'restored to contemporary fiction something of the full, broad power of novelistic representation that the dominance of female writing and … reading [had] threatened'.[33] Goode sees Scott's historical narrative (and portrayals of historical pursuits within it) as crucially tied to developing ideas about historiography, masculinity, and sentiment, writing that *The Antiquary* 'demarcates the field of history's legitimacy as one whose borders men literally ought to feel: it … implies that the legitimacy of historical

pursuits depends upon the manliness of the sentimental and sexual education that those pursuits impart'.[34] Though differently oriented, both
lines of argument show the close ties between gender and Scott's historical
portrayals; they also, however, open the door for further consideration of
the ways that Scott uses history – or, to be more precise, representations of
historical ideas and artifacts – to explore his own position as a highly
prolific author in an already highly crowded market.

What is the connection between Scott's historical 'facts', the material
objects that represent 'history' to his readers and characters, and the
proliferation of novels that marks his contemporary reception? Just as
mixing books with swords and dirks can make them the objects of a
particular kind of antiquarian study, so the juxtaposition of literary and
historical objects in Oldbuck's study, I suggest, calls attention to books as
things. This in turn transforms them from simply vehicles of narrative or
history to material objects, produced by labour and circulated and preserved by human activity. The relationship between books and the content
of writing is, in other words, decoupled by Oldbuck's antiquarian enthu-
siasms. When we first meet the Antiquary, he is perusing a folio, but his
attention makes it clear that he is, at this stage, more interested in it as an
object than a text. Rather than reading it, he examines it, 'admiring its
height and condition, and ascertaining, by a minute and individual inspection of each leaf, that the volume was uninjured and entire from title-page
to colophon' (18). Oldbuck's folio bears little resemblance to a 'bluebacked' circulating library novel, but, as we will see, Scott uses the former
to imagine possible fates for the latter.

Rob Roy's setting is hardly less book-oriented than *The Antiquary*'s.
When the young narrator, Frank Osbaldistone, arrives at his uncle's home,
a central feature of this unwelcoming manse is the library: 'The library at
Osbaldistone Hall was a gloomy room, whose antique oaken shelves bent
beneath the weight of the ponderous folios so dear to the seventeenth
century, from which ... we have distilled matter for our quartos and
octavos, and which ... may, should our sons be yet more frivolous than
ourselves, be still farther reduced into duodecimos and pamphlets' (153).
The narrator's attention to the history of the volumes, outdated now in
format as well as function, is echoed by his concern with their physical
state. Like the Antiquary's stacks and piles, these folios exist in distinctly
concrete terms, and their sheer age is attested by the physical decay of the
room that surrounds them, adorned with 'tattered tapestry', 'worm-eaten
shelves', and 'rusty grate' (153). The fire-trap accumulation of texts in
scenes like these may (not accidentally) remind us of the world-ending

'general conflagration' of the world's 'infinite heaps' of books from this book's introduction.[35] Read alongside Scott's claims about contemporary fiction, however, these moments of antiquarian encounter become even more complex: they remind us of the authority potentially conferred by age and overwhelming physical presence, but also cast doubt on the value of such markers of legitimacy. Scott's teasing point, that imposing folios can convey material identical to that in cheaper and less impressive duodecimos (the staples of the circulating library), reminds us that literary judgement is often based on non-literary signifiers. Circulating library proprietors like Lane and Newman knew this as well as Scott did: Jonathan Hill notes that, even as Scott insisted that *Ivanhoe* be published in the more prestigious octavo format, publishers often misleadingly advertised duodecimo novels as octavos.[36] Surviving Minerva Press library catalogues list books by format, with the most impressive first; novels are subsumed under the heading 'Octavo &c.' even though the vast majority of them were published in the smaller duodecimo format.[37] As Scott also reminds us with his account of the Osbaldistone library, these signifiers of value are subject to changing norms – and thus changing value – over time.

In *The Antiquary* Scott plays explicitly with these hierarchies of literary value – and particularly with the relationship between value and volume. Oldbuck's criterion for collection, we learn, is simple: 'There was, it seemed, no peculiar distinction, however trifling or minute, which might not give value to a volume, providing the indispensable quality of scarcity, or rare occurrence, was attached to it' (36). The ideal of the rare is exactly what the prolificity of popular publishing so blatantly defies, with countless books that overburden the press, prolix authors that overflow the page, and multiple volumes that weigh down the shelves of the circulating library. But Oldbuck's fixation on 'rare occurrence' tends to be comically misguided, and Scott suggests that this may also be the case for critics of novels. When we consider the persistent emphasis on numerical scale – how could so *many* novels possibly be any good? – as a marker of the unworthiness of both Scott's novels and Minerva's, it becomes increasingly easy to read the *Antiquary* as a satire of scarcity or, more precisely, as a satire of the critical valorisation of rarity and uniqueness. We find, for instance, among Oldbuck's collection of rarities, 'the Dying Speech, Bloody Murder, or Wonderful Wonder of Wonders, in its primary tattered guise, as it was hawked through the streets' (37). The financial stakes inherent in the transformation from popular to historic are dramatized when we learn that this broadside was originally 'sold for the cheap and easy price of one penny, though now worth the weight of that penny in gold' (37). Given Oldbuck's tendency to overestimate the value of his finds, we may doubt this assessment, but even – especially – if we accept it at face value, it offers a fascinating reversal of an industrial model in which a relatively low-value item accrues wealth for its owner through being sold in large quantities. The cheap, common penny broadside, hardly valued or taken seriously in its own day, now becomes both expensive and respectable, the province of intellectualism and scholarship.

We might interpret this as an optimistically imagined trajectory for Scott's novels themselves, but the novel's repeated emphasis on economic value also takes the sheen of unbiased intellectual pursuit from Oldbuck's interests and from Scott's. If simple scarcity is enough to make something interesting and valuable, then not only are specifically literary judgements rendered superfluous, but works of literature are entirely reduced to their object status: content doesn't matter, but the physical container of it does. Scott, inundating the market with dozens of novels, with multiple editions and massive print runs, challenges the kinds of critiques his novels so often engendered: they are numerous (but may one day be rare); they are unoriginal (or, perhaps, simply concerned with historical accuracy); they are mass-produced, but also physical objects subject to age and changing circumstance.[38]

'The Importance of a Title-Page'

Complaining good-naturedly about a proposed title for his newest novel – *The Nunnery* – Walter Scott, writing to his Edinburgh publisher Archibald Constable in 1820, declared, 'The only objection I know to your proposal (if it be an objection) is, that there is neither Nun nor Nunnery mentioned in the affair from beginning to end.'[39] The book in question was eventually published as *The Abbot* (1820), perhaps suggesting that Scott's opposition was stauncher than his tone here suggests, but Scott's letter also took the question of naming in a different direction:

> I remember Harry Siddons wrote a novel, which he sold to Mr. Lane, of the Minerva Press, who, not liking the title, new-christened it The Mysterious Bridal, or some such name. 'Saar', as poor Harry used to say, 'there was neither mystery nor bridal in my poor book. So egad, Saar, the consequence was I took my own book out of a circulating library for some new reading to Mrs. Siddons, and never found it out till I was far in the first volume.'[40]

Beyond the obvious comedy of an author not recognizing his own work 'till [he] was far in the first volume', Scott's choice of this anecdote is also telling in terms of his conceptualization of his own novels. Severing title from content, as, we are told, William Lane did with Siddons, and as Constable plans to do with Scott, reveals the complex relationship between novel and product, fictional story and marketable commodity. Calling attention to a title as a deliberately selected part of the advertising process, rather than as a quality springing directly or deriving innately from the content of a novel, reminds us of the business processes involved in novel production, emphasizing the difference between the work of the novelist himself and the labour required to bring a novel to the public. To put this another way, Scott's story, by highlighting a marketing strategy rather than a literary approach, calls attention to the thing-ness of the novel as a produced and marketed object.[41] Just as Scott points to the physical qualities of historical books as potential markers of value, so he character-izes his own works as physical commodities, manufactured by the bale to satisfy consumer demand. The latter self-description satirizes the critical rancour turned against Scott in the 1820s, but it is also a continuation of the author's approach from the first. Mass commercialism may seem to be the reverse of rare antiquarianism, but in fact Scott's works treat them as two sides of the same coin, two different self-conceptualizations of the novel as an object of value in an era of mass production.

As Timothy Campbell has shown, Scott's descriptions of material objects from the past, in particular, fashions in clothing and accessories, are intrinsically commercial and modern, even as they fill his books with historical detail: in a discussion of *Kenilworth* (1821) Campbell argues that the 'fashions reveal how Scott had to produce the temporal coherence of this Elizabethan period through objects that, while marked as belonging to the age, nevertheless knowingly and anachronistically reflected the serial cycles of his own later days, when dress and other commodities could more genuinely be all-of-a-moment'.[42] Just as Scott's lavish descriptions of historical fashions are, as Campbell suggests, akin to 'modern showroom [s]', in their ahistorical accumulation of objects, so Scott's portrayals of ancient tomes and antiquarian objects are invariably inflected by the commercial publishing conditions of his own day.[43]

When we focus on Scott's own marketing strategies, the manifold comparisons to the Minerva Press discussed at the beginning of this chapter become clear. Though Scott's novels were frequently compared with Minerva's on the basis of their contents, another reason for their close and contentious relationship in the press was the likeness of the two branded entities – 'Author of Waverley' and 'Minerva' – as efficient, staggeringly productive business operations. As Scott's biographer John Sutherland pithily puts it, 'By 1810' (that is, even before the publication of

Waverley), 'Scott was the completest of authors. He could write his books, publish his books, print his books, sell his books and – if he were daring enough – review (or have friends review) his books in his journal.'[44] We may rightly be reminded here of William Lane's in-house printing presses, circulating-library business, and part-ownership of his own newspaper, *The Star and Evening Advertiser*, 'the first idea', of which, in Dorothy Blakey's words, 'was to provide a reliable medium of advertising for [the owners'] own products'.[45] The Minerva Press's black-letter imprint was no less recognizable than the 'Author of Waverley' imprimatur on a title page, and reviewers and advertisers alike cite these brands when discussing books associated with them.

Scott's incredibly prolific output – he wrote twenty-two novels, a total of seventy-one volumes – also tied him to the Minerva Press; relatively few authors of the period wrote very large numbers of books, and other than Scott, most of those were associated with the Minerva.[46] The *New Monthly Magazine* complained about Scott's publishing pace in precisely these terms in 1823, writing,

> We have already taken occasion to give vent to a slight movement of impatience at the overwhelming rapidity with which the anonymous author of the, so called, 'Scotch novels' proceeds in his literary career – a career, in which the panting reviewer toils after him in vain, and the most voracious glutton of circulating lore that ever 'gave his days and nights' to the Clarindas and Theodosias of the Minerva press, can hardly avoid being distanced.[47]

Scott's emphasis on his novels' historical veracity and importance may have been in part a way of distancing himself from these mercantile associations, but he also embraces this side of his novel-writing, explicitly exploring and justifying it. Returning specifically to the prefaces to *Peveril of the Peak* and *Fortunes of Nigel* introduced in the previous section, it is clear that Scott uses these introductions to emphasize the commercial and industrial aspects of modern authorship.[48]

For Captain Clutterbuck, in the preface to *Fortunes of Nigel*, getting to know the Author of Waverley is inseparable from getting to know the workings of the book-selling business. Finally coming face to face with him in the depths of Constable's Edinburgh publishing house, Clutterbuck rejoices, 'I no longer stand in the outer shop of our bibliopolists, bargaining for the objects of my curiosity with an unrespective shop-lad, hustled among boys who come to buy Corderies and copy-books, and servant girls cheapening a penny-worth of paper, but am cordially welcomed by the bibliopolist himself.'[49] Their ensuing discussion, which focuses on the reception of the Waverley novels, is wide-ranging, but while the Author's opinions are varied and sometimes contradictory, he continually returns to a single theme, one foreshadowed by Clutterbuck's description of Constable's premises: authorship is a business, and this business requires that the reading public (the customer) be provided with books (products) that meet their expectations, in sufficient quantities and at sufficiently frequent intervals. Clutterbuck repeatedly plays devil's advocate, voicing all the critical and aesthetic arguments that might be marshalled against such a position – authors must be original! authors should value the opinions of expert critics above those of lay readers! artists shouldn't be motivated by financial gain! – but the Author rebuts each one in turn. 'I care not who knows it – I write for the public amusement', he declares at one point.[50] Like the Minerva Press and its manifold sub-enterprises, the Author of Waverley is in the business of satisfying customers on as many fronts as possible, and he justifies his position by minimizing the content or uniqueness of any one of his books, while drawing attention to the physical book itself as precisely the kind of 'dependable commodity' that Emma Clery has argued the Minerva Press first provided.[51]

Scott's authorial self-effacement is, at some moments, surprisingly drastic. 'To the public, I stand pretty nearly in the relation of the postman who leaves a packet at the door of an individual', the Author declares.[52] Indeed, in the introduction to his 1825 *Tales of the Crusaders*, he discusses a mechanical solution to the continuing necessity of rapid publication, with one character suggesting that, 'at the expense of a little mechanism, some part of the labour of composition of these novels might be saved by the use of steam'.[53] This is a model of authorship in which the author can easily be assisted – or replaced – by a steam-powered machine.

If he refuses to glorify the individual genius of the Author, so too does he belie any romanticized notions of the intellectuality of the writing process: 'the works and passages in which I have succeeded, have uniformly been written with the greatest rapidity ... the parts in which I have come feebly off, were by much the more laboured', the Author claims. This argument for speedy composition may sound familiar, and indeed Scott immediately goes on to echo the rhetoric of the authors responding to *Cœlebs* in Chapter 4: 'Besides, I doubt the beneficial effect of too much delay, both on account of the author and the public. A man should strike while the iron is hot, and hoist sail while the wind is fair.'[54]

But whereas the *Cœlebs* authors primarily focused on the fickleness of changing literary fashions, Scott is more concrete in his imagined description of the benefits of successful publication. When Clutterbuck challenges his motives, demanding, 'Are you aware that an unworthy motive may be assigned for this rapid succession of publication? You will be supposed to work merely for the lucre of gain', the Author is unfazed.[55] If indeed he earns money with his pen, he says, then that is surely 'a voluntary tax', one that is 'extorted from no one, and paid ... by those only who can afford it'.[56] Moreover, he argues, "No man of sense, in any rank of life, is, or ought to be, above accepting ... a reasonable share of the capital which owes its very existence to his exertions.'[57] In staging this argument, Scott was clearly responding to contemporary critiques – a few years later, for instance, a reviewer in the *Dublin and London Magazine* attacked him using nearly identical terms: 'Sir Walter appears to be satiated with fame, and writes now, perhaps, only for profit.'[58] However, Scott also seems to be thinking aloud here about the relationship between literature and money. He points out that the wealth he generates through his fictional endeavours does not enrich him alone, but rather spreads throughout the publishing business. Everyone from 'honest Duncan the paper manufac-turer, to the most snivelling of printer's devils' shares his earnings, the Author complains, concluding, 'I think our modern Athens much obliged to me for having established such an extensive manufacture.'[59] Clutterbuck quellingly replies, 'This would be called the language of a calico-manufacturer', but the Author responds with an even more frank defence of literature-as-business:

> I do say it, in spite of Adam Smith and his followers, that a successful author is a productive labourer, and that his works constitute as effectual a part of the public wealth, as that which is created by any other manufacture. If a new commodity ... be the result of the operation, why are the author's bales of books to be esteemed a less profitable part of the public stock than the goods of any other manufacturer?[60]

Just as the references to the author's labour echo the rhetoric used by Chapter 5's 'fashionable' novelists, so the terminology used here – 'paper', 'printer', 'bales', 'manufacture' – evokes not only the publishing business but the physical qualities of the books themselves thus produced. (In the preface to the *Tales of the Crusaders*, Scott refers to the Waverley novels as an 'immense mass of various matter', pointing to material volume, iron-ically, as evidence against his own authorship of the works: 'It is indeed to me a mystery how the sharp-sighted could suppose so huge a mass ... amounting to scores of volumes could be the work of one hand.')[61] And it is in this very quality, the physical presence of a book that might endure through time, that we see Scott's industrial-antiquarian rhetoric come full circle. Whereas Clutterbuck suggests (echoing all the real-life reviewers discussed earlier in the chapter) that the vast scale of Scott's output might have an inverse relationship to the quality of his works, the Author counters that his continuing output is actually the measure of his works' excellence: publishers and booksellers won't support an author who won't make them money, and books will only make money if they are worthy. Thus the Author dismisses all the contemporary protests about poor-quality writers flooding the market: 'as for writers, who are possessed of no merit at all, unless indeed they publish their works at their own expense ... their power of annoying the public will be soon limited by the difficulty of finding undertaking booksellers'.[62] The deciding power does not, in the end, lie with the publishers, however: 'You speak as if the public were obliged to read books merely because they are printed – your friends the booksellers would thank you to make the proposition good. The most serious grievance attending such inundations as you talk of is, that they make rags dear.'[63]

Scott takes the critical language of excess – particularly the hyperbolic prospect of literary inundation – and turns it on its head, not only reminding the reader that a book is, in the end, merely another iteration of the humble rag, but suggesting that popularity is not only a marker of value in and of itself – 'It is always something to have engaged the public attention for seven years' – but that current tastes, however dubious, also may bode well for the staying power of a work.[64] Asked explicitly by Clutterbuck, 'You are willing, then, to barter future reputation for present popularity?,' the author denies that the two kinds of success are mutually exclusive.[65] Indeed, his argument to the contrary is quite striking: 'It is some consolation to reflect, that the best authors in all countries have been the most voluminous; and it has often happened, that those who have been best received in their own time, have also continued to be acceptable to posterity.'[66]

This is quite a new argument in favour of excess: the more one writes, by this logic (and the more popular one's works are), the greater the chances that one's reputation will survive for posterity. And Scott doesn't stop here, perhaps considering that some onlookers might deny that his own recent works were all that well 'received in their own time'. Even *un*popular works may benefit from 'the alarming fertility of the press', he claims:

> The multiplicity of publications does the present age no harm, and may greatly advantage that which is to succeed us.. ... The complaints in the time of Elizabeth and James, of the alarming fertility of the press, were as loud as they are at present – yet look at the shore over which the inundation of that

age flowed, and it resembles now the Rich Strand of the Faery Queen.... Believe me, that even in the most neglected works of the present age, the next may discover treasures.[67]

Recasting the 'inundation' of his own age as merely equivalent to that of the past, Scott not only resists contemporary critiques that singled out the novel as a particularly pernicious and prolific new genre, but suggests that simply having *enough* works published may be what allows some few of them to persist into the next age. *The Antiquary*'s Elizabethan handbill, once worthless but now valuable because it is surviving and rare, comes into view again here, reminding us that, for Scott, not only is literary value in the eye of the beholder, but the odds of a book achieving such value depend directly on its conditions of production, reception, and physical duration.

Scott's deliberate paratextual framing and reframing of his novels did not end at their first publication. Most notably, the Magnum Opus editions, published monthly from 1829, with illustrated plates, new introductions, and editorial notes, offered the author an unusual opportunity to explain, with the benefit of hindsight, his goals and aims for his novels. While this chapter focuses primarily on the 1810s and early 1820s, when Scott's novels were most actively engaged with and competing against other works of contemporary fiction, rather than their later life, his Advertisement and General Preface to the Magnum Opus editions clearly reveal how, even in retrospect, the relationship between volume and literary influence shaped his thinking. He begins the Advertisement by reminding the reader not of the contents or the quality of the novels he is about to reissue, but about how numerous (and possibly lengthy) they were: 'It has been the occasional occupation of the Author of Waverley', he writes, 'to revise and correct the voluminous series of Novels which pass under that name.'[68] As he moves into the General Preface, Scott relates his own history as a reader, emphasizing how his experiences were shaped by the sheer volume of books he encountered. He identifies a primary site of his literary education as 'a circulating library in Edinburgh', which was 'peculiarly rich in works of fiction', writing, 'I was plunged into this great ocean of reading without compass or pilot.'[69] The overwhelming (if exhilarating) numbers of books in his past seem to presage the 'voluminous' books he has produced in the present, and the sheer numbers of both, like so many other references to excess, are described in ways designed to evoke emotion.

Describing his younger self as 'a glutton of books', Scott seems to channel the critiques of unthinking, devouring readers that have echoed through the chapters of this study; crucially, however, he refuses any wholesale condemnation of his reading habits, however 'vague and wild' they may have been.[70] Ferris reminds us that '[r]eading as ingestion ... function[s] as [one of] two key motifs of the trope of *female* reading' – it is striking, then, how Scott co-opts this metaphor to describe his own development as a reader, at once making light of his youthful predilections and recasting the 'gluttonous' reader as omnivorous, intellectually curious, even admirable.[71] Thus Scott emphasizes how 'satiety' with a diet of only fiction ultimately led him to read broadly and deeply, and though he argues that his tastes eventually turned to works with a greater degree of 'truth' (e.g., histories and memoirs) he seems to draw a direct line between his early passion for fiction and his abilities as a 'future romance writer', albeit one with an eye for 'a genuine ancient fragment'.[72] Recounting the long delay between his first attempted 'work of imagination in prose' and the eventual completion and publication of *Waverley*, Scott returns to oceanic metaphors to emphasize how overwhelming and unstoppable his own works eventually became (directly echoing the 'great ocean of reading' anecdote from earlier). '[T]hose who complain, not unreasonably, of the profusion of the Tales that have followed Waverley', he writes, 'may bless their stars at the narrow escape they have made, by the commencement of the inundation ... being postponed.'[73] 'Inundation', 'conflagration': we should be once again reminded here of the apocalyptic metaphors used to describe fictional proliferation, which emphasize the sheer power and inexorable expansive growth of books en masse. Scott's decision to repeatedly describe his own oeuvre in these terms is tongue-in-cheek, a way of rendering common critiques of his work harmlessly comic. But he also, quite clearly, is using these numeric assertions as a means of exerting authority, both his own as an author and his work's, in terms of lasting impact. By repeatedly reminding readers of the pleasure and value of objects preserved from the past, Scott recasts the exuberant materiality of his own proliferating texts: no longer simply industrial productions, these works, by virtue of their popularity, wide distribution, and the sheer space they take up, are poised to persist into the future as antiquarian artifacts or rediscovered treasures in their own right.

Aging the Industrial Novel

If Scott's critics compared him, favourably or unfavourably, to other contemporary novelists, so too did other contemporary novelists compare themselves to Scott. Especially in the first few years after *Waverley*, authors found it both necessary and expedient to reference the 'Author of Waverley' to explain the aims and genre of their own novels. While many cite Scott as an inspiration, at least a few writers made a point of staking their own claim to his (historical, Scottish) territory. Minerva author Mary Johnston, for instance, began her novel *The Lairds of Glenfern; or, Highlanders of the Nineteenth Century* (1816) with a defensive preface, in which she worried that 'sharp-sighted critics' might call her book '"a puerile attempt at imitating those exquisite delineations of Scottish scenery and manners which have lately appeared, under the titles of *Waverly, Discipline, &c.*" The writer trusts she has a plea to avert such a verdict. The whole of the first, and great part of the second volume, have been written nearly four years.'[74] Johnston's mention of Mary Brunton's *Discipline* (1814) is telling, reminding us as it does of another author who had an even stronger claim to the Highland scenes so strongly associated with Scott. When *Discipline* came out, only a little after *Waverley*, Brunton felt the need to declare her own originality at some length:

> The author cannot help expressing a strong feeling of regret, that the close of her story may, from its subject, seem to provoke a comparison which it is most truly her interest to avoid.... Yet she owes it to herself to state, that the story of Discipline has been planned for years; [and] that the whole held very nearly its present form before she knew the subject of Waverley.[75]

Brunton takes a self-consciously humble stance through much of the preface, but her desire to defend her own work comes through clearly. Indeed, in the posthumously published 'Memoir of Her Life' that accompanied her novel *Emmeline*, Brunton's husband outlined her anxiety at discovering that Scott had chosen such similar material, suggesting that 'she resolved at first to cancel the Highland part of her own story altogether' upon learning of it, but was ultimately convinced to retain it.[76] The memoir also includes a letter from Brunton, which lamented that *Discipline* 'is very unfortunate in coming after Waverley ... What a competitor for poor little me! The worst of all is, that I have ventured unconsciously on Waverley's own ground, by carrying my heroine to the Highlands!'[77]

Given Scott's fame, and the unfortunate timing of their respective works' releases, it is unsurprising that Brunton was anxious to think of how her own work would fare in comparison. As Johnston's matter-of-fact mention of *Discipline* alongside *Waverley* suggests, however, not only did Brunton's work enjoy a fair amount of success, but at least some onlookers viewed both her work and Scott's as early entries in a new literary fashion.

While a focus on Scotland is often the overt basis for such comparisons, many of Scott's fellow novelists also shared something else with the 'Author of Waverley'. Considering how Scott's contemporary fellow novelists talk about him and their own work reveals a focus not only on history but on a shared rhetoric of scarcity and literary value.

The anonymously authored *Forman, a Tale* (1819) follows in the footsteps of both Brunton and Johnston by positioning itself immediately in relation to Scott. The author includes both a cheeky dedication, which declares the novel to be 'humbly dedicated' but 'without permission indeed' to the better-known author, and a preface. In the latter, the author admits 'that he has endeavoured to connect fiction with historical fact, in a mode somewhat resembling a late style of delightful and most deservedly popular romances'.[78] And indeed the very first lines of the preface stake out this territory; it begins 'The original hint for the following story may be found in the proceedings upon the Widow Turner's case, for the murder of Sir Thomas Overbury, 1 State Trials, 3d Edition, p. 339.'[79] The pedantic, footnote-like specificity of the reference directly echoes Scott's own claims for historical veracity, figuring the novel as a repository of otherwise-lost or inaccessible data. *Forman*'s author doesn't try to compete with Scott on every level; he admits that while Scott's novels are 'not more admired for accuracy, as to the habits of the era they describe, than for using the very language of those periods', in his own novel 'the language of that day has not been even attempted'.[80] But while certain grounds of comparison may not favour his own work, he is unhesitating in claiming one kind of authority granted by historical topics: hypothetically asking 'why so distant a period has been chosen at all', he replies, 'For the sake of that general conviction of the reality of the necromantic art, which prevailed in James the First's time.'[81] The cultural differences between that age and the current one not only provide inspiring source material but, crucially, are said to validate the supernatural genre in which the author wishes to write.

It is clear that historical accuracy (of a certain kind) is being used to defend genre when the author indignantly declares that *Forman* will *not* contain 'mysterious circumstances to be afterwards explained away by passages in walls, pictures, skeletons, &c. &c.' but rather 'real, downright sorcery, fiends, and spectres'. This comparison explicitly references the clichéd critiques of gothic authors like Radcliffe, and then distances the present work from them. *Forman*, such a preface declares, is not a gothic novel, subject to all the mockery that identification might entail, but rather a *historical* novel, respectable, accurate and 'pretty fairly natural' (except, of course, for the 'no few impossibilities' mentioned in passing) (viii). This is Scott's have-it-both-ways advertising brought to a high level: readers want what they want, and it is the author's business to provide it. But the secret passages and mouldering books of the gothic may have a longer lifespan (may, indeed, sell better) if they are recast as historical relics, rare and valuable.

That one's work doesn't have to be specifically historical in nature to explore such dichotomies is clear if we return to Brunton, who includes a scene in which her heroine, given a rare compliment, replies, 'Thank you Sir; I shall put that into my memorandum-book, and preserve it like a Queen Anne's farthing, not much worth in itself, but precious, because she never made but one.'[82] This reference to value deriving from rarity obviously aligns with some of the claims Scott would develop in the *Antiquary*, and the comparison is still more clear when we realize that Brunton is referring to a long-lived early nineteenth-century rumour, which (falsely) persuaded countless would-be collectors that Queen Anne farthings were extremely rare and valuable.[83] Another author, a few years later, made the comparison between the two scenarios even more explicit, writing satirically, 'Another Jonathan Oldbuck, or Oldenbuck, buys a Queen Anne's farthing, and gives 300*l.* for this rarity, because the die was broken at the third piece, and yet there have been duplicates of it seen, from the Antiquarian Society of Birmingham! To another, the *old rusty carving knife and brass spurs* of Sir W. Wallace, are invaluable.'[84] Value is only ever in the eye of the beholder, such anecdotes declare, and indeed Brunton suggests as much when it comes to the novel, declaring mournfully in the Preface to *Discipline* that (despite the problems she sees with the novel as a genre) '[t]he appetite for fiction is indeed universal.'[85] Like Scott, authors like these justify their work through the idea of reader demand, but *also* point out the fallacy of assuming that such demand always represents an objective assessment of value.

In another of the letters published in the Memoir accompanying *Emmeline*, Brunton specifically ties these 'appetites' to trends in fiction, remarking satirically, 'As for the *Highlands*, you know, they are quite the rage. All the novel-reading Misses have seen and admired them in the verdure and sunshine of July.'[86] Whether this 'rage' is founded in accuracy or facts of any kind is highly doubtful, however (despite the occasional claims of Scott's fiction to historical precision). Brunton continues, 'Now, what novel-reading Miss ever had common sense enough to doubt, that what is pleasing to the eye, should be desirable in possession; or that what charms for an evening, should delight for ever?'[87] Just as a Queen Anne farthing (or an Elizabethan broadside) derives its worth only from the collector's belief in its rarity, so even misguided interest in a literary topic can result in its success. As Brunton remarks in another letter, 'In authorship luck does a great deal. Self-Control [her first novel] was more successful than many a better book has been. This may be less successful, without being less deserving.'[88] Dissociating aesthetic judgement from market success, or value from worth, here serves as a consolation. But as Scott's prefaces suggest, it is a consolation that can work in two ways: if a book is unappreciated, it may be a failure of present taste, and future days may value it more. But, simultaneously, if one's work finds contemporary favour, it may be deemed a success: What, after all, is a better indicator of value than consumer desire?

In Benjamin Frere's 1821 novel *Rank and Fashion! or The Mazes of Life,* the author begins with a lengthy prefatory dedication to the 'Author of Waverly', in which he explores some of these same ideas.[89] A satirical acknowledgement of Scott's marketplace dominance, this letter is also a fascinating recasting of Scott's own authorial rhetoric. 'When you, as a Novel Writer, became a candidate for literary fame', the dedication begins, 'I rejoiced in the vast encrease of entertainment, derivable from your productions.'[90] The 'vast encrease' obviously hints at Scott's prolific habits, and 'productions' prefigures Scott's industrial metaphors in *The Fortunes of Nigel.* Frere expands this analogy in the next line, declaring, 'But having, since, set up in the same line, I most cordially wish that your Manuscripts had undergone a sort of *Ostracism* ... and that the *casting shell* had devolved on me.'[91] Imagining literary works as cast objects, the predictably uniform results of craft, rather than art, might seem simply derogatory, but Frere's expressed wish to inherit Scott's former casting-shell suggests a more complex relationship, in which the power to produce *numerous* works, works in alignment with a pre-existing public taste, represents the ultimate in literary success.[92] Indeed, Frere elaborates on the power of mass production to reshape taste and the market itself on the following page, writing, 'the fecundity of the produce, together with its goodness, has made the Public so very fastidious, that the mental provender of other Growers find but few Consumers; and Publishers aver, in the language of the Trade, that no other Novelties will now go *down*, maugre all their attempts at puffing them *up*'.[93] Agricultural production has a slightly different valence than industrial casting, but the upshot of both comparisons is the same: sheer volume (assuming some lower bound of sufficient quality) can steer the direction of the market. Most striking, perhaps, is Frere's closing salvo. After a tongue-in-cheek declaration that he is 'concealing the smart of envy under the affectation of praise', he dedicates his book to Scott, concluding,

> Having thus publicly declared myself the ardent Admirer of your literary talents, (would to Heaven they had been piled upon the shelves of the Alexandrian Library) I beg the honor of subscribing myself, with more politeness than truth,
>   Sir,
> Your very humble,
>   very obsequious,
>   devoted Servant,
>   B. Frere.[94]

This is beating Scott at his own game: rather than figuring books as rare and valuable remainders of a lost historical culture, Frere flips the focus to the attrition of antiquity. Scott's books, however numerous, would have been lost were they indeed in that legendarily lost library – and, the comparison implies, this still may be their fate. Surviving for posterity is an uncertain venture, subject to forces that have nothing to do with merit.

Frere's hopes aside, such a disappearance seems unlikely to happen anytime soon when we see how frequently Scott, his characters, and his authorial strategies pop up in other contemporary works.[95] Novelist Anna Maria Porter introduced her *Roche-Blanche; or, Thtoe Hunters of the Pyrenees* (1822) with a note to the reader that explains how she, like Scott, uses historical artifacts as aids to the imagination: 'I found it impossible to rekindle imagination, until I should have warmed my heart by contemplating either past or present excellence. I betook me, therefore, to the huge picture gallery of history: there, two or three portraits interested me ... and, furnished with these, I was soon able to imagine others.'[96]

Burton (1825), by the improbably named 'Ronald M'Chronicle', directly engages with Scott's prefatory techniques: 'Even the author of Waverley thinks it necessary to introduce his work to the public, sometimes telling them where he found his material, and sometimes throwing a double darkness over his shadowy personage.'[97] The dual function of Scott's self-positioning is obvious here: like Porter's anecdote does for her own story, Scott's historical notes lend veracity and relevance to his tales; just as importantly, however, his persona is a marketing device, most effective when shrouded in semi-mystery. M'Chronicle has clearly grasped the double-edged rhetoric of Scott's antiquari-commercial claims, as he shows when he declares, 'Should any gentle reader, or ungentle reader (for I am not particular so they are readers at all) wish to know from whence this work sprung, or to ascertain its origin or veracity, let me assure them that it is perfectly genuine, for I had it direct from the manufactory.'[98] The competing value systems – 'genuine' suggests an authentic, rare artifact, while 'manufactory' implies mass production and replication – here iron-ically unite to support the bottom line: any reader is a good reader.

The author of the satirical *Prodigious!!! or, Childe Paddie in London* (1818) attacks the antiquarian aspect of Scott's persona in more explicit terms with rants about old books, such as, 'For after all, what are these precious relics? of which, perhaps, only one or two copies may be in existence, and the race nearly extinct, like the Mammoth; and most likely no loss to the world if they were, except to those rakers up of trash out of the charnel house of literature' (201). Refusing the transformation by which old books become 'precious relics', the author mocks the idea that age or rarity constitute markers of value. Taking a tack more akin to that of the *Cœlebs* authors in Chapter 4, this author ties age to obsolescence, and literary loss to a little-mourned extinction. The 'trash' that is elsewhere described as pouring from modern presses is here more archaeological in nature; a 'charnel house of literature', however, offers little appeal to would-be excavators. But if Scott's antiquarian arguments for value are under attack, his more commercial justifications for literary production meet with more approval; the author declares elsewhere in the book that '[s]uch astonishing and continued success speaks for itself; it proves the merit of [Scott's] works.'[99]

As examples like this demonstrate, both Scott's themes and his literary approaches rippled outward from the publication of *Waverley*. In perhaps the final irony of this publishing phenomenon, this replication ultimately led to the inversion of the model with which this chapter began: if Scott (supposedly) single-handedly quashed the hordes of novels that preceded him, soon enough he was unquestionably the cause of new hordes, some written and some inspired by him. The critics were not alone in comment-ing on this phenomenon; novelists too located themselves within this new literary movement. Horace Smith, in *Reuben Apsley* (1827), dedicates his book to Scott, declaring,

> the imitators of your honourable and generous candour may perhaps become more numerous than those who have been the copyists of your style ... In this career many have already done themselves honour by treading in your footsteps; and more, it is to be hoped, will follow. Such imitators can never be termed a servile herd: every honest friend of the Muses will wish to see them multiplied until they shall form a large fraternity of generous competitors.[100]

'Many', 'more', 'herd', 'multiplied', 'large fraternity': this is the language of plenitude – but *not*, as this author takes pains to argue, of excess. Other authors, however, were less optimistic about the effects of Scott's spreading influence. In the preface to *Manderville; or, The Hibernian Chiliarch* (1825), the author begins by reinforcing the message that following a familiar model is the best route to success: 'if, in the following pages, [readers] recognise any attempt made to copy the style of the author of "Waverley", they are to ascribe it merely to a desire ... of pursuing that track, which experience has proved to be the best'.[101] As the introduction proceeds, however, it becomes clear that the familiarity of that 'track' is more of a problem than a benefit (at least, when others follow it). Scott, the author declares, 'has paid dearly for his popularity, in witnessing the many barbarous inroads attempted on a province he has made peculiarly his own, by a Horde, who may aptly be described as the Vandals of Literature'. If 'Horde' is not strong enough language, the author soon comes up with an even clearer denunciation of the 'unnumbered pre-tenders' (iii) to 'the highest honors' of Scott's own literary 'department', calling their works 'that multiplicity of wretched abortions, which have emanated from the Press' (i–ii).

The author of *Prodigious!!!* (1818) is somewhat kinder when, after listing some impressive sales figures for Scott's works, the author continues, 'without any disparagement to Mr. Scott be it said, that he has, luckily for himself, been the founder of a rage or fashion for the legendary or minstrelsy, or tales in prose and verse, of Scottish borderers or robbers'.[102] Thomas Lauder, author of *Lochandhu, a Tale of the Eighteenth Century* (1825), brings the critique of this 'rage or fashion' back to its beginnings, opening with an epigraph taken from MacCulloch's *Letters on the Highlands of Scotland*. Describing the titular Lochandhu, the epigraph reads, in part,

> This lake is much embellished by an ancient castle.... If ever you should propose to rival the Author of Waverley in that line of art, I recommend you to choose part of your scene here. As I lay on its topmost tower ... I, too, felt as if I would have written a chapter that might hereafter be worthy the protection of Minerva – the Minerva of Leadenhall Street.[103]

Here, history serves as Scottian inspiration, which in turn serves ironically as fodder for the prolific press supposedly rendered obsolete by Scott's advancements. While the reviewer with whom I began this chapter rejoiced that Scott and his works had displaced the 'countless, nameless, equivocal things' published by the Minerva Press in the earlier nineteenth century – replacing a 'whole brood' with a singularity – reading Scott's contemporaries shows us this trend in reverse. Walter Scott's own singular success spawned in short order a vast 'brood' of its own, bringing the novel's contemporary domination to new heights even as he staked a claim for its lasting relevance.

Epilogue
Remainders

The Minerva Press, by most accounts, came to an end in 1820. A. K. Newman, Lane's business partner and then successor, retired the distinctive Minerva imprint in that year, returning to the more standard practice of publishing books under his own name. The break is not a clean one, however: in fact, two novels dated 1821 also bear the 'Minerva Press' imprimatur.[1] *Lovers and Friends; or, Modern Attachments* and *Eleanor; or, The Spectre of St. Michael's* are the last known novels to appear with the Minerva name; stranded alone among the 'A. K. Newman and Co.' and 'Longman, Hurst, Rees, Orme and Brown' title pages that preface the year's other productions, they seem already belated, an echo of former glory – or infamy. Strictly speaking, the conundrum of their existence has a simple explanation: it appears that both novels, despite their official printed dates, were actually published at the end of 1820, a theory that the existence of a December 1820 review of one of the titles seems to confirm.[2] In a symbolic sense, however, these two novels offer a way into thinking about the final problem I want to explore in this book: What happens *after* a problem of oversupply? As we have seen, the discourse of excess often functions to force new works into premature oblivion; the superfluous text is always already a part of the past. Yet, conversely, it is also eminently contemporary. Metaphors of groaning presses and creaking shelves function meaningfully only in a continual present, in which the threat they pose is ongoing. In the realm of metaphor both states can exist simultaneously, but in the real world, history moves on, and the reams of paper and stacks of cheaply bound books remain. How then should we think about the excesses of the Romantic novel, as rhetorical superfluity gives way to actual superfluity?

As examples of sheer textual overload, the final two Minerva novels serve quite well. Both are exuberantly long, a full five volumes; both appear not only under the familiar auspices of the Press but, like so many other novels of the day, with the identification of a lengthy string of previous novels written by their respective authors. The author of *Lovers and Friends*, one 'Anne of Swansea' (now identified as Anne Julia Kemble Hatton) is, in fact, one of the most prolific authors of the entire period, producing thirteen novels in a remarkable sixty volumes in the years between 1800 and 1829.[3] A full seven of these are listed on the title page of *Lovers and Friends*: Anne of Swansea is described as 'Author of Conviction, Gonzola de Baldivia, Chronicles of an Illustrious House, Secret Avengers, Secrets in Every Mansion, Cambrian Pictures, Cesario Rosalba, &C. &C.' (see Figure 6).

Miss C. D. Haynes, the author of *Eleanor*, is not quite so prolific, but her three previous novels, including one published serially in the *Lady's Magazine*, are similarly included on the title page: 'Author of Castle Le Blanc; Foundling of Devonshire; Augustus and Adelina, &C. &C.'[4] All the bolstering literary indicators of the period surround these novels, propelling them into the world atop a pile of previous attributions and between the covers of an intimidating stack of volumes. This is by no means a coincidence: as Jonathan Hill has noted, A. K. Newman frequently chose the adjective 'large' to advertise his new novels.[5] Hill includes works by both Anne Hatton and C. D. Haynes on his list of novels thus advertised, suggesting the importance of simple bulk (here presumably implying length) as an attractive selling point.[6] Many of these volumes, as we might expect from all the examples discussed in previous chapters of this book, conclude with lists of still *more* novels, 'New Publications, Printed for A. K. Newman at the Minerva-Press'.[7] Most of the novels advertised in these advertisements are not precisely 'new' – many are more than a decade old – but they amplify the sense of plenitude and lend an endorsing kind of legitimacy to each actually new novel.[8] Despite the multiple mentions of the Minerva name, however, the visually distinctive black-letter Minerva imprint is nowhere to be found in either of these two novels. On the title pages, only the title and place of publication – 'London' – are printed in this typeface, while 'Printed at the Minerva Press' is in a modern-looking italic; in the advertisements at the end of the volumes, 'The Minerva-Press' is written in an elegant cursive (see Figure 7).

The gothic connotations of the 1790s Minerva, such a shift clearly hints, are behind the press now; its brand still merits recognition, but the visual shift also emphasizes forward progress. It seems, however, that the associations of the Minerva name were not shed as easily as a distinctive typeface. 'Minerva' ultimately had to go, leaving these two belated novels as the last representatives of the press that had so dominated the market for

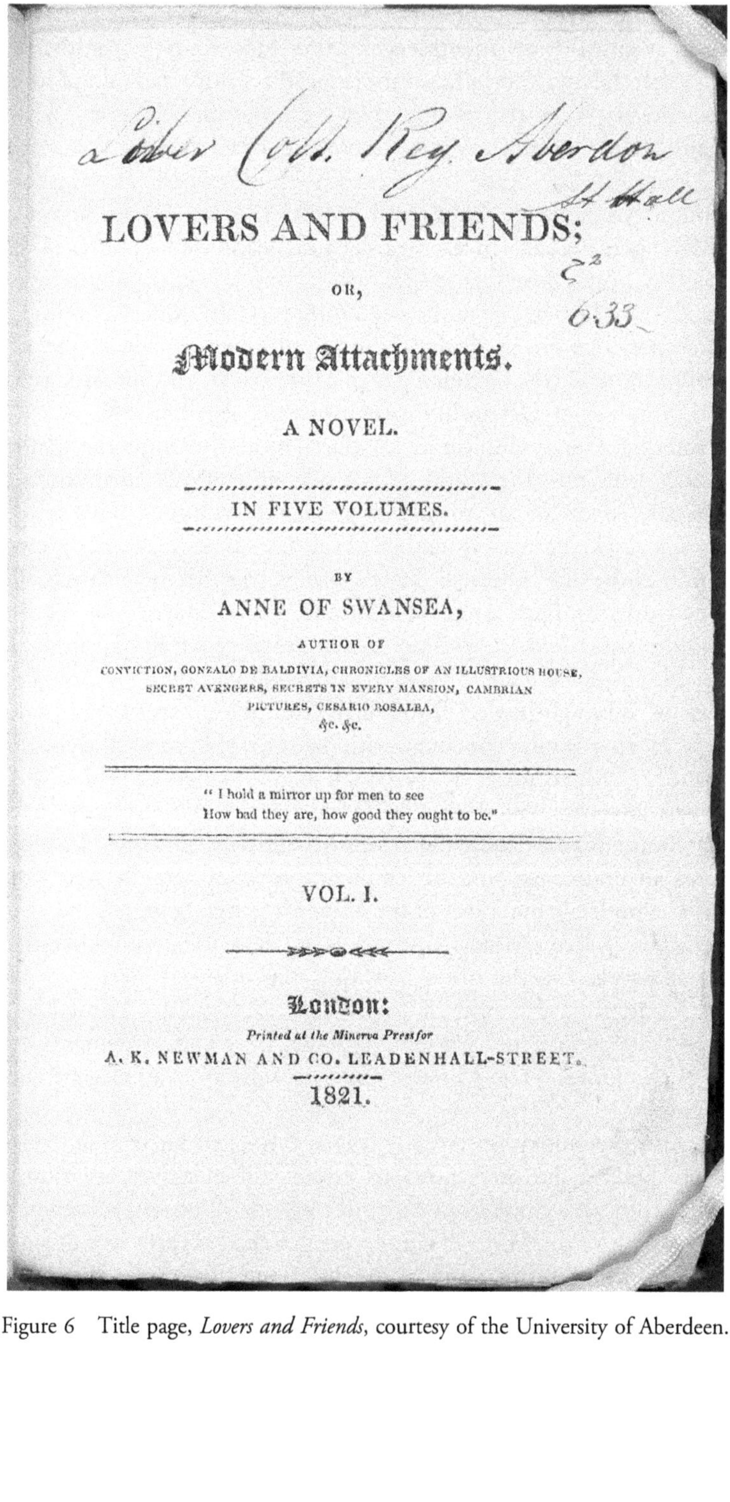

LOVERS AND FRIENDS;

OR,

𝔐𝔬𝔡𝔢𝔯𝔫 𝔄𝔱𝔱𝔞𝔠𝔥𝔪𝔢𝔫𝔱𝔰.

A NOVEL.

IN FIVE VOLUMES.

BY

ANNE OF SWANSEA,

AUTHOR OF

CONVICTION, GONZALO DE BALDIVIA, CHRONICLES OF AN ILLUSTRIOUS HOUSE,
SECRET AVENGERS, SECRETS IN EVERY MANSION, CAMBRIAN
PICTURES, CESARIO ROSALBA,
&c. &c.

" I hold a mirror up for men to see
How bad they are, how good they ought to be."

VOL. I.

London:

Printed at the Minerva Press for
A. K. NEWMAN AND CO. LEADENHALL-STREET.

1821.

Figure 6   Title page, *Lovers and Friends*, courtesy of the University of Aberdeen.

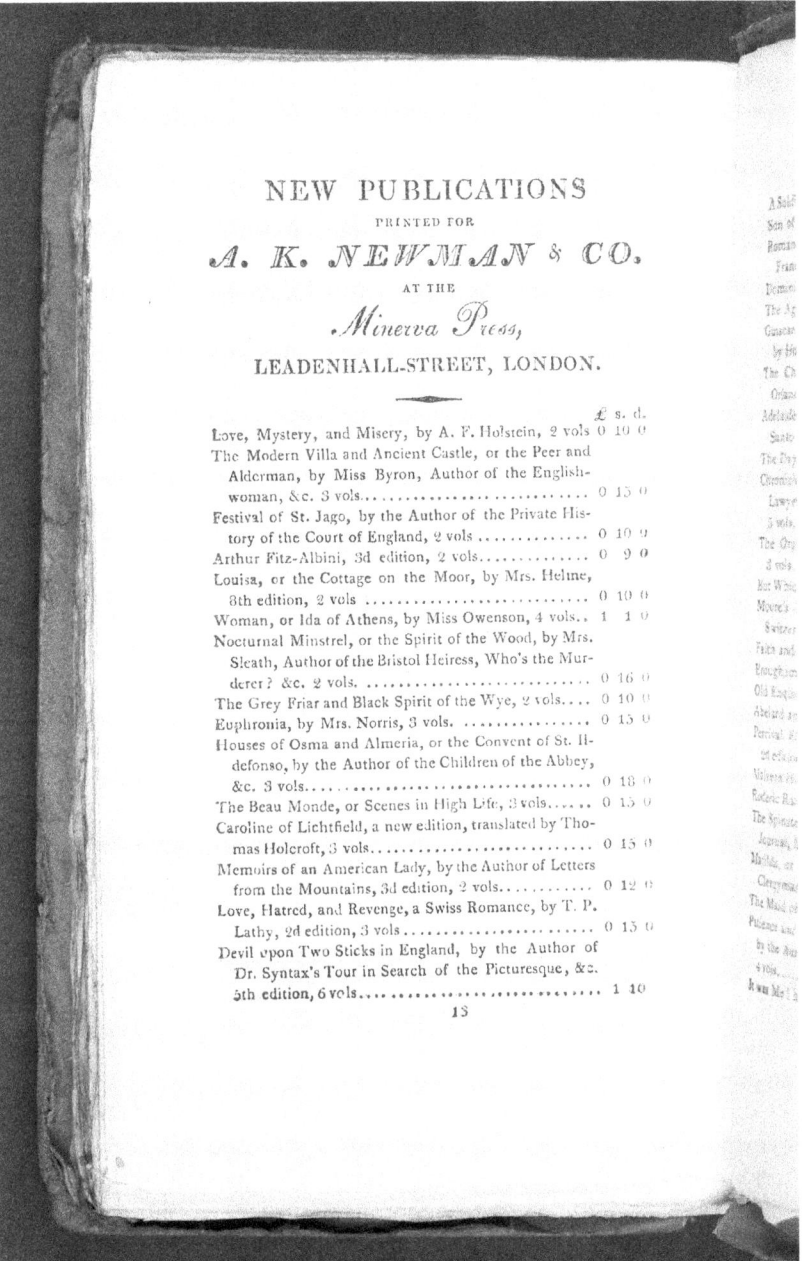

NEW PUBLICATIONS

PRINTED FOR

A. K. NEWMAN & CO.

AT THE

Minerva Press,

LEADENHALL-STREET, LONDON.

	£	s.	d.
Love, Mystery, and Misery, by A. F. Holstein, 2 vols	0	10	0
The Modern Villa and Ancient Castle, or the Peer and Alderman, by Miss Byron, Author of the English-woman, &c. 3 vols.	0	15	0
Festival of St. Jago, by the Author of the Private History of the Court of England, 2 vols	0	10	0
Arthur Fitz-Albini, 3d edition, 2 vols.	0	9	0
Louisa, or the Cottage on the Moor, by Mrs. Helme, 8th edition, 2 vols	0	10	0
Woman, or Ida of Athens, by Miss Owenson, 4 vols..	1	1	0
Nocturnal Minstrel, or the Spirit of the Wood, by Mrs. Sleath, Author of the Bristol Heiress, Who's the Murderer? &c. 2 vols.	0	16	0
The Grey Friar and Black Spirit of the Wye, 2 vols....	0	10	0
Euphronia, by Mrs. Norris, 3 vols.	0	15	0
Houses of Osma and Almeria, or the Convent of St. Ildefonso, by the Author of the Children of the Abbey, &c. 3 vols.	0	18	0
The Beau Monde, or Scenes in High Life, 3 vols......	0	15	0
Caroline of Lichtfield, a new edition, translated by Thomas Holcroft, 3 vols.	0	15	0
Memoirs of an American Lady, by the Author of Letters from the Mountains, 3d edition, 2 vols.	0	12	0
Love, Hatred, and Revenge, a Swiss Romance, by T. P. Lathy, 2d edition, 3 vols	0	15	0
Devil upon Two Sticks in England, by the Author of Dr. Syntax's Tour in Search of the Picturesque, &c. 5th edition, 6 vols.	1	10	

13

Figure 7   End-page advertisement, *Lovers and Friends*, vol. I, courtesy of the University of Aberdeen.

so many years. If A. K. Newman chose to retire the Minerva name at this moment in time in order to escape the press's increasingly negative reputation, however, this strategy was hardly successful: if anything, the Minerva's usefulness as a 'convenient epithet of contempt' only increased in the years following the press's nominal demise.[9] In fact, the absence of new Minerva novels, which might complicate or challenge a stereotypical view of the press, seems to have made it all the easier for reviewers and critics to refer to the 'Minerva novel' or the 'Minerva reader' as uniform, immediately recognizable, and eminently dismissible entities.

So striking is the continued use of 'Minerva' as a shorthand for the over-long, over-sentimental, over-produced novel, that a reader of nineteenth-century periodicals could easily take away the impression that the Press remained in operation well into the Victorian era. In one sense, in fact, there may be no such thing as a post-Minerva period, because despite the imprint's retirement, many commentators continued to refer to Newman's business by that name. I have found no explicit references to the retirement of the name in the periodicals of the early 1820s, and multiple articles make observations about the Minerva Press in the present tense or refer to A. K. Newman's new publications in reviews as 'Minerva' novels. More broadly, discussions of the contemporary literary scene frequently mention the Minerva. In 1827, for instance, to take one of many examples, the *Mirror* claimed that '[t]he poor spinsters of the Minerva press can scarcely support life by their labours, so completely are they driven out of the market by the Lady Charlottes and the Lady Bettys.'[10] In 1834, in a review of a book of quotations, the *Metropolitan Magazine* joked that '[t]he Minerva press novelists will now never want excellent mottos for headings of their chapters.'[11] Both of these examples clearly imply that the Minerva Press novelist, while an embattled and pitiable species, is still very much around (of course, this is true in a certain sense – 'Anne of Swansea' did not cease publishing when Newman removed the Minerva imprint from her title pages). The strong association between the press, the novels it published, and the novelists who wrote for it gave Minerva a life that extended beyond its intended conclusion.

Commentators in the 1820s and 1830s clearly continued to feel that overproduction of undesirable novels was a problem: as a writer in the *Lady's Monthly Museum* memorably put it in 1828: 'Since the time of Fielding, novels and romances have sprung up like the mushroom's spawn, and it is [a] matter of lamentation, that too many of them may be justly compared to the poisonous fungus.'[12] And the Minerva Press, or at least the memory of it, retained its utility as a means of referring to unwanted textual proliferation. In 1824 the *Edinburgh Magazine* drew on old and familiar reproductive metaphors to make it clear that though a particular novel being reviewed had its flaws, 'With all its defects ... it could never be confounded with the thousand and one stillborn children of the Minerva Press.'[13] In 1832, the *Metropolitan Magazine* invoked Minerva and an unstoppable flood of bad fiction, in order to claim that bad novels shouldn't deserve the title of 'novel' at all: 'It is true that any one can sit down and attempt a novel, and the Minerva press has deluged the public with them, *usque ad nauseam*; but these compositions can be no more considered as novels, or pictures of real life, than the scratchings of a school-girl in her first elements of drawing, or the daubing of some self-taught village sign-painter, can be offered as specimens of the pictorial art.'[14] The *idea* of the Minerva novel, or, more specifically, the idea that a 'deluge' of undesirable titles has obscured the merit of a few more superior titles, is quite clearly still serving a critical purpose here, more than a decade after the last actual Minerva novel appeared.

Yet even as these condescending references persisted, we do begin to see, especially by the 1830s, descriptions of the Minerva press novel – or novelist – that are more clearly in the past tense. These references share a number of key features: though they depict an obviously past time, the timetable is vague; moreover, the undesirable books or behaviours are portrayed as persisting after their nominal demise, in zombie-like fashion. While these later descriptions of the press more clearly delineate the past temporality of the Minerva Press novel, in other words, they maintain its current presence as a constant threat, constantly renewing its associations with literary excess. Not long after the retirement of the Minerva imprint, the *Literary Chronicle* described its influence in terms that emphasize physical volume, commercial (over)production, and extended narrative length:

> No species of literature thrives so luxuriantly as that of novel-writing; but a few years back it was confined almost exclusively to the sons and daughters of *Minerva*, who got their five or ten pounds per volume, or filled the shelves of a circulating library at so much per cubic foot. These were the writers who would keep the love-sick school-miss hanging between hope and despair through a thousand pages ... and this class of writers is not extinct.[15]

Even the process of relegating 'the sons and daughters of *Minerva*' to the past necessitates the acknowledgement that 'this class of writers is not extinct', and neither is their large audience. Whether imagined as botanically luxuriant or mass-produced by the cubic foot, the novels these authors produced may be beneath contempt, but they have also clearly left their mark on the literary landscape, whether physically – those thousands of pages take up considerable space, the writer reminds us – or intellectually, as a cautionary tale.

More than a decade later, the *Monthly Review* was still doing its best to hammer the nails firmly into Minerva's coffin, declaring in 1836 that a disfavoured new novel 'can alone properly claim kindred with a school where Minerva at one time superintended the press, and which, we thought, was defunct, never to be resuscitated'.[16] 'We thought' is clearly synonymous with 'we hoped', but equally clearly, in the context of the review, suggests that this hope is a rather futile one and that the Minerva's 'school' still maintains plenty of adherents. As these quotations demonstrate, the Press's continuing reputation and recognizability in the 1820s, 1830s, and beyond is, ironically, clearly fostered by the media's insistence on its irrelevance, with constant references to 'the golden days of the "Minerva Press"' or 'some early silliness belonging to the Minerva-Press School',[17] keeping the memory of the Press ever-alive in the public's mind. Humourists in the 1840s could still mock female readers by describing how 'Miss Snubbs sends for a Minerva Press novel, and makes herself miserably happy through its five volumes of delicate distresses.'[18] Even as increasing critical acceptance of the novel diminished the general anti-novel sentiments of the previous century, the perceived need to critique *specific* novels, in order to valorise other, more admirable exemplars of the genre, only seems to have increased.

In bibliographic terms, the persistence of Minerva in this role is particularly striking due to its increasing anachronism: not only had the Minerva imprint been officially retired in 1820, but by the mid-1820s, A. K. Newman had lost the title of most prolific English publisher. The Minerva (or the press formerly known as Minerva) was rapidly, dramatically eclipsed in fictional output by another publisher: Henry Colburn.[19] While Colburn's long and controversial career deserves much greater attention than I can give it here, a brief exploration of his role as the inheritor of the Minerva Press's mantle offers insight into the 'post-Minerva' period. Magazines and reviews reflect the transition from Newman to Colburn as the market's greatest (over)producer: much as Walter Scott's extreme productivity immediately drew comparisons to the Minerva, so Colburn's newly established market dominance clearly invited comparisons between the two. "We are surprised to see, among the books announced by Mr. Colburn, a new Novel … and several other books, equally worthy of the Minerva Press', opined a commentator in the

Literary Magnet.[20] That this reviewer expressed 'surprise' at Colburn's publication of these Minerva-esque titles seems likely to reflect Colburn's own efforts to distance himself from his predecessor's reputation: an earlier feature in the *New Monthly Magazine* (owned by Colburn and used by him to promote his new titles) features a character who, when speaking to his prospective readers, 'beg[s] to assure them I have never undertaken the *pathetic line* for the "Minerva Press", and have "no connexion with any other house" but the very excellent one of Mr. Colburn'.[21]

Yet despite these efforts, most contemporaries clearly thought that Colburn resembled William Lane in more than just fictional output and elaborately interconnected media publicity strategies. As John Sutherland notes, Colburn's 'personal pedigree' was publicly critiqued; he was (like Lane) 'the butt of spiteful anecdotes and lampoons'; and he was 'everywhere accused of depraving public taste' with his publications.[22] Discussions of literary quality in both cases were thus linked to stereotypes about social class, education, and morality. While Colburn appears to have been more openly unscrupulous than either Minerva publisher, his path to success, like theirs, is characterized by an emphasis on scale and, especially, a similar understanding of the essential interconnections between book publishing, advertising, and professional reviewing. As Sutherland puts it, 'in this early form of diversified book-trade operation (he was variously library-owner, retail bookseller, magazine-proprietor, publisher) Colburn anticipated what is now termed synergistic patterns of publishing'.[23]

Colburn's career, even upon this brief examination, shows that just as the Minerva's reputation persisted well beyond its actual presence, so the publishing practices that created and supported Lane's original large-scale production of novels became a permanent part of the publishing landscape. However passionately contemporaries argued that publication on the 'deluge' model was outdated, Colburn's success demonstrates that both high volume and multi-pronged marketing were elements that could still lead to success (and indeed, were perhaps increasingly necessary to achieve it). As the publisher's efforts to differentiate himself from the Minerva Press suggest, however, he was well aware of the negative associations with these techniques. Two of his most substantial modifications to the business model are easily legible as responses to the age's ongoing critiques of excess: Colburn played a substantial role in standardizing the increasingly dominant 'three-decker' novel form, rejecting the five-, six-, and seven-volume tomes of the Minerva's tenure; he also followed the trend of pricing his novels substantially higher than older publishers had done (31s 6d for a three-volume novel, for example, as compared with a maximum of 18s for a Newman three-volume title from the same period), cultivating an impression of prestige rather than of a cheap commodity.[24] Once created, the expectation that novels would be available on a large scale did not diminish, and Colburn's career demonstrates the power of building on those expectations, but also the necessity of continually navigating their less desirable side effects.

The model of succession, then, presents one answer to the question I posed at the beginning of this epilogue: after oversupply (from one source) begins to abate, another supplier may simply step into the resulting void. Colburn and a number of other publishers of popular fiction embraced this role, to varying degrees, leaving those who complained about fiction's ongoing presence with an ample supply of culprits to blame. But, as I have argued throughout this book, to think purely in reputational terms would be to miss the ongoing importance of the novel's actual, material qualities. This is just as true of the novel's afterlife: Where did all those volumes go? Eighteenth- and nineteenth-century authors, as we have seen, often imagine their books' unfortunate afterlives, from conflagration to oblivion. The popular novels of the age were perhaps particularly prescient in anticipating how irrelevant they would shortly become: even copyright libraries often didn't want them. As Peter Garside remarks, in a discussion of the potential limitations of the Nineteenth-Century Short Title Catalogue as a bibliographical source, the Catalogue 'is based on the holdings of a relatively small number of libraries, some likely to be unsympathetic to seemingly ephemeral literature when originally making accessions'.[25] Given that the NSTC is based on the 'catalogued holdings of all the main British copyright libraries', the implications for the novel are clear: even (especially) in the heyday of Romantic fiction, these publications were seen as extraneous, superfluous, unworthy of collection because irrelevant to posterity.

This exclusion is especially marked, as we might expect, after 1800, when some of the challenges of fictional proliferation became more obvious; as Garside points out, 'more than 40 per cent of titles belonging to 1801–1809 [are not] present in NSTC in the original edition given'.[26] Where did all those novels go? To track individual copies from their origins to the libraries that eventually acquired them is a task for a different (and fascinating) project, but we can see a clear hint of the selective forces at work in Jonathan Hill's research at the University of Aberdeen. The University holds a large number of popular novels from this period, including many published by the Minerva Press: 'In the second and third decades of the nineteenth century, someone at the library [in a former incarnation, as King's College] requested works of prose fiction in large quantities', taking advantage of the library's right to receive all works registered at Stationer's Hall. But, as Hill notes, this state of affairs was brief.[27] A Royal Commission investigation between 1826 and 1830 found fault with the state of the King's collection; in particular, they complained, 'trifling or pernicious works ... are sent in great abundance'.[28] Even in an institution – a library – oriented towards collection and preservation, novels were seen as both unimportant and capable of inflicting harm, assessments amplified simply by the 'abundance' in which these works appeared. In the case of library acquisitions, we can see how easily these value judgements can become a self-fulfilling prophecy.

The tie between the Minerva and the material aftermath of excess is not merely a matter of critical or institutional rejection. As Dorothy Blakey points out, 'a large part of [A. K. Newman's] trade from 1820 on was in remainders'.[29] In other words, she explains, Newman bought up unwanted books from other publishers, replacing the original title pages with his own imprint before sale. This practice explains some of the peculiar difficulties in identifying which novels come from which Press in this period, and also goes some way towards explaining why so many of the novels listed in ads like the ones in *Lovers and Friends* and *Eleanor* don't appear to have been originally published by Minerva, Lane, or Newman, despite being advertised under the Press's aegis.[30] In material terms, however, it is fascinating to consider the effects of this kind of salvage-publishing. Blakey offers an example in which the discarded pages can be distinguished from the new title and half-title with which they were bound by both 'paper and type', a scenario that vividly illustrates the point that the body of a book like this quite literally *is* excess – the unwanted surplus of another firm – offered anew to the public.[31] If trash can be transformed to a profitable product, as Newman's business model demonstrates, then the discourse of abundance and super-fluity explored throughout this book shows us how easily this 'product' might be transformed again into trash. The emphasis on the mass and materiality of these novels elides the differences between newly published novels and already-discarded detritus, with the novel perched precariously at the tipping point. After Newman's retirement in 1848, indeed, this division broke down altogether, as he sold all his stock as remainders to yet another publisher.[32] Blakey does not trace the fate of these left-over titles, but we can imagine their recycled reappearances, ever-further down the scale of prestige.

The Minerva Press's aftermath looks very different from the perspective of different stakeholders. For publishers, the Press's decline created an opportunity, an opening in the market, a model for successful marketing practices, and a cautionary tale about reputation. For librarians, warehouse owners, and, possibly, possessors of overstuffed bookshelves, the physical accumulation of Minerva titles was something to be winnowed, weeded, or recycled into something more lucrative. For readers, the Press's absence might have created a void, but (despite the claims of patronizing critics) it seems far more likely that any resultant space in a reader's agenda was seamlessly filled by the new offerings from London and Edinburgh publishers. In 1837, *Bentley's Miscellany* painted a vividly humorous picture of one more type of person who might miss the Minerva: the young woman author. According to the editors, 'A young lady who rejoices in the appellation of Czarina Amabelle St. Cloud has addressed a lengthened epistle to us, in which she feelingly deplores the gradual decline and downfall of the Minerva Press.'[33] The deliberately melodramatic name of the 'young lady' is echoed by the listed titles of her 'unpublished works', which hilariously parody the Minerva Press's distinctive two-part titles, with examples like 'A Nympholept Lover; or, The Whispering Fungus', 'The Fatal Furbelow; or, The Tempted Templar', 'Venomgorgia, the Arsenic-Eater; A Pastoral Romance', and 'The Evil Ear; A Legend of Love'.[34] The editors include 'a spirit-stirring extract from her last manuscript romance, which is indeed a masterpiece in a department of literature now unhappily but too much neglected', and remark that '[f]or a young lady under twenty years of age, Miss St. Cloud is the most voluminous writer we ever had the pleasure of meeting with.'[35]

While the intent of this piece is obviously satirical, it does raise a serious question: In the absence of the Minerva Press, did women authors (or 'voluminous' writers in general) have fewer opportunities to publish their work? Indeed, to follow this question's implications further, what had such writers done *before* Lane began to publish them? Did the Minerva merely exploit a previously untapped vein of creativity, or, through its advertisements inviting authors to submit their work for publication, did the Press effectively create a generation of authors like Czarina Amabelle St Cloud? To some extent, of course, these chicken-and-egg questions are impossible to answer: we are unlikely to be able to reconstruct the psychological motivations of many Minerva authors in retrospect, and this epilogue doesn't engage in the kind of large-scale bibliographical analysis necessary to trace the shifts in authorship profiles over many decades.[36] But there is clear evidence that Lane did seek to expand not only the number of books on the market but the number of writers who, under his auspices, became published authors. In Lane's 'Address to the Public on Circulating Libraries, &c.' from the mid-1790s, for instance, he draws a clear connection between large numbers of novels, their wide distribution, and their authorship.[37] He offers his assistance in establishing circulating libraries 'in every part of this Kingdom', given that these establishments 'have yet failed in being so universal as they might be', and assures prospective proprietors that 'many Thousand Volumes, of every Description, in Literature, are kept prepared ... for immediate circulation; – and that Works of Merit are constantly printing ... at the Minerva Press'.[38] He explicitly connects this abundant production with the cultivation of new writers to produce it, declaring, 'Authors are respectfully urged to offer their Productions, where eminent Talents will be liberally, though proportionably, encouraged, from their earliest Dawn to their meridian Splendor.'[39] As that telling phrase, 'liberally, though proportionably' suggests, Lane does seem to have ushered many budding novelists into the market – but his payment structure was not calculated to let many of them achieve financial security by means of their pen.

Elizabeth Neiman has demonstrated that during the Press's years of prominence, 'Minerva plays a special role as a gateway to publishing', pointing out that 'Minerva ... debuts 45 per cent of *all* newcomer female novelists at its zenith' and that 'many [Minerva novelists] – in comparison to their non-Minerva counterparts – continue publishing novels' after their first.[40] The Press was, in other words, successful in attracting new novelists to the market, both those who would go on to publish more novels with Minerva and those who would continue their career with other publishers. Moreover, those who did go on to publish further books with the Minerva Press bear out the stereotype of the 'voluminous' writer: Neiman's analysis reveals that 'Minerva novelists are indeed more prolific on average than other novelists' – and that female *Minerva* novelists (as opposed to female novelists in general) 'are significantly more prolific than men'.[41] It is possible that these authors published more because the speed and efficiency of the Leadenhall Street operation facilitated it, but evidence from the Royal Literary Fund suggests a less optimistic interpretation: as scholars like Jennie Batchelor and Matthew Sangster have shown, multiple Minerva Press authors were in such dire financial straits, despite the ongoing success of their writing career, that they had to plead for further monetary support.[42] Sangster notes at least six Minerva authors who appealed to the Literary Fund, pointing out that while Lane's payments to authors were reported to be relatively generous, they paled in comparison to the profits he himself made (particularly since the circulating library business, a large source of Lane's income, was dependent on lending, rather than selling, copies of novels).[43] The mobility of authors between different publishers suggests ongoing price negotiations, additional evidence that even for prolific novelists, writing alone was unlikely to provide a comfortable income stream. It also, however, clearly implies that a novelist no longer able to write for Minerva might move to a different publishing house with relatively little ado. On the other hand, certain key trends – the decline of the ultra-long novel and the increasing proportion of male to female authors, to name just a few – may indeed have limited the opportunities of some would-be 'voluminous' novelists.[44]

From ten, twenty, or thirty years on, then, the Minerva Press's demise might have been viewed as leaving a hole in the market, but it was equally likely to be framed as a new opportunity or a timely corrective to an unfortunate literary fashion. It did not, certainly, spell the end of the novel – quite the reverse – nor stem the widespread sense that there were more and more things to read being produced every day and that readers had to develop their own means of navigating them. Indeed, it is perhaps the long-developing outgrowth of this latter feeling that has led, after decades upon decades of oblivion, to the Minerva Press's recent return to at least one popular stage. In 2009, nearly 200 years after the last Minerva Press novel emerged from the press, the best-selling romance novelist Eloisa James introduced a new series, *The Essex Sisters*.[45] The four sisters whose adventures and misadventures fill the pages often discuss their reading, and what they read, frequently, are Minerva Press novels. James, the pen name of an English professor who has written publicly under her real name about the stigma attaching to romance reading and writing, makes it plain that her references to the Minerva are deliberate.[46] 'In the 1800s, the Minerva Press was busy printing books right along the lines of those I like to read', she writes.[47] The charges levied against the Press's novels by characters in the books are familiar: they are misleading, lurid, unrealistic; they are definitely a waste of time and probably damaging to a young lady's morals. The comparison clearly resonates with others in the romance community; while James may be the contemporary novelist who uses the Minerva most extensively as a plot point, other recent historical novelists who set their stories in the period of its operation also reference the Press, sending their characters to the Minerva library, identifying heroines as Minerva readers, and discussing the merits of the novels with other characters.[48] One character mocks another by declaring that he 'wouldn't know the Gutenberg Bible from a Minerva Press novel', while the stereotypes of the past are revived in the present in a scene from a different novel, which riffs on *Northanger Abbey*'s 'horrid novels' and the gothic formulae discussed in Chapter 3.[49]

This kind of referentiality is in part likely intended to establish historical accuracy, but it very clearly serves another purpose as well. Copyright libraries may no longer automatically exclude popular novels from their purview but novels that are deemed insufficiently 'literary' are still, by and large, excluded from high-profile book reviews and other markers of literary status. In referencing earlier derided novels in their own often-dismissed works, we might see these authors as following in the footsteps of their Minerva Press predecessors, defending their share of the market through in-jokes and collectivity. In pointing out this connection, I don't wish to overstate the similarities between the Minerva Press novel and modern romance fiction – such a comparison depends, for instance, on an oversimplified assumption that either group of books are uniformly read and written by women. And it occludes the multiplicity of fictional and non-fictional genres in which Minerva authors wrote (not to mention the varied sub-genres within contemporary romance). But the blend of numerical dominance and literary marginalization that characterizes both groups of novels reminds us that literary 'excess' is not only a problem of the past. The dynamics of prestige still cannot be separated from the pressures of the market. Moreover, though, authors plainly still anticipate that readers will enjoy the familiarity of frequently used plot points (no matter how critics may complain about their overuse), and understand that ironic references to their own beleaguered status can serve to unify a large readership. Invoking the Minerva Press is still, it seems, a legible shorthand for the pressures and pleasures of literary overload.

William Hazlitt's 1821 essay 'On Reading Old Books' is in part a cry of protest against the literary inundations of his age. 'I hate to read new books', Hazlitt declares at the outset, rejecting wholesale the allure of the unopened cover or the faddish title.[50] Not for him the delights of novelty; he favours instead the emotion- and memory-laden experience of reading and rereading the 'twenty or thirty volumes' that comprise his preferred library.[51] As he explains, 'those places, those times, those persons, and those feelings that come across me as I retrace the story and devour the page, are to me better far than the wet sheets of the last new novel from the Ballantyne press, or even from the Minerva press in Leadenhall-street'.[52] In his attention to the material qualities of the 'wet sheets' of a new novel and his specificity about which presses would be likely to produce these unwanted but tempting titles, Hazlitt follows the emphasis of so many of his peers on the conditions under which new novels are produced. In his resistance to novelty- and volume-focused models of reading, Hazlitt's insistence on deep and focused engagement with a delimited number of books is both nostalgic and deliberately anachronistic, embracing a way of thinking about books that is appealing exactly because it runs so strongly against the prevailing current. Hazlitt wrote this essay in 1821, the same year as *Eleanor* and *Lovers and Friends* made their appearance, in the twilight of the Minerva Press. But even as the Press itself moved further and further into the shadows of history, the concerns about novelty, prestige, quality, and quantity it inspired showed little sign of ebbing. The Minerva Press is long gone now, but the Minerva Press era – characterized above all by too many books and too little time – may be here to stay.

Notes

Introduction

1 'General Observations on Modern Novels', *LM* 18 (1787): 456.
2 Mary Meeke, preface to *Midnight Weddings* (London: Minerva Press, 1802), I:1.
3 'On Novel Reading', *The Kaleidoscope* 2.60 (21 Aug 1821): 54.
4 'Lucius', 'On Novels', *UMKP* 93 (July 1793): 8–11.
5 Ibid., 8.
6 I provide numerous examples of this kind of language in the pages that follow; for discussion of some of these specific metaphors, see, e.g., Ina Ferris, *The Achievement of Literary Authority: Gender, History, and the Waverley Novels* (Ithaca, NY: Cornell University Press, 1991), 43–44, and James Raven, *Judging New Wealth: Popular Publishing and Responses to Commerce in England, 1750–1800* (Oxford: Clarendon Press, 1992), 61–75.
7 'Hints on Reading', *LM* 20 (Feb 1789): 79. On the importance of the *Lady's Magazine* to literature and culture in this period, and the relationship between the *LM* and the Minerva Press (respectively), see Jennie Batchelor, '"To Cherish Female Ingenuity, and to Conduce to *Female* Improvement": The Birth of the Woman's Magazine', in *Women's Periodicals and Print Culture in Britain, 1690–1820s: The Long Eighteenth Century*, edited by Jennie Batchelor and Manushag N. Powell (Edinburgh: Edinburgh University Press, 2018), 377–392, and 'UnRomantic Authorship: The Minerva Press and the *Lady's Magazine*, 1770–1820', *Romantic Textualities* 23 (Summer 2020): 76–93.
8 Review of *First Impressions*, *CR* 2.32 (June 1801): 233.
9 Mary Charlton, *Rosella, or Modern Occurrences* (London: Minerva Press, 1799), I:9.
10 For a visual representation of the growth in printed materials in Britain after 1475, see James Raven, *The Business of Books: Booksellers and the English Book Trade, 1450–1850* (New Haven, CT: Yale University Press, 2007), 8, fig. 1.1 (data drawn from the *ESTC*).

11 Alexander Pope, 'The Dunciad Variorum', Book 1, ll. 134–135, in *The Poems of Alexander Pope*, edited by John Butt (New Haven, CT: Yale University Press, 1963), 362.

12 Lupton argues that 'if there is one thing characterizing the writing of this period [mid-century], it is the vivid interest that writers . . . show in representing the phenomena of bad writing, mindless reading, and ruthlessly profit-driven publishing'. Christina Lupton, *Knowing Books: The Consciousness of Mediation in Eighteenth-Century Britain* (Philadelphia: University of Pennsylvania Press, 2012), 3.

13 Raven, *The Business of Books*, 8.

14 'Hints on Reading', *LM* 20 (Jan 1789): 79 [79–81]. Also cited in Ferris, *Achievement of Literary Authority*, 42; see further discussion below.

15 David Higgins, *Romantic Magazines and Metropolitan Literary Culture* (Basingstoke: Palgrave Macmillan, 2011), 1; Andrew Piper, *Dreaming in Books: The Making of the Bibliographic Imagination in the Romantic Age* (Chicago: University of Chicago Press, 2009), 12.

16 See Raven, *Judging New Wealth*, esp. 32–34, for discussion of growth in different genres and graph comparisons of overall print production, novel publication, and the publication of magazine fiction. Lee Erickson offers an in-depth exploration of the effects of publishing changes on the reception and production of literary works of different genres in *The Economy of Literary Form: English Literature and the Industrialization of Publishing, 1800–1850* (Baltimore, MD: Johns Hopkins University Press, 1996). William St. Clair provides extensive bibliographical detail on the publishing and circulation of Romantic books and periodicals in *The Reading Nation in the Romantic Period* (Cambridge: Cambridge University Press, 2004).

17 Sodeman gives particular attention to the sentimental novel, while Clery is concerned with the gothic novel, and Ferris's argument considers how authors set out to establish 'literary authority' against the backdrop of the undesirable 'ordinary novel', but all show how the new proliferation of fiction (and perhaps particularly popular fiction by women) at the end of the eighteenth century drew critical scorn, as these works became associated with poor-quality and risible work. Melissa Sodeman, *Sentimental Memorials: Women and the Novel in Literary History* (Stanford, CA: Stanford University Press, 2015); Clery, *The Rise of Supernatural Fiction, 1762–1800* (Cambridge: Cambridge University Press, 1995); and Ferris, *Achievement of Literary Authority*. Other accounts of the novel of this period that have shaped my understanding of it in important ways include Edward Copeland, *Women Writing about Money: Women's Fiction in England, 1790–1820* (Cambridge: Cambridge University Press, 1995); Claudia Johnson, *Equivocal Beings: Politics, Gender, and Sentimentality in the 1790s: Wollstonecraft, Radcliffe, Burney, Austen* (Chicago: University of Chicago Press, 1995); and Gary Kelly, *English Fiction of the Romantic Period, 1789–1830* (London: Longman, 1989). My sense of the developing sense of Romantic literary hierarchy and the novel's place within it is particularly indebted to Gothic

scholarship, especially Clery; James Watt, *Contesting the Gothic: Fiction, Genre, and Cultural Conflict, 1764–1832* (Cambridge: Cambridge University Press, 1999); and Michael Gamer, *Romanticism and the Gothic: Genre, Reception, and Canon Formation* (Cambridge: Cambridge University Press, 2000).

18 Peter Garside, James Raven, and Rainer Schöwerling, eds., *The English Novel, 1770–1829: A Bibliographical Survey of Prose Fiction Published in the British Isles*, 2 vols. (Oxford University Press, 2000).

19 James Raven, 'Historical Introduction: The Novel Comes of Age', in *The English Novel*, vol. I, ed. Garside et al., 79. On one key fictional genre published by Lane in his early years, see Joe Lines, 'William Lane, the Ramble Novel and the Genres of Romantic Irish Fiction', *Romantic Textualities* 23 (Summer 2020): 21–38.

20 Both the visually distinctive font and the name of the Press itself (as opposed to the more standard practice of publication under the publisher's own name) set the Minerva's books apart from competitors. As Clery has argued, 'it is difficult to find another instance in the eighteenth-century book trade, perhaps in British trade in general, of a founder-owner choosing an "image" for his business, in effect creating what we would call today a "corporate identity"'. *Supernatural Fiction*, 137.

21 Raven, 'Historical Introduction', 73–74.

22 Apparently 'the figure remained there until the premises were pulled down in 1859'. Dorothy Blakey, *The Minerva Press, 1790–1820* (London: Printed for the Bibliographical Society at the Oxford University Press, 1939), 16 n. 1.

23 The most up-to-date information about the demographics of the Minerva Press's authors is provided by Elizabeth Neiman in her book *Minerva's Gothics: The Politics and Poetics of Romantic Exchange, 1780–1820* (Cardiff: University of Wales Press, 2019). Deborah McLeod provided an important earlier analysis of Minerva's output in her dissertation 'The Minerva Press' (University of Alberta, 1997). On the disdain for newly wealthy businessmen, including publishers like Lane, in this period, see Raven, *Judging New Wealth*, 48.

24 Quoted in Blakey, *The Minerva Press*, 59.

25 Raven identifies 'at least four printing presses by 1791', while Blakey notes that '"printed at the Minerva-Press" appeared on the title-pages of 1792'. Raven, 'Historical Introduction', 79; Blakey, *The Minerva Press*, 18–19, 39.

26 Numerical data here are drawn from the 'Minerva Press' entry in the index to Garside et al., eds., *The English Novel, 1770–1829,* 856.

27 See Peter Garside, 'The English Novel in the Romantic Era: Consolidation and Dispersal', in *The English Novel, 1770–1829*, vol. II, ed. Garside et al. (Oxford: Oxford University Press, 2000), 85.

28 Raven, 'Historical Introduction', 26, 73; Garside, 'The English Novel in the Romantic Era', 38, 83–85.

29 Raven, 'Historical Introduction', 26.

30 Gamer, *Romanticism and the Gothic,* 67.

31 Ferris, *Achievement of Literary Authority,* 33.

32 Ibid., 43.

33 Ibid., 43–44.

34 While both men and women wrote for the Minerva Press, the strong reputational associations between the Press and women authors (and readers) means that this process of literary marginalization – and my own discussion of it – is necessarily bound up with changing stereotypes about gender and authorship in this period. Gender is not the central focus of this book, but my work is indebted throughout to the many scholars who have brought attention to the (often marginalized) women authors of this period. Key works include Betty A. Schellenberg, *The Professionalization of Women Writers in Eighteenth-Century Britain* (Cambridge: Cambridge University Press, 2005); Jane Spencer, *The Rise of the Woman Novelist: From Aphra Behn to Jane Austen* (Oxford: Blackwell, 1986); and Janet Todd, *The Sign of Angellica: Women, Writing, and Fiction, 1660–1800* (New York: Columbia University Press, 1989). Without work like theirs, a book like this could not have been written. On the gender dynamics of reviewing in the eighteenth century, see especially Laura Runge, *Gender and Language in British Literary Criticism, 1660–1790* (New York: Cambridge University Press, 1997).

35 Erickson, *Economy of Literary Form,* 5.

36 Higgins, *Romantic Magazines,* 1.

37 Clery, *Supernatural Fiction,* 138.

38 Watt, *Contesting the Gothic,* 84.

39 Gamer, *Romanticism and the Gothic,* 67.

40 Sodeman, *Sentimental Memorials,* 5.

41 Lynch, *The Economy of Character: Novels, Market Culture, and the Business of Inner Meaning* (Chicago: University of Chicago Press, 1998), 7.

42 Edward Jacobs, *Accidental Migrations: An Archaology of Gothic Discourse* (Lewisburg, PA: Bucknell University Press, 2000), 198.

43 See also, e.g., Gamer, *Romanticism and the Gothic,* 23, and Watt, *Contesting the Gothic,* 80–84. Neiman offers a more positive reading of the Minerva novel's derivative qualities, arguing that 'Minerva's admittedly derivative themes and otherwise borrowed material … draw its authors into a shared circuit of production' (*Minerva's Gothics,* xv).

44 Neiman, *Minerva's Gothics,* 27.

45 Some of the most influential works of literary criticism on this period have focused specifically on the commercial and economic ramifications of writing and selling books within a larger literary 'marketplace' – as scholars like Deidre Lynch and Catharine Gallagher have shown, this milieu influenced not only *how* authors (perhaps particularly women authors) produced their work but how the contents of that work developed. Gallagher, *Nobody's Story: The Vanishing Acts of Women Writers in the Marketplace 1670–1820* (Oxford: Clarendon, 1994); Lynch, *The Economy of Character.*

46 On 'field' in this sense, implying not merely a large number of books, but a complex series of ongoing negotiations for prestige, profit, and influence, see

Pierre Bourdieu, *The Field of Cultural Production: Essays on Art and Literature*, ed. Randal Johnson (New York: Columbia University Press, 1993).

47 For a discussion of 'waste' and related categories in eighteenth-century literature, see the introduction to Sophie Gee, *Making Waste: Leftovers and the Eighteenth-Century Imagination* (Princeton, NJ: Princeton University Press, 2010), 1–17.

48 Thomas Malthus, *An Essay on the Principle of Population* (London: Printed for J. Johnson, 1798).

49 For a characteristic example of popular usage of the phrase, see, e.g., 'Creanda', 'A Simple Mode of Preventing an Excess of Population', *The Satirist* 5 (Dec 1809): 579.

50 Review of *Gray versus Malthus. The Principles of Population and Production Investigated*, *MR* 89 (July 1819): 273.

51 P. P. Howe, 'Malthus and the Publishing Trade', *EM* (Nov 1912): 577.

52 For a brief summary of the Act and its relationship to crime, see Mark Crosby, 'The Bank Restriction Act (1797) and Banknote Forgery', in *BRANCH: Britain, Representation and Nineteenth-Century History*, ed. Dino Franco Felluga (Jan 2013). Extension of *Romanticism and Victorianism on the Net*, accessed 11 June 2021. See also Matthew Rowlinson, *Real Money and Romanticism* (Cambridge: Cambridge University Press 2010), 50–53, and E. J. Clery, *Eighteen Hundred and Eleven* (Cambridge: Cambridge University Press, 2017), 105–110.

53 S.A., Review of *The Iniquity of Banking*, *AR* 26.3 (Sept 1797): 297.

54 Ibid.

55 Ibid., 298.

56 Ibid., 298.

57 Samuel Johnson, *A Dictionary of the English Language*, vol. I (London: Printed by W. Strahan for J. and P. Knapton et al., [1755]).

58 'Literature of the Day', *Metropolitan* 1.1 (May 1831): 17.

59 While the works being examined are quite different, the gendered resonances of 'excess' are explored in Karen Jackson Ford, *Gender and the Poetics of Excess: Moments of Brocade* (Jackson: University Press of Mississippi, 1997). See esp. p. 7 on excess and marginalization.

60 'On an Excess of Sensibility', *The Lady's Monthly Museum* 4 (Nov 1816): 275.

61 'On Novels and Romances', *The Weekly Entertainer* 22.558 (21 Oct 1793): 399.

62 Priscilla Wakefield, *Mental Improvement: or The Beauties and Wonders of Nature and Art* (London: Printed and sold by Darton and Harvey, 1794), I:121.

63 Stephen Ahern, *Affected Sensibilities: Romantic Excess and the Genealogy of the Novel, 1680–1810* (New York: AMS Press, 2007), 12.

64 M. O. Grenby includes this quotation (from the work of conservative novelist Henry James Pye) in his study of anti-Jacobin fiction, also including, for instance, novelist Edward Sayer describing 'a great multitude already assembled and committing every possible excess'. M. O. Grenby, *The Anti-Jacobin*

Novel: British Conservatism and the French Revolution (Cambridge: Cambridge University Press, 2001), 34, 32.

65 See Chapter 2 for more extensive discussion of the scholarship on Romantic ideas about fiction and revolution.

66 Franco Moretti's theory of 'distant reading', and the many digital corpus analysis projects that have followed it, provides another model for dealing with literary excess and has been influential to my own thinking about this period. Franco Moretti, *Distant Reading* (London: Verso Books, 2013).

67 Neiman, *Minerva's Gothics*, xvi.

68 Lupton, *Knowing Books*, 4. See also Thomas Keymer, *Sterne, the Moderns, and the Novel* (Oxford: Oxford University Press, 2002), for discussion of the mid-century novel's self-consciousness about materiality.

69 Richard Graves, *Columella; or, The Distressed Anchoret* (London: printed for J. Dodsley, 1779), II:243 (Graves places his preface at the end of the novel rather than at the beginning). Qtd. in Lupton, *Knowing Books,* 4.

70 Ibid.

71 Ibid., II:243-4.

72 Review of *Julia* by Anna-Maria Williams, *MR* 2.334 (July 1790): 334, also quoted in Raven, *Judging New Wealth*, 68.

73 'Lucius', 'On Novels', *UMKP* 93 (July 1793): 8.

74 Ibid., 8.

75 Ibid.

76 'Sketch of the Progress of Novel-Writing', *The Port-Folio* 9.2 (1 Feb 1820): 270.

77 'Ned Culpepper, the Tomahawk', 'Mr. Edward Lytton Bulwer's Novels; and Remarks on Novel-Writing', *Fraser's Magazine for Town and Country* 1.5 (June 1830): 510.

Chapter 1

1 Review of *Nubilia in Search of a Husband*, *The Scottish Review* 71 (Aug 1809): 595.

2 Review of *Valombrosa; or, The Venetian Nun*, *CR*, 3rd ser., 4.3 (Mar 1805): 329.

3 Derek Roper, *Reviewing before the Edinburgh, 1782–1802* (Newark: University of Delaware Press, 1978), 37. Antonia Forster similarly notes the changing landscape for reviews in her *Index to Book Reviews in England, 1775–1800* (London: British Library, 1997). The *English Novel* bibliography of 2000 gave much greater specificity to the problem, with Peter Garside noting in the introduction to its second volume that 'by the beginning of the new century the policy of all-inclusion had become well nigh untenable' (16).

4 These numbers will, of course, vary somewhat depending on one's definition of 'novel', but there seems to be little debate that percentages of novels reviewed in the major reviews dropped during the period in question.

In forthcoming work, Megan Peiser identifies multiple novels reviewed that were not included in the *English Novel* bibliography.

5 On the role of reviewers in eighteenth-century literary success before this period, see Frank Donoghue, *The Fame Machine: Book Reviewing and Eighteenth-Century Literary Careers* (Stanford, CA: Stanford University Press, 1996).

6 Holcroft, Review of *Man as He Is, MR*, 2nd ser., 10 (Mar 1793): 297, cited in Roper, *Reviewing*, 123.

7 On gender and eighteenth-century book reviewing, see Laura Runge, *Gender and Language in British Literary Criticism, 1660–1790* (New York: Cambridge University Press, 1997). While male reviewers frequently criticized women authors on the basis of gender, women critics too participated in this process. See Megan Peiser, 'Reviewing Women: Women Reviewers on Women Novelists', in *Women's Periodicals and Print Culture in Britain, 1690–1820s: The Long Eighteenth Century*, edited by Jennie Batchelor and Manushag N. Powell (Edinburgh: Edinburgh University Press, 2018), 236–249, and Mary A. Waters, *British Women Writers and the Profession of Literary Criticism, 1789–1832* (Basingstoke: Palgrave Macmillan, 2004).

8 Review of *Emily, or The Fatal Promise, a Northern Tale, CR*, 2nd ser., 5 (June 1792): 234.

9 Review of *The Follies of St James Street , MR*, 2nd ser., 4 (Jan 1791): 92.

10 Review of *The Bristol Heiress, CR*, 3rd ser., 19.1 (Jan 1810): 97.

11 Review of *The Family Party, ER* 20 (July 1792): 69.

12 Review of *Elvina, a Novel, CR*, 2nd ser., 5 (June 1792): 233.

13 OED 'wire-draw, v.' OED Online, September 2019 (accessed 7 Oct 2019).

14 Review of *Forresti; or, The Italian Cousins: A Romance, CR*, 3rd ser., 11.1 (May 1807): 96–97.

15 Review of *Edmund; or, The Child of the Castle, CR* 70 (Oct 1790): 454.

16 Review of *Hermione, or The Orphan Sisters, ER* 18 (Sept 1791): 230.

17 Review of *Fanny; or, The Deserted Daughter, ER* 19 (June 1792): 471.

18 Review of *A Butler's Diary; or, The History of Miss Eggerton, GM* 62.2 (Feb 1792): 192.

19 Review of *The Duchess of York: An English Story, MR,* 2nd ser., 8 (July 1792): 339–340.

20 See Megan Peiser, 'William Lane and the Minerva Press in the Review Periodical, 1790–1820', *Romantic Textualities: Literature and Print Culture, 1780–1840* 23 (Summer 2020): 130–131 on discussions of the identification of Minerva Press novels as a particular literary class or kind.

21 Review of *Humbert Castle, CR*, 2nd ser., 32 (June 1801): 231.

22 Review of *Anna Melvil, ER* 21 (Feb 1793): 147–148.

23 Review of *The Aunt and the Niece, CR*, 3rd ser., 3.4 (Dec 1804): 470.

24 Review of *Persiana; or, The Nymph of the Sea, CR*, 2nd ser., 2 (July 1791): 356.

25 On the importance of periodical writing in establishing literary canonicity, see Rachael Scarborough King, '"[L]et a Girl Read": Periodicals and Women's

Literary Canon Formation', in *Women's Periodicals and Print Culture*, ed. Batchelor and Powell, 221–235.

26 Review of *The Butler's Diary; or, The History of Miss Eggerton*, CR, 2nd ser., 4 (Feb 1792): 236.

27 Review of *Ariana and Maud*, CR, 2nd ser., 37 (Mar 1803): 356.

28 Review of *First Love*, CR, 2nd ser., 32 (July 1801): 352.

29 Review of *The Cypher, or The World as It Goes*, The Town and Country *Magazine* 23 (Aug 1791): 357.

30 Review of *Monimia*, CR, 2nd ser., 3 (Oct 1791): 235.

31 Review of *Charles Henly; or, The Fugitive Record*, CR 70 (Aug 1790): 219.

32 Review of *Mortimer Castle; A Cambrian Tale*, ER (Oct 1793): 307.

33 Peiser, 'William Lane', 129, table 1.

34 Review of *Woman as She Should Be; or, Memoirs of Mrs. Menville*, CR, 2nd ser., 9 (Sept 1793): 118.

35 Review of *Errors of Education*, The Town and Country Magazine 23 (Nov 1791): 507.

36 Review of *Monimia*, The Town and Country Magazine 23 (Nov 1791): 508.

37 Review of *The Baron of Manstow*, ER (Mar 1791): 232.

38 See Peiser, 'William Lane', 133, for discussion of metaphors involving textiles, weaving, sewing, and other kinds of feminine-coded work in Minerva reviews. In my essay 'Gothic before Gothic: Minerva Press Reviews, Gender, and the Evolution of Genre', in *Women's Authorship and the Early Gothic: Innovations and Legacies*, ed. Kathleen Hudson (Cardiff: University of Wales Press, 2020), I discuss how reviewers use gendered metaphors such as these to direct authors towards (and away from) certain kinds of writing.

39 Review of *Heaven's Best Gift*, The Monthly Visitor 2 (Nov 1797): 478.

40 Catherine Harris, *Edwardina, a Novel* (London: Minerva Press, 1800).

41 Review of *Edwardina*, CR, 2nd ser., 31 (Mar 1801): 354.

42 See the Epilogue for further discussion of Lane's advertising and the financial position of his authors. On the life of Romantic authors, including financial constraints and motivations, see Matthew Sangster, *Living as an Author in the Romantic Period* (Basingstoke: Palgrave Macmillan, 2021).

43 Review of *First Impressions*, CR, 2nd ser., 32 (June 1801): 233.

44 Review of *Belleville Lodge*, CR, 2nd ser., 7 (Mar 1793): 357.

45 Review of *Independence*, CR, 2nd ser., 37 (Feb 1803): 237.

46 Review of *The Family Party*, ER 20 (July 1792): 69.

47 Anna Maria Bennett, *The Beggar Girl and Her Benefactors* (London: Printed for William Lane, at the Minerva-Press, 1797).

48 Review of *Henry of Northumberland*, CR, 2nd ser., 29 (May 1800): 115.

49 Review of *The Dangers of Coquetry*, The Town and Country Magazine 22 (Oct 1790): 460.

50 Review of *The Scottish Legend*, CR, 2nd ser., 36 (Sept 1802): 117.

51 Peiser, 'William Lane', figure 3.

52 Peiser, 'William Lane.'

53 Clery, *The Rise of Supernatural Fiction, 1762–1800* (Cambridge: Cambridge University Press, 1995), 137.

54 Review of *Memoirs of Joan d'Arc*, *CR*, 3rd ser., 2.4 (Oct 1812): 411.

55 Review of *History of the Duke de Lauzun*, *CR*, 3rd ser., 13.4 (Jan–Apr 1808): 450.

56 Review of *Observations on a Journey through Spain and Italy to Naples*, *CR*, 3rd ser., 12.1 (Sept 1807): 80–81.

57 Review of *Faulkener*, *CR* 3rd ser., 13 (1808): 415.

58 See, e..g., the review of *Rhymes on Art; or, the Remonstrance of the Painter*, *CR*, 3rd. ser., 4.4 (Apr 1805): 446.

59 See Ina Ferris, *The Achievement of Literary Authority: Gender, History, and the Waverley Novels* (Ithaca, NY: Cornell University Press, 1991), 43, on the 'discursive promiscuity and fertility' of the novel.

60 Review of *The Stranger in Ireland; or, A Tour to the Southern and Western Parts of That Country in 1805*, *CR*, 3rd. ser., 9.3 (1806): 315. On gender and book reviewing in this period, in addition to King and Runge, see Pam Perkins, 'Reviewing Femininity: Gender and Genre in the Late Eighteenth- and Early Nineteenth-Century Periodical Press', in *Women's Periodicals and Print Culture*, ed. Batchelor and Powell, 250–262.

61 See James Raven, *The Business of Books: Booksellers and the English Book Trade, 1450–1850* (New Haven, CT: Yale University Press, 2007), 284, on the practice of including quotations from reviews in end-page advertisements.

62 Mary Charlton, *Phedora; or, The Forest of Minski: A Novel* (London: Minerva Press, 1798), I:n.p.

63 Ibid., vols. II and III, n.p. Vol II does not identify the *British Critic* as the review's source.

64 See Dorothy Blakey, *The Minerva Press, 1790–1820* (London: Printed for the Bibliographic Society at the Oxford University Press), 1939, 101–104, on the Minerva's use of review extracts for advertising.

65 This kind of authorial strategy was of course not limited to this period, or to novelists alone; see, e.g., George Justice's account of prefatorial manoeuvring by authors like Frances Brooke and Frances Burney earlier in the century in chapter 4 of *The Manufacturers of Literature: Writing and the Literary Marketplace in Eighteenth-Century England* (Newark: University of Delaware Press, 2002), or Jennie Batchelor's discussion of prefaces by female authors in hardship in chapter 4 of *Women's Work: Labour, Gender, Authorship, 1750–1830* (Manchester: Manchester University Press, 2010). And Michael Gamer has recently shown how Romantic poets including Charlotte Smith and Wordsworth actively engaged with the market through (among other things) re-publication and savvy use of paratextual material in *Romanticism, Self-Canonization, and the Business of Poetry* (Cambridge University Press, 2017).

66 Ronald M'Chronicle, *Burton: A Novel*, vol. I (London: A. K. Newman and Co., 1825), I:2.

67 *Laurentia, a Novel* (London: Minerva Press, 1790), I:i–ii.

68 See Batchelor, *Women's Work*, chapter 4, for ties between gender, finance, and prefatory self-positioning. On gender and author/reviewer relationships more broadly, see Runge, *Gender and Language*.

69 Eliza Parsons, *The Mysterious Warning* (London: Minerva Press, 1796), I:6.

70 Ibid., I:3.

71 George Walker, *The Haunted Castle, a Norman Romance* (London: Printed at the Minerva-Press, 1794), I:v.

72 *Iphigenia, a Novel* (London: Minerva Press, 1791), I:i.

73 Robert Bage, *Man as He Is: A Novel* (London: Minerva Press, 1792), I:iii.

74 T. J. Horsley, *Ethelwina, or The House of Fitz-Auburne: A Romance of Former Times* (London: Minerva Press, 1799), I:ii.

75 Eliza Sophia Tomlins, *Rosalind de Tracy: A Novel*, 2nd ed., vol. I (London: Minerva Press, 1799), I:iii. (Note: The first edition of the novel also includes this preface, but was published by Charles Dilly the previous year.)

76 Eliza Parsons, *Ellen and Julia* (London: Minerva Press, 1793), I:n.p.

77 Ibid.

78 André Guillaume Contant D'Orville, *Pauline; or, The Victim of the Heart: From the French of D'Orville* (London: Minerva Press, 1794), I:vi.

79 William Linley, *Forbidden Apartments* (London: Minerva Press, 1800), I:iv.

80 Anna Maria Mackenzie, *Mysteries Elucidated, a Novel* (London: Minerva Press, 1795), I:iv.

81 Ibid., I:ix.

82 Mary Ann Hanway, *Ellinor; or The World as It Is* (London: Minerva Press, 1798), I:iii–iv.

83 Sarah Lansdell, *Manfredi, Baron St. Osmund: An Old English Romance* (London: Minerva Press, 1796), I:vi–vii. Intriguingly, Anna Maria Bennett is inked out in the Bodleian/*ECCO* copy, perhaps suggesting a reader who disagreed with her inclusion on this list.

84 Ibid., vi–vii.

85 Tomlins, *Rosalind de Tracey*, I:v

86 Maria Hunter, *Ella: or, He's Always in the Way* (London: Minerva Press, 1798), I:iv.

87 Linley, *Forbidden Apartments*, I:iv–v.

88 D'Orville, *Pauline*, I:vii.

89 Francis Lathom, *The Unknown; or, The Northern Gallery* (London: Minerva Press, 1808), I:v.

90 Ibid., v.

91 See *DBF* (www.british-fiction.cf.ac.uk/index.html) for the full listing; 'Holstein' is listed here as a pseudonym, but, lacking an identification of a real author, I continue to refer to him as such in this section.

92 Anthony Frederick Holstein, *Lady Durnevor; or, My Father's Wife* (London: Minerva Press, 1813), I:iii.

93 Anthony Frederick Holstein, *Bouverie: The Pupil of the World* (London: Minerva Press, 1812), I:[i], ix.

94 Ibid., ix–x.

95 Anthony Frederick Holstein, *The Inhabitants of Earth; or, The Follies of Woman: A Novel* (London: Minerva Press, 1811), I:i.

96 Other authors of the period took an opposite approach to the same concern; see, for instance, Catherine Gallagher's account of Maria Edgeworth and her 'fear of overproduction', which led her to edit her works concisely. Gallagher, *Nobody's Story: The Vanishing Acts of Women Writers in the Marketplace 1670–1820* (Oxford: Clarendon, 1994), 262.

97 Anthony Frederick Holstein, *The Modern Kate; or, A Husband Perplexed* (London: Minerva Press, 1812), I:v–vi; *Lady Durnevor; or, My Fathers's Wife: A Novel* (London: Minerva Press, 1813), I:i.

98 Holstein, *Lady Durnevor*, I:i–ii.

99 Joseph Moser, *Turkish Tales* (London: Minerva Press, 1796), I:i–ii.

100 *Reginal di Torby, or the Twelve Robbers* (London: Minerva Press, 1803), I:vii–viii.

101 Anthony Frederick Holstein, *The Miseries of an Heiress* (London: Minerva Press, 1810), I:xvii–xviii.

102 Ibid., I:i.

103 Mary Meeke, *Something Odd! A Novel* (London: Minerva Press, 1804), I:vi.

104 Linley, *Forbidden Apartments*, I:vii.

105 Ibid., I:vii–viii.

106 Joseph Moser, *The Hermit of Caucasus* (London: Minerva Press, 1796), I:x–xi.

107 Mrs. Martin, *Melbourne* (London: Minerva Press, 1798), I:5.

108 [Carl Grosse], *Horrid Mysteries: A Story; From the German of the Marquis of Grosse* (London: Minerva Press, 1798), I:xii.

109 *Concealment; or, The Cascade of Llantwarryhn* (London: Minerva Press, 1801), I:iii.

110 *De Willenberg; or, The Talisman* (London: A. K. Newman and Co., 1821), I:ii.

111 Elizabeth Bonhote, *Bungay Castle* (London: Minerva Press, 1796), I:xviii–xix.

112 Francis Lathom, *London; or, Truth without Treason* (London: Minerva Press, 1809), I:iv.

113 Siddons, *Reginal di Torby*, I:x.

114 Henry Summersett, *Leopold Warndorf*, vol. I (London: Minerva Press, 1800), I:vi–viii.

115 Regina Maria Roche, *The Vicar of Lansdowne*, 2nd ed. (London: Minerva Press, 1800), I:iii–iv.

116 Quintin Poynet, *The Wizard Priest and the Witch* (London: A. K. Newman and Co., 1822), I:iii.

117 James MacHenry, *The Wilderness; or, The Youthful Days of Washington: A Tale of the West* (London: A. K. Newman and Co., 1823), I:iii. This author appears in the Corvey Collection/*NCCO* as 'James M'Henry'; the title page and preface bear the pseudonym 'Solomon Secondsight'.

118 Mary White, *Beatrice; or, The Wycherly Family,*(London: A. K. Newman and Co., 1824), I:i; Anna Maria Mackenzie, *Feudal Events, or Days of Yore: An Ancient Story* (London: Minerva Press, 1800), I:viii.

119 Helen Craik, *Henry of Northumberland; or, The Hermit's Cell: A Tale of the Fifteenth Century* (London: Minerva Press, 1800), I:i.

120 Francis Lathom, *The Mysterious Freebooter; or, The Days of Queen Bess: A Romance* (London: Minerva Press, 1806), I:viii–ix.

121 Siddons, *Reginal di Torby*, I:[v].

122 H. J. Jackson, *Romantic Readers: The Evidence of Marginalia* (New Haven, CT: Yale University Press, 2005); William St Clair, *The Reading Nation in the Romantic Period* (Cambridge: Cambridge University Press, 2004). See also, e.g., Richard Altick, *The English Common Reader* (Chicago: University of Chicago Press, 1957); Jan Fergus, *Provincial Readers in Eighteenth-Century England* (Oxford: Oxford University Press, 2006); and Jon Klancher, *The Making of English Reading Audiences* (Madison: University of Wisconsin Press, 1987).

123 For analysis of a fascinating group of Minerva Press novels complete with reader comments and annotations from an early American library, see Eric Daffron, 'Transatlantic Terror: James Hammond's Circulating Library and the Minerva Press Gothic Novel', *Romantic Textualities* 23 (Summer 2020): 109–123. On marginalia more generally, see particularly Jackson, *Romantic Readers*. The Book Traces Project (Andrew Stauffer) collects reader's marks, including those found in many early nineteenth century works (www .booktraces.org/). For analysis of library records and readerships, see especially David Allan, *A Nation of Readers* (London: British Library, 2008); Fergus, *Provincial Readers*; Christopher Skelton-Foord, 'Economics, Expertise, Enterprise and the Literary Scene: The Commercial Management Ethos in British Circulating Libraries, 1780–1830', in *Authorship, Commerce and the Public: Scenes of Writing, 1750–1850*, ed. E. J. Clery, Caroline Franklin, and Peter Garside (London: Palgrave Macmillan UK, 2002), 136–152; and Mark Towsey, '"All Partners May Be Enlightened and Improved by Reading Them": The Distribution of Enlightenment Books in Scottish Subscription Library Catalogues 1750–c. 1820', *Journal of Scottish Historical Studies* 28.1 (2008): 20–43.

124 The Reading Experience Database: www.open.ac.uk/Arts/reading/UK/. On print runs, see, e.g. St Clair's numerous appendices.

125 Authors including Mary Shelley and Jane Austen, for instance, left records of their reading in letters or other writings.

Chapter 2

1 Mary Wollstonecraft, *The Works of Mary Wollstonecraft*, ed. Marilyn Butler and Janet M. Todd, vol. VII (New York: New York University Press, 1989), 104.

2 See ibid., VII:14–18, on the difficulties of identifying many *AR* contributors.

3 For more in-depth discussion of the way women reviewers handled novels by women authors, see Megan Peiser, 'Reviewing Women: Women Reviewers on Women Novelists', in *Women's Periodicals and Print Culture in Britain, 1690–1820s: The Long Eighteenth Century*, edited by Jennie Batchelor and Manushag N. Powell (Edinburgh: Edinburgh University Press, 2018), 236–249.

4 Though there is no final evidence that this unsigned review is by Wollstonecraft, I accept Todd and Butler's identification of her authorship for the purposes of my argument here. For a complete listing of Maria Regina Roche's novels, see Peter Garside, James Raven, and Rainer Schöwerling, eds., *The English Novel, 1770–1829: A Bibliographical Survey of Prose Fiction Published in the British Isles* (Oxford: Oxford University Press, 2000). Christina Morin has recently shown the importance of Roche and the Minerva Press within the field of Irish gothic fiction; see Christina Morin, *The Gothic Novel in Ireland: C. 1760–1829* (Manchester: Manchester University Press, 2018), esp. chapter 4, 'Gothic Materialities: Regina Maria Roche, the Minerva Press, and the Bibliographic Spread of Irish Gothic Fiction', 154–195.

5 For further discussion of Mary Wollstonecraft and Minerva Press novels, see Elizabeth Neiman, *Minerva's Gothics: The Politics and Poetics of Romantic Exchange, 1780–1820* (Cardiff: University of Wales Press, 2019), 49–100.

6 William Godwin, *Imogen, a Pastoral Romance from the Ancient British*, ed. Jack Marken, rpt. ed. (New York: New York Public Library, 1963). Subsequent *Imogen* citations refer to this edition.

7 Review of *Imogen, a Pastoral Romance, from the Ancient British*, *MR* 72 (Mar 1785): 233–234. Cited in Godwin, *Imogen*, 17. The notable exception to this trend was the *English Review*, which praised the novel in rather strong terms. As *Imogen*'s editor, Jack Marken, points out, however, this praise is slightly suspect, given its provenance: 'Since [*Imogen*'s author] was writing for the *English Review* at this time, possibly the reviewer was attempting to please the author or, as often happened, the author wrote the review himself' (Godwin, *Imogen*, 17).

8 Reproduced in Dorothy Blakey, *The Minerva Press, 1790–1820* (London: Printed for the Bibliographic Society at the Oxford University Press, 1939), 309–314.

9 Godwin, *Imogen*, 9.

10 William Godwin, *Caleb Williams*, ed. Gary J. Handwerk and A. A. Markley (Peterborough: Broadview Press, 2000), 444.

11 William Godwin, *Memoirs of the Author of a Vindication of the Rights of Woman* (London: Printed for J. Johnson, 1798), 93.

12 For the attribution to Inchbald, see Godwin, *Caleb Williams*, ed. Handwerk and Markley, 32. Mary Ann Hanway, *Ellinor; or, The World as It Is* (London: Minerva Press, 1798).

13 Scholarship on this group has followed Gary Kelly's influential work *The English Jacobin Novel, 1780–1805* (Oxford: Clarendon Press, 1976). While Eliza Parsons' work has primarily been discussed through a gothic lens, with the author herself viewed as quite conservative, some recent scholarship has begun to understand her work, as I do, in a more politically ambiguous light; see Hoeveler's claim that *Castle Wolfenbach* is an 'ideologically bifurcated female gothic', and Neiman's argument that in another Parsons novel, *The Mysterious Warning*, as in other 'female-authored Minerva Press novels, we should expect neither consistently conventional nor radically atypical themes, but rather complex negotiations between competing discourses by women'. Parsons, *The Castle of Wolfenbach: A German Story* (1793), edited by Diane Long Hoeveler (Chicago: Valancourt Books, 2006), vii, ix; see also Elizabeth Neiman, 'The Female Authors of the Minerva Press and "Copper Currency": Revaluing the Reproduction of "Immaculate-Born Minervas"', in *Global Economies, Cultural Currencies of the Eighteenth Century*, edited by Michael Rotenberg-Schwartz and Tara Czechowski (New York: AMS, 2012), 288.

14 Antonia Forster notes that the *Analytical Review* published reviews of the following four Parsons works (one is a play) before 1800: *Anecdotes of Two Well-Known Families* (1798), *AR* 27 (1798): 644–645; *Intrigues of a Morning, AR* 13 (1792): 469; *Lucy, AR* 20 (1794): 49–52; *The Voluntary Exile, AR* 21 (1795): 296–299. Forster, *Index to Book Reviews in England, 1775–1800* (London: British Library, 1997).

15 Review of *Hermsprong, AR* 24.6 (December 1796): 608–609; see relevant discussion in Derek Roper, *Reviewing before the Edinburgh* (Newark: University of Delaware Press, 1978), 149, and James Watt, '"The Blessings of Freedom": Britain, America, and "the East" in the Fiction of Robert Bage,' *Eighteenth Century Fiction* 22.1 (2009): 64.

16 In its attention to the proliferation of dissenting voices and political forces within and without the novel, this chapter's analysis echoes some aspects of Bakhtin's work on heteroglossia; see M. M. Bakhtin, *The Dialogic Imagination: Four Essays*, trans. Michael Holquist (Austin: University of Texas Press, 1981).

17 Mark Philp, *Reforming Ideas in Britain: Politics and Language in the Shadow of the French Revolution, 1789–1815* (Cambridge: Cambridge University Press, 2014), 8.

18 See, e.g., ibid., 20–24, for a brief overview of some of the different media forms involved in the debate. M. O. Grenby, *The Anti-Jacobin Novel: British Conservatism and the French Revolution* (Cambridge: Cambridge University Press, 2001), 22, provides a more in-depth discussion of suspicions about novels being political.

19 Grenby, *Anti-Jacobin Novel*, 4.

20 Jon Mee, *Print, Publicity, and Popular Radicalism in the 1790s: The Laurel of Liberty* (Cambridge: Cambridge University Press, 2016), 12; Grenby, *Anti-Jacobin Novel*, 65.

21 Mee, *Print, Publicity, and Popular Radicalism*, 8.

22 Ibid., 37. Mee here credits the work of Mary Fairclough, *The Romantic Crowd: Sympathy, Controversy, and Print Culture* (Cambridge: Cambridge University Press, 2013), 116.

23 Mee, *Print, Publicity, and Popular Radicalism*, 37.

24 Qtd. in ibid., 37–38.

25 Fairclough, *The Romantic Crowd*, see especially pp. 82–107.

26 Ibid., 82.

27 Paul Keen, *The Crisis of Literature in the 1790s: Print Culture and the Public Sphere* (Cambridge: Cambridge University Press, 1999), 35. Here Keen is quoting Wollstonecraft, *The Works of Mary Wollstonecraft*, vol. VI, 16.

28 'On the Epistolary Mode of Novel-Writing', *LM* 18 (Oct 1787): 538.

29 Ibid.

30 Ibid.

31 Keen, *Crisis of Literature*, 56.

32 Review of *The Adventures of Hugh Trevor*, British Critic 4 (July 1794): 71. Qtd. in Keen, *Crisis of Literature*, 56.

33 Eliza Parsons, *The History of Miss Meredith: A Novel* (London: Printed for the Author and sold by T. Hookham, 1790), 'Preface.'

34 For Bage's biography, including the facts I've cited here, see Gary Kelly, 'Robert Bage', in *The Oxford Dictionary of National Biography* (Oxford University Press Online, 2006), accessed 8 Feb 2011, doi:10.1093/ref:odnb/ 1028. Information on Eliza Parsons, an obscurer figure, is available at 'Eliza Parsons', in *Orlando: Women's Writing in the British Isles from the Beginnings to the Present* (Cambridge University Press Online, 2006), accessed 14 June 2013, http://orlando.cambridge.org/; see also Jennie Batchelor, *Women's Work: Labour, Gender, Authorship, 1750–1830* (Manchester: Manchester University Press, 2010), 162–180, for a useful discussion of Parsons's applications to the Royal Literary Fund.

35 Eliza Parsons, *Woman as She Should Be; or, Memoirs of Mrs. Menville: A Novel*, 4 vols. (London: Minerva-Press, 1793); Robert Bage, *Man as He Is*, 4 vols. (London: Minerva-Press, 1792). Subsequent parenthetical citations refer to these editions.

36 Grenby, *Anti-Jacobin Novel*, 3, offers an example of an anti-Jacobin novel with a similar clearly stated moral to support his claim that it was not in fact difficult to distinguish between loyalist and radical novels; in one sense this is surely true (a maxim is an obvious statement of authorial intent), but my analysis of Bage and Parsons suggests that it is a mistake to take such a claim at face value: just because a work claims it will demonstrate something doesn't mean it actually will do so.

37 Review of *The Spirit of the Elbe*, MR, 2nd ser., 30 (Sept 1799): 93.

38 On the decline of the epistolary form, see Raven, 'Historical Introduction: The Novel Comes of Age', in *The English Novel*, ed. Garside et al., 30–31.

39 See Claudia L. Johnson, *Equivocal Beings: Politics, Gender, and Sentimentality in the 1790s: Wollstonecraft, Radcliffe, Burney, Austen* (Chicago: University of Chicago Press, 1995), 52–69, for relevant discussion of Wollstonecraft's

novels. Sarah Scott, *A Description of Millenium Hall* (London: Newbery, 1762).

40 Godwin, *Political and Philosophical Writings of William Godwin*, edited by Mark Philp (London: William Pickering, 1993), 453.

41 Grenby, *Anti-Jacobin Novel*, 49.

42 It would be simplistic to suggest that these popular novels sold well *only* because they managed to offend nobody – as other best-selling works, including *Caleb Williams* or, in a different context, *Uncle Tom's Cabin*, make clear, it certainly is possible to be both polemical and popular. (I thank Mark McGurl for suggesting the *Uncle Tom's Cabin* comparison.) What I want to emphasize here, however, is how Bage and Parsons incorporate opposing viewpoints and (as I'll suggest in the chapter's conclusion), tie that approach directly to the idea of popular reader response.

43 See Grenby, *Anti-Jacobin Novel*, 9–10 and 61–63.

44 Mary Wollstonecraft, *The Collected Letters of Mary Wollstonecraft*, ed. Janet Todd (New York: Penguin Classics, 2004), 136.

45 Ibid., 404.

46 See, for instance, Sharma, *Autobiography of Desire*, on the treatment of autobiographical components of 1790s women writers' works.

47 See Mary Hays, *Memoirs of Emma Courtney*, edited by Marilyn L. Brooks (Peterborough: Broadview Press, 2000), 11–17, and James Boaden, *Memoirs of Mrs. Inchbald: Including Her Familiar Correspondence with the Most Distinguished Persons of Her Time* (London: Richard Bentley, 1833), 140–141. Inchbald's costume ball escapade is described in Terry Castle, *Masquerade and Civilization: The Carnivalesque in Eighteenth-Century English Culture and Fiction* (Stanford, CA: Stanford University Press, 1986), 291.

48 See, e.g., Grenby, *Anti-Jacobin Novel*, 9: 'Fiction was perfectly adapted to reinforce anti-Jacobin nostrums without appearing to ram them home. But moreover, as a commodity in a competitive market, they would have been unable to do anything else – unless their authors or publishers were prepared to sustain large financial losses.'

49 Thomas Constable, *Archibald Constable and His Literary Correspondents* (Edinburgh: Edmonston and Douglas, 1873), II: 68. Quoted in Godwin, *Caleb Williams*, ed. David McCracken (New York: Norton, 1977), x–xi.

50 Bisset, *Modern Literature* III:181–182, qtd. in Grenby, *Anti-Jacobin Novel*, 20.

51 William Godwin, *Caleb Williams*, ed. Pamela Clemit (Oxford: Oxford University Press, 2009), 312. Subsequent parenthetical citations of the novel refer to this edition unless otherwise noted.

52 J.B., 'On Novels and Novel Writers', *EM* 75 (May 1819): 404.

53 On English literacy and its rise over the eighteenth century, see, e.g., Richard Altick, *The English Common Reader* (Chicago: University of Chicago Press, 1957), esp. chapters 2 and 3.

54 J.B., 'Upon Novels and Novel Writers', *EM* 75 (May 1819): 405.

55 Robert Bage, *James Wallace*, vol. III (London: W. Lane, 1788), 164.

56 Such claims do have some basis in reality, but as Altick notes (with reference to a nearly identical quotation from the bookseller Lackington), they vastly overstate the case, especially when thinking about rural readers (Altick, *English Common Reader*, 39).

57 Robert Bage, *Barham Downs* (Tamworth: Printed by and sold for B. Shelton, 1784), I:322. This quotation and some additional parts of this section first appeared in my article, 'Robert Bage's Novel Merchandise: Commercialism, Gender, and Form in Late Eighteenth-Century Fiction', in *The Eighteenth-Century Novel*, edited by Albert J. Rivero and George Justice (New York: AMS Press, 2012), IX:171–192.

58 Robert Bage, *Mount Henneth* (London: T. Lowndes, 1782), II:130.

59 Ibid.

60 Mee, *Print, Publicity, and Popular Radicalism* 42.

61 John Barrell, *The Spirit of Despotism: Invasions of Privacy in the 1790s* (Oxford: Oxford University Press, 2006), 4.

62 Fairclough, *The Romantic Crowd*, 7.

63 Godwin, *Caleb Williams*, ed. Handwerk and Markley, 9.

64 Ibid., 450.

65 For discussion of the metaphor of consumption as it related to (especially female) reading, see Ina Ferris, *The Achievement of Literary Authority: Gender, History, and the Waverley Novels* (Ithaca, NY: Cornell University Press, 1991), 37–39.

66 Wollstonecraft, *Collected Letters*, 404.

67 See William Warner, *Licensing Entertainment: The Elevation of Novel Reading in Britain, 1684–1750* (Berkeley: University of California Press, 1998), 292, on the relationship between 'formula fiction' and the 'legitimate novel'.

68 Fairclough, *Romantic Crowd*, 82.

69 James Mackintosh, Review of the *Lives of Edward and John Philips, Nephews and Pupils of Milton, &c.*, *The Edinburgh Review* 25.50 (Oct 1815): 487; quoted in Godwin, *Caleb Williams*, ed. Handwerk and Markley, 564.

70 Ibid.

71 Review of *Things as They Are*, CR, 2nd ser., 11 (July 1794): 290; review of *Things as They Are*, MR, 2nd ser., 15 (Oct 1794): 146.

72 Review of *Things as They Are*, British Critic 4 (July 1794): 71, emphasis added.

73 Review of *Things as They Are*, CR, 2nd ser., 11 (July 1794): 290, emphasis added.

74 Fairclough, *Romantic Crowd*, 99.

75 Hays, *Memoirs*, 37–38.

76 Grenby, *Anti-Jacobin Novel*, 9–10.

77 Godwin's preface to the Bentley's Standard Novels edition of *Fleetwood* (1832), quoted from Godwin, *Caleb Williams*, ed. Handwerk and Markley, 445.

Chapter 3

1 [William Lane], 'A Tale Addressed to the Novel Readers of the Present Day', [1794?], New York Society Library, Hammond Collection, Ham O412 W4. For further discussion of this advertisement, see Deborah McLeod, 'The Minerva Press' (PhD diss., University of Alberta, 1997), 4; Kurt E. Milberger, '"The first impression, you, yourself, will buy": The Gunninghiad, *Virginius and Virginia* and the Art of Scandal at the Minerva Press', *Romantic Textualities: Literature and Print Culture, 1780–1840* 23 (Summer 2020): 39–59; and Michael Sadleir, '"Minerva Press" Publicity: A Publisher's Advertisement of 1794', *The Library*, 2nd ser., 21 (1940), 207–215. These three analyses are based on Sadleir's edition of the pamphlet held in the British Library; here I cite a second extant copy that I located thanks to the detailed cataloguing of the New York Society Library. This version does not include Lane's 'Address to the Public' at the end. I am very grateful to Barbara Bieck for her assistance in digitizing and sharing this copy with me during the pandemic.

2 Lane, 'A Tale', 3.

3 Peter Teuthold [Kahlert, Karl Friedrich], *The Necromancer, or The Tale of the Black Forest*, 2 vols. (London: Minerva-Press, 1794); Joseph Moser, *The Turkish Tales*, 2 vols. (London: Minerva-Press, 1794); Anon., *Edward De Courcy, an Ancient Fragment*, 2 vols. (London: Minerva-Press, 1794); Anon., *Count Roderic's Castle; or Gothic Times*, 2 vols (London: Minerva-Press, 1794); Anon., *Castle Zittaw, a German Tale*, 3 vols. (London: Minerva-Press, 1794).

4 Lane, 'A Tale', 2.

5 James Raven, *The Business of Books: Booksellers and the English Book Trade 1450–1850* (New Haven, CT: Yale University Press, 2007), 285, provides another example of Lane's blending of fiction and advertisement in *The Follies of St James Street*.

6 Jane Austen, *Northanger Abbey*, ed. Barbara Benedict and Deirdre Le Faye (Cambridge: Cambridge University Press, 2006), 205. Subsequent parenthetical citations refer to this edition.

7 Ibid., 108; 33. For further discussion of the 'Horrid Novels', see Michael Sadleir, *The Northanger Novels: A Footnote to Jane Austen* (Oxford: Oxford University Press, 1927); Douglass H. Thomson and Frederick S. Frank, 'Jane Austen and the Northanger Novelists', in *Gothic Writers: A Critical & Bibliographical Guide*, ed. Douglass H. Thomson, Jack G. Voller, and Frederick S. Frank (Westport, CT: Greenwood Press, 2001), 33–47; and Natalie Neill, '"The trash with which the press now groans": *Northanger Abbey* and the Gothic Best Sellers of the 1790s', *Eighteenth-Century Novel* 4 (2004): 163–192.

8 Elizabeth Neiman, 'A New Perspective on the Minerva Press's "Derivative" Novels: Authorizing Borrowed Material', *European Romantic Review* 26.5 (2015): 634.

9 Edward Jacobs, 'Anonymous Signatures: Circulating Libraries, Conventionality and the Production of Gothic Romances', *English Literary History*, 62.3 (1995): 616. More recently, Jacobs has argued that Radcliffe 'authored several innovations in print culture', suggesting that 'she reinvented genericism' with her distinctive and reproducible narratives. 'Ann Radcliffe and Romantic Print Culture', in *Ann Radcliffe, Romanticism and the Gothic*, ed. Dale Townshend and Angela Wright (Cambridge: Cambridge University Press 2014), 49–66.

10 Deirdre Lynch, 'Gothic Libraries and National Subjects', *Studies in Romanticism*, 40.1 (2001): 31–32; see also Melissa Sodeman, *Sentimental Memorials: Women and the Novel in Literary History* (Stanford, CA: Stanford University Press, 2015), 3. Other scholars who have recently considered the Romantic novel's remarkable web of generic relationships include Franz Potter, *The History of Gothic Publishing* (Basingstoke: Palgrave Macmillan, 2005); Anthony Mandal, *Jane Austen and the Popular Novel: The Determined Author* (Basingstoke: Palgrave Macmillan, 2007); Yael Shapira, 'Isabella Kelly and the Minerva Gothic Challenge', *Romantic Textualities* 23 (Winter 2020): 168–184; Victoria Ravenwood, '"Historical Anecdotes Are the Most Proper Vehicles for the Elucidation of Knowledge": The "Historical Gothic" and the Minerva Press, 1790–99', *Romantic Textualities* 23 (Summer 2020): 60–75; and Diane Long Hoeveler, 'Gothic Adaptation, 1765–1830', in *The Gothic World*, ed. Glennis Byron and Dale Townshend (New York: Routledge, 2013), 185–198.

11 Edward Copeland, *Women Writing about Money: Women's Fiction in England, 1790–1820* (Cambridge: Cambridge University Press, 1995), 6.

12 E. J. Clery, *The Rise of Supernatural Fiction, 1762–1800* (Cambridge: Cambridge University Press, 1995), 137.

13 Michael Gamer, *Romanticism and the Gothic: Genre, Reception, and Canon Formation* (Cambridge: Cambridge University Press, 2000), 24.

14 James Watt, *Contesting the Gothic: Fiction, Genre, and Cultural Conflict, 1764–1832* (Cambridge: Cambridge University Press, 1999), 80; see also Clery on the ways that discussions of 'the sameness of Gothic fiction' showed 'larger concerns about the regulation of cultural production and the disciplining of readers' (5).

15 See especially Edward Jacobs, *Accidental Migrations: An Archaeology of Gothic Discourse* (Lewisburg, PA: Bucknell University Press, 2000), on the ties between the gothic genre and its modes of material circulation.

16 I discuss some early Lane works that were reviewed in terms of their relationship to earlier gothic authors in 'Gothic before Gothic: Minerva Press Reviews, Gender, and the Evolution of Genre', in *Women's Authorship and the Early Gothic: Legacies and Innovations*, ed. Kathleen Hudson (Cardiff: University of Wales Press), 43–64.

17 For discussion of reviews of Radcliffe's novels, see Derek Roper, *Reviewing before the Edinburgh, 1788–1802* (London: Methuen & Co., 1978), 132–139.

See Townshend and Wright, eds., *Ann Radcliffe, Romanticism and the Gothic*, 32 n. 1, on the dating of *The Italian*, which bears a 1797 date on its title page but, as they argue (following Robert Miles) appears to have been published in late 1796. Anne Radcliffe, *The Italian; or, The Confessional of the Black Penitents: A Romance*, ed. Robert Miles (London: Penguin, 2000).

18 On the dominance of Lane's press versus other publishers in the period 1790–1820, see the introductions to Peter Garside, James Raven, and Rainer Schöwerling, eds., *The English Novel, 1770–1829: A Bibliographical Survey of Prose Fiction Published in the British Isles* (Oxford: Oxford University Press, 2000), I:26, 73 and II:38, 83–85.

19 Review of the *Count De Santerre*, *Monthly Visitor* 2 (July 1797): 74, 77. While some Romantic reviewers have been subsequently identified, throughout this book I generally cite reviews in terms of each publication's corporate identity, to reflect the anonymity experienced by readers.

20 Radcliffe-inspired plays from the era include, for instance, *Fountainville Forest* (1794) and *The Mysteries of the Castle: A Dramatic Tale in Three Acts* (1795), both performed at Covent Garden. See also Diego Saglia, '"A portion of the name": Stage Adaptations of Radcliffe's Fiction, 1794–1806', in Townshend and Wright, eds., *Ann Radcliffe, Romanticism and the Gothic*, 219–236.

21 On sales of Radcliffe's novels, especially *Udolpho*, see William St Clair, *The Reading Nation in the Romantic Period* (Cambridge: Cambridge University Press, 2004), 631–632.

22 Rictor Norton, *Mistress of Udolpho: The Life of Ann Radcliffe* (London: Leicester University Press, 1999), 171.

23 See, e.g., Yael Shapira, 'Beyond the Radcliffe Formula: Isabella Kelly and the Gothic Troubles of the Married Heroine', *Women's Writing* 26.3 (2019): 245–263. Sue Chaplin offers a helpful discussion of 'the appropriations and renegotiations of the Radcliffean Gothic by women writers ... between 1793 and 1798' in 'Ann Radcliffe and Romantic-Era Fiction', in Townshend and Wright, eds., *Ann Radcliffe, Romanticism and the Gothic*, 203–218.

24 As Gamer points out, even the distinction between 'critical' and 'popular' reception in this period is complex, given that 'individuals often occupy both [sides of the divide] simultaneously by reading, reviewing, and writing gothic texts' (25).

25 Review of *The Abbey of St. Asaph*, *CR*, 2nd ser., 14 (July 1795): 349. This review, as well as several of those mentioned in the following paragraphs, is also cited in Rictor Norton, *Mistress of Udolpho: The Life of Ann Radcliffe* (London: Leicester University Press, 1999), 152–170.

26 Shapira notes that this reviewer's claim 'seems convincing enough if we read only the novel's third volume'; if we read it in its entirety, however, Kelly's work and Radcliffe's 'contain two distinct Gothic formulas' that 'differ from each other significantly' ('Beyond the Radcliffe Formula', 4–5).

27 Review of *The Castle of Hardayne: A Romance*, *AR* 23.1 (Jan 1796): 55.

28 Review of *Santa Maria*, *MR*, 2nd ser., 23 (June 1797): 210.

29 Review of *Oakendale Abbey, Monthly Visitor* 2 (Nov 1797): 478.
30 Review of *The Orphan of the Rhine, CR,* 2nd ser., 27 (Nov 1799): 356.
31 As Megan Peiser argues, summing up Minerva novels pejoratively as a 'class' or 'tribe' of their own – often using originality as a criterion for so doing – is common practice in the era's major reviews. Peiser, 'William Lane and the Minerva Press in the Review Periodical, 1790–1820', *Romantic Textualities: Literature and Print Culture, 1780–1840* 23 (Aug 2020): 124–148, 130.
32 Review of the *Count De Santerre, Monthly Visitor* 2 (July 1797): 74.
33 Review of *Hubert de Sevrac, CR,* 2nd ser., 23 (Aug 1798): 472.
34 Review of the *Count De Santerre, Monthly Visitor* 2 (July 1797): 74, 77.
35 Review of *Dusseldorf; or The Fratricide, CR,* 2nd ser., 24 (Oct 1798): 236.
36 Review of *The Haunted Cavern: A Caledonian Tale, CR,* 2nd ser., 15 (Dec 1795): 480.
37 Angela Wright, *Britain, France and the Gothic, 1764–1820: The Import of Terror* (Cambridge: Cambridge University Press, 2013), 78.
38 Ibid., 79, 93.
39 Ibid., 79.
40 Review of *Austenburn Castle, CR,* 2nd ser., 16 (Feb 1796): 222.
41 Wright, *Britain, France and the Gothic,* 84.
42 See Roper, *Reviewing before the Edinburgh,* 37, and Garside's introduction to vol. II of *The English Novel,* 16, for discussion of the ways increasing novel output affected reviewers. The role of the Minerva Press's books as conveniently synonymous with all things literarily undesirable has been noted in many works of gothic criticism; see, for example, Gamer, *Romanticism,* 67, and Watt, *Contesting the Gothic,* 80–84.
43 Review of *Valombrosa, or The Venetian Nun, CR,* 3rd ser., 4.3 (Mar 1805): 329, emphases added.
44 The use of 'imitators of Radcliffe' or closely related phrases to characterize 1790s gothics is ubiquitous in gothic criticism; to give just a few representative examples, see Kate Ferguson Ellis, *The Contested Castle: Gothic Novels and the Subversion of Domestic Ideology* (Urbana: University of Illinois Press, 1989), 207; Gary Kelly, *English Fiction of the Romantic Period, 1789–1830* (London: New York: Longman, 1989), 52; Rictor Norton, *Gothic Readings: The First Wave, 1764–1840* (London: Leicester University Press, 2000), 89. On eighteenth-century imitation more broadly, see, e.g., Robert L. Mack, *The Genius of Parody: Imitation and Originality in Seventeenth- and Eighteenth-Century English Literature* (Basingstoke: Palgrave Macmillan, 2007). Colin Burrow's *Imitating Authors: Plato to Futurity* (Oxford University Press, 2019) traces the longer history of literary imitation.
45 I follow the *ESTC*'s 'title' designation here – given the extreme variability of eighteenth-century titling practices, many of the results might strictly be considered subtitles or additional title-page descriptors. Urging imitation upon readers is also common in titles, so a substantial percentage of these works fall into this category, e.g., titles that encourage the 'imitation of Christ'.

46 Stéphanie-Félicité de Genlis, *The Castle of Kolmeras* (London: Minerva Press, 1804), 4. Subsequent parenthetical citations refer to this edition.

47 Wright, *Britain, France and the Gothic*, 102–103.

48 T. J. Horsley Curties, *Ancient Records; or, The Abbey of Saint Oswythe: A Romance* (London: Minerva-Press, 1801), I:i–ii.

49 See, for instance, the *Critical Review*'s sarcastic comments in the Review *of Ancient Records*, *CR*, 2nd ser., 32 (June 1801): 232.

50 In addition to justifying himself at great length in the preface, Curties also takes the opportunity to derogate female novelists in general, declaring that 'when female invention will employ itself in images of the grosser sort, it is a fatal prediction of relaxed morals, and species of – at least – literary prostitution'. Curties, *Ancient Records*, I:vi–vii.

51 *Eloise de Montblanc* (London: Minerva Press, 1796), I:i–ii.

52 George Justice's discussion of the paratexts of Burney and Brooke is relevant here for its account of the delicate balance between humility and self-promotion these authors had to maintain. *The Manufacturers of Literature: Writing and the Literary Marketplace in Eighteenth-Century England* (Newark: University of Delaware Press, 2002), esp. 157–170.

53 A. Hutchinson, *Exhibitions of the Heart* (London: Printed for the author and sold by Kearsley, 1799), I:147–148.

54 Francis Lathom, *Men and Manners*, a new edition (London: Wright and Symonds, 1800), I:212.

55 Ibid., I:213, 210.

56 Review of *Valombrosa, or The Venetian Nun*, *CR*, 3rd ser., 4.3 (Mar 1805): 329, emphases added.

57 Edward Du Bois, *St. Godwin: A Tale of the Sixteenth, Seventeenth, and Eighteenth Century* (Dublin: Wogan, 1800), 27.

58 For further discussion of Radcliffe's relationship with France, actual and perceived, see Wright, *Britain, France and the Gothic,* especially chapter 4.

59 *CR*, 2nd ser., 14 (July 1795): 349.

60 *CR*, 2nd ser., 24 (Oct 1798): 236.

61 *CR*, 2nd ser., 20 (July 1797): 353.

62 Review of *The Midnight Bell*, *CR*, 2nd ser., 23 (Aug 1798): 472.

63 See Jacobs, *Accidental Migrations*, 207: 'once readers had read one of Radcliffe's works … they knew what kinds of tricks to watch for, not only in works by Radcliffe but also in topically and physically similar "novels and romances" grouped with them in book catalogs and on library shelves'.

64 See Neiman, 'A New Perspective', 635, on Minerva novelists' relationship to 'popular formulas' and their 'revisions of value-laden conventions', as well as her larger arguments in *Minerva's Gothics* about 'an even subtler (because not always intentional) site of collaboration between author and text: the genre expectations that produce authorial agency, even as they constrain it' (xvii).

65 Marilyn Butler, *Romantics, Rebels, and Reactionaries: English Literature and Its Background, 1760–1830* (New York: Oxford University Press, 1982), 29.

66 The inclusion of the first and last novels on this list in Austen's *Northanger Abbey* has ensured that, as 1790s gothic novels go, they are well known to current scholars; both authors, however, with all of their works, were also included in the Minerva Press's 1798 Prospectus on a list of 'particular and favorite Authors', along with Robert Bage and Eliza Parsons, both discussed in Chapter 2. The Prospectus is reproduced in Dorothy Blakey, *The Minerva Press, 1790–1820* (London: Printed for the Bibliographic Society at the Oxford University Press, 1939), 309–14.

67 Eliza Parsons, *Lucy: A Novel* (London: Minerva Press, 1794), I:24–25. Subsequent references are parenthetically cited by volume and page number.

68 Regina Maria Roche, *Clermont: A Tale*, ed. Natalie Schroeder (Chicago: Valancourt Books, 2006), 104.

69 Eliza Parsons, *Castle of Wolfenbach*, ed. Diane Long Hoeveler (Chicago: Valancourt Books, 2006), 30.

70 Avril Horner and Sue Zlosnik, *Gothic and the Comic Turn* (Basingstoke: Palgrave Macmillan 2005), 4.

71 For further discussion of the Radcliffean novels' use of poetic quotation, see Leah Price, *The Anthology and the Rise of the Novel: From Richardson to George Eliot* (Cambridge: Cambridge University Press, 2000).

72 Ann Radcliffe, *The Mysteries of Udolpho*, ed. Bonamy Dobrée (Oxford: Oxford World's Classics, 1980), 168, 322, 365.

73 For a much more detailed discussion of gothic literature's approach to social problems, see Ellen Malenas Ledoux, *Social Reform in Gothic Writing: Fantastic Forms of Change, 1764–1834* (Basingstoke: Palgrave Macmillan, 2013). Chapter 2, 'A Castle of One's Own', contains a particularly resonant discussion of gothic heroines, gendered oppression, and class status. See also Ravenwood, 'Historical Anecdotes', 64, on gothic portrayals of the effects of the 'horrors of war' on women.

74 Jennie Batchelor discusses Parsons in 'The Claims of Literature: Women Applicants to the Royal Literary Fund, 1790–1810', *Women's Writing*, 12.3 (2003): 505–520, and in her book *Women's Work* she considers the central importance of *work* to the self-conception of many female authors in this period. Edward Copeland shows that preoccupation with financial issues, and the emergence of financial themes in fictional plots, is characteristic of many novels of this era, perhaps particularly Minerva Press novels, in *Women Writing about Money*, see esp. 43–47 on Parsons.

75 See also Ledoux, *Social Reform*, esp. 77–92, on the gothic and social class.

76 Here we can see that less well-known female authors were also participating, if in slightly different ways, in the process of writing books that 'memorializ[e], quite self-consciously, the conditions of their writing' (13) that Sodeman identifies in the works of authors like Radcliffe and Charlotte Smith. See also Lupton, who (discussing a slightly earlier period) argues that 'A special account is needed of why these kinds of writing, produced largely for profit, reflect so closely on their status as paper products, on the marketplace for which they [were] written, and on the misbehaviour and appetites of their

authors and readers'. Christina Lupton, *Knowing Books: The Consciousness of Mediation in Eighteenth-Century Britain* (Philadelphia: University of Pennsylvania Press, 2012), 3.

77 Mary Charlton, *Rosella, or Modern Occurrences* (London: Minerva Press, 1799). For a related discussion of *Rosella*, see McLeod, 'The Minerva Press', 80–84.

78 For a compelling account of female quixotism as a mode of empowerment among female reader-authors of this period, see Jodi Wyett, 'Female Quixotism Refashioned: *Northanger Abbey*, the Engaged Reader, and the Woman Writer', *The Eighteenth Century* 56.2 (2015): 261–276.

79 *Plain Sense* is the title of a best-selling work by Frances Jacson, which reached at least three editions in the 1790s (London: Minerva Press, 1795).

80 See, for instance, Charlotte Smith's *Ethelinde, or The Recluse of the Lake* (London: T. Cadell, 1789), Mrs Hughes's *Jemima, a Novel* (London: Minerva Press, 1795), as well as the anonymously published *Frederica; or, The Memoirs of a Young Lady* (London: J. Ridgeway, 1792) and *Frederica Risberg, a German Story* (London: Minerva Press, 1793). This is a somewhat eclectic group of publishers; Cadell, and especially Ridgeway, published novels on a much smaller scale than Lane in the 1790s, and neither was primarily known for publishing novels, though Cadell did publish fiction or blends of poetry and fiction by a number of relatively high-profile woman authors including Smith, Ann Radcliffe, Anna Seward, and Helen Maria Williams. See James Raven, 'Historical Introduction: The Novel Comes of Age', in Garside et al., eds., *The English Novel*, 73, for the highest-producing novel publishers of the 1790s.

81 I am grateful to Helen Plimmer and the other contributors to 'Corinne' for their helpful synopses of Minerva plots, which initially helped me to narrow down the possibilities for these identifications; more recently, my indefatigable research assistants Amanda Zarni and Anna Pravdica were invaluable in tracking the specific intertextual references cited here. Helen Plimmer, 'Corvey "Adopt an Author": Anna Maria Bennet', *Corinne* 1 (May 1998), accessed 2 Mar 2012, http://extra.shu.ac.uk/corvey/corinne/.

82 Anna Maria Mackenzie, *Mysteries Elucidated, a Novel,* 3 vols. (London: Minerva-Press, 1795).

83 Deidre Shauna Lynch, 'Gothic Fiction', in *The Cambridge Companion to Fiction in the Romantic Period*, ed. Richard Maxwell and Katie Trumpener (Cambridge: Cambridge University Press, 2008), 47.

84 This copy of *Rosella* is also available via *ECCO*; one example of identifying marginalia can be seen on page 216/image 218, though many of the other marginal comments are written lightly and aren't visible in the scanned version.

85 Lane, 'A Tale', 3.

86 The scholarship on this topic is extensive: on gothic adaptation (and gothic plagiarism), see, for instance, Diane Long Hoeveler, 'Gothic Adaptation, 1764–1830', in *The Gothic World*, ed. Glennis Byron and Dale Townshend

(London: Routledge, 2014), 185–198, and Lauren Fitzgerald, 'The Gothic Villain and the Vilification of the Plagiarist: The Case of The Castle Spectre', *Gothic Studies* 7.1 (2005): 5–17.

87 Review of *Castle Spectre, a Drama in Five Acts*, *AR* 28.2 (Aug 1798): 190.

88 Review of *The Monk*, *MR*, 2nd ser., 23 (Aug 1797): 451.

89 Dale Townshend and Angela Wright offer a usefully concise account of Radcliffe's early reception, including discussion of some of the passages I cite here, in *Ann Radcliffe, Romanticism and the Gothic*, chapter 1, 6–11.

90 Review of *The Romance of the Forest*, *ER* 20 (Nov 1792): 52.

91 See Jacobs, 'Ann Radcliffe and Romantic Print Culture', 61, for discussion of the legitimating function of Radcliffe's Shakespearean epigraphs.

92 Review of *The Castles of Athlin and Dunbayne*, *MR* 81 (Dec 1789): 563.

93 Review of *A Sicilian Romance*, *CR*, 2nd ser., 1 (Mar 1791): 350.

94 Review of *The Italian, British Critic* 10 (Sept 1797): 270. This kind of critique is especially interesting in light of Jerrold Hogle's contention that *The Italian* directly engages with 'Walpolean elements'. 'Recovering the Walpolean Gothic: *The Italian; or, The Confessional of the Black Penitents*', in Townshend and Wright, eds., *Ann Radcliffe, Romanticism and the Gothic*, 151–167.

95 Review of *The Italian, CR*, 2nd ser., 23 (June 1798): 168–169.

96 Townshend and Wright, eds., *Ann Radcliffe, Romanticism and the Gothic*, 11.

97 Ibid., 13, quoting from 'Obit.: Ann Radcliffe', *The New Monthly Magazine and Literary Journal* 9.29 (May 1823): 232.

98 Jacobs, *Accidental Migrations*, 617–618. Jacobs' extended discussion of 'female imitation' is also very relevant here, though our interpretative angle, particularly on Radcliffe, differs in some points.

99 Review of *Tancred, a Tale of Ancient Times*, *ER* 18 (Aug 1791): 114.

100 See the introduction for further discussion and images of this distinctive imprint and its evolution in the early 1790s, as well as Clery, *Supernatural Fiction*, 137–138.

101 J. Fox, Jr., *Tancred: A Tale of Ancient Times* (London: Minerva Press, 1791), II:n.p. While many publishers engaged in advertising, J. M. S. Tompkins singles out Lane as particularly active in this arena, writing, 'By 1790 the fly-leaves of novels, particularly those published by William Lane at what was presently to become the Minerva Press, are full of advertisements of Legendary Tales, Old English Tales, Historical Stories and Historical Romances'. Tompkins, *The Popular Novel in England*, rpt. ed. (London, Methuen and Co., 1961), 238.

102 Review of *The Abbey of St. Asaph, CR*, 2nd ser., 14 (July 1795): 349.

103 Curties, *Ancient Records*, I:i–ii. Subsequent references are cited parenthetically. The British Library's copy of *Ethelwina* contains this ad, as does the Corvey Collection's (digitized in *ECCO* and *NCCO*, respectively), along with numerous other ads in vols. 1 and 2.

104 JoEllen DeLucia, 'Radcliffe Incorporated: Ann Radcliffe, Mary Ann Radcliffe, and the Minerva Author', *Romantic Textualities: Literature and*

Print Culture, 23 (Summer 2020): 129. www.romtext.org.uk/articles/rt23_ no8/ (accessed June 2022). DeLucia's research reveals the benefits of the 'Radcliffe' name (even falsely attributed) as a selling point in posterity.

105 Neiman notes that 'as early as 1813' this began to change, as Lane included novels by other publishers in his advertisements for new novels (*Minerva's Gothics*, 18).

106 J. Fox, Jr., *The Bastard of Normandy* (London: Hookham, 1793) I:n.p. (British Library/*ECCO* copy).

107 *Edelfrida* (London: Hookham, 1792), III:n.p. To date I have located just one copy with this advertisement intact: the British Library's copy (digitized in *ECCO*) contains it, while copies at both Houghton and the Beinecke do not.

108 Jacobs offers a fascinating account of Radcliffe's transition from anonymous authorship to named publication and how this process ties to publisher, fame, and status ('Anonymous Signatures', 620–622).

109 *The Cavern of Death: A Moral Tale*, 3rd ed. (Cork: Printed by J. Connor, Circulating Library, Castle Street, 1795), n.p. (first edition: London: Bell, 1794). (University of Cambridge Library/*ECCO* copy).

110 Justice, *Manufacturers of Literature*, 158.

111 Lane, 'Tale', 7.

112 Ibid. The reference here is to Anna Maria Mackenzie's novel *Mysteries Elucidated* (London: Minerva Press, 1795).

113 William Lane, 'A Tale: Addressed to the Novel Readers of the Present Time,' *The Lady & Gentleman's Pocket Magazine of Literary and Polite Amusement* (1 Nov 1796): 224–229.

114 Ibid., 224.

115 Circulating library proprietors were well known for making sweeping and not always accurate claims about the generous size of their catalogues; see David Allan, *A Nation of Readers* (London: British Library, 2008), 132.

Chapter 4

1 Review of Mary Wollstonecraft's *Posthumous Works*, *MR*, 2nd ser., 27 (Nov 1798): 325.

2 John Laurens Bicknell, *Original Miscellanies* (London: Printed for Cadell, Davies, and Blackwood, 1820), 14.

3 Hannah More, *Cœlebs in Search of a Wife*, ed. Patricia Demers (Peterborough: Broadview Press, 2007), 8. For a representative discussion of the novel, see Review of *Coelebs in Search of a Wife*, *CR*, 3rd ser., 16.3 (Mar 1809): 252–264.

4 Review of *Cœlebs*, *MR*, 2nd ser. 58 (Feb 1809): 128–136 (via *DBF*); this and subsequent *DBF* reviews can be found in the 'Reviews' tab of the relevant novel entry.

5 Quoted in Mary Gwladys Jones, *Hannah More* (Cambridge: Cambridge University Press, 1952), 193 (via 'Hannah More', *The Orlando Project*).

6 A number of bibliographical sources mention this trend, although none lists all the novels I cite here. See Garside, 'English Novel in the Romantic Era', pp. 58–59; and the More entry in the Orlando Project, as well as the material Patricia Demers includes in her edition of *Cœlebs* (*Cœlebs in Search of a Wife*, ed. Patricia Demers [Broadview Press, 2007]), particularly excerpts of reviews and three of the response novels, with short plot summaries. See also Demers 29, n. 2.

7 See, e.g., Carl Fisher, 'Innovation and Imitation in the Eighteenth-Century Robinsonade', in *The Cambridge Companion to Robinson Crusoe*, ed. John Ricchetti (Cambridge: Cambridge University Press, 2018), 99–111.

8 William B. Warner, *Licensing Entertainment: The Elevation of Novel Reading in Britain, 1684–1750* (Berkeley: University of California Press, 1998), 176.

9 *Cœlebs in Search of a Wife*, ed. Demers, 37. Subsequent parenthetical references refer to this edition except where otherwise noted.

10 *Cœlebs in Search of a Wife*, ed. Demers, 33.

11 On More's *Cheap Repository Tracts* and 1790s anti-Jacobin culture, see Ian Haywood, *The Revolution in Popular Literature: Print, Politics and the People, 1790–1860* (Cambridge: Cambridge University Press, 2004), chapter 3. M. O. Grenby details accusations against More *by* anti-Jacobin conservatives in *The Anti-Jacobin Novel: British Conservatism and the French Revolution* (Cambridge: Cambridge University Press, 2001), 15–16.

12 Grenby, *The Anti-Jacobin Novel*, 24.

13 On Methodism and literature earlier in the eighteenth century, see Misty G. Anderson, *Imagining Methodism in Eighteenth-Century Britain: Enthusiasm, Belief, & the Borders of the Self* (Baltimore, MD: Johns Hopkins University Press, 2012); on satirical anti-Methodist response texts, see Brett McInelly, *Textual Warfare and the Making of Methodism* (Oxford: Oxford University Press, 2014); on women's writing and Methodism, see Andrew Winckles, *Eighteenth-Century Women's Writing and the Methodist Media Revolution: 'Consider the Lord as Ever Present Reader'* (Liverpool: Liverpool University Press, 2019).

14 McInelly, *Textual Warfare and the Making of Methodism*, 36.

15 Winckles, *Eighteenth-Century Women's Writing*, 3.

16 'A Modern Antique', *Celia in Search of a Husband*, 2 vols. (London: Printed at the Minerva-Press, 1809), I:i. Subsequent parenthetical references refer to this edition.

17 Ibid., I:ii.

18 Neil McKendrick, John Brewer, and J. H. Plumb, *Birth of a Consumer Society: The Commercialization of Eighteenth-Century England* (London: Europa Publications; Bloomington: Indiana University Press, 1982), 1. I discuss the novel's ties to consumer culture and its conceptualization as a fashionable object in more depth in Chapter 5.

19 William Mudford, *Nubilia in Search of a Husband* (London: J. Ridgeway and Sherwood, Neely and Jones, 1809).

20 Sir George Rover [pseud.], *Cœlebs Suited* (London: Printed for Edmund Lloyd, 1809), iv, emphasis added.

21 See *Cœlebs in Search of a Wife*, ed. Demers, 22 and 27 (citing Anne Stott and Charlotte Yonge, respectively).

22 Letter 67, 30 Jan 1809, in *Jane Austen's Letters*, ed. Deirdre Le Faye (Oxford: Clarendon Press, 1995), 172. Thanks to Devoney Looser and the other participants in the 2012 NEH Summer Seminar, 'Jane Austen and Her Contemporaries', for pointing me towards Austen's engagement with More's work.

23 [Jane Best], *Celia Suited* (London: Printed by T. Harper for H. Colburn, 1810).

24 Ibid., I:iv.

25 Ibid.

26 Ibid., I:iii.

27 Anon., *Cœlebs Married* (London: Published and sold by G. Walker, 1814), iv.

28 Ibid., iii–iv.

29 [Harriet Corp], *Cœlebs Deceived* (London: Printed for the Author, 1817).

30 See 'Advertisement' (n.p.) for *Cœlebs Deceived*. I have not yet been able to determine whether or not this claim (of previous publication) is true by locating the actual periodical containing the novel. On the importance of religious periodicals to the reception of the novel during this period, see, e.g., Samuel F. Pickering, 'Literature and Theology: The "Christian Observer" and the Novel, 1802–1822', *Historical Magazine of the Protestant Episcopal Church* 43.1 (1974): 16.

31 Ibid., I:viii

32 Ibid., I:x.

33 Ibid.

34 Ibid., I:viii–ix.

35 Ibid., I:ix.

36 Ibid., I:ix.

37 A Modern Antique, *Celia in Search*, I:iv.

38 Grenby, *The Anti-Jacobin Novel*, 198.

39 *Coelebs Deceived*, viii.

40 Ibid., viii.

41 *CR*, 3rd ser., 17 (Aug 1809): 439 (via *DBF*).

42 *MR*, 2nd ser., 59 (July 1810): 299.

43 *CR*, 3rd ser., 17 (Aug 1809): 439 (via *DBF*); *MR*, 2nd ser., 59 (July 1810): 299–304 (via *DBF*).

44 Review of *Nubilia in Search of a Husband*, *The Satirist* 5 (Aug 1809): 176.

45 Review of *Nubilia in Search of a Husband*, *Universal Magazine* 12.68 (July 1809): 34.

46 Ibid.

47 Ibid.

48 Review of *Nubilia in Search of a Husband*, *The Satirist* 5 (Aug 1809): 175.

49 Review of *Celia in Search of a Husband*, *The British Critic* 34 (Oct 1809): 410.

50 Review of *Celia in Search of a Husband*, *CR*, 3rd ser., 18 (Oct 1809): 219–220 (via *DBF*).

51 See, e.g., R.H., 'The Errors of the Author of Nubilia Vindicated', *Universal Magazine* 12.71 (Oct 1809): 267–268, and 'Justus', 'Reply to R.H. in Defence of Nubillia', *Universal Magazine* 12.72 (Nov 1809): 377–379.

52 'Correspondence', *Anti-Jacobin Review and Magazine* 34.137 (Nov 1809): 336.

53 On the temporality and periodicity of periodicals, see, e.g., Jennie Batchelor, '"To Cherish Female Ingenuity, and to Conduce to *Female* Improvement": The Birth of the Woman's Magazine', in *Women's Periodicals and Print Culture in Britain, 1690–1820s: The Long Eighteenth Century*, ed. Jennie Batchelor and Manushag N. Powell, 377–392 (Edinburgh: Edinburgh University Press, 2018), 379–381, and Manushag Powell, *Performing Authorship in Eighteenth-Century English Periodicals* (Lewisburg, PA: Bucknell University Press, 2012), 227–229.

54 *La Belle Assemblée* published an excerpt of *Cœlebs* in their February issue (1809) and then began publishing *Hymenaea in Search of a Husband* in increments the following month. Anon., 'Hymenæa in Search of a Husband', *La Belle Assemblée* (Mar 1809): 72–76.

55 'Literary Intelligence', *GM* 79 (Oct 1809): 936.

56 William Mudford, 'The Author's Defence of *Nubilia*', *Anti-Jacobin Review and Magazine* 33.133 (July 1809): 328.

57 Review of *Celia in Search of a Husband, CR*, 3rd ser., 18 (Oct 1809): 220.

58 Ibid.

59 Ibid., emphases added.

60 Chapter 6 discusses how this 'rage' for antiques translated into a complex figuration of the popular novel *as* a potential antique.

61 The Antique's desire to look on without 'mixing' contrasts with the approach taken by Addison, who wrote in the *Spectator*, No. 1, 'where-ever I see a cluster of people I always mix with them, though I never open my lips but in my own Club'. Denise Gigante, *The Great Age of the English Essay: An Anthology* (New Haven, CT: Yale University Press, 2008), 45.

62 See, e.g., *Celia* I:129 and I:158, as well as the Review of *Cælia in Search of a Husband, MR*, 2nd ser., 60 (Oct 1809): 212.

63 Caroline Burney [pseud.?], *Lindamira in Search of a Husband, a Satirical Novel* (London: J. F. Hughes, 1810), III:86. Subsequent parenthetical citations refer to this edition.

64 Patrica Demers, in her edition of *Cœlebs*, identifies most of these titles, published between 1753 and 1805, and explains that they include popular 'sentimental, Gothic, and farcical works', many by women (57).

65 'Rosa Matilda' has since been identified as the novelist Charlotte Dacre.

66 See McKendrick et al., eds., *Birth of a Consumer Society*: 'Where once women had merely dreamed of following the prevailing London fashions, they could now follow them daily in the advertisements in the provincial press, and actually buy them from the ever-increasing number of commercial outlets dedicated to satisfying their wants and their needs' (1).

67 Robert Torrens, *Cælibia Choosing a Husband* (London: For J. F. Hughes, 1809).

68 For some of the novel's many references to its predecessor, see especially pages II:166–171, where the characters discuss whether or not they have read *Cœlebs*; one finds it painfully over-moral, while another details the foolish changes she has made to her household in order to emulate its characters.

69 *Coelebs Married*, 122–123.

70 *Nubilia*, second edition, 480–481.

71 *Cœlebs Deceived*, I:vii.

72 Ibid.

73 *Celia*, I:iv.

74 Jane Austen, *Northanger Abbey, Lady Susan, The Watsons, Sanditon*, ed. James Kinsley and John Davie (Oxford: Oxford World's Classics, 2008), 3.

75 I am grateful to the audience at NASSR 2012 (Neuchâtel, Switzerland) for their feedback on an early version of this chapter tying Austen's fears of obsolescence to the *Cœlebs* novels. Timothy Campbell offers a closely related reading of this passage from *Northanger Abbey* in *Historical Style: Fashion and the New Mode of History, 1740–1830* (Philadelphia: University of Pennsylvania Press, 2016), 69–71.

76 Campbell, *Historical Style*, 70.

77 See Garside, 'English Novel in the Romantic Era', 83, for a table of the most prolific fiction publishers of this decade.

78 Ibid., 70.

79 Sarah Green, *Scotch Novel Reading; or, Modern Quackery: A Novel Really Founded on Facts* (London: Printed for A. K. Newman and Co., 1824), I:91, and Innes Hoole, *Scenes at Brighton; or, 'How Much?': A Satirical Novel* (London: Printed for A. K. Newman and Co., 1821), II:150.

80 Anthony Frederick Holstein, The *Discontented Man; or, Love and Reason: A Novel* (London: Printed at the Minerva Press for A. K. Newman and Co., 1815), III:14.

81 Mary Meeke, *Stratagems Defeated: A Novel* (London: Printed at the Minerva-Press for A. K. Newman and Co., 1811), IV:54–55.

82 [George Gordon, Lord Byron], *Don Juan*, canto 1, verse XVI (London: Printed by Thomas Davison, 1819), 9.

83 *Happiness*, 3rd ed. (London: Printed for Francis Westley, sold by Longman, Hurst, Rees, Orme, & Brown, 1821), I:123.

84 Meeke, *Strategems Defeated*, IV:156.

85 [Elizabeth Thomas], *Mortimer Hall; or, The Labourer's Hire* (London: Printed at the Minerva-Press for A. K. Newman and Co., 1811), III:99–100.

86 Garside lists Sherwood & Co. fourth, with 5.6 per cent of the market, in the ranks of most prolific publishers, 1810–1819. 'The English Novel in the Romantic Era', 84.

87 Alicia Lefanu, *Tales of a Tourist* (London: Printed for A. K. Newman and Co., 1823), III:156.

88 Ibid.

89 *Happiness*, I:67.

90 'Priscilla Parlante', *Ferdinand and Ordella: A Russian Story* (London: Printed for Samuel Tipper, 1810), I:xvi.

91 Ibid., xl.

92 Anthony Frederick Holstein, *Miseries of an Heiress* (London: Printed at the Minerva Press for A. K. Newman and Co., 1810), I: ix–x.

93 Ibid., x.

94 Ibid.

95 Ibid.

96 Ibid.

97 *Cœlebia Choosing a Husband* (1809) and *Lindamira* (1810) are the two Hughes titles.

98 Sydney Owenson, *Woman; or, Ida of Athens*, vol. I (London: Longman, Hurst, Rees and Orme, 1809).

99 Review of *Nubilia*, *The Satirist* 5 (Aug 1809): 176.

100 Letter from Jane to Cassandra Austen, 17–18 Jan 1809, in *Jane Austen's Letters*, ed. Deirdre Le Faye (Oxford: Clarendon Press, 1995), 166. I am grateful to one of my anonymous readers for calling my attention to this letter.

101 Review of *Nubilia*, *Literary Panorama* 6 (Sept 1809): 1105.

Chapter 5

1 *Asmodeus; or, The Devil in London: A Sketch* (London: Printed by J. Dean for J. F. Hughes, 1808), I: viii.

2 'Domestic Intelligence', *EM* 41 (June 1802): 500.

3 Ibid., 500. Cited in 'Quizzing-Glass', *OED Online* (Mar 2013), accessed 22 Apr 2013, www.oed.com.

4 'Domestic Intelligence', 499.

5 Maxine Berg, *Luxury and Pleasure in Eighteenth-Century Britain* (Oxford: Oxford University Press, 2005), 247–248.

6 Neil McKendrick, John Brewer, and J. H. Plumb, *The Birth of a Consumer Society: The Commercialization of Eighteenth-Century England* (Bloomington: Indiana University Press, 1982), 10.

7 For discussion of the rise of consumerism, luxury goods, and commercialism in eighteenth- and nineteenth-century London, see McKendrick, et al., *Birth of a Consumer Society*; as well as Maxine Berg and Elizabeth Eger, eds., *Luxury in the Eighteenth Century: Debates, Desires and Delectable Goods* (Basingstoke: Palgrave Macmillan, 2003); John Brewer and Roy Porter, eds., *Consumption and the World of Goods* (London: Routledge, 1993).

8 Nicholas Mason helpfully sums up the disagreements in 'Consumer Culture: Getting and Spending in the Romantic Age', in *A Concise Companion to the Romantic Age*, ed. Jon P. Klancher (Chichester: Wiley-Blackwell, 2009), 189–209.

9 Jan De Vries, *The Industrious Revolution: Consumer Behavior and the Household Economy, 1650 to the Present* (Cambridge: Cambridge University Press, 2008), ix.

10 James Raven compellingly analyses the relationship between fiction and changing trends in *Judging New Wealth: Popular Publishing and Responses to Commerce in England, 1750–1800* (Oxford: Clarendon Press, 1992), chapter 8, 'Reactions to Fashion and Luxury'.

11 While I focus more on the representation and production of luxury objects themselves than the construction of characters in the novels that feature them, my discussion here is related to Deidre Lynch's argument that 'Literary character's history … converges in particular, unpredictable ways with the history that sees imports of luxury goods into Britain … double in quantity between 1715 and 1800. It converges too with a history that sees reading and writing themselves become commercialized, fashionable activities.' Lynch, *The Economy of Character: Novels, Market Culture, and the Business of Inner Meaning* (Chicago: University of Chicago Press, 1998), 5.

12 Edward Copeland, *Women Writing about Money: Women's Fiction in England, 1790–1820* (Cambridge: Cambridge University Press, 1995), 3. I wholeheartedly share Copeland's sense of the centrality of money, labour, and consumerism to Romantic women's fiction, although here I am more interested in exploring the continuities between the 'genteel' novel, the 'didactic' novel, and the 'Minerva' novel than in establishing distinctions between these overlapping groups; in particular, I argue, novels across the spectrum portray fiction as centrally imbricated in larger systems of fashion, labour, and commerce.

13 *Hardenbrass and Haverill; or, The Secret of the Castle: A Novel* (London: Sherwood, Neely and Jones, 1817), IV:183–184.

14 Mrs Ross, *Paired Not Matched; or, Matrimony in the Nineteenth Century: A Novel* (London: Printed at the Minerva-Press, for A. K. Newman and Co., 1815), I:138–139.

15 For further examples of outrageous overdressing in novels of the period, as well as analysis of the structures of wealth and class mobility that these depictions satirized, see Raven, *Judging New Wealth*, 141–143.

16 See Copeland, *Women Writing about Money*, chapter 4, for a more in-depth discussion of Austen's engagement with scenes of consumption.

17 Jane Austen, *Pride and Prejudice*, ed. Pat Rogers and Janet Todd (Cambridge: Cambridge University Press, 2006), 31, 80.

18 The term 'Silver Fork novel' to refer to novels focusing on luxury goods and fashionable life was coined by William Hazlitt in 1827. For a general introduction, see Tamara Wagner, 'The Silver-Fork Novel', *The Victorian Web*, accessed 25 Mar, 2013, www.victorianweb.org/genre/silverfork.html.

19 Cheryl A. Wilson, *Fashioning the Silver Fork Novel* (London: Pickering & Chatto, 2012), 17. The Silver Fork novel has been the subject of at least two scholarly books in the past decade, Wilson's as well as Edward Copeland, *The Silver Fork Novel: Fashionable Fiction in the Age of Reform* (Cambridge:

Cambridge University Press, 2012). Wilson characterizes the Silver Fork preoccupation with fashion in terms that closely overlap with my reading of the novels in this chapter; she 'approach[es] the silver fork genre from multiple perspectives on "fashion": fashion as in "to fashion" or to make – studying the construction of the genre and the silver fork formula; fashion as in "*ton*" or the world of fashion – studying the relationship between the novels and the fashionable world; and fashion as in "to be popular" – studying the literary marketplace, publishing practices and commercialization of fiction during this period' (5). There are differences between the two genres, however, particularly in their depiction of 'fashioning' – Minerva authors tended to be somewhat lower in socioeconomic class than Silver Fork authors, and the tensions between the working classes and the wealthy bourgeoisie and aristocracy also represented in the novels are thus, unsurprisingly, more dramatic than in their later iterations. See Wilson, *Fashioning the Silver Fork Novel*, 6–8, for a summary of the class negotiations inherent in the Silver Fork genre; for a vivid account of the class and financial situations of some Minerva novelists, see Jennie Batchelor, *Women's Work: Labour, Gender, Authorship, 1750–1830* (Manchester: Manchester University Press, 2010), chapter 4.

20 Raven, *Judging New Wealth*, 63.

21 'A Modern Antique', *The English Exposé; or, Men and Women 'Abroad' and 'At Home'* (London: Minerva-Press, 1814), I:29.

22 See Raven, *Judging New Wealth*, chapter 8. Raven points to 'imprecision in the meaning of luxury' (167–168) as one cause of the ambiguous relationship between novels and fashion.

23 Ibid., 154.

24 Serena Dyer and Chloe Wigston Smith, *Material Literacy in Eighteenth-Century Britain: A Nation of Makers* (New York: Bloomsbury Publishing, 2020), 6. See also Chloe Wigston Smith, 'The Haberdasher's Plot: The Romance of Small Trade in Frances Burney's Fiction', *Tulsa Studies in Women's Literature* 37.2 (2018): 271–293, and *Women, Work and Clothes in the Eighteenth-Century Novel* (Cambridge: Cambridge University Press, 2013).

25 Batchelor, *Women's Work*, 11.

26 This chapter's focus on the importance of objects in early nineteenth-century fiction overlaps with recent scholarship on the relationship between objects and literature. See, for instance, the recent double issue of *Eighteenth-Century Fiction* on 'Material Fictions', edited by Eugenia Zuroski and Michael Yonan (31.1–2 Fall 2018 and Winter 2019).

27 On writing as work, see, e.g., Batchelor, *Women's Work*; Clifford Siskin, *The Work of Writing: Literature and Social Change in Britain, 1700–1830* (Baltimore, MD: Johns Hopkins University Press, 1998); Betty A. Schellenberg, *The Professionalization of Women Writers in Eighteenth-Century Britain* (Cambridge: Cambridge University Press, 2005); Cheryl Turner, *Living by the Pen: Women Writers in the Eighteenth Century* (London: Routledge, 1992).

28 Review of *Tales of Fashionable Life*, by Miss Edgeworth, *The Polyanthos* 1 (1 Nov 1812): 59.

29 Critiquing fashion, however, is very different from eschewing engagement with labour or commerce overall; indeed, as Catherine Gallagher argues, Edgeworth was keenly aware of 'the "productivist" economic theories of the political economists, who stressed that human labor created value, and she applied their ideas to her own work as an author'. *Nobody's Story: The Vanishing Acts of Women Writers in the Marketplace 1670–1820* (Oxford: Clarendon, 1994), 257. Copeland, even more pointedly, sums up Edgeworth's story 'The Purple Jar', featuring a heroine with 'total, dizzying delight in shopping', by asking 'where the greatest burden of anxiety really rests in that story: with [the heroine], or with her poor author, whose earnest labor to attach "use" to consumption provides so feeble a dam against the enchanting powers that attract her heroine'? *Women Writing about Money*, 3.

30 Maria Edgeworth, *Belinda*, ed. Kathryn J. Kirkpatrick (Oxford: Oxford University Press, 1994, reissued 2008), 9. Subsequent parenthetical citations refer to this edition.

31 On the importance of advertisement to Romantic literature, see Nicholas Mason, *Literary Advertising and the Shaping of British Romanticism* (Baltimore, MD: Johns Hopkins University Press, 2013); Mason discusses the Minerva Press specifically in pp. 120–122.

32 Smith, 'The Haberdasher's Plot', 271–272.

33 For years, 'Miss Byron' has been taken to be the same author as the 'Modern Antique,' with both names attributed to a 'Medora Gordon Byron' in many bibliographies and library catalogues. While the first assumption seems possible (and is tenuously supported by a small amount of evidence from the period), the second seems to be a bibliographic red herring.

34 Byron, *Hours of Affluence, and Days of Indigence: A Novel*, 4 vols. (London: Printed at the Minerva-Press, for Lane, Newman, and Co., 1809), I:1. Subsequent references are cited parenthetically.

35 W. H. Rayner, *Virtue and Vice: A Novel*, 2 vols. (London: W. Thiselton, 1806); Miss Barrell, *Riches and Poverty: A Tale* (London: Tipper and Robins, 1808); E. Senate, *Family Pride and Humble Merit: A Novel, Founded on Facts, and Partly Taken from the French*, 3 vols. (London: Sherwood, Neely and Jones, 1810).

36 Miss Byron, *The Alderman and the Peer; or Ancient Castle and Modern Villa*, 3 vols. (London: Printed at the Minerva-Press, for A. K. Newman and Co., 1810); Rayner, *Virtue and Vice*; Barrell, *Riches and Poverty*; Senate, *Family Pride and Humble Merit*.

37 On a bibliographic level, the novel's bifurcation raises other questions: Would the circulation practices of the Minerva library have favoured such a novel? How many subscribers who read volumes 1 and 2 would actually read 3 and 4? Would some readers have read the second two volumes first, a practice that would pose obvious difficulties with a traditional novel, but hardly any at all with this one? What about a mid-volume break between stories? The British

Library's copy has all four volumes bound into one, which makes for a different reading experience than beginning each volume separately, as I initially did with the Corvey copy digitized in Nineteenth Century Collections Online. For plot summaries of both of these novels, see my entries in *The Cambridge Guide to the Eighteenth-Century Novel*, ed. April London (Cambridge University Press, forthcoming).

38 See, for instance, the collection of quotes cited in McKendrick et al., *Birth of a Consumer Society*, 9–10. The astonishment of visitors to London at the new state of affairs in the late eighteenth century seems to reflect this anxiety as well; Neil McKendrick, quoting a German professor, G. C. Lichtenberg, visiting England at the time, argues that 'the luxury and extravagance of the lower and middling classes had "risen to such a pitch as never before seen in the world"'. Ibid., 10.

39 Berg, *Luxury and Pleasure,* 247.

40 Ibid., 7. See also McKendrick et al., *Birth of a Consumer Society*: 'In imitation of the rich the middle ranks spent more frenziedly than ever before, and in imitation of them the rest of society joined in as best they might' (11).

41 A single-lensed glass, akin to a monocle, but often held up to the eye using an attached stick, the quizzing-glass first begins to appear in English literature around the turn of the nineteenth century (see *OED*, 'quizzing glass').

42 Edgeworth, *Belinda*, 3.

43 My argument in the following sections is informed by Copeland's work on female 'fictions of employment' (see esp. *Women Writing about Money*, 159–212), although our senses of the ultimate purpose and effect of the Minerva Press novel's financial preoccupations are somewhat different. In particular, I differ in my understanding of the relationship between novel-writing and other kinds of work – Copeland calls depictions of 'women as authors' 'the sorest and rarest of topics' with only a 'very occasional example' in the era's fiction (12). Certainly, these plots are rare, but work by Elizabeth Neiman, for example, explores examples beyond those cited by Copeland (see, e.g. Neiman, *Minerva's Gothics: The Politics and Poetics of Romantic Exchange, 1780–1820* [Cardiff: University of Wales Press, 2019], 28–42), and my own analysis suggests that even where author-characters do not directly appear, allusions to women's writing and the conditions of literary production pervaded many Minerva novels. Moreover, as I argue in this chapter, the ties between novels and other kinds of produced commercial objects help us to see how many novels about fashion that feature other kinds of women workers may also be intended as commentary on women authors.

44 Copeland, *Women Writing about Money*, 86.

45 See Neiman, *Minerva's Gothics*, 26–42, for further discussion of Minerva novels depicting struggling would-be novelists.

46 I want to emphasize here the ways that Byron seems directly to invite the reader to equate work *on* and work *in* novels – a conflation reminiscent of Jenny Batchelor's argument that 'it is vital that we distinguish those "fictions

of employment" *within* eighteenth-century novels from those fictions of employment that we have created *about* the eighteenth-century novel. Batchelor, *Women's Work*, 11.

47 Jonathan Hill, 'Minerva at Aberdeen', *Romantic Textualities* 16 (Summer 2006): 21–39. See also Batchelor, *Women's Work*, chapter 4, and Copeland, *Women Writing about Money*, on Minerva authors and financial difficulties.

48 Edward Copeland argues that Minerva authors agree 'that Great Merchants are admirable, but petty tradesmen need not apply'; in the books I analyse here wealthy merchants certainly are often valorised, but I also find quite a few sympathetic representations of less prominent tradespeople. Copeland, *Women Writing about Money*, 85.

49 Mrs Martin, *The Enchantress, or Where Shall I Find Her? A Tale* (London: Printed at the Minerva-Press, for William Lane, Leadenhall-Street, 1801).

50 Ibid., I:1.

51 See Copeland, *Women Writing about Money*, esp. chapter 3; as he argues, several Minerva authors 'embrace a vision that celebrates their urban heroine's origins in the ranks of commerce' (11).

52 Barbara Hofland, *A Father as He Should Be: A Novel* (London: Printed at the Minerva-Press for A. K. Newman and Co., 1815), I:1.

53 Mrs Thomson, *The Pride of Ancestry; or, Who Is She?: A Novel*, vol. IV (Printed for Parsons & Son, 1804).

54 Miriam Malden, *Jessica Mandaville; or, The Woman of Fortitude*, 5 vols. (Richmond: Printed by and for G. A. Wall, and sold by Longman, Hurst, Rees and Orme, 1804).

55 Ibid., I:1.

56 Ibid.

57 Mary Meeke, *Conscience: A Novel* (London: Printed at the Minerva-Press for A. K. Newman and Co., 1814).

58 *Emily; or, The Wife's First Error and Beauty & Ugliness, or The Father's Prayer and the Mother's Prophecy: Two Tales* (London: Printed at the Minerva Press for A. K. Newman and Co., 1819), III:3–4.

59 Richard Altick, *The English Common Reader: A Social History of the Mass Reading Public, 1800–1900*, 2nd ed. (Columbus: Ohio State University Press), 57. On William Lane's own early retail practices, see Kurt E. Milberger, 'The First Impression, You, Yourself, Will Buy": The Gunninghiad, Virginius and Virginia and the Art of Scandal at the Minerva Press', *Romantic Textualities* 23 (5 July 2020): 39–69, 45.

60 David Allan, *A Nation of Readers* (London: British Library, 2008), 126.

61 See Lee Erickson's discussion of circulating libraries in *The Economy of Literary Form: English Literature and the Industrialization of Publishing, 1800–1850* (Baltimore, MD: Johns Hopkins University Press, 1996), chapter 8, esp. 137.

62 Ibid., 127.

63 Ibid.

64 Christopher Skelton-Foord, 'Economics, Expertise, Enterprise and the Literary Scene: The Commercial Management Ethos in British Circulating

Libraries, 1780–1830', in *Authorship, Commerce and the Public: Scenes of Writing, 1750–1850*, ed. E. J. Clery, Caroline Franklin, and Peter Garside (London: Palgrave Macmillan UK, 2002), 148.

65 Barbara Hofland, *Says She to Her Neighbour, What?* (London: Printed at the Minerva-Press, for A. K. Newman and Co., 1812), III:215.

66 Edward Mangin, *George the Third: A Novel*, vol. I (London: Printed for James Carpenter, 1807), I:4.

67 Ibid.

68 *Nobility Run Mad, or Raymond and His Three Wives* (London: Minerva-Press for Lane and Newman, 1802), I:1–2.

69 Tammy C. Whitlock, *Crime, Gender and Consumer Culture in Nineteenth-Century England* (Aldershot: Ashgate, 2005), 52.

70 Paul Keen, *The Crisis of Literature in the 1790s: Print Culture and the Public Sphere* (Cambridge: Cambridge University Press, 1999), 96.

71 George Jones, *Supreme Bon Ton and Bon Ton by Profession: A Novel* (London: John C. Spence, 1820) I:117–118.

72 Ibid., 125.

73 H. B. Wheatley writes, 'Nowadays picture galleries, jewellers and silver-smiths of artistic products must be considered as one of the chief features of the street, but formerly Bond Street was the headquarters of the circulating libraries, and the "librarians" were a power in the land.... It is a strange thing that a history of the Bond Street librarians and booksellers has never been produced.' Henry B. Wheatley, *Short History of Bond Street Old and New* (London: Fine Art Society, 1911), 20.

74 *Asmodeus; or, The Devil in London* (London: Printed by J. Dean for J. F. Hughes, 1808), I:153.

75 Ibid., 154–155.

76 Mary Meeke, *Midnight Weddings: A Novel* (London: Printed at the Minerva-Press, for William Lane, 1802), I:4. Clery describes this passage's unabashed willingness to cater to the consumer as inspiring 'a *frisson* of transgression', while Copeland uses it as an example of 'the influence of Lane's commercial judgement'. Clery, *The Rise of Supernatural Fiction, 1762–1800* (Cambridge: Cambridge University Press, 1995), 139; Copeland, *Women Writing about Money*, 78.

Chapter 6

1 Review of *Walladmor, The Eclectic Review* 24 (July 1825): 18–19.

2 This twentieth-century shift is often attributed to the discussion of Scott in György Lukács, *The Historical Novel*, trans. Hannah and Stanley Mitchell (London: Merlin Press, 1962). More recent scholars to bring attention to Scott's accomplishment include Ian Duncan, *Modern Romance and Transformations of the Novel: The Gothic, Scott, Dickens* (Cambridge: Cambridge University Press, 1992); Ina Ferris, *The Achievement of Literary*

Authority: Gender, History, and the Waverley Novels (Ithaca, NY: Cornell University Press, 1991); and Jane Millgate, *Walter Scott: The Making of the Novelist* (Toronto: University of Toronto Press, 1984). Ina Ferris's work, though differently oriented (and more directly concerned with gender) than my own, is especially relevant to the arguments I make in this chapter, especially her discussions of the way that Scott balanced historical and fictional authority and handled critiques based on his prolific production, feminized readers, and commercial rhetoric.

3 Continuing research on the historical and national novel has already made it clear that Scott was drawing on pre-existing literary genres to a much greater extent than has often been acknowledged; see, e.g., Ian Dennis, *Nationalism and Desire in Early Historical Fiction* (New York: St. Martin's Press, 1997); Fiona Price, *Reinventing Liberty: Nation, Commerce and the British Historical Novel from Walpole to Scott* (Edinburgh: Edinburgh University Press, 2016); Anne H. Stevens, *British Historical Fiction before Scott* (Basingstoke: Palgrave Macmillan, 2010); and Katie Trumpener, *Bardic Nationalism* (Princeton, NJ: Princeton University Press, 1997), chapter 3. In this chapter I focus specifically on the way that Scott's use of history and antiquarianism intersects with ongoing trends in characterizing literary 'excess' in material and mercantile terms.

4 Ferris, *Achievement of Literary Authority*; Price, *Reinventing Liberty*; Stevens, *British Historical Fiction before Scott*.

5 William St Clair, *The Reading Nation in the Romantic Period* (Cambridge: Cambridge University Press, 2004), 636–644.

6 Anthony Mandal, *Jane Austen and the Popular Novel: The Determined Author* (Basingstoke: Palgrave Macmillan, 2007), 34 and 169.

7 St Clair, *Reading Nation*, 245.

8 Megan Peiser, 'William Lane and the Minerva Press in the Review Periodical, 1790–1820', *Romantic Textualities: Literature and Print Culture, 1780–1840* 23 (Aug 2020): 124–148, 142–143.

9 Ferris, *Achievement of Literary Authority*, 238. See also James Watt, *Contesting the Gothic: Fiction, Genre, and Cultural Conflict, 1764–1832* (Cambridge: Cambridge University Press, 1999), 155–157.

10 As Ferris points out, the terms in which Scott's achievement (particularly his historical focus) was lauded were highly gendered; this is not to say, however, that women had no foothold in the field of history. For more on women writers of historical novels, see discussion below; on women writing history more generally in the eighteenth century, see Devoney Looser, *British Women Writers and the Writing of History, 1670–1820* (Baltimore, MD: Johns Hopkins University Press, 2000).

11 James Raven, *Business of Books: Booksellers and the English Book Trade 1450–1850* (New Haven, CT: Yale University Press, 2007), 321.

12 Review of *The Jesuit*, *GM* (Sept 1832): 239.

13 'Dramatic Taste', *Fraser's Magazine for Town and Country* 1.1 (Feb 1830): 128.

14 Garside et al., *BFD*, 'Walter Scott, *Waverley:* Anecdotal Records', accessed 6 Jan 2023, www.british-fiction.cf.ac.uk/titleDetails.asp?title=1814A054.

15 Garside et al., *BFD*, 'Walter Scott, *Waverley:* Publishing Records', accessed 6 Jan 2023, www.british-fiction.cf.ac.uk/titleDetails.asp?title=1814A054.

16 Review of *Waverley, The Scourge; or, Literary, Theatrical, and Miscellaneous Magazine* 8 (Oct 1814): 298.

17 For a similar argument with reference to the gothic elements in Scott's poetry, see Michael Gamer, *Romanticism and the Gothic: Genre, Reception, and Canon Formation* (Cambridge: Cambridge University Press, 2000), esp. 186–188.

18 Review of *The Fortunes of Nigel, The Literary Speculum* 2 (July 1822): 125.

19 Review of *Woodstock, The London Magazine* 5.18 (June 1826): 180.

20 Review of *Redgauntlet, The Kaleidoscope* 5.212 (20 July 1824): 19.

21 Review of *Woodstock, MR*, n.s., 2.6 (May 1826): 83.

22 Review of *Redgauntlet, The Westminster Review* 2.3 (July 1824): 179–180.

23 William Hazlitt, *The Complete Works of William Hazlitt*, ed. P. P. Howe et al., vol. 20 (London: J. M. Dent and Sons, 1930), 386.

24 Review of *Woodstock, The London Magazine* 5 (June 1826): 173–174.

25 Review of *Woodstock, or The Cavalier; A Tale of the Year 1657, The Westminster Review* 5 (Apr 1826): 410.

26 Walter Scott, *The Fortunes of Nigel* (Edinburgh: Archibald Constable and Co., 1822), I:v–vii. Subsequent parenthetical citations refer to this edition.

27 Scott uses the 'Driasdust' spelling in *Peveril of the Peak*, but employs 'Dryasdust' in *Fortunes of Nigel*. I have used the latter spelling throughout, except when quoting directly from *Peveril*.

28 Walter Scott, *Peveril of the Peak* (Edinburgh: Archibald Constable and Co., 1822). Subsequent parenthetical citations refer to this edition.

29 Scott's relationship to the Gothic has been the subject of much interesting scholarship; works include Duncan, *Modern Romance*; Gamer, *Romanticism and the Gothic*, chapter 5; Fiona Robertson, *Legitimate Histories: Scott, Gothic, and the Authorities of Fiction* (Oxford: Oxford University Press, 1994); and Watt, *Contesting the Gothic*, chapter 5.

30 Deidre Lynch, "Gothic Libraries and National Subjects," *Studies in Romanticism* 40.1 (2001): 31.

31 For discussion of Scott's commercial orientation, see, for instance, Ferris, *Achievement of Literary Authority*, 250–252; Kathryn Sutherland, 'Fictional Economies: Adam Smith, Walter Scott and the Nineteenth-Century Novel', *ELH* 54.1 (Spring 1987): 97–127; and Lawrence Poston, 'The Commercial Motif of the Waverley Novels', *ELH* 42.1 (Apr 1975): 62–87. The latter articles offer related, though differently oriented, readings of some of the passages I discuss here, including the preface to *Fortunes of Nigel*.

32 Walter Scott, *The Antiquary*, ed. Nicola J. Watson (Oxford: Oxford University Press, 2002), 32. Subsequent references to this edition are cited parenthetically.

33 Ina Ferris, 'Re-Positioning the Novel: "Waverley" and the Gender of Fiction', *Studies in Romanticism* 28.2 (Summer 1989): 298.

34 Mike Goode, 'Dryasdust Antiquarianism and Soppy Masculinity: The Waverley Novels and the Gender of History', *Representations* 82.1 (2003): 53.

35 Qtd. in Christina Lupton, *Knowing Books: The Consciousness of Mediation in Eighteenth-Century Britain* (Philadelphia: University of Pennsylvania Press, 2012), 4.

36 Jonathan Hill, 'Minerva at Aberdeen', *Romantic Textualities* 16 (Summer 2006): 24–25.

37 See, e.g., *A Catalogue of the Minerva General Library, Leadenhall-Street, London* ([London]: [1795?]), 348 (Bodleian Library/*ECCO*).

38 See St Clair, *Reading Nation*, appendix 9, 632–644, for statistics on Scott's publication history.

39 Walter Scott, *The Letters of Sir Walter Scott, 1787–1832*, ed. H. J. C. Grierson, Davidson Cook, and W. M. Parker, vol. VI (London: Constable & Co., 1932), 145.

40 Ibid.

41 Recent scholarship in book history increasingly calls attention to the book's object status; see, for instance, Leah Price, *How to Do Things with Books in Victorian Britain* (Princeton, NJ: Princeton University Press, 2012), and Dennis Duncan and Adam Smyth, eds., *Book Parts* (Oxford: Oxford University Press, 2019).

42 Timothy Campbell, *Historical Style: Fashion and the New Mode of History, 1740–1830* (Philadelphia: University of Pennsylvania Press, 2016), 214.

43 Ibid., 219.

44 John Sutherland, *The Life of Walter Scott: A Critical Biography* (Oxford: Blackwell, 1995), 139.

45 Dorothy Blakey, *The Minerva Press, 1790–1820* (London: Printed for the Bibliographic Society at the Oxford University Press, 1939), 10–11.

46 Peter Garside, 'English Novel in the Romantic Era: Consolidation and Dispersal', in *The English Novel, 1770–1829: A Bibliographical Survey of Prose Fiction Published in the British Isles*, vol. II, ed. Peter Garside, James Raven, and Rainer Schöwerling, 15–103 (Oxford: Oxford University Press, 2000), 64. See also Elizabeth Neiman, *Minerva's Gothics: The Politics and Poetics of Romantic Exchange, 1780–1820* (Cardiff: University of Wales Press, 2019), who concludes that 'Minerva novelists are indeed more prolific on average than other novelists' (9).

47 Review of *Reginald Dalton*, *The New Monthly Magazine* 8.32 (Jan 1823): 459.

48 On Scott's prefaces, see Walter Scott, *The Prefaces to the Waverley Novels*, ed. Mark A. Weinstein (Lincoln: University of Nebraska Press, 1978), and Patricia Sullivan Gaston, *Prefacing the Waverley Prefaces: A Reading of Sir Walter Scott's Prefaces to the Waverley Novels* (New York: P. Lang, 1991).

49 Walter Scott, *The Fortunes of Nigel* (Edinburgh: Archibald Constable and Co., 1822), I:ii. Subsequent parenthetical citations refer to this edition.

50 Ibid., I:xxii.

51 Clery, *Supernatural Fiction*, 137.

52 Scott, *Fortunes of Nigel*, I:xxii.

53 Scott, *Tales of the Crusaders* (Edinburgh: Archibald Constable and Co., 1825), viii.

54 Scott, *Fortunes of Nigel*, I:xiv.

55 Ibid., I:xxxvi.

56 Ibid., I:xxxvi.

57 Ibid., I:xl.

58 Review of *Woodstock, Dublin and London Magazine* (June 1826): 271.

59 Scott, *Fortunes of Nigel*, I: xxxvii.

60 Ibid., I:xxxvii–xxxviii.

61 Scott, *Tales of the Crusaders*, I:iii–iv.

62 Scott, *Fortunes of Nigel*, I:xlvi.

63 Ibid., I:xlv.

64 Ibid., I:xliii–xliv.

65 Ibid., I:xliv.

66 Ibid., I:xliv–xlv.

67 Ibid., I:xlv–xlvi.

68 Walter Scott, *Introductions and Notes from The Magnum Opus, Waverley to A Legend of the Wars of Montrose*, ed. J. H. Alexander, with P. D. Garside and Claire Lamont (Edinburgh: Edinburgh University Press, 2012), 6.

69 Ibid., 9.

70 Ibid., 10.

71 Ferris, *Achievement of Literary Authority*, 38, emphasis added.

72 Scott, *Introductions*, 8, 69.

73 Ibid., 11.

74 Mary Johnston, *The Lairds of Glenfern; or, Highlanders of the Nineteenth Century* (London: Printed for A. K. Newman and Co., 1816), I:v–vi.

75 Mary Brunton, *Discipline*, 2nd ed. (Edinburgh: Printed by George, Ramsay and Co., 1815), I:ix.

76 Mary Brunton, *Emmeline: With Some Other Pieces; To Which Is Prefixed a Memoir of Her Life Including Some Extracts from Her Correspondence* (Edinburgh: Printed for Manners and Miller and Archibald Constable and Co., and John Murray 1819), lxv–lxvi.

77 Ibid., lxxvi.

78 Anon., *Forman, a Tale* (London: Ogle, Duncan, and Co., 1819), vii.

79 Ibid.

80 Ibid., viii.

81 Ibid.

82 Brunton, *Discipline*, I:77.

83 On the Queen Anne farthing, see C. Wilson Peck, 'The Pattern Halfpennies and Farthings of Anne', *British Numismatic Journal*, 3rd ser., 9 (1958): 152–171.

84 Anon., *Prodigious!!! or, Childe Paddie in London*, vol. I (London: Printed for the author, and sold by W. Lindsell, 1818), 199–200.

85 Brunton, *Discipline*, I:v.

86 Brunton, *Emmeline*, lxxvii–lxxviii.

87 Ibid., lxxvii–lxxviii.

88 Ibid., lxxvi.

89 Benjamin Frere, *Rank and Fashion! or, The Mazes of Life: A Novel* (London: Printed for William Fearman, 1821).

90 Ibid., I:i–ii.

91 Ibid., I:ii.

92 Frere here articulates a position on the value of repetitive and automatic production of works of art that stands in interesting opposition to Walter Benjamin's later argument in 'The Age of Mechanical Reproduction' in *Illuminations: Essays and Reflections*, ed. Hannah Arendt, trans. Harry Zohn (New York: Mariner Books, Houghton Mifflin Harcourt, 2019 [1968]), 166–195.

93 Frere, *Rank and Fashion*, I:iii.

94 Ibid., I:iv.

95 See, e.g. Miss M'Leod, in her *Tales of Ton*, who features a young clergyman attempting to read *Waverley* in a stage-coach. Miss M'Leod, *Tales of Ton*, ser. 2, vol. III (London: Printed for A. K. Newman and Co., 1821), 197–200. *Almack's* (1827) features a plotline with a mysterious stranger who claims to be the 'Author of Waverley'. [Marianne Spencer Hudson], *Almack's, a Novel*, 2nd ed. (London: Saunders and Otley, 1827), III:272. R. N. Kelly, *Frederick Dornton; or, The Brothers: A Novel* (London: A. K. Newman and Co., 1822), I:6, features still another example.

96 Anna Maria Porter, *Roche-Blanche; or, The Hunters of the Pyrenees: A Romance* (London: Longman, Hurst, Rees, Orme, and Brown, 1822). Porter, like Brunton before her, claims this history-to-fiction process as her own, but then cites a similar statement made by Scott in order to highlight the commonalities in their process (I:ix-x). Scholarship on Anna Maria Porter and her sister (also a novelist) in the past two decades has made it clear that the relationship between them and Scott was not a case of one-sided inspiration; Scott clearly drew much of his approach from earlier works such as Porter's *Thaddeus of Warsaw* (1803). See, e.g., Devoney Looser, 'The Porter Sisters, Women's Writing, and Historical Fiction', in *The History of British Women's Writing, vol. V: 1750–1830*, ed. Jacqueline Labbe (Basingstoke: Palgrave Macmillan, 2010), 233–253; Thomas McLean, 'Nobody's Argument: Jane Porter and the Historical Novel', *Journal for Early Modern Cultural Studies* 7.2 (Fall 2007): 88–103; and Fiona Price, chapter 5, 'The End of History?: Scott, His Precursors and the Violent Past', in *Reinventing Liberty: Nation, Commerce and the British Historical Novel from Walpole to Scott* (Edinburgh: Edinburgh University Press, 2016), 170–206.

97 Ronald M'Chronicle, *Burton: A Novel* (London: Printed for A. K. Newman and Co., 1825), I:2–3.

98 Ibid., I:6.

99 Anon., *Prodigious!!! or, Childe Paddie in London*, vol. II (London: Printed for the author, and sold by W. Lindsell, 1818), 164.

100 Horace Smith, *Reuben Apsley*, vol. I (London: Henry Colburn, 1827), I:vi–vii.
101 Francis S. Higginson, *Manderville; or, The Hibernian Chiliarch*, vol. I (London: Printed and published by Thomas Dolby, 1825), i.
102 *Prodigious!!!*, I:163–164.
103 Thomas Dick Lauder, *Lochandhu: A Tale of the Eighteenth Century*, vol. I (London: Printed for Archibald Constable and Co., and Hurst, Robinson and Co., 1825), [xiv].

Epilogue

1 See Peter Garside, 'The English Novel in the Romantic Era: Consolidation and Dispersal', in *The English Novel, 1770–1829: A Bibliographical Survey of Prose Fiction Published in the British Isles*, ed. Peter Garside, James Raven, and Rainer Schöwerling, vol. II (Oxford: Oxford University Press, 2000), 85–86.
2 Garside cites the *English Catalogue of Books 1801–1836*, ed. Robert Alexander Peddie and Quintin Waddington (London, 1914; Kraus Reprint, New York, 1963), here, which lists both novels as actually published in November 1820 (cited in Garside et al., 'The English Novel', 43, 45). Review of *Lovers and Friends; or, Modern Attachments*, *The Lady's Monthly Museum* 12 (Dec 1820): 325.
3 Garside, 'The English Novel', 64.
4 See Garside et al., eds., *English Novel*, 463, on the serialization of *The Castle of Le Blanc*.
5 Jonathan Hill, 'Minerva at Aberdeen', *Romantic Textualities* 16 (Summer 2006): 24.
6 Ibid., 24–25.
7 Vols. 2 and 3 of *Eleanora* and vols. 1 and 3–5 of *Lovers and Friends* contain end-page advertisements (see, e.g., Corvey Collection/*NCCO* copies; also University of Aberdeen, *Lovers and Friends*).
8 See Elizabeth Neiman, *Minerva's Gothics: The Politics and Poetics of Romantic Exchange, 1780–1820* (Cardiff: University of Wales Press, 2019), 17–18, on the re-advertisement of older works as new in Minerva novels.
9 Dorothy Blakey, *The Minerva Press, 1790–1820* (London: Printed for the Bibliographic Society at the Oxford University Press, 1939), 1.
10 'Signs of the Times', *The Mirror* 10.282 (10 Nov 1827): 327–328.
11 Review of *The Literary Cyclopedia*, *The Metropolitan Magazine* 9.34 (Feb 1834): 51.
12 'Works of Fiction', *The Lady's Monthly Museum* 28 (Nov 1828): 274.
13 Review of *The Albigenses, a Romance*, *Edinburgh Magazine* 14 (Feb 1824): 209.
14 F.M., 'On Novels and Novel Writing', *Metropolitan* 5.19 (Nov 1832): 233.
15 Review of *Ringan Gilhaize; or, The Covenanters*, *The Literary Chronicle* 209 (17 May 1823): 305.

16 Review of *The Forsaken*, *MR*, 4th ser., 3.4 (Dec 1836): 628.

17 'Lady Morgan's *Book of the Boudoir*', *The Examiner*, no. 1132 (11 Oct 1829): 643.

18 Review of *Cecil Hyde*, *The Metropolitan Magazine* 9.34 (Feb 1834): 41.

19 Garside, 'The English Novel', 89. On Colburn's life and business practices, see John Sutherland and Veronica Melnyk, *Rogue Publisher: The 'Prince of Puffers': The Life and Works of the Publisher Henry Colburn* (Brighton: Edward Everett Root, 2018).

20 'Chit-Chat; Literary and Miscellaneous', *Literary Magnet* 3 (Jan 1827): 60.

21 'The Life and Times of Peter Priggins, College Scout and Bedmaker', *New Monthly Magazine* 60.237 (Sept 1840): 67.

22 John Sutherland, 'Henry Colburn, Publisher', *Publishing History* 19 (1 Jan 1986): 59, 60.

23 Ibid., 80.

24 Garside, 'The English Novel', 93–94, and Sutherland, 'Henry Colburn', 79.

25 Ibid., 25.

26 Ibid., 25 n. 22.

27 Hill, 'Minerva at Aberdeen', 22.

28 Qtd. in ibid., 22.

29 Blakey, *The Minerva Press*, 46.

30 Other possible sources of confusion include instances when the Minerva printed a later edition but not the first, and the fact that the Minerva *library* included novels by many different publishers.

31 Blakey, *The Minerva Press*, 46.

32 Ibid., 47.

33 'A Fragment of Romance', *Bentley's Miscellany* 1 (Jan 1837): 165–168 [165].

34 Ibid.

35 Ibid.

36 Elizabeth Neiman provides the most detailed recent assessment of the Minerva Press's authorship profile over time; see especially *Minerva's Gothics*, chapter 1, 'Bringing the Data to Scale: Analyzing a "Minerva Effect on the Novel Market"', pp. 3–26.

37 William Lane, 'An Address to the Public on Circulating Libraries,' [1795?] British Library, C.184.f.25(2).

38 Ibid., 1–2.

39 Ibid., 2.

40 Neiman, *Minerva's Gothics*, 16, 5.

41 Ibid., 9.

42 See, e.g., Jennie Batchelor, *Women's Work: Labour, Gender, Authorship, 1750–1830* (Manchester: Manchester University Press, 2010), esp. chapter 2, and Matthew Sangster, *Living as an Author in the Romantic Period* (Basingstoke: Palgrave Macmillan, 2021), esp. chapter 4.

43 Sangster, *Living as an Author*, 207.

44 See Garside, 'The English Novel', 74 and 91, for graphs of changing gender breakdown of authors, and novels by number of volumes, respectively.

45 Eloisa James, *Much Ado about You, Kiss Me, Annabel, The Taming of the Duke, Pleasure for Pleasure* (New York: Avon Books, 2004, 2005, 2006, 2006). The Minerva Press references cluster in the latter three novels, particularly the fourth.

46 Mary Bly, 'A Fine Romance', *New York Times*, 12 Feb 2005, A17. www .nytimes.com/2005/02/12/opinion/a-fine-romance.html.

47 James, Inside *Pleasure for Pleasure.* www.eloisajames.com/extras/inside-plea sure-for-pleasure/, 20 June 2020.

48 See, e.g., Wilma Counts, *The Memory of Your Kiss* (New York: Lyrical Press, 2015), 1; Sabrina Darby, *Woo'd in Haste* (New York: Avon Impulse, 2014); Barbara Metzger, *Valentines and Road to Ruin* (New York: Signet Regency Romance, 2004), 24.

49 Miranda Neville, *Confessions from an Arranged Marriage* (New York: Avon Books, 2012), 30; Loretta Chase, *Don't Tempt Me* (New York: HarperCollins 2009), 173.

50 William Hazlitt, 'Table-Talk', *The London Magazine* 3.14 (Feb 1821): 128.

51 Ibid.

52 Ibid., 130. Compare Deirdre Lynch's discussion of 're-reading' in Coleridge and Austen, in *Economy of Character: Novels, Market Culture, and the Business of Inner Meaning* (Chicago: University of Chicago Press, 1998), 132.

Bibliography

Primary Sources (Non-Periodical)

Anon. *Asmodeus; or, The Devil in London*. 3 vols. London: J. F. Hughes, 1808.

Castle Zittaw, a German Tale. 3 vols. London: Minerva-Press, 1794.

The Cavern of Death: A Moral Tale, 3rd ed. Cork: Printed by J. Connor, 1795.

Cœlebs Married. London: Published and sold by G. Walker, 1814.

Cœlebs in Search of a Mistress. London: Thomas Tegg, 1814.

Count Roderic's Castle; or Gothic Times. 2 vols. London: Minerva-Press, 1794.

Edelfrida. 4 vols. London: Hookham, 1792.

Edward De Courcy, an Ancient Fragment. 2 vols. London: Minerva-Press, 1794.

Eloise de Montblanc. 4 vols. London: Minerva Press, 1796.

Forman, a Tale. 3 vols. London: Ogle, Duncan, and Co., 1819.

Frederica; or, The Memoirs of a Young Lady. London: J. Ridgeway, 1792.

Frederica Risberg, a German Story. 2 vols. London: Minerva-Press, 1793.

Happiness: A Tale, for the Grave and the Gay, 3rd ed. 2 vols. London: Longman, Hurst, Rees, Orme, and Brown, 1821.

Iphigenia, a Novel. 3 vols. London: Minerva Press, 1791.

The Jewish Maiden: A Novel. 4 vols. London: A. K. Newman and Co., 1830.

Nobility Run Mad, or Raymond and His Three Wives. 4 vols. London: Minerva-Press, 1802.

Prodigious!!! or, Childe Paddie in London. 3 vols. London: W. Lindsell, 1818.

A Sequel to Cœlebs; or, The Stanley Letters. London: M. Jones, 1812.

Austen, Jane. Letter 65, 17–18 Jan 1809. In *Jane Austen's Letters*, 166. Edited by Deirdre Le Faye. Oxford: Clarendon Press, 1995.

Letter 67, 30 Jan 1809. In *Jane Austen's Letters*, 172. Edited by Deirdre Le Faye. Oxford: Clarendon Press, 1995.

Northanger Abbey. Edited by Barbara Benedict and Deirdre Le Faye. Cambridge: Cambridge University Press, 2006.

Northanger Abbey, Lady Susan, The Watsons, Sanditon. Edited by James Kinsley and John Davie. Oxford: Oxford World's Classics, 2008.

Pride and Prejudice. Edited by Pat Rogers and Janet Todd. Cambridge: Cambridge University Press, 2006.

Sense and Sensibility. Edited by Edward Copeland. Cambridge: Cambridge University Press, 2006.

[Bage, Robert]. *Barham Downs*. 2 vols. Tamworth: Printed by and Sold for B. Shelton, 1784.

    Hermsprong; or, Man as He Is Not. 3 vols. London: Minerva-Press, 1792.

    James Wallace. 3 vols. London: W. Lane, 1788.

    Man as He Is: A Novel. 4 vols. London: Minerva-Press, 1792.

    Mount Henneth. 2 vols. London: T. Lowndes, 1782.

Barrell, Miss. *Riches and Poverty: A Tale*. London: Tipper and Robins, 1808.

Bennet, Elizabeth. *Emily; or, The Wife's First Error and Beauty and Ugliness, or The Father's Prayer and the Mother's Prophecy: Two Tales*. 4 vols. London: Printed at the Minerva Press for A. K. Newman and Co., 1819.

Bennett, Anna Maria. *The Beggar Girl and Her Benefactors*. 7 vols. London: Printed for William Lane, at the Minerva Press, 1797.

[Best, Jane]. *Celia Suited*. 2 vols. London: Printed by T. Harper for H. Colburn, 1810.

Bicknell, John Laurens. *Original Miscellanies*. London: Printed for Cadell, Davies, and Blackwood, 1820.

Bisset, Robert. *Modern Literature: A Novel*. 3 vols. London: Longman, 1804.

Boaden, James. *Memoirs of Mrs. Inchbald: Including Her Familiar Correspondence with the Most Distinguished Persons of Her Time*. London: Richard Bentley, 1833.

Bonhote, Elizabeth. *Bungay Castle: A Novel*. 2 vols. London: Minerva Press, 1796.

Brunton, Mary. *Discipline: A Novel*, 2nd ed. 3 vols. Edinburgh: Printed by George Ramsay & Co., Longman, Hurst, Rees, Orme, and Brown 1815.

    Emmeline: With Some Other Pieces; To Which Is Prefixed a Memoir of Her Life Including Some Extracts from Her Correspondence. Edinburgh: Manners and Miller, Archibald Constable and Co., and John Murry, 1819.

    Self-Control: A Novel. 2 vols. Edinburgh: Printed by George Ramsay & Co. for Manners and Miller; and Longman, Hurst, Rees, Orme, and Brown, London, 1811.

Burney, Caroline [pseud.?]. *Lindamira in Search of a Husband, a Satirical Novel*. 3 vols. London: J. F. Hughes, 1810.

Byron, Lord. *Don Juan*, canto 1. London: Printed by Thomas Davison, 1819.

Byron, Miss. [*See also* 'A Modern Antique']. *The Alderman and the Peer; or Ancient Castle and Modern Villa*. 3 vols. London: Minerva-Press, 1810.

    Hours of Affluence, and Days of Indigence: A Novel. 4 vols. London: Printed at the Minerva Press for Lane, Newman and Co., 1809.

Charlton, Mary. *Phedora; or, The Forest of Minski: A Novel*. 4 vols. London: Minerva Press, 1798.

    Rosella, or Modern Occurrences. 4 vols. London: Minerva-Press, 1799.

Constable, Thomas. *Archibald Constable and His Literary Correspondents*. 3 vols. Edinburgh: Edmonston and Douglas, 1873.

Corp, Harriet. *Coelebs Deceived*. 2 vols. London: Baldwin, Cradock and Joy, 1817.

Craik, Helen. *Henry of Northumberland; or, The Hermit's Cell: A Tale of the Fifteenth Century*. 3 vols. London: Minerva Press, 1800.

Curties, T. J. Horsley. *Ancient Records; or, The Abbey of Saint Oswythe: A Romance.* 4 vols. London: Minerva-Press, 1801.

Ethelwina, or The House of Fitz-Auburne: A Romance of Former Times. 3 vols. London: Minerva Press, 1799.

The Scottish Legend, or The Isle of Saint Clothair. 4 vols. London: Minerva Press, 1802.

Dacre, Charlotte. *Confessions of the Nun of St. Omer.* 3 vols. London: Hughes, 1805.

De Genlis, Stéphanie-Félicité. *The Castle of Kolmeras.* London: Minerva Press, 1804.

D'Orville, André Guillaume Contant. *Pauline; or, The Victim of the Heart: From the French of D'Orville.* 2 vols. London: Minerva Press, 1794.

Du Bois, Edward. *St. Godwin: A Tale of the Sixteenth, Seventeenth, and Eighteenth Century.* Dublin: Wogan, 1800.

Edgeworth, Maria. *Belinda.* 3 vols. London: J. Johnson, 1801.

Belinda. Edited by Kathryn J. Kirkpatrick. Oxford: Oxford University Press, 1994, reissued 2008.

[Foster, E. M.]. *Concealment; or, The Cascade of Llantwarryhn: A Tale.* 2 vols. London: Printed at the Minerva Press for William Lane, 1801.

Fox, J[oseph], Jr. *The Bastard of Normandy.* 2 vols. London: Hookham, 1793.

Tancred: A Tale of Ancient Times. 2 vols. London: Minerva Press, 1791.

Frere, Benjamin. *Rank and Fashion! or, The Mazes of Life: A Novel.* 3 vols. London: William Fearman, 1821.

Godwin, William. *Caleb Williams.* Edited by David McCracken. New York: Norton, 1977.

Caleb Williams. Edited by Gary J. Handwerk and A. A. Markley. Peterborough: Broadview Press, 2000.

Caleb Williams. Edited by Pamela Clemit. Oxford: Oxford University Press, 2009.

Fleetwood; or, The New Man of Feeling. London: Richard Bentley, 1832.

Imogen, a Pastoral Romance from the Ancient British, ed. Jack Marken, rpt. ed. New York: New York Public Library, 1963.

Memoirs of the Author of a Vindication of the Rights of Woman. London: Printed for J. Johnson, 1798.

Political and Philosophical Writings of William Godwin. Edited by Mark Philp. London: William Pickering, 1993.

Graves, Richard. *Columella; or, The Distressed Anchoret.* 2 vols. London: Printed for J. Dodsley, 1779.

Green, Sarah. *Scotch Novel Reading.* 3 vols. London: A. K. Newman and Co., 1824.

[Grosse, Carl]. *Horrid Mysteries: A Story; From the German of the Marquis of Grosse.* 4 vols. London: Minerva Press, 1798.

Hales, J. M. *De Willenberg; or, The Talisman: A Tale of Mystery.* 4 vols. London: A. K. Newman and Co., 1821.

Hanway, Mary Ann. *Ellinor; or, The World as It Is.* 4 vols. London: Minerva Press, 1798.

Harris, Catherine. *Edwardina, a Novel.* 2 vols. London: Minerva Press, 1800.

Hays, Mary. *Memoirs of Emma Courtney.* Edited by Marilyn L. Brooks. Peterborough: Broadview Press, 2000.

Higginson, Francis. *Manderville; or, The Hibernian Chiliarch* 2 vols. London: Printed and Published by Thomas Dolby, 1825.

Hofland, Barbara. *A Father as He Should Be: A Novel.* 4 vols. London: Printed at the Minerva-Press for A. K. Newmand and Co., 1815.

    Says She to Her Neighbor, What? 4 vols. London: Printed at the Minerva-Press for A. K. Newmand and Co., 1812.

Holstein, Anthony Frederick [pseud.?]. *Bouverie: The Pupil of the World: A Novel.* 5 vols. London: Minerva Press, 1812.

    The Discontented Man; or, Love and Reason: A Novel. 3 vols. London: Printed at the Minerva-Press for A. K. Newmand and Co., 1815.

    The Inhabitants of Earth; or, The Follies of Woman: A Novel. 3 vols. London: Minerva Press, 1811.

    Lady Durnevor; or, My Father's Wife: A Novel. 3 vols. London: Minerva Press, 1813.

    The Miseries of an Heiress: A Novel. 4 vols. London: Printed at the Minerva-Press for A. K. Newman and Co., 1810.

    The Modern Kate; or, A Husband Perplexed. 2 vols. London: Minerva Press, 1812.

Hoole, Innes. *Scenes at Brighton; or, 'How Much?': A Satirical Novel.* 3 vols. London: A. K. Newman and Co., 1821.

[Hudson, Marianne Spencer]. *Almack's, a Novel.* 2nd ed. 3 vols. London: Saunders and Otley, 1827.

[Hughes, Mrs]. *Jemima, a Novel.* 2 vols. London: Minerva Press, 1795.

Hunter, Maria. *Ella; or, He's Always in the Way.* 2 vols. London: Minerva Press, 1798.

Hutchinson, Miss. *Exhibitions of the Heart.* 4 vols. London: Kearsley, 1799.

[Jacson, Frances]. *Plain Sense.* 3 vols. London: Minerva-Press, 1795.

Johnson, Samuel. *A Dictionary of the English Language.* 2 vols. London: Printed by W. Strahan for J. and P. Knapton et al., [1755].

Johnston, Mary. *The Lairds of Glenfern; or, Highlanders of the Nineteenth Century: A Tale.* 2 vols. London: Printed for A. K. Newman and Co., 1816.

[Jones, George]. *Supreme Bon Ton and Bon Ton by Profession.* 3 vols. London: John C. Spence, 1820.

Kelly, R. N. *Frederick Dornton; or, The Brothers: A Novel.* 4 vols. London: A. K. Newman and Co., 1822.

[Lane, William]. 'An Address to the Public on Circulating Libraries', [1795]. British Library, C.184.f.25(2).

    'A Tale Addressed to the Novel Readers of the Present Times', [1794?]. New York Society Library, Hammond Collection, Ham O412 W4.

    'A Tale Addressed to the Novel Readers of the Present Times', [1795]. British Library, C.184.f.25(1).

Lansdell, Sarah. *Manfredi, Baron St. Osmund: An Old English Romance.* 2 vols. London: Minerva Press, 1796.

Lathom, Francis. *London; or, Truth without Treason*. 4 vols. London: Minerva Press, 1809.

    Men and Manners. 4 vols. London: Wright and Symonds, 1799.

    The Mysterious Freebooter; or, The Days of Queen Bess: A Romance. 4 vols. London: Minerva Press, 1806.

    The Unknown; or, The Northern Gallery: A Romance. 3 vols. London: Minerva Press, 1808.

[Lauder, Thomas Dick.] *Lochandhu, a Tale of the Eighteenth Century*. 3 vols. London: Printed for Archibald Constable and Co., and Hurst, Robinson and Co., 1825.

Lefanu, Alicia. *Tales of a Tourist: Containing the Outlaw, and Fashionable Connexions*. 4 vols. London: A. K. Newman and Co., 1823.

Linley, William. *Forbidden Apartments: A Tale*. 2 vols. London: Minerva Press, 1800.

[MacHenry, James.] *The Wilderness; or, The Youthful Days of Washington: A Tale of the West*. 3 vols. London: A. K. Newman and Co., 1823.

Mackenzie, Anna Maria. *Feudal Events, or Days of Yore: An Ancient Story*. 2 vols. London: Minerva Press, 1800.

    Mysteries Elucidated, a Novel. 3 vols. London: Minerva-Press, 1795.

Malden, Miriam. *Jessica Mandaville; or, The Woman of Fortitude*. 5 vols. London: Printed by and for G. A. Wall and sold by Longman, Hurst, Rees, and Orme, 1804.

Malthus, Thomas. *An Essay on the Principle of Population*. London: Printed for J. Johnson, 1798.

[Mangin, Edward.] *George the Third: A Novel*. 3 vols. London: James Carpenter, 1807.

[Martin, Mrs]. *The Enchantress, or Where Shall I Find Her? A Tale*. London: Minerva Press, 1801.

    Melbourne: A Novel. London: Minerva Press, 1798.

[Matilda, Rosa]. *See* Dacre, Charlotte.

M'Chronicle, Ronald [pseud.]. *Burton: A Novel*. 3 vols. London: A. K. Newman and Co., 1825.

Meeke, Mary. *Conscience: A Novel*. 4 vols. London: Printed at the Minerva-Press for A. K. Newman and Co., 1814.

    Midnight Weddings: A Novel. 3 vols. London: Minerva Press, 1802.

    Something Odd! A Novel. 3 vols. London: Minerva Press, 1804.

    Strategems Defeated: A Novel. 4 vols. London: Printed at the Minerva-Press for A. K. Newman and Co., 1811.

Minerva Literary Repository, Library and Printing-Office. 'A Catalogue of the Minerva General Library, Leadenhall-Street, London'. [London]: n.p., [1795?].

M'Leod, Miss. *Tales of Ton, Second Series*. 4 vols. London: A. K. Newman and Co., 1821.

'A Modern Antique'. [*See also* Byron, Miss]. *Celia in Search of a Husband*. 2 vols. London: Minerva Press, 1809.

    The English Exposé; or, Men and Women 'Abroad' and 'At Home'. 4 vols. London: Minerva-Press, 1814.

More, Hannah. *Cœlebs in Search of a Wife*. Edited by Patricia Demers. Peterborough: Broadview Editions, 2007.

Moser, Joseph. 2 vols. *The Hermit of Caucasus: An Oriental Romance*. London: Minerva Press, 1796.

   Turkish Tales. 2 vols. London: Minerva Press, 1794.

Mudford, William. *Nubilia in Search of a Husband*. London: J. Ridgway; Sherwood, Neely, and Jones; and J. Booth, 1809.

Owenson, Sydney. *Woman; or, Ida of Athens*. 4 vols. London: Longman, Hurst, Rees and Orme, 1809.

'Parlante, Priscilla'. *Ferdinand and Ordella: A Russian Story*. 2 vols. London: Samuel Tipper, 1810.

Parsons, Eliza. *The Castle of Wolfenbach: A German Story* (1793). Edited by Diane Long Hoeveler. Chicago: Valancourt Books, 2006.

   Ellen and Julia. 2 vols. London: Minerva Press, 1793.

   The History of Miss Meredith: A Novel. 2 vols. London: T. Hookham, 1790.

   Lucy: A Novel. 3 vols. London: Minerva Press, 1794.

   The Mysterious Warning, a German Tale. 4 vols. London: Minerva Press, 1796.

   Woman as She Should Be; or, Memoirs of Mrs. Menville: A Novel. 4 vols. London: Minerva-Press, 1793.

   Women as They Are: A Novel. 4 vols. London: Minerva Press, 1796.

Pope, Alexander. 'The Dunciad Variorum'. In *The Poems of Alexander Pope*. Edited by John Butt. New Haven, CT: Yale University Press, 1963, 317–460.

Porter, Anna Maria. *Roche-Blanche; or, The Hunters of the Pyrenees*. 3 vols. London: Longman, Hurst, Rees, Orme, and Brown, 1822.

Poynet, Quintin. *The Wizard Priest and the Witch: A Romance*. 3 vols. London: A. K. Newman and Co., 1822.

Radcliffe, Ann. *The Italian; or, The Confessional of the Black Penitents: A Romance*. Edited by Robert Miles. London: Penguin, 2000.

   The Mysteries of Udolpho. Edited by Bonamy Dobrée. Oxford: Oxford World's Classics, 1980.

Rayner, W. H. *Virtue and Vice: A Novel*. 2 vols. London: W. Thiselton, 1806.

Roche, Regina Marie. *Clermont: A Tale* (1796). Edited by Natalie Schroeder. Chicago: Valancourt Books, 2006.

   The Vicar of Lansdowne; or, Country Quarters. 2nd ed. 2 vols. London: Minerva Press, 1800.

Rover, George [pseud.]. *Coelebs Suited*. London: Edmund Lloyd, 1809.

'Sabina'. *Laurentia, a Novel*. 2 vols. London: Minerva Press, 1790.

[Scott, Sarah]. *A Description of Millenium Hall*. London: Newbery, 1762.

Scott, Walter. *The Antiquary*. Edited by Nicola J. Watson. Oxford: Oxford University Press, 2002.

   The Fortunes of Nigel. 3 vols. Edinburgh: Archibald Constable and Co., 1822.

   Introductions and Notes from the Magnum Opus: Waverley to a Legend of the Wars of Montrose. Edited by J. H. Alexander, with P. D. Garside and Claire Lamont. Edinburgh: Edinburgh University Press, 2012.

Ivanhoe. Edited by Ian Duncan. Oxford: Oxford University Press, 1996.

The Lay of the Last Minstrel. London: Longman, Hurst, Orme, and Brown, 1805.

The Letters of Sir Walter Scott, 1787–1832. Edited by H. J. C. Grierson, Davidson Cook, and W. M. Parker. London: Constable & Co., 1932.

Peveril of the Peak. 4 vols. Edinburgh: Archibald Constable and Co., 1822.

The Prefaces to the Waverley Novels. Edited by Mark A. Weinstein. Lincoln: University of Nebraska Press, 1978.

Rob Roy. Edited by Ian Duncan. Oxford: Oxford University Press, 1998.

Tales of the Crusaders. 4 vols. Edinburgh: Archibald Constable and Co., 1825

Senate, E. *Family Pride and Humble Merit: A Novel, Founded on Facts, and Partly Taken from the French*. 3 vols. London: Sherwood, Neely and Jones, 1810.

[Siddons, Henry]. *Reginal di Torby and the Twelve Robbers: A Romance*. 2 vols. London: Minerva Press, 1803.

Smith, Charlotte. *Ethelinde, or The Recluse of the Lake*. 5 vols. London: T. Cadell, 1789.

The Old Manor-House. 4 vols. London: J. Bell, 1793.

[Smith, Horatio]. *Reuben Apsley*. 3 vols. London: Henry Colburn, 1827.

Summersett, Henry. *Leopold Warndorf: A Novel*. 2 vols. London: Minerva Press, 1800.

Teuthold, Peter [Kahlert, Karl Friedrich]. *The Necromancer, or The Tale of the Black Forest*. 2 vols. London: Minerva-Press, 1794.

[Thomas, Elizabeth.] *Mortimer Hall; or, The Labourer's Hire: A Novel*. 4 vols. London: Printed at the Minerva-Press for A. K. Newman and Co., 1811.

Thomson, Mrs. *The Pride of Ancestry; or, Who Is She?: A Novel*. 4 vols. London: Parsons & Son, 1804.

Tomlins, Elizabeth Sophia. *Rosalind de Tracy: A Novel*. 2nd ed. 3 vols. London: Minerva Press, 1799.

Torrens, Robert. *Coelibia Choosing a Husband*. 2 vols. London: J. F. Hughes, 1809.

[Walker, George]. *The Haunted Castle, a Norman Romance*. 2 vols. London: Printed at the Minerva-Press, 1794.

White, Mary. *Beatrice; or, The Wycherly Family*. 4 vols. London: A. K. Newman and Co., 1824.

Wollstonecraft, Mary. *The Collected Letters of Mary Wollstonecraft*. Edited by Janet Todd. New York: Penguin Classics, 2004.

The Works of Mary Wollstonecraft. Edited by Marilyn Butler and Janet M. Todd. New York: New York University Press, 1989.

Periodical Reviews and Articles

'Chit-Chat; Literary and Miscellaneous'. *Literary Magnet* 3 (Jan 1827): 59–64.

'Correspondence'. *Anti-Jacobin Review and Magazine, or, Monthly Political, and Literary Censor, 1798–1810* 34.137 (Nov 1809): 336.

'Creanda'. 'A Simple Mode of Preventing an Excess of Population'. *The Satirist, or, Monthly Meteor* 5 (Dec 1809): 579.

'Culpepper, Ned, the Tomahawk'. 'Mr. Edward Lytton Bulwer's Novels; and Remarks on Novel-Writing'. *Fraser's Magazine for Town and Country* 1.5 (June 1830): 509–532.

'Domestic Intelligence'. *The European Magazine, and London Review* 41 (June 1802): 498–500.

'Dramatic Taste'. *Fraser's Magazine for Town and Country* 1.1 (Feb 1830): 125–128.

'A Fragment of Romance'. *Bentley's Miscellany* 1 (Jan 1837): 165–168.

'General Observations on Modern Novels'. *The Lady's Magazine* 18 (1787): 456.

Hazlitt, William. 'Table-Talk'. *The London Magazine* 3.14 (Feb 1821): 128–134.

Holcroft, Thomas. Review of *Man as He Is*. *The Monthly Review,* 2nd ser., 10 (Mar 1793): 297–302.

Howe, P. P. 'Malthus and the Publishing Trade'. *The English Review* (Nov 1912): 577.

'Hints on Reading'. *The Lady's Magazine* 20 (Jan 1789): 79–81.

'Hymenæa in Search of a Husband'. *La Belle Assemblée* (Mar 1809): 72–76.

J.B. 'On Novels and Novel Writers'. *The European Magazine* 75 (May 1819): 404–405.

'Justus'. 'Reply to R.H. in Defence of Nubilia'. *Universal Magazine* 12.72 (Nov 1809): 377–379.

'Lady Morgan's *Book of the Boudoir*'. *The Examiner* 1132 (11 Oct 1829): 643.

Lane, William. 'A Tale: Addressed to the Novel Readers of the Present Time'. *The Lady & Gentleman's Pocket Magazine of Literary and Polite Amusement* (1 Nov 1796): n.p.

'The Life and Times of Peter Priggins, College Scout and Bedmaker'. *New Monthly Magazine* 60.237 (Sept 1840): 66–82.

'Literary Intelligence'. *Gentleman's Magazine* 79 (Oct 1809): 933–936.

'Literature of the Day'. *Metropolitan* 1.1 (May 1831): 17.

'Lucius'. 'On Novels'. *Universal Magazine of Knowledge and Pleasure* 93 (July 1793): 8–11.

'M'. 'On Novels and Novel Writing'. *Metropolitan* 1.1 (Nov 1832): 17–22.

Mackintosh, James. Review of the *Lives of Edward and John Philips, Nephews and Pupils of Milton, &c*. *The Edinburgh Review* 25.50 (Oct 1815): 487.

'Obit.: Ann Radcliffe'. *The New Monthly Magazine and Literary Journal* 9.29 (May 1823): 232.

'On an Excess of Sensibility'. *The Lady's Monthly Museum* 4 (Nov 1816): 274–276.

'On Novel Reading'. *The Kaleidoscope* 2.60 (21 Aug 1821): 54–55.

'On Novels and Romances'. *The Weekly Entertainer* 22.558 (21 Oct 1793): 399–400.

Review of *The Abbey of St. Asaph*. *The Critical Review,* 2nd ser., 14 (July 1795): 349.

Review of *The Adventures of Hugh Trevor*. *British Critic* 4 (July 1794): 71.

Review of *The Albigenses, a Romance*. *Edinburgh Magazine* 14 (Feb 1824): 209–215.

Review of *Ancient Records*. *The Critical Review*, 2nd ser., 32 (June 1801): 232.

Review of *Anecdotes of Two Well-Known Families*. *Analytical Review* 27 (June 1798): 644–645.

Review of *Anna Melvill*. *English Review* 21 (Feb 1793): 147–148.

Review of *Ariana and Maud*. *The Critical Review*, 2nd ser., 37 (Mar 1803): 356.

Review of *The Aunt and the Niece*. *The Critical Review*, 3rd ser., 3.4 (Dec 1804): 470–471.

Review of *Austenburn Castle*. *The Critical Review*, 2nd ser., 16 (Feb 1796): 222.

Review of *The Baron of Manstow*. *English Review* 17 (Mar 1791): 232.

Review of *Belleville Lodge*. *The Critical Review*, 2nd ser., 7 (Mar 1793): 357.

Review of *The Bristol Heiress*. *The Critical Review*, 3rd ser., 19 (Jan 1810): 97.

Review of *A Butler's Diary; or, The History of Miss Eggerton*. *The Gentleman's Magazine* 62.2 (Feb 1792): 192.

Review of *The Butler's Diary; or, The History of Miss Eggerton*. *The Critical Review* 4 (Feb 1792): 236.

Review of *The Castle of Hardayne: A Romance*. *Analytical Review* 23 (Jan 1796): 55.

Review of *Castle Spectre, a Drama in Five Acts*. *Analytical Review* 28 (Aug 1798): 179–191.

Review of *The Castles of Athlin and Dunbayne*. *The Monthly Review* 81 (Dec 1789): 563.

Review of *Cecil Hyde*. *The Metropolitan Magazine* 9.34 (Feb 1834): 41.

Review of *Celia in Search of a Husband*. *British Critic* 34 (Oct 1809): 410.

Review of *Celia in Search of a Husband*. *The Critical Review*, 3rd ser., 18.2 (Oct 1809): 219–220.

Review of *Celia in Search of a Husband*. *The Lady's Monthly Museum* 7 (Nov 1809): 270.

Review of *Celia in Search of a Husband*. *The Satirist, or, Monthly Meteor* 5 (Aug 1809): 182.

Review of *Charles Henly; or, The Fugitive Record*. *The Critical Review* 70 (Aug 1790): 219.

Review of *Coelebs in Search of a Wife*. *The Critical Review*, 3rd ser., 16.3 (Mar 1809): 252–264.

Review of *Coelebs in Search of a Wife*. *The Monthly Review*, 2nd ser., 58 (Feb 1809): 128–136.

Review of *Cœlia in Search of a Husband*. *The Monthly Review*, 2nd ser., 60 (Oct 1809): 212.

Review of *The Count De Santerre*. *Monthly Visitor* 2 (July 1797): 73–77.

Review of *The Cypher, or The World as It Goes*. *The Town and Country Magazine* 23 (Aug 1791): 357.

Review of *The Dangers of Coquetry*. *The Town and Country Magazine* 22 (Oct 1790): 460.

Review of *The Duchess of York: An English Story*. *The Monthly Review*, 2nd ser., 8 (July 1792): 339–340.

Review of *Dusseldorf; or, The Fratricide. The Critical Review*, 2nd ser., 24 (Oct 1798): 236.

Review of *Edmund; or, The Child of the Castle. The Critical Review* 70 (Oct 1790): 454.

Review of *Edwardina. The Critical Review*, 2nd ser., 31 (Mar 1801): 354–355.

Review of *Elvina, a Novel. The Critical Review*, 2nd ser., 5 (June 1792): 233.

Review of *Emily, or The Fatal Promise, a Northern Tale. The Critical Review*, 2nd ser., 5 (June 1792): 234.

Review of *Errors of Education. The Town and Country Magazine* 23 (Nov 1791): 507.

Review of *Ethelwina. The Critical Review*, 2nd ser., 14 (July 1795): 349.

Review of *The Family Party. English Review* 20 (July 1792): 69.

Review of *Fanny, or The Deserted Daughter. The English Review* 19 (June 1792): 471.

Review of *Faulkener. The Critical Review*, 3rd ser., 13 (1808): 415–420.

Review of *First Impressions. The Critical Review*, 2nd ser., 32 (June 1801): 232–233.

Review of *First Love. The Critical Review*, 2nd ser., 32 (July 1801): 352.

Review of *The Follies of St James Street. The Monthly Review*, 2nd ser., 4 (Jan 1791): 92.

Review of *Forresti; or, The Italian Cousins: A Romance. The Critical Review*, 3rd ser., 11 (May 1807): 96–97.

Review of *The Forsaken. The Monthly Review*, 4th ser., 3.4 (Dec 1836): 628.

Review of *The Fortunes of Nigel. The Literary Speculum* 2 (July 1822): 125.

Review of *Gray versus Malthus. The Principles of Population and Production Investigated. Monthly Review* (July 1819): 273–283.

Review of *Great Britain in 1833. The Edinburgh Review* 58.117 (Oct 1833): 151–163.

Review of *The Haunted Cavern: A Caledonian Tale. The Critical Review*, 2nd ser., 15 (Dec 1795): 480.

Review of *Heaven's Best Gift. The Monthly Visitor* 2 (Nov 1797): 478.

Review of *Henry of Northumberland. The Critical Review*, 2nd ser., 29 (May 1800): 115.

Review of *Hermione; or, The Orphan Sisters. English Review* 18 (Sept 1791): 230.

Review of *History of the Duke de Lauzun. The Critical Review*, 3rd ser., 13.4 (Apr 1808): 449–457.

Review of *Hubert de Sevrac. The Critical Review*, 2nd ser., 23 (Aug 1798): 472.

Review of *Humbert Castle. The Critical Review*, 2nd ser., 32 (June 1801): 231.

Review of *Imogen, a Pastoral Romance, from the Ancient British. The Monthly Review* 72 (Mar 1785): 233–234.

Review of *Independence. The Critical Review*, 2nd ser., 37 (Feb 1803): 237.

Review of *Intrigues of a Morning. Analytical Review* 13 (1792): 469.

Review of *The Italian. British Critic* 10 (Sept 1797): 266–270.

Review of *The Italian. The Critical Review*, 2nd ser., 23 (June 1798): 166–169.

Review of *The Jesuit. The Gentleman's Magazine* (Sept 1832): 239.

Review of *Julia* by Anna-Maria Williams. *The Monthly Review* 2.334 (July 1790): 334–336.

Review of *The Literary Cyclopedia*. *The Metropolitan Magazine* 9.34 (Feb 1834): 51.

Review of *Lovers and Friends; or, Modern Attachments*. *The Lady's Monthly Museum* 12 (Dec 1820): 325.

Review of *Lucy*. *Analytical Review* 20 (1794): 49–52.

Review of Mary Wollstonecraft's *Posthumous Works*. *The Monthly Review*, 2nd ser., 27 (Nov 1798): 325–327.

Review of *Massouf*. *The Critical Review*, 2nd ser., 36 (Sept 1802): 117.

Review of *Memoirs of Joan d'Arc*. *The Critical Review*, 3rd ser., 2.4 (Oct 1812): 409–411.

Review of *The Midnight Bell*. *The Critical Review*, 2nd ser., 23 (Aug 1798): 472.

Review of *Monimia*. *The Critical Review*, 2nd ser., 3 (Oct 1791): 235.

Review of *Monimia*. *The Town and Country Magazine* 23 (Nov 1791): 507–508.

Review of *The Monk*. *The Monthly Review*, 2nd ser., 23 (Aug 1797): 451.

Review of *Mortimer Castle; A Cambrian Tale*. *English Review* (Oct 1793): 307.

Review of *Nubilia*. *Literary Panorama* 6 (Sept 1809): 1105.

Review of *Nubilia in Search of a Husband*. *The Satirist* 5 (Aug 1809): 174–182.

Review of *Nubilia in Search of a Husband; Including Sketches of Modern Society*. *The Critical Review* 3.17 (Aug 1809): 439.

Review of *Nubilia in Search of a Husband; Including Sketches of Modern Society*. *The Monthly Review*, 2nd ser., 2.59 (July 1810): 299–304.

Review of *Nubilia in Search of a Husband; Including Sketches of Modern Society*. *The Scottish Review* 71 (Aug 1809): 595–598.

Review of *Nubilia in Search of a Husband; Including Sketches of Modern Society*. *The Universal Magazine* 12.68 (July 1809): 34.

Review of *Oakendale Abbey*. *Monthly Visitor* 2 (Nov 1797): 478–479.

Review of *Observations on a Journey through Spain and Italy to Naples*. *The Critical Review* 12.1 (Sept 1807): 71–84.

Review of *The Orphan of the Rhine*. *The Critical Review*, 2nd ser., 27 (Nov 1799): 356.

Review of *Persiana; or, The Nymph of the Sea*. *The Critical Review*, 2nd ser., 2 (July 1791): 356.

Review of *Redgauntlet*. *The Kaleidoscope* 5.212 (20 July 1824): 19.

Review of *Redgauntlet*. *The Westminster Review* 2.3 (July 1824): 179–180.

Review of *Reginald Dalton*. *The New Monthly Magazine* 8.32 (Jan 1823): 459–463.

Review of *Rhymes on Art; or, The Remonstrance of the Painter*. *The Critical Review*, 3rd ser., 4.4 (April 1805): 444–446.

Review of *Ringan Gilhaize; or, The Covenanters*. *The Literary Chronicle* 209 (17 May 1823): 305–307.

Review of *The Romance of the Forest*. *The English Review* 20 (Nov 1792): 52.

Review of *Santa Maria*. *The Monthly Review*, 2nd ser., 23 (June 1797): 210.

Review of *The Scottish Legend*. *The Critical Review*, 2nd ser., 36 (Sept 1802): 117.

Review of *A Sequel to Coelebs*. *The Monthly Review*, 2nd ser., 71 (July 1813): 319–320.

Review of *A Sicilian Romance*. *The Critical Review*, 2nd ser., 1 (Mar 1791): 350.

Review of *The Spirit of the Elbe*. *The Monthly Review*, 2nd ser., 30 (Sept 1799): 93.

Review of *The Stranger in Ireland; or, A Tour to the Southern and Western Parts of That Country in 1805*. *The Critical Review*, 3rd ser., 9.3 (Nov 1806): 315.

Review of *Tales of Fashionable Life*. *The Polyanthos* 1 (Nov 1812): 59.

Review of *Tancred, a Tale of Ancient Times*. *The English Review* 18 (Aug 1791): 114.

Review of *Things as They Are*. *British Critic* 4 (July 1794): 71.

Review of *Things as They Are*. *The Critical Review*, 2nd ser., 11 (July 1794): 290.

Review of *Things as They Are*. *The Monthly Review*, 2nd ser., 15 (Oct 1794): 146.

Review of *Valombrosa; or, The Venetian Nun*. *The Critical Review*, 3rd ser., 4.3 (Mar 1805): 329–330.

Review of *The Voluntary Exile*. *Analytical Review* 21 (1795): 296–299.

Review of *Walladmor*, '"Freely Translated into German from the English of Sir Walter Scott", and Now Freely Translated from the German into English'. *The Eclectic Review* 24 (July 1825): 18–19.

Review of *The Wanderer of the Alps*. *The Critical Review*, 2nd ser., 20 (July 1797): 352–353.

Review of *Waverley*. *The Scourge; or, Literary, Theatrical, and Miscellaneous Magazine* 8 (Oct 1814): 298.

Review of *Woodstock*. *Dublin and London Magazine* (June 1826): 271.

Review of *Woodstock*. *The London Magazine* 5.18 (June 1826): 180.

Review of *Woodstock*. *The Monthly Review* 2.6 (May 1826): 83.

Review of *Woodstock*. *The Westminster Review* 5 (Apr 1826): 410.

Review of *Woman as She Should Be; or, Memoirs of Mrs. Menville*. *The Critical Review*, 2nd ser., 9 (Sept 1793): 118.

R.H. 'The Errors of the Author of Nubilia Vindicated'. *Universal Magazine* 12.71 (Oct 1809): 267–268.

'S.A.'. Review of *The Iniquity of Banking*. *The Analytical Review* 26.3 (Sept 1797): 297–298.

'Signs of the Times'. *The Mirror*, 10.282 (10 Nov 1827): 327–328.

'Sketch of the Progress of Novel-Writing'. *The Port-Folio* 9.2 (1 Feb 1820): 266–286.

[Wollstonecraft, Mary]. Review of *Hermsprong*. *Analytical Review* 24.6 (Dec 1796): 608–609.

'Works of Fiction'. *The Lady's Monthly Museum* 28 (Nov 1828): 272–280.

Other Works

Ahern, Stephen. *Affected Sensibilities: Romantic Excess and the Genealogy of the Novel, 1680–1810*. New York: AMS Press, 2007.

Allan, David. *A Nation of Readers*. London: British Library, 2008.

Altick, Richard. *The English Common Reader*. Chicago: University of Chicago Press, 1957.

Anderson, Misty G. *Imagining Methodism in Eighteenth-Century Britain: Enthusiasm, Belief, & the Borders of the Self*. Baltimore, MD: Johns Hopkins University Press, 2012.

Bakhtin, M. M. *The Dialogic Imagination: Four Essays*. University of Texas Slavic Series 1. Translated by Michael Holquist. Austin: University of Texas Press, 1981.

Barrell, John. *The Spirit of Despotism: Invasions of Privacy in the 1790s*. Oxford: Oxford University Press, 2006.

Batchelor, Jennie. 'The Claims of Literature: Women Applicants to the Royal Literary Fund, 1790–1810'. *Women's Writing* 12.3 (2003): 505–520.

'"To Cherish Female Ingenuity, and to Conduce to *Female* Improvement": The Birth of the Woman's Magazine'. In *Women's Periodicals and Print Culture in Britain, 1690–1820s: The Long Eighteenth Century*, edited by Jennie Batchelor and Manushag N. Powell, 377–392. Edinburgh: Edinburgh University Press, 2018.

'UnRomantic Authorship: The Minerva Press and the *Lady's Magazine*, 1770–1820'. *Romantic Textualities* 23 (Summer 2020): 76–93.

Women's Work: Labour, Gender, Authorship, 1750–1830. Manchester: Manchester University Press, 2010.

Benjamin, Walter. 'The Work of Art in the Age of Mechanical Reproduction'. In *Illuminations: Essays and Reflections*, edited by Hannah Arendt, translated by Harry Zohn, 166–195. New York: Mariner Books, Houghton Mifflin Harcourt, 2019 [1968].

Berg, Maxine. *Luxury and Pleasure in Eighteenth-Century Britain*. Oxford: Oxford University Press, 2005.

Berg, Maxine, and Elizabeth Eger, eds. *Luxury in the Eighteenth Century: Debates, Desires and Delectable Goods*. Basingstoke: Palgrave Macmillan, 2003.

Blakey, Dorothy. *The Minerva Press, 1790–1820*. London: Printed for the Bibliographic Society at the Oxford University Press, 1939.

Bly, Mary. 'A Fine Romance'. *New York Times*, 12 Feb 2005, A17. www.nytimes.com/2005/02/12/opinion/a-fine-romance.html.

Bourdieu, Pierre. *The Field of Cultural Production: Essays on Art and Literature*. Edited by Randal Johnson. New York: Columbia University Press, 1993.

Brewer, John, and Roy Porter, eds. *Consumption and the World of Goods*. London: Routledge, 1993.

Brown, Susan, Patricia Clements, and Isobel Grundy, eds. 'Hannah More'. In *Orlando: Women's Writing in the British Isles from the Beginnings to the Present*. Cambridge: Cambridge University Press Online, 2006.

Burrow, Colin. *Imitating Authors: Plato to Futurity*. Oxford: Oxford University Press, 2019.

Butler, Marilyn. *Romantics, Rebels, and Reactionaries: English Literature and Its Background, 1760–1830*. New York: Oxford University Press, 1982.

Campbell, Timothy. *Historical Style: Fashion and the New Mode of History, 1740–1830*. Philadelphia: University of Pennsylvania Press, 2016.

Castle, Terry. *Masquerade and Civilization: The Carnivalesque in Eighteenth-Century English Culture and Fiction*. Stanford, CA: Stanford University Press, 1986.

Chaplin, Sue. 'Ann Radcliffe and Romantic-Era Fiction'. In *Ann Radcliffe, Romanticism and the Gothic*, edited by Dale Townshend and Angela Wright, 203–218. Cambridge: Cambridge University Press, 2014.

Chase, Loretta. *Don't Tempt Me*. New York: HarperCollins, 2009.

Clery, E. J. *Eighteen Hundred and Eleven*. Cambridge: Cambridge University Press, 2017.

   The Feminization Debate in Eighteenth-Century England: Literature, Commerce and Luxury. Palgrave Studies in the Enlightenment, Romanticism, and Cultures of Print. Houndmills: Palgrave Macmillan, 2004.

   The Rise of Supernatural Fiction, 1762–1800. Cambridge: Cambridge University Press, 1995.

Clery, E. J., Caroline Franklin, and Peter Garside, eds. *Authorship, Commerce and the Public: Scenes of Writing 1750–1850*. London: Palgrave Macmillan, 2002.

Copeland, Edward. *The Silver Fork Novel: Fashionable Fiction in the Age of Reform*. Cambridge: Cambridge University Press, 2012.

   Women Writing about Money: Women's Fiction in England, 1790–1820. Cambridge: Cambridge University Press, 1995.

Counts, Wilma. *The Memory of Your Kiss*. New York: Lyrical Press, 2015.

Crosby, Mark. 'The Bank Restriction Act (1797) and Banknote Forgery'. In *BRANCH: Britain, Representation and Nineteenth-Century History*. Edited by Dino Franco Felluga, Jan 2013. Extension of *Romanticism and Victorianism on the Net*. Accessed June 11, 2021.

Daffron, Eric. 'Transatlantic Terror: James Hammond's Circulating Library and the Minerva Press Gothic Novel'. *Romantic Textualities* 23 (Summer 2020): 109–123.

Darby, Sabrina. *Woo'd in Haste*. New York: Avon Impulse, 2014.

De Vries, Jan. *The Industrious Revolution: Consumer Behavior and the Household Economy, 1650 to the Present*. Cambridge: Cambridge University Press, 2008.

DeLucia, JoEllen. 'Radcliffe Incorporated: Ann Radcliffe, Mary Ann Radcliffe, and the Minerva Author'. *Romantic Textualities: Literature and Print Culture, 1780–1840* 23 (2020): 94–108.

Dennis, Ian. *Nationalism and Desire in Early Historical Fiction*. New York: St. Martin's Press, 1997.

Donoghue, Frank. *The Fame Machine: Book Reviewing and Eighteenth-Century Literary Careers*. Stanford, CA: Stanford University Press, 1996.

Duncan, Dennis, and Adam Smyth, eds. *Book Parts*. Oxford: Oxford University Press, 2019.

Duncan, Ian. *Modern Romance and Transformations of the Novel: The Gothic, Scott, Dickens*. Cambridge: Cambridge University Press, 1992.

Dyer, Serena, and Chloe Wigston Smith. *Material Literacy in Eighteenth-Century Britain: A Nation of Makers*. New York: Bloomsbury Publishing, 2020.

Ellis, Kate Ferguson. *The Contested Castle: Gothic Novels and the Subversion of Domestic Ideology*. Urbana: University of Illinois Press, 1989.

Erickson, Lee. *The Economy of Literary Form: English Literature and the Industrialization of Publishing, 1800–1850*. Baltimore, MD: Johns Hopkins University Press, 1996.

Fairclough, Mary. *The Romantic Crowd: Sympathy, Controversy, and Print Culture*. Cambridge Studies in Romanticism 97. Cambridge: Cambridge University Press, 2013.

Fergus, Jan. *Provincial Readers in Eighteenth-Century England*. Oxford: Oxford University Press, 2006.

Ferris, Ina. *The Achievement of Literary Authority: Gender, History, and the Waverley Novels*. Ithaca, NY: Cornell University Press, 1991.

    'Re-Positioning the Novel: "Waverley" and the Gender of Fiction'. *Studies in Romanticism* 28.2 (Summer 1989): 291–301.

Fitzgerald, Lauren. 'The Gothic Villain and the Vilification of the Plagiarist: The Case of Castle Spectre'. *Gothic Studies* 7.1 (2005): 5–17.

Ford, Karen Jackson. *Gender and the Poetics of Excess: Moments of Brocade*. Jackson: University Press of Mississippi, 1997.

Forster, Antonia. *Index to Book Reviews in England, 1775–1800*. London: British Library, 1997.

Gallagher, Catherine. *Nobody's Story: The Vanishing Acts of Women Writers in the Marketplace 1670–1820*. Oxford: Clarendon, 1994.

Gamer, Michael. *Romanticism and the Gothic: Genre, Reception, and Canon Formation*. Cambridge: Cambridge University Press, 2000.

    Romanticism, Self-Canonization, and the Business of Poetry. Cambridge: Cambridge University Press, 2017.

Garside, P. D., J. E. Belanger, and S. A. Ragaz, eds. *British Fiction, 1800–1829: A Database of Production, Circulation & Reception*, designer A. A. Mandal. www.british-fiction.cf.ac.uk. 15 July 2020.

    'Walter Scott, *Waverly*: Anecdotal Records'. *British Fiction Database*, accessed 6 January 2023.

Garside, Peter. 'The English Novel in the Romantic Era: Consolidation and Dispersal'. In *The English Novel, 1770–1829: A Bibliographical Survey of Prose Fiction Published in the British Isles*, vol. II, edited by Peter Garside, James Raven, and Rainer Schöwerling, 15–103. Oxford: Oxford University Press, 2000.

Garside, Peter, James Raven, and Rainer Schöwerling, eds. *The English Novel, 1770–1829: A Bibliographical Survey of Prose Fiction Published in the British Isles*. 2 vols. Oxford: Oxford University Press, 2000.

Gaston, Patricia Sullivan. *Prefacing the Waverley Prefaces: A Reading of Sir Walter Scott's Prefaces to the Waverley Novels*. New York: P. Lang, 1991.

Gee, Sophie. *Making Waste: Leftovers and the Eighteenth-Century Imagination*. Princeton, NJ: Princeton University Press, 2010.

Gigante, Denise. *The Great Age of the English Essay: An Anthology.* New Haven, CT: Yale University Press, 2008.

Goode, Mike. 'Dryasdust Antiquarianism and Soppy Masculinity: The Waverley Novels and the Gender of History'. *Representations* 82.1 (2003): 52–86.

Grenby, M. O. *The Anti-Jacobin Novel: British Conservatism and the French Revolution.* Cambridge: Cambridge University Press, 2001.

Haywood, Ian. *The Revolution in Popular Literature: Print, Politics and the People, 1790–1860.* Cambridge: Cambridge University Press, 2004.

Higgins, David. *Romantic Magazines and Metropolitan Literary Culture.* Basingstoke: Palgrave Macmillan, 2011.

Hill, Jonathan. 'Minerva at Aberdeen'. *Romantic Textualities* 16 (Summer 2006): 21–39.

Hoeveler, Diane Long. 'Gothic Adaptation, 1764–1830'. In *The Gothic World,* edited by Glennis Byron and Dale Townshend, 185–198. New York: Routledge, 2013.

Hogle, Jerrold. 'Recovering the Walpolean Gothic: *The Italian; or, The Confessional of the Black Penitents*'. In *Ann Radcliffe, Romanticism and the Gothic,* edited by Dale Townshend and Angela Wright, 151–167. Cambridge: Cambridge University Press, 2014.

Horner, Avril, and Sue Zlosnik. *Gothic and the Comic Turn.* Basingstoke: Palgrave Macmillan, 2005.

Hudson, Hannah Doherty. 'The English-Woman' (1808); 'Celia in Search of a Husband' (1809); 'Hours of Affluence and Days of Indigence' (1809); 'The Alderman and the Peer' (1810); 'The Englishman' (1812); 'The English Exposé' (1814); 'The Bachelor's Journal' (1815); and 'Genevieve; or, The Orphan's Visit' (1818). In *The Cambridge Guide to the Eighteenth-Century Novel,* edited by April London. Cambridge: Cambridge University Press, forthcoming.

'Gothic before Gothic: Minerva Press Reviews, Gender, and the Evolution of Genre'. In *Women's Authorship and the Early Gothic: Innovations and Legacies,* edited by Kathleen Hudson, 43–64. Cardiff: University of Wales Press, 2020.

'Imitation, Intertextuality, and the Minerva Press's Popular Fiction'. *Romantic Textualities: Literature and Print Culture, 1780–1840* 23 (Aug 2020): 149–167.

'Robert Bage's Novel Merchandise: Commercialism, Gender, and Form in Late Eighteenth-Century Fiction'. In *The Eighteenth-Century Novel,* vol. IX, edited by Albert J. Rivero and George Justice, 171–192. New York: AMS Press, 2012.

Jackson, H. J. *Romantic Readers: The Evidence of Marginalia.* New Haven, CT: Yale University Press, 2005.

Jacobs, Edward. *Accidental Migrations: An Archaeology of Gothic Discourse.* Lewisburg, PA: Bucknell University Press, 2000.

'Ann Radcliffe and Romantic Print Culture'. In *Ann Radcliffe, Romanticism and the Gothic,* edited by Dale Townshend and Angela Wright, 49–66. Cambridge: Cambridge University Press, 2014.

'Anonymous Signatures: Circulating Libraries, Conventionality and the Production of Gothic Romances'. *English Literary History* 62.3 (1995): 616.

James, Eloisa. *Kiss Me, Annabel*. New York: Avon Books, 2005.

Much Ado about You. New York: Avon Books, 2004.

Pleasure for Pleasure. New York: Avon Books, 2006.

The Taming of the Duke. New York: Avon Books, 2006.

Johnson, Claudia L. *Equivocal Beings: Politics, Gender, and Sentimentality in the 1790s: Wollstonecraft, Radcliffe, Burney, Austen*. Chicago: University of Chicago Press, 1995.

Jones, Mary Gwladys. *Hannah More*. Cambridge: Cambridge University Press, 1952.

Justice, George. *The Manufacturers of Literature: Writing and the Literary Marketplace in Eighteenth-Century England*. Newark: University of Delaware Press, 2002.

Keen, Paul. *The Crisis of Literature in the 1790s: Print Culture and the Public Sphere*. Cambridge Studies in Romanticism 36. Cambridge: Cambridge University Press, 1999.

Kelly, Gary. *English Fiction of the Romantic Period, 1789–1830*. London: Longman, 1989.

The English Jacobin Novel, 1780–1805. Oxford: Clarendon Press, 1976.

'Robert Bage'. In *The Oxford Dictionary of National Biography*. Oxford University Press Online, 2006, accessed 8 Feb 2011, doi:10.1093/ref:odnb/1028.

Keymer, Thomas. *Sterne, the Moderns, and the Novel*. Oxford: Oxford University Press, 2002.

King, Rachael Scarborough. '"[L]et a Girl Read": Periodicals and Women's Literary Canon Formation'. In *Women's Periodicals and Print Culture in Britain, 1690–1820s: The Long Eighteenth Century*, edited by Jennie Batchelor and Manushag N. Powell, 221–235. Edinburgh: Edinburgh University Press, 2018.

Klancher, Jon. *The Making of English Reading Audiences*. Madison: University of Wisconsin Press, 1987.

Ledoux, Ellen Malenas. *Social Reform in Gothic Writing: Fantastic Forms of Change, 1764–1834*. Basingstoke: Palgrave Macmillan, 2013.

Lines, Joe. 'William Lane, the Ramble Novel and the Genres of Romantic Irish Fiction'. *Romantic Textualities* 23 (Summer 2020): 21–38.

London, April, ed. *The Cambridge Guide to the Eighteenth-Century Novel*. Cambridge: Cambridge University Press, forthcoming.

Looser, Devoney. *British Women Writers and the Writing of History, 1670–1820*. Baltimore, MD: Johns Hopkins University Press, 2000.

'The Porter Sisters, Women's Writing, and Historical Fiction'. In *The History of British Women's Writing, vol. V: 1750–1830*, edited by Jacqueline Labbe, 233–253. Basingstoke: Palgrave Macmillan, 2010.

Lukács, György. *The Historical Novel*. Translated by Hannah and Stanley Mitchell. London: Merlin Press, 1962.

Lupton, Christina. *Knowing Books: The Consciousness of Mediation in Eighteenth-Century Britain*. Philadelphia: University of Pennsylvania Press, 2012.

Lynch, Deirdre Shauna. *The Economy of Character: Novels, Market Culture, and the Business of Inner Meaning*. Chicago: University of Chicago Press, 1998.

'Gothic Fiction'. In *The Cambridge Companion to Fiction in the Romantic Period*, edited by Richard Maxwell and Katie Trumpener, 47–64. Cambridge: Cambridge University Press, 2008.

'Gothic Libraries and National Subjects'. *Studies in Romanticism* 40.1 (2001): 29–48.

Mack, Robert L. *The Genius of Parody: Imitation and Originality in Seventeenth- and Eighteenth-Century English Literature*. Basingstoke: Palgrave Macmillan, 2007.

Mandal, Anthony. *Jane Austen and the Popular Novel: The Determined Author*. Basingstoke: Palgrave Macmillan, 2007.

Mason, Nicholas. 'Consumer Culture: Getting and Spending in the Romantic Age'. In *A Concise Companion to the Romantic Age*, edited by Jon P. Klancher, 189–209. Chichester: Wiley-Blackwell, 2009.

Literary Advertising and the Shaping of British Romanticism. Baltimore, MD: Johns Hopkins University Press, 2013.

McInelly, Brett C. *Textual Warfare and the Making of Methodism*. Oxford: Oxford University Press, 2014.

McKendrick, Neil, John Brewer, and J. H. Plumb. *The Birth of a Consumer Society: The Commercialization of Eighteenth-Century England*. London: Europa Publications; Bloomington: Indiana University Press, 1982.

McLean, Thomas. 'Nobody's Argument: Jane Porter and the Historical Novel'. *Journal for Early Modern Cultural Studies* 7.2 (Fall 2007): 88–103.

McLeod, Deborah. 'The Minerva Press'. PhD thesis, University of Alberta, 1997.

Mee, Jon. *Print, Publicity, and Popular Radicalism in the 1790s: The Laurel of Liberty*. Cambridge Studies in Romanticism 112. Cambridge: Cambridge University Press, 2016.

Metzger, Barbara. *Valentines and Road to Ruin*. New York: Signet Regency Romance, 2004.

Milberger, Kurt E. '"The First Impression, You, Yourself, Will Buy": The Gunninghiad, Virginius and Virginia and the Art of Scandal at the Minerva Press'. *Romantic Textualities* 23 (5 July 2020): 39–69.

Millgate, Jane. *Walter Scott: The Making of the Novelist*. Toronto: University of Toronto Press, 1984.

Moretti, Franco. *Distant Reading*. London: Verso Books, 2013.

Morin, Christina. *The Gothic Novel in Ireland: C. 1760–1829*. Manchester: Manchester University Press, 2018.

Nangle, Benjamin Christie. *The Monthly Review, Second Series, 1790–1815*. Clarendon Press, 1955.

Neill, Natalie. "'The trash with which the press now groans": *Northanger Abbey* and the Gothic Best Sellers of the 1790s'. *Eighteenth-Century Novel* 4 (2004): 163–192.

Neiman, Elizabeth. 'The Female Authors of the Minerva Press and "Copper Currency": Revaluing the Reproduction of "Immaculate-Born Minervas"'. In *Global Economies, Cultural Currencies of the Eighteenth Century*, edited by Michael Rotenberg-Schwartz and Tara Czechowski, 275–294. AMS Studies in the Eighteenth Century 64. New York: AMS, 2012.

Minerva's Gothics: The Politics and Poetics of Romantic Exchange, 1780–1820. Cardiff: University of Wales Press, 2019.

'A New Perspective on the Minerva Press's "Derivative" Novels: Authorizing Borrowed Material'. *European Romantic Review* 26.5 (2015): 633–658.

Neville, Miranda. *Confessions from an Arranged Marriage*. New York: Avon Books, 2012.

Norton, Rictor. *Gothic Readings: The First Wave, 1764–1840*. London: Leicester University Press, 2000.

Mistress of Udolpho: The Life of Ann Radcliffe. London: Leicester University Press, 1999.

'Parsons, Eliza'. *Orlando: Women's Writing in the British Isles from the Beginnings to the Present*. Cambridge University Press Online, 2006, accessed 14 June, 2013. http://orlando.cambridge.org/.

Peck, C. Wilson. 'The Pattern Halfpennies and Farthings of Anne'. *British Numismatic Journal*, 3rd ser., 9 (1958): 152–171.

Peddie, Robert Alexander, and Quintin Waddington, eds. *English Catalogue of Books 1801–1836*. London: S. Low, Marston, 1914; New York: Kraus Reprint Corp., 1963.

Peiser, Megan. 'Reviewing Women: Women Reviewers on Women Novelists'. In *Women's Periodicals and Print Culture in Britain, 1690–1820s: The Long Eighteenth Century*, edited by Jennie Batchelor and Manushag N. Powell, 236–249. Edinburgh: Edinburgh University Press, 2018.

'William Lane and the Minerva Press in the Review Periodical, 1790–1820'. *Romantic Textualities: Literature and Print Culture, 1780–1840* 23 (Aug 2020): 124–148. www.romtext.org.uk/articles/rt23_n08/.

Perkins, Pam. 'Reviewing Femininity: Gender and Genre in the Late Eighteenth- and Early Nineteenth-Century Periodical Press'. In *Women's Periodicals and Print Culture in Britain, 1690–1820s: The Long Eighteenth Century*, edited by Jennie Batchelor and Manushag N. Powell, 250–262. Edinburgh: Edinburgh University Press, 2018.

Philp, Mark. *Reforming Ideas in Britain: Politics and Language in the Shadow of the French Revolution, 1789–1815*. Cambridge: Cambridge University Press, 2014.

Pickering, Samuel F. 'Literature and Theology: The "Christian Observer" and the Novel, 1802–1822'. *Historical Magazine of the Protestant Episcopal Church* 43.1 (1974): 29–43.

Piper, Andrew. *Dreaming in Books: The Making of the Bibliographic Imagination in the Romantic Age*. Chicago: University of Chicago Press, 2009.

Plimmer, Helen. 'Corvey "Adopt an Author": Anna Maria Bennet'. *Corinne* 1 (May 1998), accessed 2 Mar 2012. http://extra.shu.ac.uk/corvey/corinne/.

Poston, Lawrence. 'The Commercial Motif of the Waverley Novels'. *ELH* 42.1 (Apr 1975): 62–87.

Potter, Franz. *The History of Gothic Publishing*. Basingstoke: Palgrave Macmillan, 2005.

Powell, Manushag N. *Performing Authorship in Eighteenth-Century English Periodicals*. Lewisburg, PA: Bucknell University Press, 2012.

Price, Fiona. *Reinventing Liberty: Nation, Commerce and the British Historical Novel from Walpole to Scott*. Edinburgh: Edinburgh University Press, 2016.

Price, Leah. *The Anthology and the Rise of the Novel: From Richardson to George Eliot*. Cambridge: Cambridge University Press, 2000.

How to Do Things with Books in Victorian Britain. Princeton, NJ: Princeton University Press, 2012.

Raven, James. *The Business of Books: Booksellers and the English Book Trade 1450–1850*. New Haven, CT: Yale University Press, 2007.

'Historical Introduction: The Novel Comes of Age'. In *The English Novel, 1770–1829: A Bibliographical Survey of Prose Fiction Published in the British Isles*, vol. I, edited by Peter Garside, James Raven, and Rainer Schöwerling, 15–121. Oxford: Oxford University Press, 2000.

Judging New Wealth: Popular Publishing and Responses to Commerce in England, 1750–1800. Oxford: Clarendon Press, 1992.

Ravenwood, Victoria. '"Historical Anecdotes Are the Most Proper Vehicles for the Elucidation of Knowledge": The "Historical Gothic" and the Minerva Press, 1790–99'. *Romantic Textualities* 23 (Summer 2020): 60–75.

The Reading Experience Database. www.open.ac.uk/Arts/reading/UK/.

Robertson, Fiona. *Legitimate Histories: Scott, Gothic, and the Authorities of Fiction*. Oxford: Oxford University Press, 1994.

Roper, Derek. *Reviewing before the Edinburgh*. Newark: University of Delaware Press, 1978.

Rowlinson, Matthew. *Real Money and Romanticism*. Cambridge: Cambridge University Press 2010.

Runge, Laura L. *Gender and Language in British Literary Criticism, 1660–1790*. New York: Cambridge University Press, 1997.

Sadleir, Michael. '"Minerva Press" Publicity: A Publisher's Advertisement of 1794'. *The Library*, 2nd ser., 21 (1940): 207–215.

The Northanger Novels: A Footnote to Jane Austen. Oxford: Oxford University Press, 1927.

XIX Century Fiction: A Bibliographical Record Based on His Own Collection, vol. II. London: Constable & Co., 1951.

Saglia, Diego. '"A portion of the name": Stage Adaptations of Radcliffe's Fiction, 1794–1806'. In *Ann Radcliffe, Romanticism and the Gothic*, edited by Dale Townshend and Angela Wright, 219–236. Cambridge: Cambridge University Press, 2014.

Schellenberg, Betty A. *The Professionalization of Women Writers in Eighteenth-Century Britain*. Cambridge: Cambridge University Press, 2005.

Shapira, Yael. 'Beyond the Radcliffe Formula: Isabella Kelly and the Gothic Troubles of the Married Heroine'. *Women's Writing* 26.3 (2019): 245–263.

'Isabella Kelly and the Minerva Gothic Challenge'. *Romantic Textualities* 23 (Winter 2020): 168–184.

Sharma, Anjana. *Autobiography of Desire: English Jacobin Women Novelists of the 1790s*. New Delhi: Macmillan, India, 2004.

Siskin, Clifford. 'Eighteenth-Century Periodicals and the Romantic Rise of the Novel'. *Studies in the Novel* 26.2 (1994): 26.

The Work of Writing: Literature and Social Change in Britain, 1700–1830. Baltimore, MD: Johns Hopkins University Press, 1998.

Skelton-Foord, Christopher. 'Economics, Expertise, Enterprise and the Literary Scene: The Commercial Management Ethos in British Circulating Libraries, 1780–1830'. In *Authorship, Commerce and the Public: Scenes of Writing, 1750–1850*, ed. E. J. Clery, Caroline Franklin, and Peter Garside, 136–152. London: Palgrave Macmillan UK, 2002.

Smith, Chloe Wigston. 'The Haberdasher's Plot: The Romance of Small Trade in Frances Burney's Fiction'. *Tulsa Studies in Women's Literature* 37.2 (2018): 271–293.

Women, Work and Clothes in the Eighteenth-Century Novel. Cambridge: Cambridge University Press, 2013.

Sodeman, Melissa. *Sentimental Memorials: Women and the Novel in Literary History*. Stanford, CA: Stanford University Press, 2015.

Spencer, Jane. *The Rise of the Woman Novelist: From Aphra Behn to Jane Austen*. Oxford: Blackwell, 1986.

St Clair, William. *The Reading Nation in the Romantic Period*. Cambridge: Cambridge University Press, 2004.

Stauffer, Andrew. *The Book Traces Project*. www.booktraces.org/.

Stevens, Anne H. *British Historical Fiction before Scott*. Basingstoke: Palgrave Macmillan, 2010.

Stott, Anne. *Hannah More: The First Victorian*. Oxford: Oxford University Press, 2003.

Sutherland, John. 'Henry Colburn, Publisher'. *Publishing History* 19 (1 Jan 1986): 59–84.

The Life of Walter Scott: A Critical Biography. Oxford: Blackwell, 1995.

Sutherland, John, and Veronica Melnyk. *Rogue Publisher: The 'Prince of Puffers', the Life and Works of the Publisher Henry Colburn*. Brighton: Edward Everett Root, 2018.

Sutherland, Kathryn. 'Fictional Economies: Adam Smith, Walter Scott and the Nineteenth-Century Novel'. *ELH* 54.1 (Spring 1987): 97–127.

Thomson, Douglass H., and Frederick S. Frank. 'Jane Austen and the Northanger Novelists'. In *Gothic Writers: A Critical & Bibliographical Guide*, edited by Douglass H. Thomson, Jack G. Voller, and Frederick S. Frank, 33–47. Westport, CT: Greenwood Press, 2001.

Todd, Janet. *The Sign of Angellica: Women, Writing, and Fiction, 1660–1800*. New York: Columbia University Press, 1989.

Tompkins, J. M. S. *The Popular Novel in England, 1770–1800*. Rpt. ed. London: Methuen and Co., 1961.

Townshend, Dale, and Angela Wright. *Ann Radcliffe, Romanticism and the Gothic*. Cambridge: Cambridge University Press, 2014.

Towsey, Mark. "'All partners may be enlightened and improved by reading them': The Distribution of Enlightenment Books in Scottish Subscription Library Catalogues, 1750–c. 1820'. *Journal of Scottish Historical Studies* 28.1 (2008): 20–43.

Trumpener, Katie. *Bardic Nationalism*. Princeton, NJ: Princeton University Press, 1997.

Turner, Cheryl. *Living by the Pen: Women Writers in the Eighteenth Century*. London: Routledge, 1992.

Wagner, Tamara. 'The Silver-Fork Novel'. *The Victorian Web*, accessed 25 Mar. 2013. www.victorianweb.org/genre/silverfork.html.

Warner, William Beatty. *Licensing Entertainment: The Elevation of Novel Reading in Britain, 1684–1750*. Berkeley: University of California Press, 1998.

Waters, Mary A. *British Women Writers and the Profession of Literary Criticism, 1789–1832*. Basingstoke: Palgrave Macmillan, 2004.

Watt, James. "'The Blessings of Freedom": Britain, America, and "the East" in the Fiction of Robert Bage'. *Eighteenth Century Fiction* 22.1 (2009): 49–69.

   Contesting the Gothic: Fiction, Genre, and Cultural Conflict, 1764–1832. Cambridge: Cambridge University Press, 1999.

Wheatley, Henry B. *Short History of Bond Street Old and New*. London: Fine Art Society, 1911.

Whitlock, Tammy C. *Crime, Gender and Consumer Culture in Nineteenth-Century England*. Aldershot: Ashgate, 2005.

Wilson, Cheryl A. *Fashioning the Silver Fork Novel*. London: Pickering & Chatto, 2012.

Winckles, Andrew. *Eighteenth-Century Women's Writing and the Methodist Media Revolution: 'Consider the Lord as Ever Present Reader'*. Liverpool: Liverpool University Press, 2019.

Wright, Angela. *Britain, France and the Gothic, 1764–1820: The Import of Terror*. Cambridge: Cambridge University Press, 2013.

Wyett, Jodi. 'Female Quixotism Refashioned: *Northanger Abbey*, the Engaged Reader, and the Woman Writer'. *The Eighteenth Century* 56.2 (2015): 261–276.

Yonge, Charlotte. *Hannah More*. Boston: Roberts Brothers, 1888.

Zuroski, Eugenia, and Michael Yonan, eds. 'Material Fictions'. Special double issue of *Eighteenth Century Fiction* 31.1–2 (Fall 2018 and Winter 2019): 1–18, 253–270.

Index

CAMBRIDGE STUDIES IN ROMANTICISM

General Editor
James Chandler, *University of Chicago*

For EU product safety concerns, contact us at Calle de José Abascal, 56–1°,
28003 Madrid, Spain or eugpsr@cambridge.org.

www.ingramcontent.com/pod-product-compliance
Ingram Content Group UK Ltd.
Pitfield, Milton Keynes, MK11 3LW, UK
UKHW020431240426